D0855886

HOW TO THINK SERIOUSLY ABOUT THE PLANET

The Case for an Environmental Conservatism

Roger Scruton

OXFORD
UNIVERSITY PRESS

OXFORD
UNIVERSITY PRESS

Oxford University Press, Inc., publishes works that further
Oxford University's objective of excellence
in research, scholarship, and education.

Oxford   New York
Auckland   Cape Town   Dar es Salaam   Hong Kong   Karachi
Kuala Lumpur   Madrid   Melbourne   Mexico City   Nairobi
New Delhi   Shanghai   Taipei   Toronto

With offices in
Argentina   Austria   Brazil   Chile   Czech Republic   France   Greece
Guatemala   Hungary   Italy   Japan Poland   Portugal   Singapore
South Korea   Switzerland   Thailand   Turkey   Ukraine   Vietnam

First published in hardback in Great Britain in 2011 by Atlantic Books, Ltd.
Published by Oxford University Press, Inc.
198 Madison Avenue, New York, New York 10016

www.oup.com

Oxford is a registered trademark of Oxford University Press

Library of Congress Cataloging-in-Publication Data
Scruton, Roger.
How to think seriously about the planet : the case for an environmental
conservatism / Roger Scruton.
p.   cm.
Rev. ed. of: Green philosophy.
Includes bibliographical references (p.   ) and index.
ISBN 978-0-19-989557-1 (alk. paper)
1. Environmental ethics. 2. Conservation of natural resources—Philosophy.
I. Scruton, Roger. Green philosophy. II. Title.
GF80.S37   2012
333.7201—dc23   2011051383

1 3 5 7 9 8 6 4 2

Printed in the United States of America
on acid-free paper

Contents

	Preface	I
ONE	Local Warming	5
TWO	Global Alarming	38
THREE	The Search for Salvation	72
FOUR	Radical Precaution	104
FIVE	Market Solutions and Homeostasis	137
SIX	The Moral Economy	183
SEVEN	*Heimat* and Habitat	209
EIGHT	Beauty, Piety and Desecration	253
NINE	Getting Nowhere	292
TEN	Begetting Somewhere	325
ELEVEN	Modest Proposals	376
	Appendix 1: Global Justice	403
	Appendix 2: How Should We Live?	409
	Bibliography	414
	Index	443

Preface

The problems of the environment seem so far beyond our reach that we lurch from opinion to opinion and policy to policy with nothing to cling to, save the thread of our shared concern. We believe the scaremongers, since no one can be as gloomy as that without a reason. We believe the sceptics, since they offer hope, and remind us that the scaremongers have made an emotional investment in their gloom. And we watch as governments, NGOs and pressure groups both augment our anxieties and offer to assuage them.

Without the resources of government it is hard to address such problems as climate change, oil spills, plastic pollution and the loss of biodiversity. But history tells us that large-scale projects in the hands of bureaucrats soon cease to be accountable, and that regulations imposed by the state have side effects that often worsen what they aim to cure. Moreover, the same people who promise vast schemes for clean energy and reduced pollution, also promise vast schemes to expand airports, build roads and subsidize the motor industry. The fact is that, when problems pass to governments, they pass out of our hands. Our own understanding was shaped by local needs, not global uncertainties: it is the product of day-to-day emergencies, and its wisdom is the wisdom of survival.

But there is a lesson in this for the environmentalists. No large-scale project will succeed if it is not rooted in our small-scale practical reasoning. For it is *we* in the end who have to act, who have to accept and co-operate with the decisions made in our name, and who have to make whatever sacrifices will be required for the sake of future generations. It seems to me that current environmental movements, many of which demand far-reaching and even unimaginable government projects, as well as fundamental changes in our way of life, have failed to learn this lesson. Their schemes, like their cries of alarm, frighten the ordinary citizen without recruiting him, and he stands in the midst of a thousand warnings hoping to get through to the end of his life without going insane from the noise.

In this book I develop another way of looking at environmental problems, one that is, I hope, in keeping with human nature and also with the conservative philosophy that springs from the routines of everyday life. I do not offer detailed solutions to particular problems. Instead I propose a perspective on those problems that will make them seem like *our* problems, which *we* can start to solve, using our given moral equipment. That, it seems to me, is the enduring message of conservatism. And if it is greeted with hostility by those who cannot encounter a problem without advocating radical solutions with themselves in charge, then that is only further proof of its validity.

My intention in this book is to present the environmental question as a whole and in all its ramifications. Hence I have drawn on philosophy, psychology and economics, as well as on the writings of ecologists and historians. I argue that environmental problems must be addressed by all of us in our everyday circumstances, and should not be confiscated by the state. Their solution is possible only if people are motivated to confront them, and the task of government is to create the conditions in which the right kind of motive can emerge and solidify. I describe this motive (or rather, family of motives) as oikophilia, the love and feeling for home, and I set out the conditions in which oikophilia arises and the task of the state in making room for it. I defend local initiatives against global schemes, civil association against political activism, and small-scale institutions of friendship against large-scale and purpose-driven campaigns. Hence my argument runs counter to much of the environmental literature today, and may be greeted with scepticism by readers who nevertheless share my central concerns. For this reason I have explored the first principles of practical reasoning, and the ways in which rational beings can reach co-operative solutions to problems that cannot be addressed either by the individual or by the centralized state. I am critical equally of top-down regulations and goal-directed movements, and see the environmental problem as arising from the loss of equilibrium that ensues when people cease to understand their surroundings as a home. This loss has many causes; but not the least among them is the wrong use of legislation, and the fragmentation of society that comes about when the bureaucrats take charge of it.

Work on this book has been made possible by my position as resident scholar at the American Enterprise Institute, where I have been fortunate to find the collegiate atmosphere and open-minded opposition of which I was in need. I have benefited from conversations with many colleagues there, and in particular from discussions with Kenneth P. Green, Lee Lane, Stephen Hayward and Christopher C. DeMuth. I also wish to thank Kimberly Hudson and Keriann Hopkins for invaluable editorial assistance, and Tony Curzon Price, Angelika Krebs, Ian Christie, Alicja Gęscinska, Mark Sagoff and David Wiggins, who patiently read through earlier drafts and rightly reproached me for my many errors, not all of which have been corrected.

Scrutopia, July 2010.

ONE

Local Warming

The environmental movement has recently been identified, both by its supporters and by many of its opponents, as in some way 'on the left': a protest on behalf of the poor and the powerless against big business, consumerism and the structures of social power. But that image is highly misleading. In Britain the environmental movement has its roots in the Enlightenment cult of natural beauty and in the nineteenth-century reaction to the Industrial Revolution, in which Tories and radicals played an equal part; and the early opposition to industrial farming joined guild socialists like H. J. Massingham, Tories like Lady Eve Balfour, secular gurus like Rudolf Steiner, and eccentric radicals like Rolf Gardiner, who borrowed ideas from left and right and who has even been identified (by Patrick Wright) as a kind of fascist.[1]

1   H. J. Massingham, *The Wisdom of the Fields*, London, 1945; *The Faith of a Fieldsman*, London, 1951; Eve Balfour, *The Living Soil*, London, 1943; Patrick Wright, 'An Encroachment too Far', in Anthony Barnett and Roger Scruton, eds., *Town and Country*, London, 1999.

American environmentalism incorporates the nature worship of John Muir, the radical individualism of Thoreau, the transcendentalism of Emerson, the 'ecocentrism' of Aldo Leopold and the social conservatism of the Southern Agrarians – a group of writers typified by the nostalgic poet Allen Tate, and represented in our day by Wendell Berry.[2] French environmentalism is the child of *pays réel* conservatives like Gustave Thibon and Jean Giono, while the German Greens have inherited some of the romanticism of the early twentieth-century *Wandervogel* movement, as well as the vision of home and settlement so beautifully expressed by the German Romantic poets and taken up in our time both by the ex-Nazi Martin Heidegger and, in more lucid and liberal vein, by his Jewish student Hans Jonas.[3]

Moreover, environmentalists today are aware of the ecological damage done by revolutionary socialism – as in the forced collectivization, frenzied industrialization and gargantuan plans to shift populations, rivers and whole landscapes that we have witnessed in the Soviet Union and China.[4] Left-leaning thinkers will not regard those abuses as the inevitable result of their ideas.

2 Wendell Berry, *The Gift of Good Land: Further Essays Cultural and Agricultural*, San Francisco, 1981; Aldo Leopold, *A Sand County Almanac and Sketches Here and There*, New York, 1949.

3 I discuss Heidegger's and Jonas's views in Chapter 7.

4 See Murray Feisbach, *Ecocide in the USSR*, New York, 1992, and the devastating commentary on the information then available by John Gray, *Beyond the New Right*, London and New York, 1993, pp. 130–3. The facts are set out in *World Resources 1992–3*, the report of the World Resources Institute, Oxford and New York, 1992.

Nevertheless, they will recognize that more work is needed, if the normal conscience is to be persuaded that socialism is the answer, rather than one part of the problem. At the same time, they seldom recognize any affinity with 'the right', and often seem to regard 'conservatism' as a dirty word, with no semantic connection to the 'conservation' that they favour.

The explanation, I believe, is that environmentalists have been habituated to see conservatism as the ideology of free enterprise, and free enterprise as an assault on the earth's resources, with no motive beyond short-term gain. Furthermore, there is a settled tendency on the left to confuse rational self-interest, which powers the market, with greed, which is a form of irrational excess. Thus the Green Party manifesto of 1989 identifies the 'false gods of markets, greed, consumption and growth', and says 'a Green Government would replace the false gods with co-operation, self-sufficiency, sharing and thrift'.[5] This manifesto echoes a widespread feeling that to rely exclusively on markets to solve our problems is to drift inevitably in an anti-social direction. And this accusation goes hand in hand with the view that there are other, more altruistic motives that can be called upon, and which *would* be called upon by a left-wing government. I agree that there are those other motives. But I doubt that they would be called upon by a left-wing government.

Those who have called themselves conservatives in the political context are in part responsible for this misperception. For they

5   *The Economist*, 24 June 1989.

7

have tended to see modern politics in terms of a simple dichotomy between individual freedom on the one hand, and state control on the other. Individual freedom means economic freedom, and this, in turn, means the freedom to exploit natural resources for financial gain. The timber merchant who cuts down a rainforest, the mining corporation that decapitates a mountain, the motor manufacturer that churns out an unending stream of cars, the cola producer that sends out a million plastic bottles each day – all are (or at any rate seem to be) obeying the laws of the market, and all, unless checked, are destroying some part of our shared inheritance. Because, in a market economy, the biggest actors do the most damage, environmentalists turn their hostility on big businesses, and on the free economies that produce them. Abolish the market economy, however, and the normal result is enterprises that are just as large and just as destructive but which, because they are in the hands of the state, are usually answerable to no sovereign power that can limit their predations. It is a plausible conservative response, therefore, not to advocate economic freedom at all costs, but to recognize the costs of economic freedom, and to take all steps to reduce them.

We need free enterprise, but we also need the rule of law that contains it, and law must keep pace with the threats. When enterprise is the prerogative of the state, the entity that controls the law is identical with the entity that has the most powerful motive to evade it – a sufficient explanation, it seems to me, of the ecological catastrophe of socialist economies. Studies have shown that free economies, with private property rights and an enforceable rule of law, not only consume far less energy per comparable product than economies where private property is insecure or absent, but also are able to adapt far more rapidly to the demand for clean energy, and for the reduction of emissions.[6] And while markets cannot solve all our environmental problems, and are indeed the cause of some of them, the alternatives are almost always worse.

There is another and better reason for thinking that conservatism and environmentalism are natural bedfellows. Conservatism, as I understand it, means the maintenance of the social ecology. It is true that individual freedom is a part of that ecology, since without it social organisms cannot adapt. But freedom is not the only goal of politics. Conservatism and conservation are two aspects of a single long-term policy, which is that of husbanding resources and ensuring their renewal. These resources include the social capital embodied in laws, customs and institutions; they also include the material capital contained in the environment, and the economic capital contained in a free but law-governed economy. According to this view, the purpose of politics is not to rearrange society in the interests of some overarching vision or ideal, such as equality, liberty or fraternity. It is to maintain a vigilant resistance to the entropic forces that

6   Aaron Wildavsky and Adam Wildavsky, 'Risk and Safety', in *The Concise Encyclopedia of Economics*, www.econlib.org/library/Enc/RiskandSafety. html; Michiel Schwarz and Michael Thompson, *Divided We Stand: Redefining Politics, Technology and Social Choice*, University Park, 1990.

threaten our social and ecological equilibrium. The goal is to pass on to future generations, and meanwhile to maintain and enhance, the order of which we are the temporary trustees.[7]

This means that conservatism, in the eyes of its critics, will seem doomed to failure, being no more than an attempt to escape the Second Law of Thermodynamics. Disorder is always increasing, and every system, every organism, every spontaneous order will, in the long term, be randomized. However, even if true, that does not make conservatism futile as a political practice, any more than medicine is futile, simply because 'in the long run we are all dead', as Keynes famously put it. Rather, we should recognize the wisdom of Lord Salisbury's terse summary of his philosophy, and accept that 'delay is life'. Conservatism is the politics of delay, the purpose of which is to maintain in being, for as long as possible, the life and health of a social organism.

Moreover, as thermodynamics also teaches us, entropy can be countered indefinitely at the local level by injecting energy and exporting randomness. Conservatism emphasizes historical loyalties, local identities and the kind of long-term commitment that arises among people by virtue of their localized and limited affections. While socialism and liberalism are inherently global in their aims, conservatism is inherently local: a defence of some pocket

7   Such is the view of political order that I defend in *The Meaning of Conservatism*, London, 1981. In a powerful analysis John Gray has linked conservatism of this kind with the environmental movement, and distanced both from the 'neo-liberalism' of the free-marketeers: see 'Towards a Green Conservatism', in *op. cit.*

of social capital against the forces of anarchic change. And it is precisely this local emphasis that uniquely suits conservatism to the task of addressing environmental problems.

Another way of putting the point is that, for the conservative, politics concerns the maintenance and repair of homeostatic systems – systems that correct themselves in response to destabilizing change. Markets are homeostatic systems; so too are traditions, customs and the common law; so too are families, and the 'civil associations' that make up the stuff of a free society.[8] Conservatives are interested in markets, and prefer market forces to government action wherever the two are rivals. But this is not because of some quasi-religious belief in the market as the ideal form of social order or the sole solution to social and political problems; still less is it because of some cult of *homo economicus* and the 'rational self-interest' that supposedly governs him. It is rather because conservatives look to markets as self-correcting social systems, which can confront and overcome shocks from outside, and in normal cases adjust to the needs and motives of their members.

There are other such systems, however. There are the long-term associations over time that form the traditions and institutions of a self-governing society. There is representative government in the hands of officers who must pay the price of their mistakes. And there are the legal instruments that return the

8   I take the term 'civil association' from Michael Oakeshott. See the second part of *On Human Conduct*, Oxford, 1975.

costs of mistakes to the people who make them. In later chapters I will explore some of these systems, and the states of mind that sustain them. It is only by respecting and exploiting those states of mind that we can develop a successful environmental policy. For they introduce into human affairs the crucial element of stewardship. They provide some of the negative feedback without which markets can become the anti-social and exploitative machines that their opponents suppose them always to be.

It follows that conservatism admits of many varieties. Conservatives in America emphasize economic freedoms, and associate this emphasis with a rugged individualism and a belief in the virtues of risk-taking and enterprise. Conservatives in Europe have favoured tradition, custom and civil society, emphasizing the need to contain enterprise within a durable social order. This difference of emphasis can lead to conflicting policies. Thus there is a tendency in American conservatism to prefer 'market solutions', whether or not they pose a threat to traditional forms of community and social equilibrium. Americans collectively possess an abundance of land and natural resources, and this has enabled them to put problems of scarcity and overpopulation out of mind, believing that there will always be space and resources for some new experiment. Europe is an assemblage of constricted states, settled throughout recorded history and with precious habitats, both human and animal, cared for and fought for over centuries. European conservatives are acutely aware of the constraints that surround them, and of the dangers of 'breaking out'. This does not mean that they reject market solutions. It means that they will pay more attention than their American counterparts to the things that make markets possible: to law, tradition and the moral life. Likewise Europeans, heirs to precious cities embellished over centuries, do not have the same attitude to the human habitat as Americans. I return to these differences in Chapter 8, since they point to matters from which American conservatives have something important to learn.[9]

The conservative understanding of political action that I propose is formulated in terms of trusteeship rather than enterprise, of conversation rather than command, of friendship rather than the pursuit of some common cause.[10] Those ideas lend themselves readily to the environmental project, and it always surprises me that so few environmentalists seem to see this. It is as obvious to a conservative that our reckless pursuit of individual gratification jeopardizes the social order as that it jeopardizes the planet. It is obvious too that the wisest policies are those that strive to protect and keep in place the customs and institutions that place a brake on our appetites, renew the sources of social contentment

9 In the American context the radical individualism of Ayn Rand should be distinguished from the conservative emphasis on freedom, as exemplified by Milton and Rose Friedman in *Free to Choose: A Personal Statement*, New York, 1980. The first is a metaphysical and absolutist vision, which puts self-affirmation at the top of the agenda; the second is an easygoing belief in choice as the precondition of a free society.

10 Trusteeship is associated with Burke, Möser and Gierke; conversation with Oakeshott; friendship with Aristotle. All are trying to reconstruct political authority as something intrinsically welcome to those who are subject to it.

and forbid us to pass on the costs of what we do to those who did not incur them.

The major difficulty, from the environmental point of view, is that social equilibrium and ecological equilibrium are not the same idea, and not necessarily in harmony. Two examples illustrate the problem. Democracies appear to achieve equilibrium only in a condition of economic growth. Periods of stagnation, rapid inflation or impoverishment are also periods of radical discontent, in which resentment and deprivation lead to instability. Hence the first concern of democratic governments is to encourage economic growth, regardless of its environmental costs. It is true that serious poverty is a major cause of environmental degradation and that a certain level of prosperity is necessary if people are to free the energy and resources required to protect their environment.[11] Studies have suggested that the curve postulated by Simon Kuznets, which shows income inequality at first rising and then falling as societies develop, is exhibited also by key environmental factors. Above an average annual per capita income of $4,000 to $5,000, it has been suggested, environmental degradation steadily declines.[12] Nevertheless, whether expressed as a prediction or as a recommendation, the statement

11 See W. Beckerman, *In Defence of Economic Growth*, London, 1974; Jack M. Hollander, *The Real Environmental Crisis*, Berkeley, 2003.

12 This argument was enthusiastically made by the World Bank's *World Development Report*, 1992. It has come under criticism subsequently: see the article by David I. Stern, 'The Environmental Kuznets Curve', www.ecoeco.org/pdf/stern.pdf.

that there are 'limits to growth' has an air of intuitive plausibility. Optimists will set these limits further in the future than pessimists, and the ongoing argument between them will delay any consensus.[13] But it is evident that, beyond a certain point, what is needed may be not more growth but less – and less is precisely what no democratic government can afford to promise. We see this in the attitude of recent British governments to airports, business parks and roads, the environmental impact of which is put out of mind, once these things have been packaged in the language of 'growth'. We see it in the American response to the Kyoto Protocol. It is not only big business that puts the pressure on the American Senate not to ratify such agreements. It is also the desire of the Senators to be re-elected.[14] This is not to say that the Protocol was the right solution to the problems that it addressed. But it is to acknowledge a serious difficulty facing all attempts to find binding treaties that will constrain consumption around the globe. Why should a politician put his signature to a treaty when the effect of doing so is that he will be out of office, and therefore unable to press for its enforcement?

13 The most famous of the pessimists are D. H. Meadows *et al.*, *The Limits to Growth*, London, 1972, and E. J. Mishan, *The Economic Growth Debate: An Assessment*, London, 1977. The optimists are well represented by H. S. D. Cole, *et al.*, eds., *Thinking About the Future: A Critique of the Limits to Growth*, London, 1973. I return to the 'limits to growth' question in Chapter 11.

14 According to a study by William Nordhaus, participation in the Kyoto Treaty would cost the USA $2.3 trillion over the coming decades, over twice the combined cost to all other participants. W. D. Nordhaus, 'Global Warming Economics', *Science*, 294, 5545, 9 November 2001.

Nor is democracy the only problematic case. Other forms of social equilibrium may equally pose a threat to the environment, not because they depend on economic growth, but because they depend on population growth, or on the consumption of some dwindling resource such as a rainforest. Consider the traditional Islamic societies observed in North Africa and parts of the Middle East. These achieve equilibrium only when families enjoy spheres of private sovereignty, under the tutelage of a patriarch whose social standing is constantly enhanced by evidence of his reproductive powers. Each family must be forever adding to its retinue of sons if it is to retain its position. The result, in modern conditions, is a population explosion that is rapidly destroying the environment of Muslim Arabia and North Africa, spilling over into a Europe whose institutions and traditions are in friction with the Muslim way of life, and now putting in question half a century of uneasy dictatorship.[15]

There is a tendency among environmentalists to single out the big players in the market as the principal culprits: to pin environmental crime on those – like oil companies, motor manufacturers,

15 '... the majority of the poor population in Arab Low Development Countries live in rural areas surviving on low-productivity, subsistence agriculture and related activities. Levels of human capital are very low and population growth is rapid, which multiplies the number of unskilled workers. Such economies are often caught in a vicious circle of population growth, environmental degradation and natural resource depletion that ultimately can destabilize the social and political order.' *Arab Human Development Report 2009: Challenges to Human Security in the Arab Countries*, UNDP Regional Bureau for Arab States, p. 118, www.arab-hdr.org/publications/other/ahdr/ahdr2009e.pdf.

logging corporations, agribusinesses, supermarkets – that make their profits by exporting their costs to others (including others who are not yet born). But this is to mistake the effect for the cause. In a free economy such ways of making money emerge by an invisible hand from choices made by all of us. It is the demand for cars, oil, cheap food and expendable luxuries that is the real cause of the industries that provide these things. Of course it is true that the big players externalize their costs whenever they can. But so do we. Whenever we travel by air, visit the supermarket, or consume fossil fuels, we are exporting our costs to others, and to future generations. A free economy is driven by individual demand. And in a free economy individuals, just as much as big businesses, strive to pass on their costs to others, while keeping the benefits. The solution is not the socialist one, of abolishing the free economy, since this merely places massive economic power in the hands of unaccountable bureaucrats, who are equally in the business of exporting their costs, while enjoying secure rents on the social product.[16] The solution is to adjust our demands, so as to bear the costs of them ourselves, and to find the way to put pressure on businesses to do likewise. And we can correct ourselves in this way only if we have motives to do so – motives strong enough to restrain our appetites.

This tells us nothing, however, about what we must do to make our dealings friendlier to the environment. To defend slow food, slow transport and low energy consumption in a society

16 On the theory of 'rent seeking', see Chapters 3 and 4.

addicted to fast food, tourism, luxury and waste is to risk the anger of those who need to be converted. Not only are there no votes to be won by seeking to close airports, to narrow roads or to impose a local food economy by fiat, but there is the serious risk of making matters worse, by representing environmental protection as the cause of nostalgic cranks. All environmental activists are familiar with this reaction. Yet I am surprised they do not see that it is a version of the very same reaction directed towards social conservatives, when they defend the beleaguered moral order that was – until a few decades ago – passed from generation to generation as a matter of course. Environmentalists and conservatives are both in search of the motives that will defend a shared but threatened legacy from predation by its current trustees.

Rational self-interest is not, I think, the motive that we are seeking, although, as I will argue, it has an important part to play. Rational self-interest is subject to the well-known free rider and prisoner's dilemma syndromes, and can avert 'the tragedy of the commons'[17] only in special circumstances. Social contract theorists, from Hobbes to Rawls, have attempted to overcome the problems of social choice, but always they come up against some version of the original difficulty: why is it more reasonable to bide by the contract than to pretend to bide by it?[18]

17 Garrett Hardin, 'The Tragedy of the Commons', *Science*, 162.1, 1968, pp. 243–8.

18 Thomas Hobbes, *Leviathan*, 1651; John Rawls, *A Theory of Justice*, 1971, 2005.

The need is for non-egotistical motives that can be elicited in ordinary members of society, and relied upon to serve the long-term ecological goal. Burke proposed 'the hereditary principle', as protecting important institutions from pillage or decay, and believed that people have a natural tendency to accept the limits that this principle places on their conduct. Hegel argued for the priority of non-contractual obligations, of the kind that sustain the family, and believed that similar obligations could be recuperated and exercised at the political level. In similar vein, de Maistre gave a central place to piety, as a motive that puts divinely ordained traditions and constitutions above the temptations of self-interest.[19]

Those suggestions[20] are unlikely to carry full conviction today, though each tries to frame a picture of human motivation that does not make rational self-interest the sole ground for political decision-making. But we should take a lesson from Burke, Hegel and de Maistre. We should recognize that environmental protection is a lost cause if we cannot find the incentives that would lead people in general, and not merely their self-appointed representatives, to advance it. Here is where environmentalists and conservatives can and should make common cause. That common cause is territory – the object of a love that has found its strongest political expression through the nation state.

19 Edmund Burke, *Reflections on the French Revolution*, 1790; G. W. F. Hegel, *Outlines of the Philosophy of Right*, 1820; Joseph de Maistre, *Le Principe Générateur des Constitutions*, 1809.

20 I return to them in Chapters 7 and 8.

Many environmentalists will acknowledge that local loyalties and local concerns must be given a proper place in our decision-making, if we are to counter the adverse effects of the global economy. Hence the oft-repeated slogan: 'Think globally, act locally.' However, environmentalists will tend to baulk at the suggestion that local loyalty should be seen in national terms, rather than as the small-scale expression of a humane universalism. Yet there is a very good reason for emphasizing nationality. For nations are communities with a political shape. They are predisposed to assert their sovereignty, by translating the common sentiment of belonging into collective decisions and self-imposed laws. Nationality is a form of territorial attachment, but it is also a proto-legislative arrangement. Moreover, nations are collective agents in the sphere of global decision-making. Through membership in a nation the individual has a voice in global affairs.

It is through developing this idea, of a territorial sentiment that contains the seeds of sovereignty within itself, that conservatives make their distinctive contribution to ecological thinking. Were conservatism to adopt a slogan, it should be 'feel locally, think nationally'. This does not mean that conservatives are nationalists, in the manner of the nineteenth-century romantics who adopted that creed.[21] They are aware of the historical and transitory nature of the nation state, of the need to contain and

21 And whose antics are thoroughly discredited by Adam Zamoyski in *Holy Madness: Compatriots, Patriots and Revolutionaries, 1776–1871*, London and New York, 2001.

soften its belligerence, and of the threat that it poses to local loyalties and civil associations. But they recognize that, in the current environmental crisis, there is no agent to take the needed measures, and no focus of loyalty to secure consent to them, other than this one.

A useful contrast is provided by George Monbiot, who has trenchantly argued the case for some kind of global politics, through which ordinary people can fend off the disasters that are being concocted within the global economy, and give voice to their desire for a safe, equitable and sustainable economic order.[22] I suspect that this would be the preferred way forward for those who have retained a vestige of the old socialist agenda, and who still wish to combine environmental rectitude with social justice. However, this approach is premised on two highly questionable assumptions: first, that sustainability and social justice can be combined; and second, that ordinary people, given the choice, would opt for sustainability rather than the gratification of their present desires. In some circumstances they would, of course. But it is precisely those circumstances that the global economy erodes. By disrupting old patterns of settlement and managed environments globalization undermines the values and expectations on which a stable way of life depends. This is as true of global politics as it is true of the global economy.[23]

22 George Monbiot, *The Age of Consent*, London, 2003.

23 For an eloquent assessment of the adverse effects of globalization on the identity, and therefore the environment, of the English nation, see Paul Kingsnorth, *Real England*, London, 2008.

The conservative approach is more reasonable, even if less ambitious. Rather than attempt to rectify environmental and social problems at the global level, conservatives seek a reassertion of local sovereignty over known and managed environments. This involves affirming the right of nations to self-government, and to the adoption of policies that will chime with local loyalties and customs. It also involves opposing the all-pervasive tendency of modern government towards centralization, and actively returning to local communities some of the powers confiscated by central bureaucracies – including those confiscated by transnational institutions like the World Trade Organization (WTO), the United Nations and the European Union. The attachment to territory and the desire to protect that territory from erosion and waste remain powerful motives that are presupposed in all demands for sacrifice that issue from the mouths of politicians.[24] For such motives grow from a strong root, which is love for one's home. As I argue in Chapter 7, this motive is not single or simple, and its many-layered structure reflects the psychic archaeology of human settlement. But it is possible to describe the motive and its many components, to amplify it, and to put it to work in the new and dangerous conditions of our emerging world.

In Chapter 10 I consider the examples of England and North America in order to show the way in which patriotic sentiments have protected highly vulnerable environments through fostering the motive of stewardship, and how that motive has both operated

24 See Roger Scruton, *The Need for Nations*, London, 2004.

independently of the state and often been undermined by the state. Sentiments of territorial attachment, I argue, have helped to maintain an inherited equilibrium that is both social and ecological; and their repudiation in recent decades is one major cause of the growing entropy. At this local, national, level, coherent environmental policies and coherent conservative policies coincide.

Indeed, it is only at this local level that it is realistic to hope for improvement. For there is no evidence that global political institutions have done anything to limit the global entropy – on the contrary, by encouraging communication around the world, and by eroding national sovereignty and legislative barriers, they have fed into that global entropy and weakened the only true sources of resistance to it. I know many environmentalists who agree with me that the WTO and the World Bank are potential threats to the environment, not merely by breaking down self-sufficient and self-reproducing peasant economies, but also by eroding national sovereignty wherever this places an obstacle before the goal of free trade.[25] Many also seem to agree with me that traditional communities deserve protection from sudden and externally engineered change, not merely for the sake of their sustainable economies, but also because of the values and loyalties that constitute the sum of their social capital.

25 Criticisms of these institutions from the left are assembled on the websites of the Global Justice Center and the Global Justice Ecology Center. See also the informed scepticism expressed by Joseph Stiglitz, *Globalization and Its Discontents*, New York and London, 2002, and *Making Globalization Work*, New York and London, 2006.

The odd thing is that so few environmentalists follow the logic of this argument to its conclusion, and recognize that we too deserve protection from global entropy, that we too must retain what we can of the loyalties that attach us to our territory, and make of that territory a home. Yet, in so far as we have seen any successful attempts to reverse the tide of ecological destruction, these have issued from national or local schemes to protect territory recognized as 'ours' – defined, in other words, through some inherited entitlement. I am thinking of the following: the initiative of American nature lovers, acting upon the United States Congress, to create national parks, the action by Iceland to protect the breeding ground of the Atlantic cod, the legislation that freed Ireland from polythene bags, the clean energy initiatives in Sweden and Norway, the Swiss planning laws that have enabled local communities to retain control over their environments and to manage those environments as a shared possession, the British 'Green Belt' policies that brought an end to urban sprawl, the initiatives of lobster-catchers in Maine and cod-fishers in Norway to establish self-regulating fisheries with local people in charge. These are small-scale achievements, but they are real, and could, if replicated more widely, change the face of the earth for the better.[26] Moreover, they are successful because they appeal

26 Some of these consensual solutions have been the subject of an important study by Elinor Ostrom. I engage with her arguments in Chapter 5. Some have also been documented in Chapter 5 of William A. Shutkin, *The Land That Could Be: Environmentalism and Democracy in the Twenty-First Century*, Cambridge, MA, 2001.

to a natural motive – the shared love of a shared place.

That, it seems to me, is the goal towards which serious environmentalism and serious conservatism both point – namely, home, the place where we are and that we share, the place that defines us, that we hold in trust for our descendants, and that we don't want to spoil. Many of those who have seen this connection between conservatism and environmentalism have also – like Patrick Wright – been suspicious of it.[27] And local environmentalism between the wars – especially in Germany – was undeniably part of the collectivist turn, even if only circumstantially connected to the nationalist frenzy.[28] However, it is time to take a more open-minded and imaginative vision of what conservatism and environmentalism have to offer each other. For nobody seems to have identified a motive more likely to serve the environmentalist cause than this one, of the shared love for our home. It is a motive in ordinary people. It can provide a foundation both for a conservative approach to institutions and a conservationist approach to the land. It is a motive that might permit us to reconcile the demand for democratic participation with the respect for future generations and the duty of trusteeship. It is, in my view, the only serious resource that we have, in our fight to maintain local order in the face of globally stimulated

27 See 'An Encroachment too Far', in Barnett and Scruton, eds., *op. cit.*
28 See here the somewhat unrelenting history of the ecological movement in Germany given by Anna Bramwell in *Ecology in the 20th Century: A History*, New Haven, 1989.

decay. And it is worth adding that, in so far as thermodynamics has a story to tell, it is this one.

I describe this motive (or family of motives) as oikophilia, the love of the *oikos*, or household. The Greek word appears, in Latinate form, in 'economy' and 'ecology'; but I use it to describe the deep stratum of the human psyche that the Germans know as *Heimatgefühl*. Self-styled conservatives have been much criticized – often rightly – for their belief that all political decisions are really economic decisions, and that market solutions are the only solutions there are. Yet the conservative emphasis on economics begins to make sense if we put the *oikos* back in *oikonomia*. Respect for the *oikos* is the real reason why conservatives dissociate themselves from currently fashionable forms of environmental activism. Radical environmentalists tend to be suspicious of national feeling. They repudiate old hierarchies and strive to remove the dead from their agenda, being largely unmoved by Burke's thought that, in doing so, they also remove the unborn. They tend to define their goals in global and inter-national terms, and support NGOs and pressure groups that will fight the multinational predators on their own territory and with weapons that make no use of national sovereignty.

German suspicion of *Heimatgefühl* goes further. Many German intellectuals will agree with Bernhard Schlink that a dangerous seed of utopianism lies planted in recent invocations of the *Heimat*. The home has been conceived as a 'no place', built from unsatisfiable emotional needs and therefore always a threat to the mere realities that disappoint the one who longs for it.[29] The fifty-five hours of Edgar Reitz's cinematic trilogy *Heimat* do not entirely dispel that impression, but they illustrate the argument that will be central to this book. I will explore the sentiment of oikophilia in its *available modern forms*, and I will define the real environmental task as one of sustaining that sentiment, and protecting it from all that wars against it – from oikophobia (the repudiation of the home), from technophilia (the urge to obliterate the home with functional appliances), from consumerism (the triumph of instrumental reasoning that turns somewhere into anywhere), and from the desire to spoil and desecrate that is one of the permanent diseases of human nature.

Since its origins in the writings of Hume, Smith and Burke intellectual conservatism has emphasized the importance of small associations, autonomous institutions and the various trusts and colleges that lie beyond the reach of the state. The emphasis was shared by de Maistre and Hegel on the Continent and made pivotal to his analysis of American democracy by Tocqueville. What those thinkers had in mind was civil association: gatherings of people that exist for the sake of membership – sometimes, but by no means always, with a common purpose – conducting their affairs without interference from the state, and usually without the desire for political prominence. Such associations form the stuff of civil society, and conservatives emphasize them precisely because they are the guarantee that society will renew itself

29 See Bernhard Schlink, *Heimat als Utopie*, Frankfurt, 2000.

without being led and controlled by the state.[30] Although, legally speaking, these 'little platoons', as Burke called them, are NGOs, they are conceived in entirely different terms from the big NGOs that have, until recently, dominated environmental campaigns. The NGO shows in its name that it is *not* a government organization; but the very emergence of this name indicates the extent to which NGOs have been in the habit of competing with government for a share of the action. Many of them also have political aspirations, wishing to recruit their members to purposes that can be achieved only through far-reaching legislative change.

The difference here can be simply put by saying that, while civil associations exist for the sake of their members, the big NGOs often exist purely for the sake of their goals. Such NGOs may offer nothing to their members besides demands for money. The distinction can be illustrated by reviewing some examples. Typical among activist NGOs is the International Fund for Animal Welfare (IFAW), an NGO founded in 1969 that campaigns around the world on behalf of animals. IFAW recruits members through shocking adverts. These describe the plight of bears condemned by their Chinese captors to suffer agonizing extractions of their spleen, the mass slaughter of seals on Canadian ice floes, or anything else that will cause the average animal lover to give money to the person who promises to stop such things. The principal co-founder of IFAW, Brian Davies,

---

30 Hence the explicit distinction between State and Civil Society (*bürgerliche Gesellschaft*) in Hegel's *Outlines of the Philosophy of Right*.

received $2.5 million from the Fund on his retirement, in return for the right to use his name – a right that many people would be happy not to exercise. The Fund itself continues to finance political campaigns across the world, one of which, the campaign to ban hunting with hounds in England, was recently successful. (IFAW's political wing, the Political Animal Lobby, gave £1 million to the Labour Party in exchange for a promise to instigate the ban. It is worth noting that this kind of corruption of the political process elicits no cries of outrage when donor and recipient are both 'on the left'. IFAW's worldwide income and expenditure is around $100 million annually.)

IFAW is one extreme instance of an NGO devoted to causes the value of which it cannot debate, since it has no forum for discussion, and the results of which might be damaging to its own putative goals – as a ban on the seal cull in Canada may very well be damaging to animal welfare in that country, as well as destructive of a human habitat vital to the Inuit people of the coast.[31] IFAW is accountable to no one other than its leadership, exists purely in the realm of politics, and cannot debate the long-term effects of its short-term purposes. It requires nothing of its supporters other than their money, and acts as an uncompromising, single-issue pressure group in all the places where it enters

31 Such is the argument given by the Canadian government, at least, which claims that the cull is not only economically important, but also necessary in order to maintain the environment and ecosystems on which the seals depend: www.dfo-mpo.gc.ca/fm-gp/seal-phoque/reports-rapports/facts-faits/facts-faitsSE-eng.htm.

the fray. It is organized internationally, and takes account of no issue other than the one that defines its stated purpose. Hence it attacks the very foundations of democratic politics, the purpose of which is to reconcile conflicts, to achieve workable compromises, and to take collective responsibility for a settled community and its many interests. The same can be said of the big multinational environmental groups such as Greenpeace, Friends of the Earth and Earth First!, which, precisely because they escape national jurisdictions and the burdens of realistic politics, can easily become threats to the homeostatic systems that they ought to be protecting.

A useful illustration is provided by the case of Greenpeace versus Shell, over the matter of the Brent Spar oil platform, which Shell had proposed to dispose of by sinking it in the sea. Greenpeace countered with a massively orchestrated hate campaign against Shell, involving boycotts, advertising, leaflets and pressure on shareholders, in order to prevent the sinking of the platform. The reason given was that the platform contained many thousand tonnes of oil and would be an environmental hazard for years to come: a reason that turned out to be false. No suggestion was made that Greenpeace and Shell should sit down together and discuss the problem. This was a fight to the death, between the forces of light and the forces of darkness.

Greenpeace won, and the platform was lifted and conveyed to a Norwegian fjord, an unsightly wreck that was eventually dismantled at a cost of £43 million (as opposed to the £3 million required to sink it). Because of the energy required to dismantle the rig, and the polluting side effects of doing so, this was the worst way, from the environmental point of view, of dealing with the problem. (Indeed, some environmentalists now recommend that old oil platforms be sunk in the oceans, since they provide beneficial habitats for fish.) Having cost Shell millions of dollars, and unjustly damaged its reputation, Greenpeace, on proof that the platform after all contained no oil, offered an airy apology and went on to its next campaign.[32]

This is not to say that the big NGOs are always wrong in their campaigns or that multinational companies always behave responsibly. On the contrary, Greenpeace and Friends of the Earth have drawn attention to real abuses, and used their high profile to good effect in educating the public. As companies get bigger, developing the capacity to move from jurisdiction to jurisdiction, evading their liabilities in each, so does their accountability dwindle. Shareholders rarely ask questions, and certainly not about the environmental consequences of actions that are bringing them a return on their investment. It is one of the weaknesses in the conservative position, as this has expressed itself in America, that its reasonable enthusiasm for free enterprise is seldom tempered by any recognition that free enterprise among citizens of a single nation state is very different from free enterprise conducted by a

32 *BBC News*, 25 November 1998. See also Shell Press Release, 'Shell welcomes the letter of apology from Greenpeace', *Brent Spar Dossier*, 2008, p. 112, www-static.shell.com/static/gbr/downloads/e_and_p/brent_spar _dossier.pdf.

multinational company, in places to which the company and its shareholders have no civic tie. It is this carelessness towards 'other places' that underlies environmental catastrophes like BP's oil-rig spill in the Gulf of Mexico, or the 'slash and burn' cropping by multinational agribusinesses in the Amazon rainforest.

Nevertheless, the activist NGOs have an accountability deficit that is the natural consequence of their way of working. The contrast with civil associations is illustrated by the Women's Institute, which was founded in 1915 to provide support to British women in the countryside, during the difficult years of the Frist World War. This now has 205,000 members in Britain, organized in local branches throughout the country, and which has been imitated across the English-speaking world. The WI has no purpose other than to encourage its members to gather around socially beneficial projects, and to form mutually supportive local clubs. It responds to suggestions from below, is accountable for its funds to those who provide them, and steers clear of politics. It shapes the moral character and the social aspirations of its members by providing an enduring institution that unites them across space and time. It feeds spontaneously into their patriotic feelings, and offers them friendship and support in times of trouble. It is, in short, an instrument of peace, and, being 'depoliticized', it lends itself to the conservative instinct, offering solace to those who wish to keep their heads down and get on with their lives.

Yet I have no doubt that the WI has done an immense amount

of good, not only for its members, but also for their shared habitat. It has played an active part in promoting the local food movement, not through campaigns, but through the opportunities that it provides to farmers and their families. Its members are first to get together to support environmental initiatives in their neighbourhood, and its whole emphasis, despite its nationwide organization, is on local activities and things 'close to home'. Likewise I have no doubt that IFAW has done as much harm as good, not only to the rural communities of England, but also to the Inuit of Canada and the coastal hunters of Namibia, who have been targeted by its campaigns. And it is quite possible that wild animals are, on the whole, worse off as a result of its actions, and that the animals that might most have benefited – the imprisoned bears of Asia – are beyond the reach of its campaigns. As for Greenpeace, the jury, to my mind, is out.

Not every big NGO is open to that kind of criticism. Many of the best-known NGOs steer clear of politics, or lift some of the burdens that government must otherwise bear – the Red Cross, for example, and the educational and medical charities that have played such an important part in building functional civil societies in Europe and America. But it is significant that I use the word 'charity' to describe these institutions, and it is significant too that, ever since the preamble to the Charitable Uses Act of 1605, English law has acknowledged their social significance and granted exemption from taxes that might otherwise have impeded their work. Indeed, we rarely use the 'NGO' label in describing this kind of institution, for the very reason that we do not see them as competing with government or as pressing for political results. They are active, but not activist.

Of course, there are many distinctions to be drawn here among the various ways in which the need to associate and the need to act jointly for the common good can be expressed, fulfilled and exploited. Behind the tentative contrast that I have been drawing between the activist NGO and the civil association there lies another and more interesting distinction between two competing conceptions of politics. There are people who see politics as mobilizing society towards a goal. And there are others who see politics as a procedure for resolving conflicts and reconciling interests, but one that has no overarching goal of its own. The first group includes all revolutionaries, many democratic socialists, for whom political action should guide society towards an equal and fraternal order, and maybe some of those whom John Gray calls 'neo-liberals', whose ruling concern is to rearrange communities and institutions on free market principles, regardless of their innate tendency in some other direction.[33] The second group includes most conservatives and also those called 'classical liberals' in the typology of political science. In this book I shall be defending the second kind of politics. Wise government, I maintain, should not have a goal beyond that of reconciling, as best it can, the goals of its citizens. Only in emergencies can societies be conscripted to a shared purpose and emergencies spell the end of

33 See Gray, *op. cit.*

civil politics. People on the left tend to define their political stance in terms of an agenda – a list of changes that will create a 'new society' in place of the old. Many environmentalists in recent times have shared that approach, pressing for a dominant agenda that will reshape society in keeping with the norms of environmental rectitude. After all, if you see yourself as representing the uncountable numbers of future people you may feel a justified impatience towards arrangements designed for the convenience of those living now.

Such environmental movements, therefore, tend to be NGO-shaped; while conservative political initiatives tend to be civil-shaped – not so much movements as forms of association, like the WI. This distinction is not absolute, and there are many associations that are part purposive, part purposeless, in the manner of sports clubs, churches and reading groups. But the distinction bears upon the environmental issue in important ways. The most influential agenda-driven NGOs are powerful, largely unaccountable, and unable to discuss the validity of their goals, since they are defined in terms of them; civil associations are, on the whole, unconcerned with political power, accountable to their members, and able to adjust in response to criticism. They are not means to some end, but ends in themselves, as people are. Typically NGOs move forward on a slope, and need to maintain an impetus if they are not to crumble. Civil associations are homeostatic systems, which usually recover from their own mistakes and return towards equilibrium when they are disturbed.

Environmental problems arise largely because human purposes, pursued in a linear way, destroy homeostatic systems. Hence it is the route marked out by the civil association, rather than that followed by the activist NGO, that ought to be followed. The purpose of this book is to describe that route, and to encourage the reader to set foot on it.

Conservatives tend to see the campaigning NGOs like Greenpeace and Earth First! not merely as institutions without internal equilibrium, but also as threats to the equilibrium of others, on account of their desire to pin on the big actors blame that should in fact be distributed across us all. And by casting the conflict in the form of a zero-sum game between themselves and the enemy, they obscure what it is really about, which is the accountability of both. It seems to me that the dominance of international decision-making by unaccountable bureaucracies, unaccountable NGOs and multinational corporations accountable only to their shareholders (who may have no attachment to the environment that the corporations threaten) has made it more than ever necessary for us to follow the conservative path. We need to retreat from the global back to the local, so as to address the problems that we can collectively identify as ours, with means that we can control, from motives that we all feel. That means being clear as to who *we* are, and why we are in it together and committed to our common survival. I respect George Monbiot's attempt to identify this first-person plural in planetary terms, just as I respect the Enlightenment conception of the human being, as a rational agent motivated by universal principles. As a conservative, however, I bow to the evidence of history, which tells me that human beings are creatures of limited and local affections, the best of which is the territorial loyalty that leads them to live at peace with strangers, to honour their dead and to make provision for those who will one day replace them in their earthly tenancy.

TWO

Global Alarming

That is all very well, you might say. But our problems are no longer of the kind that can be solved at the local level, or by relying on the old-fashioned attachments that appeal to conservatives. Climate change has lifted the issue of the environment entirely clear of normal politics, and presented us with the vision of a catastrophe that will negate all our old ways of securing our common welfare. An environmental policy devoted to recycling bottles, cleaning rivers and defending red squirrels from grey has a certain charm, and may in this or that particular take inspiration from a vision of Old England, Dixieland or *la douce France*. Meanwhile, however, Old England, Dixieland and *la douce France* are destined to disappear beneath the rising oceans, or to burn to a cinder under violent suns. The worst-case scenarios that are now offered and revised day by day are so truly alarming that they seem to throw all our plans and policies into disarray, and while the fear and apprehension are shared by people of all political persuasions, no single philosophy or ideology seems to offer the solution for which everybody craves. What should be our response to this? Before proceeding with the body of my argument it is vital to address that question. For if we have no answer to it, then all discussion of the environment and its place in political thinking will be meaningless.

It is pertinent to point out that alarms of this kind are a recurring feature of human societies, and that there is a good reason for this. For alarms turn problems into emergencies, and so bring the ordinary politics of compromise to a sudden stop. Faced with an emergency we prepare ourselves to obey orders, to follow leaders and to protect our backs. People who pursue a politics of top-down control therefore find emergencies extremely useful. This is surely one reason why alarms are so often sounded, and so quickly replaced. Thus in 1968 Paul Ehrlich initiated a worldwide movement of anxiety with his book *The Population Bomb*, which predicted that global overpopulation would cause massive famines as early as the seventies.[34] Demographic studies, showing that birth-rate declines as wealth increases, were largely ignored in the ensuing panic, and it is only now that the truth is widely accepted that famines are for the most part political phenomena, the result of military conflict, of state control of the food economy or, as in Soviet Ukraine, of a policy of genocide.[35]

Again in 1972 a number of scientists began to predict a

34 Paul Ehrlich, *The Population Bomb*, New York, 1968.
35 See Hollander, *op. cit.*, ch. 2.

catastrophic cooling of the earth, and in no time the prediction had become a widespread scare. 'Major cooling widely considered to be inevitable' was the *New York Times* headline, and *Science Digest* of 1973 told its readers to brace themselves 'for another ice age'.[36] *The Cooling*, by the American science writer Lowell Ponte, published in 1976, attempted to summarize the evidence and to prepare us for the worst, informing its readers that 'the cooling has already killed hundreds of thousands of people in poor nations'.[37] In their entertaining book on mass panics, *Scared to Death*, Christopher Booker and Richard North enjoy pointing out that many of those who had devoted their energies to warning the world against global cooling were, within a year or two, spreading alarms about global warming instead.

Such examples illustrate something that all wise people know, which is that the truth of a proposition is often the least important among the many motives for believing it. Panics arise when there is an interest in promoting them, and they pass from person to person with the irresistible force of a contagious disease. Indeed, thinkers like Richard Dawkins and Dan Sperber have taken the analogy with contagious diseases seriously, and proposed to

36 Walter Sullivan, 'Scientists Ask Why World Climate is Changing; Major Cooling May be Ahead', *New York Times*, 21 May 1975; Douglas Colligan, 'Brace Yourself for Another Ice Age', *Science Digest*, February 1973, pp. 57–61.

37 See Christopher Booker and Richard D. North, *Scared to Death: From BSE to Global Warming: Why Scares Are Costing Us the Earth*, London, 2009, pp. 332–3.

explain the spread of ideas in terms of the power of mental items to reproduce themselves in human brains, bypassing any consideration of their rational warrant.[38] And when explaining mass panics there is certainly a great need for what Sperber calls an 'epidemiology of belief'. Nevertheless, the fact that a belief passes from one person to the next without the need for rational argument does not mean that it is false. People were wrong to panic over global cooling then; but maybe they are right to fear global warming now.

Concern over climate change has been a recurrent feature in social and political prognostications at least since the time of Thomas Jefferson.[39] Only recently, however, has this concern entered everyday political debates, to the extent at times of all but dominating the political agenda. Books on climate change and global warming appear at the rate of one a week, as real experts and self-appointed experts compete for a share of the vast public interest (and public expenditure) that this subject has engendered. The explosion has been likened to that of religious tracts during the European plagues. But whereas the doomsday literature of medieval Europe promised only religious solutions to the evils that it threatened – solutions to be found in the soul of the reader,

38 Richard Dawkins's theory of the 'meme' is expounded in *The Selfish Gene*, London, 1976; Dan Sperber's thoughts on the epidemiology of representations can be found in his *Explaining Culture*, Oxford, 1995.

39 See James Rodger Fleming, *Historical Perspectives on Climate Change*, Oxford, 1998, and Sir Hubert Lamb, *Climate: Past, Present and Future*, vols. 1 and 2, London, 1972, 1977.

and directed to another world than this one – the literature of climate change calls for political action here and now. Inevitably, therefore, the science has been polluted by political interests. By the time they enter the space of journalism the particles of scientific information have passed through the cyclotron of ideology, and been accelerated to fission-speed.[40]

It is foolish to suppose that inconvenient truths will be easily believed by the person whose worldview they threaten. Someone hostile to big business, industrialism, consumerism and the capitalist free-for-all will be tempted to believe that these things are propelling us towards catastrophe, and that the catastrophe can be averted only by a complete change of life. Someone who believes in the free market, and who has perhaps invested his own capital in some part of it, will be tempted to believe that it is not *this* that is the cause of global warming, and that the predictions are in any case exaggerated.[41] When Al Gore makes a bid for leadership of the American left with an alarmist film on global warming, and Rush Limbaugh dismisses global warming as a 'hoax' put about by 'pseudo-scientists', then it is time to take a cool look at the facts and forget the motives that we all have for distorting or avoiding them.

40 In an interesting survey Mick Hulme has gathered together all the causes, rational, temperamental and cultural, that will inevitably prevent us from agreeing about a problem so 'wicked' in its ramifications as global warming. See *Why We Disagree About Climate Change*, Cambridge, 2009.

41 For the two contrasting positions here see www.commontragedies. wordpress.com and www.cei.org.

The worst-case scenario, according to which global temperatures could rise by six degrees Celsius in the course of the coming
century, has been set out by Mark Lynas in *Six Degrees*.[42] This
book, the work of a journalist who has devoted much time to
studying the science and speaking to some of those who have
produced it, and who backs up the theories with eye-witness
accounts of melting glaciers, flash floods, devastating droughts
and lethal heatwaves, argues that global warming is certainly
taking place, that its rate is accelerating, that its primary cause is
human activity leading to the production of greenhouse gases
(notably carbon dioxide and methane), and that we are fast
approaching the 'tipping point' after which our ecosystems will
pass irreversibly into a potentially catastrophic disequilibrium. In
the worst-case scenario that Lynas envisages the planet will by the
end of the century be largely barren, denuded of all species other
than a few pockets of human beings clinging to the last depleted
habitats, and lashed by hurricanes of a staggering intensity,
whipped up above the warm and de-oxygenated oceans in which
no fish can live. Lynas argues that global warming will by then
have reached its 'runaway' stage, as methane, previously trapped
beneath the frozen surface of the Arctic tundra, pours into the
atmosphere. With unmistakeable relish he describes an apocalypse
that, though influenced by science fiction, is rooted, so he
believes, in scientific fact.

42 Mark Lynas, *Six Degrees: Our Future on a Hotter Planet*, Washington DC,
2007.

Lynas's book is genuinely scary, and readers come away from it in fear and trembling. Published in 2007 it has already had a profound impact on the debate. Just where the 'six degree' prophecy originated is a matter of doubt, though it is aired here and there in the first report of the Intergovernmental Panel on Climate Change (IPCC), an organization established in 1988 by the World Meteorological Organization and the United Nations Environment Programme. In any case, the 'six degree' mantra is now regularly cited by the radical campaigning groups, and whether or not Lynas is responsible for this, he has certainly provided a vivid and alarming picture of what it might mean.

Equally influential has been James Hansen, a climatologist at NASA, the US space research centre, whose report to a Congressional Committee on Climate Change in 1988 set the tone for subsequent public discussions. In a series of papers, and a striking book, Hansen has made the case for an 'eleventh hour' view of global warming, placing the blame explicitly on man-made carbon emissions, and advocating concerted international action if the world is to be saved from an irreversible disaster.[43] Hansen has combined his scientific work with political advocacy of a dramatic kind, even getting himself arrested during a recent protest against a coal-mining operation in West Virginia, while his intemperate dismissal of those whom he calls 'climate change

43 James Hansen, *Storms of My Grandchildren: The Truth About the Coming Climate Catastrophe*, New York, 2009.

44

deniers' has not earned him universal respect in the scientific community.[44]

One of Hansen's more dogged critics has been Richard Lindzen, professor of meteorology at MIT, who has been for some years trying to show that there is no scientific consensus for the belief in global warming.[45] And Lindzen's arguments have been amplified by Patrick J. Michaels and Robert C. Balling, Jr, in *The Satanic Gases*, published in 2000. The authors are academic climatologists who present difficult theories and recondite facts in an attempt to persuade the reader that we will see only a modest global warming during the twenty-first century, similar to that which occurred during the last third of the twentieth century, and occurring largely in the winter, hence producing beneficial side effects in the production of food and the management of resources. Title apart, the book is dry, dull and calculated to lower the rate of the reader's pulse. It created no stir and has been largely ignored by the politicians, though Michaels has been a consultant scientist to the IPCC. Its central thesis has been supported, however, by a fair number of reputable scientists, some of the more important of whom are

44 See Nicholas Dawidoff's article about Freeman Dyson, 'The Civil Heretic', *New York Times Magazine*, 25 March 2009, in which Dyson is sharply dismissive of Hansen. Dyson is himself widely dismissed, of course, by the 'warmist' community.

45 Richard S. Lindzen, 'Global Warming: The Origin and Nature of the Alleged Scientific Consensus', Proceedings of the OPEC Seminar on the Environment, 1992, available on the Cato Institute website.

described in a recent book by Lawrence Solomon, entitled *The Deniers*.[46]

If the sceptics are right, the argument advanced by Hansen and Lynas is no better than scaremongering – a point vehemently made by another NASA climatologist, Roy Spencer, in a book whose fighting subtitle adds a further degree to the rising temperature: *Climate Confusion: How Global Warming Hysteria Leads to Bad Science, Pandering Politicians and Misguided Policies that Hurt the Poor*.[47] So whom should we believe: the 'warmists' or the sceptics? How can you and I know, without devoting the rest of our lives to the study of climatology? Even then we will be entering a field in which there seems to be very little consensus about anything, and only competing 'computer models' without genuine 'laws of motion' of the kind familiar from the other physical sciences.[48]

Bjørn Lomborg has famously added his own contribution to the debate, arguing in *The Sceptical Environmentalist* that global

---

46 Lawrence Solomon, *The Deniers*, Minneapolis, 2010. See also the work of Fred S. Singer of The Independent Institute, cited in the bibliography.

47 Roy Spencer, *Climate Confusion: How Global Warming Hysteria Leads to Bad Science, Pandering Politicians and Misguided Policies that Hurt the Poor*, New York, 2008.

48 The predictive power of the then (2000) current models is plausibly, though somewhat cantankerously, questioned by Patrick J. Michaels and Robert Balling, *The Satanic Gases: Clearing the Air about Global Warming*, Washington DC, 2000, ch. 4. And the notorious 'hockey stick' graph of global temperature change has been subjected to devastating criticism in Andrew Montford, *The Hockey Stick Illusion*, London, 2010.

warming is real, but less catastrophic than environmentalists tend to claim, since it lies within the scope of human adaptability.[49] This argument has earned Lomborg the rage and ostracism of his fellow environmentalists, and even a custard pie in the face (thrown, as it happens, by Mark Lynas)[50] at one attempt to explain himself. Professor Lindzen has likewise been the subject of character assassination by James Hansen. At least one prominent liberal journalist has likened all 'climate sceptics' to 'holocaust deniers',[51] while Al Gore has enthusiastically adopted the label 'denier' in order to dismiss the sceptics as irresponsible, and in any case in the pay of the 'big polluters'. If you trawl through the websites devoted either to asserting or to denying the reality of climate change you will find emissions of heat and gas on both sides that leave the ordinary reader gasping for a breath of cool air. The response of moderate thinkers to this situation – for example of the left-leaning Tony Giddens in his book *The Politics of Climate Change* and of the right-leaning Kenneth P. Green, in his *Plain English Guide to the Science of Climate Change* – is to acknowledge that global warming is occurring, that it is necessary to monitor it, to seek to understand its causes, and to do what we

49 Bjørn Lomborg, *The Skeptical Environmentalist: Measuring the Real State of the World*, Cambridge, 2001. On the negative response to Lomborg, see David Thomas, 'Anti-Christ of the Green Religion', *Daily Telegraph*, 20 January 2002.

50 See *The Ecologist* for March 2003.

51 Ellen Goodman, 'No Change in Political Climate', *Boston Globe*, 9 February 2007.

can to rectify its worst effects.[52] But such thinkers agree that the science is in its infancy and that we cannot predict with certainty what might happen if human beings continue to discharge greenhouse gases into the atmosphere at the current rate.

One source, however, is worth considering, since it has acquired a unique authority among environmentalists – the Assessment Reports of the IPCC. To date there have been four such reports, and they provide the basic factual material on which politicians and negotiators draw in any discussions of climate change at the treaty level. There is no gainsaying the care that goes into preparing them or the scientific industry on which they draw, and it is not surprising if Giddens, among others, takes them as authoritative. The IPCC's findings have a head start over the doubts expressed by its critics, in that the most widely consulted textbook on climate change is written by Sir John Houghton, former chairman of the IPCC's Scientific Assessment Working Group.[53] The IPCC's assessment reports formed the basic input into the British government's Review of the Economics of Climate Change, commissioned from Nicholas Stern and released in 2006, as well as many of the discussions to which that review has given rise.[54]

52 Anthony Giddens, *The Politics of Climate Change*, Cambridge, 2009; Kenneth P. Green, *Plain English Guide to the Science of Climate Change*, Washington DC, 2001.

53 Sir John Houghton, *Global Warming*, 4th ed., Cambridge, 2009.

54 See Nicholas Stern, *Stern Review on the Economics of Climate Change*, 700-page report released October 2006. The report was published as *The*

For many people the existence of the IPCC – an unprecedented example of scientific and political co-operation – represents the first major step towards a solution to the problem of climate change. But the IPCC has critics too, who were not reassured by the fact that the organization shared the 2007 Nobel Peace Prize with Al Gore. The website climatedepot.com, managed by Marc Morano and devoted to identifying, retailing and amplifying the arguments of the sceptics, has done its best to discredit the IPCC. It has recently published pirated internal documents suggesting that scientists at the Climate Research Unit at the University of East Anglia, on which the Panel relies for its global temperature measurements, have been prepared to falsify evidence for political ends.[55] Since then the chairman of the IPCC, Indian climatologist Rajendra Pachauri, has been heavily criticized for (among other things) issuing wildly inaccurate data concerning the melting of the Himalayan glaciers.[56]

Even before those episodes, the favourable opinion of the IPCC's reports was not shared by all climatologists: certainly not

Economics of Climate Change, Cambridge, 2007. The report forms the background to the wide-ranging discussions in Dieter Helm and Cameron Hepburn, eds., *The Economics and Politics of Climate Change*, Oxford, 2010.

55 See www.climatedepot.com, where information concerning what is fast becoming known (alas) as the 'climategate' scandal is triumphantly blazoned.

56 *BBC News*, 5 February 2010. Pachauri (who is also director of the Yale Climate and Energy Institute) has responded to criticism in *Yale Environment 360*, 20 April 2010.

by the 800 sceptics listed on climatedepot.com, or the prominent 'deniers' collected by Lawrence Solomon. The IPCC secretariat selects both the scientists that it consults and the questions that it asks of them; peer-reviewed journals that dispute any of its findings are not, as a rule, incorporated in the assessment, and its summaries, even of issues where there are equally persuasive opinions in contradiction with each other, invariably refer to 'the weight of the evidence' – a phrase that is bound to awaken suspicion, since it masks the fact that we are dealing with competing hypotheses, and not just conflicting observations. While the scientific papers themselves will usually be expressed in terms of ranges (of possible temperature change, quantities of greenhouse gas emitted, rates of industrial expansion, and so on), the summaries generally lean towards the higher figures. The final executive summary, which is all that the politicians have the time to read or the knowledge to grapple with, are produced by the secretariat, consulting only the lead authors of the assessment, under conditions of unanimous agreement. The assessment is then subject to two rounds of political review before being issued. To think that a summary report, issued in these circumstances, has the authority of a scientific document is surely to underestimate the enormous pressure from national interests, lobbyists, and the warming climate of opinion that will be felt – and manifestly is felt – at every stage of the process. Hence the Panel's last report, which holds that 'most of the observed increase in global average temperatures since the mid-twentieth century is very likely due to the observed increase in anthropogenic greenhouse gas concentrations', has not escaped the accusation of bias.[57]

Without claiming any special authority I venture the following interpretation of those and related sources. The 'greenhouse effect' (the retention of outgoing radiation by carbon dioxide, methane and similar gases) was already established by John Tyndall in the 1860s and is accepted by the scientific community. The quantity of greenhouse gases in the atmosphere is increasing, at least in part because of human activity, notably the burning of fossil fuels. Moreover, global warming during the last decades of the twentieth century is a fact, even if the extent of the human contribution is disputed. Global warming and global cooling are, in the long-term scheme of things, fairly routine occurrences. There is geological and fossil evidence of major and rapid fluctuations in temperature, prior to the relatively stable Holocene

57 See Richard S. Lindzen and Yong-Sang Choi, 'On the Determination of Climate Feedbacks from ERBE Data', *Geophysical Research Letters*, 36.16, August 2009, and Roy W. Spencer and William D. Braswell, 'Potential Biases in Feedback Diagnosis from Observations Data: A Simple Model Demonstration', *Journal of Climate*, 21, November 2008, pp. 5624–8. The IPCC report, published by Cambridge University Press in 2007, is available at www.ipcc.ch/pdf/assessment-report/ar$/wgl/ar4-wgl-spm.pdf. Previous IPCC reports, which made similar claims, have been criticized for their bias by Booker and North, *Scared to Death*, op. cit., pp. 344–52. The almost identical conclusion of the 2000 report has been quoted as incontrovertible fact by Sir Crispin Tickell, one of the most urgent of the activists, for example in Jennifer Jenkins, *Remaking the Landscape: The Changing Face of Britain*, London, 2002, p. 52.

period in which we are living.[58] Greenhouse gas emissions are only one factor in altering the balance of incoming and outgoing radiation on which the earth's temperature depends. Changes in solar output and cosmic wind and the angle and inclination of the earth with respect to the sun are also important, the first not well understood; important too are volcanic activity, uptake of carbon dioxide by the oceans and atmospheric water vapour.[59] Add the effects of greenhouse gas emissions by animals (termites, ruminants, humans) and of carbon sequestration by plants and other photosynthetic organisms such as plankton, take into account changes in the reflectivity of the earth's surface due to the way we use and clear the land and to the emission of heat-reflecting pollutants and sulphate aerosols, and it becomes clear that climate change, even if it is substantially accelerated by the industrial production of greenhouse gases, is probably not uniquely the result of them.[60]

Moreover, it is also clear that *some* human activities have a cooling effect overall, and that the attempt to stabilize the climate

58 See L. A. Frakes, *Climates Throughout Geological Time*, Amsterdam, 1979. For an instructive map of the earth's climate history see Christopher R. Scotese, 'The Paleomap Project', www.scotese.com/climate.htm.

59 On the effect of sun spots, solar winds and fluctuations in solar radiation, see Henrik Svensmark and Nigel Calder, *The Chilling Stars: A New Theory of Climate Change*, Thriplow, 2007.

60 Though, as David J. C. MacKay points out in *Sustainable Energy – Without the Hot Air*, Cambridge, 2009, p. 24, the salient point is not how much carbon dioxide enters the atmosphere, but whether the additional amount due to human energy consumption *accumulates* there.

could be pursued by *adding* to the things we do to it, rather than by subtracting what we do already. This point has suggested the possibility of taking unilateral action to counteract global warming through some work of geo-engineering. Those who are sceptical towards international treaties or the ability of the big polluters to adhere to them are likely to entertain this possibility, even if only reluctantly and as a last resort. We should be clear, however, that anthropogenic cooling will not solve all the problems created by carbon emissions. For atmospheric carbon dioxide is in part recycled through the oceans, resulting in the acidification of the water. Increased acidification causes changes to the oceanic ecosystem of a kind that we do not fully understand. If atmospheric carbon dioxide continues to rise, coral reefs will certainly corrode and many marine species may be driven to extinction. (It has already been established that acidification by sulphur dioxide emissions has killed freshwater lakes throughout the industrialized world.)[61]

Global warming was at first seen as a gradual phenomenon, to which we might adapt through a change in lifestyle and precautionary measures to protect coastal areas and threatened ecosystems. However, recent discussion has focused on the possibility of the 'tipping points' described by Lynas, on reaching which some climate system undergoes radical change. For example, the thermohaline circulation of the world's oceans might suddenly change direction, so that the warm waters of the

61 John McCormick, *Acid Earth*, London, 1989.

Gulf Stream no longer protect Europe from Arctic winters. Or the melting of the Greenland and Siberia Ice Shields might release the billions of tons of methane that are currently trapped beneath them, and which result from the decay under pressure of vast primeval forests.[62] In these circumstances global warming will be taken over by a 'positive feedback' mechanism, in which warming promotes further warming, until all the methane has been released.[63] Should this happen there could be no response other than some unimaginable feat of geo-engineering. This in turn will lead to changes in rainfall pattern that we are currently unable to predict, and which might spell catastrophe for many parts of the globe.[64] Even if the alarmists are overstating their case, therefore, these possibilities are so dire that we are duty bound to consider how they might be averted. The global warming that is occurring may not be all man-made; but it is still *our problem*. The question therefore arises: what measures will prevent or mitigate it, and if we cannot take them, how do we face the future?

To date, the energies of politicians, NGOs and international

---

62 R. W. Corell *et al.*, 'Emerging Challenges – Methane from the Arctic: Global Warming Wildcard', *UNEP Year Book 2008: An Overview of Our Changing Environment*, United Nations Environment Programme, Stevenage, 2008.

63 For a popular-science account of such things, see Fred Pearce, *With Speed and Violence: Why Scientists Fear Tipping Points in Climate Change*, Boston and Uckfield, 2007.

64 Philip J. Rasch *et al.*, 'An Overview of Geoengineering of Climate Using Stratospheric Sulphate Aerosols', *Philosophical Transactions of the Royal Society*, 366.1882, 1992, 4007–37.

bodies have been devoted to strategies for slowing the rate at which greenhouse gases enter the atmosphere, with the hope of slowing the rate to zero before irreversible damage has been done. The goal of the Kyoto Protocol is to stabilize the atmospheric quantities of carbon at 500 parts per million by 2050 (currently the rate is 375 and rising, from an estimated 275 prior to the Industrial Revolution). Interestingly enough, we already know of many ways in which energy can be produced with greatly reduced carbon emissions. But political exhortation, global summiting and alarmist campaigning have not changed people's incentives, and emissions have continued as before.[65]

Most of the studies devoted to the 'economics of climate change' are devoted to the costs of stabilizing atmospheric carbon at the level sought by the Kyoto Protocol, which the IPCC has proposed as likely to lead to a global temperature rise of two degrees Celsius during the course of the twenty-first century.[66] James Hansen argues that the safe level of atmospheric carbon dioxide – which he estimates at 350 parts per million – has already been surpassed, and that it will be difficult, if not impossible, to confine global warming to the two degrees proposed.[67] Faced with an impending evil, human beings either ignore it or seek to avert it. The right response might be, however, to adapt to it. Adaptation is invariably the last strategy to emerge, and usually

65 See MacKay, *op. cit.* I return to this estimable work in later chapters.

66 Thus Stern, *op. cit.*, and Helm and Hepburn, eds., *op. cit.*

67 Hansen, *op. cit.*

only after all the mistakes have been made. Indeed, according to the theory of evolution, it is precisely the mistakes that cause the adaptation – only too late for those who make them. Jared Diamond has vividly described societies that have depleted their environmental resources and then, not slowly or gently, but suddenly and catastrophically, collapsed.[68] Thus the Easter Islanders ignored the progressive deforestation of their island until it was impossible to survive there. Many people fear that we are all about to follow their example.

The publicity release for Al Gore's propaganda film *An Inconvenient Truth* began thus: 'Humanity is sitting on a ticking time bomb. If the vast majority of the world's scientists are right, we have just ten years to avert a major catastrophe that could send our entire planet into a tail-spin of epic destruction involving extreme weather, floods, droughts, epidemics and killer heatwaves beyond anything we have ever experienced.' Such statements are far from uncommon, and if the alarmists are right about the time-scale, then we must adopt immediate and far-reaching measures. However, in the present state of our knowledge, we cannot be sure what measures lie within our power or what effects might result from them. Hence the urge to haste leads to vast schemes, the effect of which on the climate is far less knowable than their effect on the prosperity, and therefore the capacity to act, of those who adopt them. This, it seems to me, is one of the greatest

68 See Jared Diamond, *Collapse: How Societies Choose or Fail to Survive*, London, 2005.

dangers that we currently face. There is only one nation in the world that has the economic strength, the adaptability, the accountability to its citizens, and the political will to address the problem. And that nation – the United States of America – is passing through an extended economic crisis at the very moment when the greatest need is for the costly research and far-reaching policies that only the United States can afford and that, indeed, only the United States has the political will to pursue.

As I write, the US Congress is considering the American Climate and Energy Security Act, presented by Congressmen Waxman and Markey. This bill – heavily influenced by input from climate activists and radical NGOs – aims to reduce the total of American greenhouse gas emissions to 83 per cent below 2005 levels by the year 2050 – in other words to a total of 1 billion tons per year. It has been calculated that the last year in which the US emitted only 1 billion tons of greenhouse gases was 1910, when the population was a quarter of the size, and the total GDP one twenty-fifth the size, of the levels reached today.[69] To achieve the target, therefore, people six times as wealthy as their forebears will have to generate (per capita) a quarter of the emissions generated by those relatively impoverished and therefore energy-conserving ancestors. How is this to be done without turning all expectations upside down? Meanwhile, in the rest of the world, it

69 See Stephen Hayward and Kenneth P. Green, 'Waxman-Markey: An Exercise in Unreality', *AEI Energy and Environment Outlook*, 3 July 2009, www.aei.org/outlook/100057.

is business as usual, with China adding two large coal-fired power stations per week to an energy base already 80 per cent dependent on coal, and with the number of cars estimated to increase by 2.3 billion worldwide between now and 2050.[70]

The American proposals emanate a sense of dream-like unreality. Unreal targets, pursued in ignorance of the means to achieve them, and without any conception of how the attempt to do so will impinge on popular sentiment, on competing goals and on the many other factors that wise government must consider, have dominated the remedies to climate change, both in the schemes of politicians and in the exhortations of the activists. There are reasons for this unreality, one being that proposals are too often made without being priced. And until they are priced competing goals (reducing emissions, providing affordable energy, maintaining a competitive economy, and so on) cannot be offset in any calculable way – there being no measure of the extent to which one good must be forgone in order to achieve some stated advance towards another.

But how, it may be asked, do we assign prices to environmental goods?[71] Until we do so, it will be hard to influence the politicians, whose decisions are invariably justified in economic terms. Hence much of the political thinking about climate change

---

70 See Dieter Helm, 'Climate-change Policy: Why Has So Little Been Achieved?', in Helm and Hepburn, eds., *op. cit.*

71 For some of the problems here see David W. Pearce and R. K. Turner, *Economics of Natural Resources and the Environment*, Hemel Hempstead, 1990.

has been bound up with attempts to cost the actions we might take in the face of it. In 1993 W. D. Nordhaus, an economist at MIT, introduced the 'Dynamic integrated model of climate and the economy', with the purpose of modelling the economic cost of global warming, and the benefits attached to the various ways of mitigating it.[72] In 2006 the Stern report to the UK government made a similar effort to price the various policies that might be effective in bringing carbon emissions under control, and came up with the surprising figure that the goal could be achieved at the low cost of 1 per cent of global GDP. Stern promptly altered this figure to 2 per cent. Subsequent authors, however, have expressed little confidence in either figure. How can you cost such things as the loss of biodiversity or the extinction of species, let alone the social upheavals that are the likely result of radically affecting people's expectations?[73] Indeed, for many people part of the un-reality of current debates comes from the dominant place that economists have assumed in shaping the environmental agenda –

72 The model is set out in W. D. Nordhaus, *Managing the Global Commons: The Economics of Climate Change*, Cambridge, MA, 1994. See also Eban S. Goodstein, *Economics and the Environment*, Hoboken, 2004.

73 See Dieter Helm's careful and persuasive critique, *op. cit.* Stern's original estimate has been recently defended in other terms by Hector Pollitt and Chris Thoung, 'Modelling a UK 80% Greenhouse Gas Emissions Reduction by 2050', *New Scientist*, 3 December 2009. Their argument has been criticized by Kenneth P. Green and Aparna Mathur, 'A Green Future for Just Pennies a Day?', *The American*, 19 February 2010, www.american.com/archive/2010/february/a-green-future-for-just-pennies-a-day.

as though the only values involved are economic, and as though we can price the earth and all that it means by measuring our willingness to pay for this or that among its gifts to us.[74] Economists are not to blame for their ascendancy in current discussions. When considering complex social problems either we price the things that we value or we don't. If we don't, then we cannot easily resolve the many conflicts of interest that abound in modern societies. If we do price them, using some 'social welfare function' that is sensitive to the different force and seriousness of the many relevant social goods, then the result is necessarily a piece of economics.[75]

Whatever we think of the costing problem, it is debatable whether we can simply arrest the processes that promote global warming. To do so would be to introduce stasis into a vastly complex dynamic system whose workings we do not understand. We can make guesses at what we might do, but their effect in the longer term is something that we cannot predict. Most greenhouse gases enter the atmosphere from other sources than human activity. Although we might be able to slow down the rate in which we humans add to the total, this would change only *one*

74 For a far-reaching critique of the welfare economist's approach to environmental problems, see Mark Sagoff, *Price, Principle and the Environment*, Cambridge, 2004. I discuss Sagoff's arguments in Chapters 7 and 8.

75 On this point see the review of Sagoff's book by David Pearce, *Environmental & Resource Economics*, 31.3, 2005, pp. 385–8. And see Pearce's own earlier defence of economic costing in David Pearce *et al.*, *Blueprint for a Green Economy*, London, 1989, ch. 3.

factor that is known to contribute to global warming. Certainly we should do it, if we can. So far, however, none of the nation states most responsible for greenhouse gas emissions has been able to meet reduction targets – whether self-imposed or accepted under the Kyoto Protocol. The reason for this is clear: any far-reaching policy requires energy for its implementation. And if the only energy available is carbon-based, no policy aimed at a substantial reduction in carbon emissions can succeed. Only the discovery of affordable clean energy can solve the problem, and until that discovery is made all treaties will be useless.[76]

Not surprisingly, therefore, there has been a move – tentative as yet – to explore the possibility of *countering* the warming process, rather than arresting it. For example, it has been suggested that we could counter the effect of greenhouse gases by augmenting atmospheric aerosols that reflect heat away from the planet, by seeding the oceans with iron filings that cause carbon-absorbing plankton to expand, or by spraying salt from the oceans into the sky, so providing condensation nuclei that will whiten the clouds over the oceans and reflect more radiation back towards the sun. Some scientists have suggested that we can explain the apparent constancy of global surface temperature between 1998 and 2008 by the presence of such factors, and notably by the large amounts of sulphate aerosols released from the coal-fired power

76 See the argument in MacKay, *op. cit.*

stations of China.[77] To use these facts as a basis for geo-engineering naturally raises problems of its own, and the suggestion has been the target of serious criticism, notably by the climatologist Alan Robock at Rutgers University.[78] And it is surely true that, in our current state of ignorance, we cannot be certain of the side effects. Nevertheless the suggestion deserves serious consideration, not least because it promises to buy time, during which the search for clean energy might be brought to a successful conclusion.

Geo-engineering of that kind is often dismissed out of hand – even with a measure of indignation.[79] For it seems to be letting us off the hook too easily, allowing us not merely to go on producing greenhouse gases but to add to our sins by producing something else as an antidote. For many people the curbing of

77 See Robert K. Kaufmann *et al.*, in Bibliography. For advocates of this kind of geo-engineering see Singer, S. Fred; Starr, C.; Revelle, R., 'What To Do About Greenhouse Warming: Look Before You Leap', *Cosmos*, 1991, pp. 28–33. John Latham, 'Amelioration of global warming by controlled enhancement of the albedo and longevity of low-level maritime clouds', *Atmospheric Science Letters*, 2002, pp. 52–8.

78 See Robock's testimony on geo-engineering to the House Committee on Science and Technology, Nov. 5th 2009, available on the Rutgers website at http://www.csp.rutgers.edu/ csp-posts/archives/77.

79 See Dale Jamieson, 'The Ethics of Geo-Engineering', *People and Place*, 1.2, 13 May 2009. Jamieson's views are based in considerations of global justice. Others follow Doug Parr, chief scientist of Greenpeace, who describes geo-engineering as 'outright dangerous'. Jamieson and Parr are right to be concerned about the ethical aspect of meddling with our planet on the scale required; some of the ethical issues are discussed by David R. Morrow *et al.*, 'Towards Ethical Norms and Institutions for Climate Engineering Research', *Environmental Research Letters*, 4, 2009, pp. 1–8.

human activity is the goal. We are the problem, and it is our intrusion into Eden that spelled disaster for the world. This emphasis on the negative is something to which I will return, since it seems to reveal another motive than the one confessed to – one more deeply rooted in our social feelings, and one which calls on emotions that we do not necessarily understand. Nevertheless, it is, in the circumstances, singularly unhelpful to warn against impending catastrophe while denouncing the most viable-seeming defence against it. There is evidence that certain kinds of geo-engineering are likely to be many times more cost effective than emission controls, with the added advantage that their effect will be manifest immediately, and not after years or decades – during which the climate may reach one of the 'tipping points' that the alarmists fear.[80] At the very least, we should be researching this option, if only as 'Plan B'. Moreover, some forms of geo-engineering – carbon sequestration from the atmosphere, for example – will simply undo the damage, rather than adding a new form of damage to the old.

It could not possibly be part of a rational response to global warming simply to say: let nothing change. On the contrary, a great many things *must* change if we are to live with the unprece-

80 See J. Eric Beckel, 'The Climate Engineering Option: Economics and Policy Implications', work in progress, available from ebickel@mail.utexas.edu Beckel analyses the economic profile of techniques of 'solar radiation management', and what kind of investment is needed in research and development to meet the IPCC's temperature reduction targets.

dented prosperity, longevity and reproductive success that make our species such a burden to the planet. However, we are being invited to extract climate change from the pile of our environmental problems and to exalt it above all the others. The effect is to neutralize our rooted and temperate ways of accommodating change. The assumption is that we are dealing with a new kind and a new order of change, and one to which we *cannot* adapt. And if that is so it would of course mark a serious departure for our species, which has survived by adapting, and which has added to the list of its biological adaptations an enormous coda of social and political adaptations, of which the market economy, the rule of law, scientific method and religion are but four, responsible between them for the vast expansion of our species and therefore for our current environmental problems.[81] It is the thought that all our adaptations – biological, social, cultural and spiritual – may now be ineffective that is so disturbing. But this thought is in no way supported by the recent history of environmental change. 'Resilience solutions', therefore, ought to be part of the repertoire of every thinking environmentalist.[82]

Consider the vast environmental transformations that occurred in Britain during the nineteenth century, when our populations moved en masse to the manufacturing cities and

81 Some other adaptations that have powerful environmental consequences: music, dancing, prayer.

82 And have been developed by several ecologists and political scientists, notably C. S. Holling and Aaron Wildavsky, whose views I discuss in Chapter 4.

whole areas of the countryside were abandoned. Early observers like William Cobbett prophesied a complete collapse of agriculture and a spoiling of the landscape, together with a losing battle against moral corruption, disease and enslavement in the growing conurbations. Within two generations, however, people were beginning to adapt to this new environment. New and less labour-intensive forms of agriculture emerged, while reforms in the law of settled land made it possible for entrepreneurial farmers to buy self-sufficient sections of the moribund estates. The harnessing of energy from coal brought an unprecedented rise in the standard of living not only in the towns but across the country, as the railways began to link the towns and to bring employment and markets to the places between them.

Although political decisions helped the process of adaptation, they did not initiate it, and were themselves the result of campaigns and movements that originated in civil society. British society adapted to the Industrial Revolution in the same way as it had set the revolution in motion: by private enterprise and civil association. Already by the end of the eighteenth century the Friendly Societies – charitable foundations offering mortgages to low income families – had begun to address the problem of crowding and homelessness in the cities. During the next fifty years the network of Anglican and Nonconformist schools expanded to offer education to a majority of the nation's children. Thanks to charitable initiatives, including the foundation in 1832 of the British Medical Association, the health of the population rapidly improved. Philanthropic agitation led to the Factory Acts, the first of which was passed in 1802. These (notably the Act of 1844) countered the worst abuses and compelled employers of children both to limit their hours of work and to ensure that they acquired a basic education. By the end of the century new centres of civilization, like Victorian Manchester and Leeds, had become home to all their residents, to be celebrated in our art and literature and fully integrated into the affections of the people.

The process that led to the growth of those cities was prodigal of hardships, injustices and ill-health, and received biting commentary from Dickens in the description of Coketown (*Hard Times*, 1869). But it was equally prodigal of faith, hope and charity, and of the environmental initiatives that led to the public control of sanitation and waste. It provides an exemplary illustration of the way in which civil society adjusts to environmental change, and manages change in the interests of its members. Commentators like Mrs Gaskell and Charles Dickens had no equivalent in previous centuries, not because things were better then, but because they were worse. The factories liberated children from the farms, where they were worked just as hard and with less hope of rescue. Children working in factories came under the eye of educated people who could afford the luxury of compassion, and within a few decades the Factory Acts had rescued them from slavery.[83]

83 See Matt Ridley, *The Rational Optimist: How Prosperity Evolves*, London, 2010, p. 220.

Surely we should not rule out the hope of adapting to climate change in a way similar to that exemplified by the response to the Industrial Revolution? Of course, if Lynas's prophecies are fulfilled, adaptation will not be possible. Old England will survive only in the way it survives in the taxi-driver's diary that is the subtext of Will Self's novel *The Book of Dave*. Many European and American cities grew as London and Bristol did, as outlets to the sea and to the goods that trade by sea. If sea levels rise such cities will be affected in ways that will be both costly and painful. But what would enable us to adapt to the change? Surely the very thing that enabled us to adapt to the Industrial Revolution, namely the growth of new forms of local attachment, new forms of civil association, new ways of co-operating with our neighbours in free and law-abiding groups. Either the changes that are to come will be manageable or they will not. And if they are manageable it is because our inherent social motives can embrace them, and not because the state has some power that we don't have, to manage them on our behalf.

My purpose in this chapter has been to suggest that the likelihood of global warming does not serve to lift environmental problems out of the spheres where the conservatism that I advocate gains a foothold – the spheres of inherited affections, national sovereignty, free enterprise and civic initiatives. Let us assume that it is true that man-made greenhouse gases pose a near and present danger to humanity, by threatening to create conditions to which we cannot adapt. Then we must learn to live in another way, so as to produce less gas; failing that, we must follow the path of geo-engineering, and look for ways to counteract our emissions by cooling the planet, meanwhile striving to adapt to whatever change is unavoidable. The first of those ways involves sacrifice; the second involves research and determination, and a large element of risk. But neither can be embarked on except in the context of a clear and acknowledged first-person plural. These are strategies that we must adopt, and must adopt *together*. It is precisely to the definition and maintenance of this 'we' that conservative politics of the kind I shall defend is directed. Sacrifices are undertaken by self-identifying communities; large-scale projects (such as will be required by geo-engineering) are the enterprises of wealthy capitalist countries. Either way, change, adaptation and remedial efforts will be the work of self-identifying nation states, and in particular of those nation states in which public spirit, enterprise and economic activity are all strong enough to bear a burden that might be at least as great as that involved in fighting a defensive war.

Global warming is a transnational problem, and raises questions about treaties and international co-operation. But this is another reason for being concerned about the eleventh-hour prophecies with which we are now repeatedly bombarded. The sparse treaty-making power of the nation states is being devoted to the pursuit of a binding agreement that very few of them are able or willing to honour and which would, if successful, substantially reduce the energy needed for the solution of other environmental problems. And these other problems – maybe just as serious – remain undiscussed, even though many of them could be solved by treaty. An example is the problem of plastic. As poisonous in its way as any greenhouse gas, plastic is entering the environment at an ever-increasing rate, with few if any provisions to control it. Although the effect on landfill sites may have been exaggerated,[84] the worst aspect of plastic is the ease with which wrappings, bags and containers escape into the environment. There are parts of Europe, Asia and the Middle East where fields, trees and hedgerows are entangled with sheeting and bags, and an area of the Pacific Ocean twice the size of Texas is supposedly now veneered with plastic rubbish, causing untold destruction to fish, sea birds and other marine life.[85] Yet the problem of plastic is one that we could solve, both nationally and globally. If no attempt is being made to solve it, this is in part because of the great climate 'emergency' upon which all our treaty-making energies are being uselessly expended.

Even when treaties are in place that address some other potentially soluble problem, global alarming ensures that nobody knows about them, and governments do little or nothing to act on them. An example is the Convention on Biodiversity, opened for

84 See the apology for plastic, and for those who make use of it, in Richard D. North, *Life on a Modern Planet: A Manifesto for Progress*, Manchester, 1995, pp. 169–71. For a contrary view, visit the Plastic Pollution Coalition website: www.earthisland.org/index.php/aboutUs/.

85 See Curtis Ebbesmeyer and Eric Scigliano, *Flotsametrics and the Floating World*, Washington DC, 2009. The size and density of The Great Pacific Garbage Patch are both disputed: see Wikipedia article.

signature at the Rio Meeting in 1992, and entering into force in 1993. This Convention initiated a much-needed series of international meetings to discuss what can be done to prevent the extinction of species and the depletion of vital habitats.[86] The meetings are rarely reported in the press, few politicians are aware of their existence and their recommendations are seldom acted upon. Yet the disappearance of species and the loss of biodiversity are changes with potentially calamitous consequences for the planet and its human passengers.

Global warming is a problem that engages with a fundamental moral idea to which conservatives attach great importance: the idea that those responsible for damage should also repair it. If global warming is caused by carbon emissions, then those nations that emit the highest per capita quantities of carbon have the greatest responsibility to repair the damage, by limiting their emissions in future and paying compensation for damage already done. That judgement has played a significant role in both Kyoto and the Copenhagen Climate Change Conference. But it does not undermine the 'we' of nationality or replace it with some transnational substitute. On the contrary, it shows that this, like every environmental question, is addressed to, and answered by, nations, acting for the people upon whose attachments and motives they can call. The substantial sacrifices that many would

---

86 Like other measures discussed at the Rio meeting, the Convention on Biodiversity incorporated a version of the Precautionary Principle, the adverse effects of which I discuss in Chapter 4.

like to impose on the people of richer countries could be accepted only as *our* duty, where the first-person plural is that of national attachment.[87]

Moreover, serious environmental problems almost invariably flow unimpeded across national borders, giving rise to questions of equity and compensation that have rarely, to date, been answered. Consider the pollution of the oceans, the side effects of pesticides and deforestation, the transfer of infectious diseases and alien species along with the migrations of people. But the response to all such threats, I shall argue, begins at home, in responsible stewardship. In further development of that theme I shall consider climate change as one problem among others, and suggest that the conservative response to it is the response that is most likely to be effective.

87 See Appendix I: Global Justice.

THREE

The Search for Salvation

One lesson to be learned from the disputes over climate change is
that science does not end our disagreements, even when they seem
to be disagreements about the facts. There are many reasons for
this and these reasons are pertinent to the debate over global
warming.[88] One suggestion, which will concern me at several
places in this book, is that there are fundamental and enduring
differences between people concerning the perception and esti-
mation of risk. It is worth exploring this suggestion now, since it
will help to steer the argument away from partisan politics.

During the eighties there emerged within sociology and political science an enterprise called 'cultural theory', which
distinguished four ways in which human beings approach social
problems. The book that initiated this approach – *Risk and Culture*
by Mary Douglas and Aaron Wildavsky – appeared in 1983. It
was followed in 1990 by *Divided We Stand*, by Michiel Schwarz

88 See Hulme, *op. cit.*

and M. G. (Michael) Thompson, and the approach was taken up by John Adams in his 1995 book *Risk*.[89] Douglas and Wildavsky distinguish four forms of social rationality:

1. That of the individualists, who look for opportunities and freedoms, and who are disposed to hold people responsible for their acts.

2. That of the egalitarians, who seek a solution that will not make distinctions between people, and who are apt to entrust problems to the state, as the impartial provider and distributor of goods.

3. That of the believers in hierarchy, who look round for the responsible authority who will take the matter out of their hands.

4. That of the fatalists, who don't think that anything worthwhile can be achieved since the Fates do not respond to human interests.

Simultaneously with the work of Douglas and Wildavsky the ecologist C. S. Holling explored the contrasting 'myths of nature' entertained by Canadian forest managers. His results, extended later by Michael Thompson, suggested that there are also four such myths – nature as benign, ephemeral, perverse and

---

89 Mary Douglas and Aaron Wildavsky, *Risk and Culture: An Essay on the Selection of Technological and Environmental Dangers*, Berkeley, 1983; Schwarz and Thompson, *op. cit.*; John Adams, *Risk*, London, 1995.

capricious – which map onto the four forms of human rationality.[90] Thus individualists, who believe that people are or ought to be risk-takers, responsible for what they do, tend to see nature as benign, and human beings as adaptable. Egalitarians are suspicious of risk-takers, who constantly rearrange the world in their own interests and divide society into successes and failures. And they justify their suspicion by representing nature as precarious and to be disturbed at our peril. For egalitarians risk-taking is liable to push things to a 'tipping point' and so to spell disaster for us all.

Cultural theory aims to be a purely factual enterprise, neither recommending nor condemning the human types that it describes. I put no trust in its scientific credentials, but it has one very great merit in the current context. It captures tendencies within social and political thinking that help to show why there is a real, lasting and rooted difference between 'left' and 'right'. And it provides a language with which both left and right can discuss their shared concerns without regarding their opponents as inhuman. You may think that the terms 'left' and 'right' have been emptied of meaning by recent politics. In my view, however, the terms are as necessary today as they were when first applied in the French Revolution: they do not describe theories or goals, but *identities*, revealed in the structure of collective choice.

90 These results are applied to the climate change debate by M. G. Thompson and S. Rayner, 'Cultural Discourses', in S. Rayner and E. Malone, eds., *Human Choice and Climate Change, vol. 1: The Societal Framework*, Columbus, 1998, pp. 265–344.

Cultural theory also helps us to see that some of the normative issues about which we are ceaselessly reasoning may reflect attitudes that lie deeper than reason. It is surely undeniable that the contrast between the individualist and the egalitarian underlies many of our political disagreements, not least those over environmental policy. Nineteenth-century socialism was a protest against the unequal distribution of power and property in capitalist societies. This egalitarian attack on capitalism was countered by an individualist defence of it. Capitalism, its defenders argued, should not be seen as an unjust exploitation of the producers, but as the exercise of free enterprise under conditions of risk, with individuals taking full responsibility for failure as well as reaping the rewards of their success. The arguments on both sides are familiar and I do not need to rehearse them. The point is that their weight seems to depend upon the person to whom they are addressed. The egalitarian will be swayed in one direction, the individualist in another, by arguments that are accessible and intelligible to both. This does not mean that there is no distinction between right and wrong, true and false, valid and invalid. But it does suggest that to pass from a judgement that is right, true or valid to a consensus in its favour will never be easy.

Those distinctions of character have carried over into the debates concerning the environment. Egalitarians, who might once have blamed unbridled capitalism for the inequities of industrial society, now blame unbridled capitalism for the unjust appropriation of the earth, which by rights belongs to everyone,

75

future people included. Individualists, who might once have defended the market as the engine of prosperity, now defend it as the right way to protect the environment, by ensuring that polluters bear the cost of what they do, and by providing incentives to minimize waste. Those who criticized state control of the economy now criticize state control of the environment. And something of the old left–right antagonism has therefore got a purchase in the new field of environmental politics. For many egalitarians big business and the consumer society have retained their negative standing, even if the market economy has finally established itself in their thinking as a necessary part of any durable social order.

The distinction between the egalitarian and the individualist corresponds in part to the division between left and right – between 'liberal' and 'conservative', to use the American labels – in modern politics. This is not the whole truth, however, not even from the standpoint of cultural theory, which recognizes two further 'viable ways of life', those of the hierarchist and the fatalist. And in real people motives become 'viable' only in context, and only when mixed. The conservatism that I endorsed in Chapter 1 is not simply a matter of individualism, even if it emphasizes freedom and responsibility as core components in a life properly lived. It also favours custom, tradition and institutions, and the hierarchies that inevitably flow from them. And it is not without its own egalitarian sympathies – at least, in aspiring towards a rule of law under which everyone is offered equal protection. If conservatism is in conflict with the 'left', as this has been commonly identified, it is over the scope of the egalitarian aim, the use of the state to enforce it, and the threat posed by equality to communal and sacral values.[91]

Associated with radical egalitarianism is the social motive that Nietzsche called *ressentiment* – the sense that power and privilege are affronts to those who do not possess them, and must be pulled from their eminence, so that equality can be established in their stead.[92] Nietzsche believed *ressentiment* to be a defining feature of the Christian worldview and of the 'slave morality' preached by Jesus. This contention was decisively refuted by Max Scheler, who nevertheless upheld Nietzsche's view that resentment lies at the heart of modern politics, being responsible for the goals as well as much of the rhetoric of socialism.[93] In modern democracies, envious comparisons and slighted feelings have a head start over conciliation, and this has been one major cause of the conflict between left and right in our time. Conservatives see politics as an agenda-free brokering of rival interests, whose goal is peace. That

91 Though that too is simplifying. Recent research by empirical psychologists suggests that, when it comes to social attitudes, there is a systematic and evolutionally based distinction between liberals and conservatives; see Jonathan Haidt, *The Happiness Hypothesis: Finding Modern Truth in Ancient Wisdom*, New York, 2006, and Jonathan Haidt and Jesse Graham, 'Planet of the Durkheimians: Where Community, Authority and Sacredness Are the Foundations of Morality', in J. T. Jost *et al.*, eds., *Social and Psychological Bases of Ideology and System Justification*, New York, 2009.

92 Friedrich Nietzsche, *Beyond Good and Evil: Prelude to a Philosophy of the Future*, 1886.

93 Max Scheler, *Ressentiment*, New York, 1961.

conception of politics has not prevailed among politicians on the left, who have often called for massive social transformations, and a political programme organized around an agenda, to be achieved by a 'struggle' with the hierarchies and structures that stand in the way. Such a struggle is exactly what resentment demands: not the raising of the underdog only, but the humbling of the *Überhund* on top of him.

Nietzsche's theory is more biological than cultural. He is tracing our psychological dispositions to primordial 'adaptations', which were functional once, but are no longer functional in the world that we have made. *Ressentiment* might have bestowed coherence on the Pleistocene tribe, but it is a divisive force in a free society. It is suspicious of success, and disposed to blame those with power for the sufferings of those without it. *Ressentiment* is one of the reasons why people on the left are reluctant to accept markets, social hierarchies, the world of finance and big business, or to see in those things anything but the greed of those who profit from them and the oppression of those who don't.

In recent history radical egalitarians have also tended to be internationalists, looking for that vantage point outside the national settlement, from which the privileged and the powerful could be levered from their perch. They have been suspicious of both traditional loyalties and the effects of free enterprise, which maintain inequalities of privilege and power. And they have adhered to complex and far-reaching agendas, which often have the total reordering of society as their goal.[94] But there is a significant division within the ranks of the left. Hiding behind the noisy avant-garde there has always been, and in the English-speaking world especially, another and quieter form of egalitarianism, one that puts the local before the global, civil society before the state, and private initiatives before legal edicts. The avant-garde seeks to take hold of the political and legal structures that will secure the social goal. Behind the scenes, however, are those small alliances of friends and neighbours, those groups who are making space for themselves in the nooks and crannies on which the eye of officialdom seldom falls.

In Britain and America the environmental movement on the left has been more closely associated with this localized form of action – as in the followers of Richard Jefferies and Aldo Leopold. Although eager to combine environmental rectitude with egalitarian distribution, this quieter leftism has avoided overt politics, and sought for those places on the edge of society where it can show by example how to live in another, less damaging and more socially scrupulous way.

Thus, taking inspiration from the writings of the Russian anarchist Peter Kropotkin, the British writer Colin Ward has advocated small-scale initiatives, outside the purview of the state, in which 'mutual aid' takes the place of legislative edicts, to bring

94 Examples in the case of environmental politics include Monbiot, *op. cit.*, and David Orr, *Earth in Mind: On Education, Environment, and the Human Prospect*, Washington DC, 1993.

about goals that are both environmentally friendly and in conformity with social justice.[95] Ward's writings have influenced a generation of British environmentalists, including Ken Worpole, Simon Fairlie and Ian Christie, who have tried to develop real alternatives to the environmentally destructive and socially exclusive ways of using natural resources.[96] I will return to their endeavours later, since it seems to me that this 'civil' form of left environmentalism opens the way to an alliance in which conservatives and free-marketeers could also be included.

When considering inputs into environmental politics from the left, however, we should not ignore the legacy of socialism. For several decades before, during and after the Second World War many Europeans believed in the socialist project. They saw politics as a means to social transformation, rather than as a homeostatic process through which interests are brokered. The wealthy, the privileged, the 'bourgeois', the privately educated and the successful were routinely targeted as people to be controlled, impeded and brought down. In Britain post-war Labour governments felt called upon to create a 'new society', rather than to shore up the corrupt and hierarchical one that had survived the conflict with Germany.

95 See Colin Ward, *Arcadia for All: The Legacy of a Makeshift Landscape*, Nottingham, 2004, and Colin Ward and David Crouch, *The Allotment: Its Landscape and Culture*, 3rd ed., Nottingham, 1997.

96 Ken Worpole, *Richer Futures: Fashioning a New Politics*, London, 1999; Simon Fairlie, *Low Impact Development: Planning and People in a Sustainable Countryside*, Charlbury, 1996; Ian Christie et al., *From Here to Sustainability*, London, 2001.

Many egalitarians still see politics in those terms, as the pursuit of an agenda, with equality at the top of it. And resentment still has a prominent place in their rhetoric, with environmental destruction blamed on free enterprise and the market, described not in those terms but as 'consumerism', 'selfishness' and 'greed'. This lowering of the tone lowers also the tone of those opposed to it. Thus to the attacks of the egalitarians the individualists respond by defending controversial businesses, such as supermarkets and agribusinesses, and the consumer culture that goes with them, while dismissing global warming as a hoax. The question then becomes submerged in a wider ideological conflict, between egalitarian 'justice' and individualist 'freedom', even though our environmental problems have nothing much to do with either value. The real evil against which both sides should be united is the habit of treating the earth as a thing to be used but not revered. Instead they are fighting over competing claims to use it.

There is another and deeper cause of the antagonism that egalitarians feel towards the world of business. Because they see nature as precariously balanced and jeopardized by the hubris of the risk-takers, egalitarians have a tendency to move in a 'salvationist' direction. Faced with the predations of big business, and the unpredictable outcomes of the market, they often suffer from a sense of impending catastrophe, and issue calls to action that mobilize motives and methods that can be justified only in large-scale emergencies. At the same time they give voice to a total distrust of old priorities and familiar compromises. The heartfelt sense of alarm is not a result of collecting the evidence, but at best the cause of it. The alarm comes first, the evidence later. And it is the alarm that is adhered to as the evidence changes. In consequence compromise solutions and small-scale adjustments are all too often discounted as ways of evading the problem.

Recall the sequence of events in the French Revolution. Those who took power from the King and the Court – the Girondins, as they came to be known – were for the most part reasonable, compromising people, who sought an accommodation with the existing order and the rectification of long-standing abuses. But they were quickly displaced by the Jacobins, under the leadership of Saint-Just and Robespierre, who spoke the language of emergency, warned the French people of imminent destruction if something were not immediately done, and promised a new order that would entirely rid them of the deeper causes of social conflict.[97] Great emergencies require top-down solutions. They can be met only by mobilizing society as a whole, and establishing a command-structure that will unite the people around a single goal. And if you wish for such a command-structure, maybe with yourself and your friends (who will soon cease to be your friends) at the top of it, then you are well advised to invent the great emergency that will require it.

That is the motivation that we see in all the twentieth-century

---

97 See François Furet, *Penser la Révolution française*, Paris, 1978; Roger Scruton, 'Man's Second Disobedience', in *The Philosopher on Dover Beach*, Manchester, 1999.

revolutions. It seethes on the surface of Lenin's rhetoric, and indeed is contained in the title (stolen from Chernyshevsky) of the pamphlet with which Lenin first thrust himself on the world: 'What is to be done?'[98] Just that question resounded through subsequent revolutionary movements, attached to different emergencies and different radical solutions by those who exploited it. And always – whether Stalin, Hitler, Mao or Pol Pot was asking the question, or whether Trotsky, Schmitt, Sartre or Zinn was backing it up – the question had the single meaning that radical policies, controlled from the top, are what the world requires. Furthermore, this control from the top is never described as such; it is always presented as control from below, by the people, for whom the revolutionary elite is merely the 'vanguard', anxious to capture power only in order to relinquish it to those who have the better claim.

There is something deep in human nature to which this emergency-mongering appeals: a residue of ancient fears and collective panics, deposited during the dark origins of our species. The collective alert, in which the alpha-male leads a mass movement of fight or flight, is an old adaptation, dysfunctional now in times of political order and rational discourse, but not the less real for being useless. Throughout our civilization, and despite the wonderful apparatus of government that has come down to us from Greek democracy, Roman law and the Judaeo-Christian discipline of forgiveness and neighbour-love, we have seen mass

98 V. I. Lenin, 'What is to be done?', in *Iskra*, 4, May 1901.

movements of panic, some initiated by the real threats of war, invasion or plague, but just as many arising in the imagination, as thoughts of the last judgement, of witchcraft and the Devil's work, of the Second Coming or the prophesied Armageddon, sweep across the trembling masses of the credulous and the ill-informed.[99] The one who runs into the street crying 'The End is nigh!' is sure of an audience, as is the one who, like Lenin, stands on a soap-box shouting 'What is to be done?' The quiet voice of the Anglo-Saxon poet, who told us that 'this too shall pass' is heard only later, when the damage has been done.[100] In all its forms, whether secular or religious, this intransigent doomsday posture involves a full-scale repudiation of life as it is.

Nor is it only the egalitarians who are tempted by political salvationism. Individualists too may give way to it, calling for radical transformations, with themselves (or rather, fellow individualists) in charge. In the influential writings of Ayn Rand we find a kind of Nietzschean contempt for ordinary dependent beings and a supremacist assertion of the world-transforming risk-taker, who will save us from the degeneracy into which we are being led by envy and resentment. In the same spirit as Lenin, Rand bombarded the American public with doomsday tracts, telling them that their timid democracy was on a path to destruc-

99 Norman Cohn, *The Pursuit of the Millennium*, Oxford, 1957; J. Maddox, *The Doomsday Syndrome*, London, 1972.

100 See again the comprehensive survey of panics by Booker and North, *op. cit.* The precise words of Deor (tenth century) are *Þæs ofereode, þisses swa mæg!* – 'that was got over, so shall be this'.

tion, and that only the risk-taking heroes should stand at the helm.[101] Rand remains as influential in America today as she was in the post-war years, when America was emerging as the world's leading superpower.

Salvationist politics have played a major part in the environmental movements of our day.[102] From Meyer-Abich's call for a revolution on behalf of nature, to the eco-anarchism of Richard Sylvan (né Routley), radical eco-warriors have demanded total life-changing commitment from their followers.[103] In its more mystical forms, the cult of Gaia comes close to recapturing the pagan view of the earth as a goddess, whose animating principles run through all of us.[104] The scientific, or pseudo-scientific, evidence on which the cult has drawn seems to purify its mystical side, and make it into a fitting substitute for the old religions, one that can be believed sincerely by a fully modern mind: such, it seems to me, is the appeal of the 'deep ecology' movement founded by the Norwegian philosopher and one-time logical

---

101 See especially *Atlas Shrugged*, Rand's ever-popular novel.

102 See Bron Taylor, *Dark Green Religion: Nature Spirituality and the Planetary Future*, Berkeley, 2009.

103 Klaus Michael Meyer-Abich, *Aufstand für die Natur*, Munich, 1990; Richard Sylvan and David Bennett, *The Greening of Ethics*, Cambridge, 1994; Richard and Val Routley, 'Human Chauvinism and Environmental Ethics', in Don Mannison *et al.*, *Environmental Philosophy*, Canberra, 1980.

104 See James Lovelock, *Gaia: A New Look at Life on Earth*, Oxford, 1979, and the same author's recent *The Revenge of Gaia*, New York, 2006. Lovelock himself sees the 'Gaia hypothesis' – namely, that the earth and the life upon it comprise a single homeostatic system, currently taking 'revenge' against our human excesses – as a scientific and not a religious belief.

positivist, Arne Naess.[105] Such movements aim to unite people around a collective goal, and offer the comforts of solidarity to those who have hitherto suffered from feelings of helplessness and alienation. They grow by inviting on to the stage of politics the passions of the group, and by replicating the primordial religious experience invoked by Durkheim in *The Elementary Forms of the Religious Life*, which is the experience of membership.

The doomsday literature and the imperatives of salvation are two sides of a single coin. The great salvific religions proceed, first by presenting sinners with a description of their case that seems to allow no remedy but only despair, and then by offering hope in the form of a total doctrine, the path of purity and submission, which is the unique way to redemption. The doomsday scenario has the effect of removing all belief in small-scale and negotiated remedies, and creating in their place a great and comprehensive longing for salvation. And then salvation is offered, in terms that require nothing save obedience. The doctrine goes on to speak of dangers: among us there are those companions of the Devil whose false remedies are so many traps for the unwary, and who must be rooted out and exterminated if the way of salvation is not to be obscured.[106] Pursuit and persecution of the heretic have therefore occupied a large part of the

105 See the account in George Sessions, *Deep Ecology for the Twenty-First Century*, Boston, 1995, and the discussion in Chapter 6 below.

106 Eric Hoffer, *The True Believer: Thoughts on the Nature of Mass Movements*, New York, 1951; Booker and North, *op. cit.*

activities required by revolutionary movements from 1789 to the present day, and once the salvationist illusion has triumphed politics turns to witch hunting, faction forming and pursuit of 'the enemy within'. It goes without saying that this is of no help in our present circumstances. But the tendency is there and it is well to understand it.

The current emphasis on climate change should be considered in this light. Global warming is not the kind of small-scale issue that can be addressed by individuals, or which slots into the normal modes of practical reasoning. It is a *transcendental* issue, concerning the state of mankind as such. Like original sin, it weighs on us all, and like original sin it might seem to require a salvationist solution. Moreover, it connects immediately with the sins that mean most to egalitarians and with which many conservatives too are far from happy: consumerism, the luxury lifestyle, the obscenities of waste. Climate change hovers above the sinner in his sports utility vehicle like a vision of judgement, and it is a vision that comprehends the whole world. Hence climate change has been not merely believed in but *seized upon*, as a convenient way of turning a political problem into a moral and spiritual challenge, a wake-up call to mankind as a whole, which can be addressed only by action so radical as to amount to a change of life. And when people propose some less demanding response to the problem, they may be greeted with surprise and indignation, since they are undermining the faith. For the salvationists, it is *only* a change of life that will meet the prevailing need, which is as much a spiritual as a material one. Global warming sounds in their thinking as a call of angelic trumpets from the sky. *Du mußt dein Leben ändern* – 'you must change your life': Rilke's summary of the religious imperative, spoken to the poet from an antique torso of Apollo, speaks also from much of the radical literature of the environmentalists.[107] Yet rarely does the literature address the question of how ordinary people could obey such a command.

Uniting behind a purpose facilitates sacrifice, gives clear goals and strategies, and produces the kind of comradeship that is witnessed in armies and religious missions. The desire for this kind of comradeship has surely been implanted in us by evolution. People who did not have the capacity to unite in this way would be overwhelmed by emergencies, unable to defend themselves against attack, and probably destined in the circumstances of the hunter-gatherer to starve.

But old adaptations are precisely what we need to remedy and balance, now that we have achieved the supreme adaptation that is reason. Goal-directed membership has the disadvantage that the purpose itself cannot easily be subjected to critical examination, that its internal defects and contradictions must, in the interest of unity, be passed over, and that critics are inevitably treated as

---

107 Rilke's line forms the title of a book by the German philosopher Peter Sloterdijk, in which he addresses the question of how to live, in an era of bestiality and 'atmosterrorism', when the environment that is our means of life can be taken from us by force. Peter Sloterdijk, *Du mußt dein Leben ändern*, Frankfurt, 2009. Rilke's 'Archaischer Torso Apollos' occurs in *Neue Gedichte*, 1907.

enemies, as those who 'do not belong', and who fall outside the scope of the first-person plural. This surely accounts for the negativity of so many radical campaigns, which are often far clearer concerning what they are *against* than what they are for. It is easy to destroy, hard to create. It is easy to identify the targets of resentment and to pull them down; harder to work towards a world in which people will live in peace with those who do not share their opinions or who are more fortunate than themselves.

When people join together in a partnership or a club, they establish a form of collective liability, and the law has devised procedures whereby to recognize this liability in the courts. People who make decisions on behalf of the partnership or the club become accountable to the other members, and the club shapes its rules accordingly. Agenda-driven movements, however, are not like this. They involve a flow of collective sentiment, which might peak here and there in the shape of leaders and spokesmen, but which rushes ever onwards like an invading army, seldom pausing to restore the moral order that lies fragmented in its wake. The result is the erosion of accountability – both to the followers and to those whose interests they damage.

Nothing in politics stands still, and increasingly left-wing environmentalists are dissociating themselves from the campaigning NGOs, and preferring the small-scale work that both supports and expresses the low-impact way of life. The movements for low carbon communities, slow food and permaculture have recruited many who identify themselves as 'on the left'. Indeed, this shift away from radical, government-shaped solutions should be welcomed by conservatives, since it promises the thing that environmentalists of both persuasions need, which is a way of sharing our problems and co-operating in solving them.

As environmentalists are increasingly disposed to recognize, top-down solutions create incentives that do not exist in circumstances of free co-operation. The point has been established in a series of important works by J. M. Buchanan and Gordon Tullock, who show the way in which the top-down imposition of goals creates administrative positions that produce a rent on the common product.[108] The expansion of government by the creation of commissions, committees and administrative posts has led in almost every European country to a situation in which more than half of GDP is dispensed to state dependants. Rents obtained from the state are secure, since they are guaranteed by the legal order – at least until the legal order collapses. Hence there emerges a new structure of incentives, as people endeavour to obtain positions within the system. This in turn creates new motives for collective action – unionization designed to exclude interlopers; ideological tests (as in modern universities) designed to limit competition; punishments for whistle-blowers, and so on.

108 James Buchanan and Gordon Tullock, *The Calculus of Consent: Logical Foundations of Constitutional Democracy*, Ann Arbor, 1962. See also Gordon Tullock, 'The Welfare Costs of Tariffs, Monopolies, and Theft', *Western Economic Journal*, 5.3, June 1967; James Buchanan, 'Rent-seeking, Non-compensated Transfers, and Laws of Succession', *Journal of Law and Economics*, 26, April 1983, pp. 71–85; *Cost and Choice: An Inquiry in Economic Theory*, Indianapolis, 1999.

All this we are witnessing in the growth of the European Union, and in the next chapter I give some examples that will show how the incentive structure of such a bureaucracy is highly likely to impede its public goals – although not the private goals of the bureaucrats who announce them.

Comparable adverse effects arise in business oligopolies, and it is often the sight of directors and chief executives elaborately cushioned from the devastation that their businesses cause that turns people against the free market idea. However, in a properly administered legal order, a business can neither control nor evade the laws under which it operates, and there is therefore a *solution* to problems caused by the misconduct of business that is not available to problems caused by the mischievous actions of state bureaucracies. Furthermore, it is increasingly apparent that good behaviour in business is a commercial asset, and even in a big business in which rents are relatively secure, the recipient may be expected to pay for them by good behaviour.[109]

The problems here (famously summarized by Terence in the rhetorical question *quis custodiet ipsos custodes?* – 'who will guard those guardians?') are not specifically problems for environmental politics. But it is worth reflecting on the way in which Terence's question was answered in socialist economies, such as that imposed by the Soviet Communist Party or that which prevailed for fifty or more years in China. Although there are few such economies remaining, the environmental devastation that

109 Ted Malloch, *Spiritual Enterprise*, New York, 2009.

they caused remains as a permanent testimony to the folly of centralized government under monopoly control. In a socialist economy, the division of powers between executive, legislative and judicial arms of government is either non-existent or easily set aside in the interests of 'public policy'. In such an economy there is no real distinction between an emergency and the ordinary conduct of economic life, since the government takes charge of both, and applies in day-to-day decision-making the same top-down principles that in a free society might be plausibly justified only in a crisis. Even if it imposes stringent laws to protect the environment, the government can amend those laws at will and evade them with impunity, so that they offer no real barrier to environmental degradation.

During the communist years it was a criminal offence in Poland to discharge effluent from factories and sewers into the rivers; but the factories and the sewers were controlled by the state, which was in turn controlled by the Communist Party. Hence nobody was ever penalized under the anti-pollution laws, since it was legally impossible to bring the Communist Party to judgement, and politically dangerous to try. The rivers in consequence were entirely dead, and river water could not be used even to irrigate the land. With the subsequent growth of private property in the factories and an independent judiciary, the rivers have begun to change, and some are again acquiring fish.[110] Likewise

110 See the Library of Congress summary of the Polish situation at www.countrystudies.us/poland/25.htm. Commentators have drawn atten-

there were laws and regulations in place in the Soviet Union that, if applied, might have prevented the Chernobyl accident. But those uniquely entitled to invoke and apply them were also those with the motive to evade them, and as a result one of the greatest environmental disasters to occur in recent years became all but inevitable.[111] From the poisoning of the Czech forests by acid rain, to the destruction of the Black Sea sturgeon, and from the eroded and depleted soil of the collective farms to the soulless concrete 'monotowns' built around blighted industries, the evidence is incontrovertible that the centrally planned economy is an environmental disaster.[112]

Even in a democratic society in which private property and the rule of law enforce a proper separation between the one who threatens harm and the one who prevents or punishes it, the

tion to the way in which China, in response to international pressure, has been passing laws and establishing institutions to further environmental protection, but doing nothing to enforce those laws or respond to the advice received. For more details, see Fred C. Bergsten *et al.*, *China's Rise: Challenges and Opportunities*, Washington DC, 2008.

111 The story is told reasonably clearly by Wikipedia, under 'Chernobyl', while detailed scientific information can be found in the document *Chernobyl Forum*, issued by the UN in 2006. The Chernobyl accident was only one of many, and, in terms of long-term consequences, probably not the worst. The Russian province of Chelyabinsk, closed to foreigners until 1992, has been described as the most contaminated spot on the planet, following three horrifying nuclear accidents and the persistent disposal of radioactive waste in lakes and rivers. See the documentary by Slawomir Grünberg at www.logtv.com.

112 See Leon Aron, 'Russia's "Monotowns" Time-Bomb', *AEI Russian Outlook*, October 2009, www.aei.org/outlook/100080.

evidence is that state bureaucracies become a danger to the environment as soon as they acquire the role of controlling rather than containing what is done. A nice illustration is provided by the story of Ravenna Park in Seattle. This was established in 1887 by Mr and Mrs William W. Beck, who bought several parcels of land on the outskirts of the city, in order to preserve and provide public access to the giant fir trees growing there – some 400 feet high and 20 feet in diameter. They built a pavilion for concerts and nature lectures, and charged a 25¢ entrance fee to the park, which would be visited by around 10,000 people every day. In 1911 the city, in response to conservationist pressure, bought the park under a compulsory purchase order for $135,663. Almost at once the giant trees began disappearing, cut down and sold by park employees, sometimes with a bureaucratic rubber stamp that condemned a particular tree as a 'threat to public safety'. By 1925 none of the trees remained. An effective private investment that had conserved an important environmental asset, and created a lively public interest in maintaining it, had been destroyed by public ownership in a matter of fourteen years.[113]

This pattern has been repeated around the world with the takeover of well-managed resources by the state, and the subsequent loss of the mechanisms whereby the costs of maladministration are inflicted on the culprit. Notorious in this connection has been the British Forestry Commission, established

113 This and other instructive cases are described in Terry Anderson and Donald Leal, *Free Market Environmentalism*, London, 2001.

during the First World War under conditions of national emergency, and charged with taking control of forests and the production of timber throughout the country.[114] The inability of the Commission to adapt to an economy in which timber is no longer of the first importance, to manage the complex environments entrusted to its charge, or to maintain either the visual beauty or the biodiversity of the vast areas of land under its control is now well known. Although the Commission was established with the purpose of maintaining and preserving British woodlands, it has been shown that, during the fifties and sixties, when it controlled most of the marketable timber, the rate of destruction of the woodlands was greater than ever before, and entirely without historical parallel.[115] Public bodies are able to externalize their costs in a way that private bodies seldom manage, and this fact alone makes them unreliable trustees of our collective assets. Of course, private firms are also in the habit of externalizing their costs – and often they lobby government for the regulations and procedures that will ease the attempt. Moreover, the familiar devices of modern business – limited liability, shareholding, bonus payments and secured pensions – can give rise to large rents with small accountability. To this familiar problem, however, state control is not a remedy. On the contrary, it is a way of augmenting the disease.

114 See Oliver Rackham, *The History of the Countryside: The Full Fascinating Story of Britain's Landscape*, London, 1986. See also Massingham, *The Faith of a Fieldsman*, pp. 63, 243–5.

115 Rackham, *op. cit.*, pp. 93–7.

The lesson to be drawn from the dysfunctional results of state control is not the simple one, that everything must be privatized and that the market must prevail. The negative results of statism derive from a deeper cause than the confiscation of property rights and the resulting distortion of market mechanisms. They derive from the destruction of feedback. The market is simply one example of a homeostatic system that receives and responds to 'negative feedback' when things go wrong. In a market economy investors withdraw their savings from failing industries, and place them in industries that might succeed; as a result, costly failures are eliminated, and the system returns quickly to equilibrium when the wrong decisions are made. This well-known mechanism (which depends upon individuals assuming the risk of their own decisions) parallels the homeostatic systems that maintain animals in being, through the negative feedback provided by pain, fear and stress.[116] But the market is only one way in which feedback loops grow within human communities, and it is one of the tasks of this book to identify other ways in which people spontaneously adjust to social pressures and environmental changes, in order to maintain the equilibrium that they need. I shall also try to show how state initiatives, in the form of subsidies and regulation, often destroy the feedback loops needed for their own success. The state can lay down the constraints that enterprises must obey, but ought not to acquire an interest in their disobedience.

116 See Hans Selye, *The Physiology and Pathology of Exposure to Stress*, Montreal, 1950.

The distinction between left and right is wrongly described by modern commentators as a distinction between the state and the market. As I earlier suggested, it is in part a distinction between two human types, the one seeing politics as the collective pursuit of an egalitarian goal, the other seeing it as a free association between individuals, in which absent generations and present hierarchies have a place. Hence the two forms of membership: movements with causes, and civil associations that are ends in themselves.[117] My claim is that the first of those is a threat to homeostasis, the second a form of it. If we see environmental questions from that second perspective, then the emphasis shifts from control to incentive. We solve environmental problems not by appointing someone to take charge of them, but by creating the incentives that will lead people to solve them for themselves. The problem with centralized control is not merely that it reduces or extinguishes accountability, but also that it creates incentives that militate against its own success. In every case government has a part to play, but its proper role is not to take charge of the problem, but to create the framework and the constraints that enable people to take charge of it themselves.

When the state imposes central control it becomes immediately exposed to lobbying from rival interest groups and single-issue fanatics, and will favour the group that makes the

---

117 The connections between homeostasis and the existence of organisms as 'ends in themselves' is made, somewhat obscurely, by Kant, in the second part of *Critique of Judgement*.

most noise, stirs up the most trouble or gives the most money to the ruling clique. The more distant the legislature from the people the greater will be the distortion. The European Union, with its 180,000 pages of regulations, many of them absurd but most of them useful to lobbyists, illustrates the process. In a normal legislature lobbying is often an object of suspicion to the ordinary voter. Not so the lobbying in Brussels. For lobbying is the only outside pressure that the bureaucrats feel: there is no popular sentiment or electoral process that might impede its impact. And the rewards of lobbying are enormous. A manufacturer of specialized car seats for children, for example, that can secure a regulation imposing such seats by law, does not merely steal a competitive advantage in one country: if the law is issued by Brussels, it gives a competitive advantage in twenty-seven countries, with no need to lobby place by place. The example illustrates the way in which competitive advantage can be pursued under the guise of 'health and safety'. For the very reason that the legislative powers of the Commission can address any issue that affects the single market, private lobbying can disguise itself as public spirit. Increasingly firms lobby for regulations that tie the hands of the competition, rather than regulations that ensure a 'level playing field', and this negative approach operates at the level of national governments as well as individual businesses.

It is not only the inherently corrupting circumstances of the EU that distorts incentives in this way, however. A recent American illustration is provided by 'endangered species legislation', which enables environmental groups to lobby one by one for their favourite species. By this means it is possible to put an absolute brake on farming or development in places where some vulnerable species is in jeopardy. The result is a policy that is counter-productive because it is absolute, in circumstances where only a compromise could serve the environmental cause. A case in hand is the San Joaquin Valley in California – irrigated through massive public works projects that caused a once desert region to bloom. Environmental groups argue that the pumping of water for irrigation purposes threatens the autumn spawning grounds of the endangered delta smelt (a tiny fish that is of little use to anything save itself). Litigation by such groups is forcing the local authorities to curtail the supply of water to the farms. In 2008, according to Tulare County Supervisor Allen Ishida, California was thereby forced to let 26 million cubic feet of fresh-water supplies run away into the ocean – enough to supply the entire Silicon Valley for two years. Further attempts to protect fish species as endangered will lead to more curbs on irrigation, and revenue losses to farmers in the San Joaquin Valley were in the order of $500 million in 2008, and could reach $3 billion if litigation is successful.[118]

That is only one example of a disproportionate benefit conferred on one component of the environment – the delta smelt – by the top-down approach to protecting it. Legislation does not

118 See Max Schulz, 'Emptying Reservoirs in the Middle of a Drought', *American Spectator*, September 2009.

move as fast as the problems it is designed to solve or mitigate, and pressure groups can use old legislation (in this case the US Endangered Species Act of 1973) to advance their favourite causes, indifferent to the other interests that ought to be balanced in any policy outcome. In 1993 the federal government forbad private landowners from creating firebreaks around their homes in California's Riverside County for fear of disturbing the protected Stephens' kangaroo rat, which had taken up residence there. When as a result wildfires swept through the county, both the homes and the rats were destroyed.[119]

Endangered species legislation has had similar effects outside the United States. The protection afforded to the badger in the United Kingdom has made it all but impossible to respond effectively to the diseases that have swept through the badger population, now that it has grown to fill its ecological niche. The diseases include TB, which many argue is passed from the badgers to cattle, and which is witnessed in the constant outbreaks of bovine TB in British pastures. This in turn has a demoralizing effect on cattle farmers, who lose interest in caring for the pastures, which in turn are abandoned or allowed to drift towards the kind of 'horsiculture' that reduces them to scrub.

119 Dean Kleckner, 'Species Law Was Its Own Worst Enemy', *Chicago Tribune*, 11 December 1993. There were further issues of human management after these fires, when post-fire aerial seedings introduced non-native species to the decimated areas. See J. E. Keeley *et al.*, 'Overview of Management Issues Raised by the 1993 Wildfires in Southern California', in *Brushfires in California Wildlands: Ecology and Resource Management*, Fairfield, WA, 1995.

Favouritism arises from the very nature of bureaucracies, which proceed by the disaggregation of tasks, assigning to one office problems that cannot thereafter be considered by another. In a devastating book, Christopher Booker and Richard North have shown the way in which self-regulating practices are one by one destroyed when brought under the control of outside regulators.[120] Their examples place a question mark over the very idea that we can solve environmental problems by regulation alone. The question of how to distinguish good from bad regulation has indeed become one of the most vexing issues in environmental politics, and one to which I return in the next chapter.

Perhaps the most unfortunate aspect of the centralized approach to environmental problems is that, while advancing a non-compromising agenda, it ignores the need to provide ordinary people with a motive for adopting it. The impression is created that the only way to protect the environment is by putting pressure on government, through campaigns that require precise goals and legislative targets. Ordinary people do not take part in such things, and are not easily animated to stir up trouble for their fellow citizens by pressing for legislation that will inconvenience them. It is because they have acquired the habit of noticing this, indeed, that so many environmentalists have been drawn to the anarchist tradition, and have argued that the way forward lies in small-scale volunteer initiatives outside the control, and maybe

120 Christopher Booker and Richard D. North, *The Mad Officials*, London, 1994.

even outside the awareness, of the state.[121] But such people are not the ones who make the noise or attract political attention, since the avoidance of political attention is part of their goal.

It has often been noticed, indeed, that activist campaigns, which tend to be conducted in the name of the people as a whole, neither consult the people nor show much interest in noticing them – a point that was already obvious to Burke, in considering the insolence of the French revolutionaries. Such campaigns are affairs of elites who are seeking to triumph over real or imaginary adversaries, and who make an impact on politics because they share, in their hearts, the old socialist view that things must be changed from the top downwards, and that the people themselves are not to be trusted now, but only later, when the revolutionary vanguard has completed its task.

It is true that the people are not to be trusted when solutions to their problems are monopolized by the state. For state solutions create a structure of arcane and impersonal directives, which encourage people to evade them by whatever means they can. State solutions are usually rotten with free riders, rent seekers, people who see the advantage of adopting them in appearance, while escaping them in fact. And this is one of the constant laments of all environmentalists: every solution that seems perfect in theory seems to fall apart when put in the hands of government. This is the more obviously true the larger the problem

121   The best source is Simon Fairlie's website, www.tlio.org.uk, and his book, *Low Impact Development* cited in n.96, p. 80.

to be solved. Paradoxically, therefore, the distrust of ordinary economic activity leads to a larger distrust of the bureaucracies that have grown in order to regulate it, even though they have grown largely as a result of political pressure from the left. The result has been a new kind of 'organized hesitation', a pursuit of precaution for its own sake, and a kind of active injection of paralysis into the regulatory process. Before proceeding it is worth examining how this came about.

FOUR

Radical Precaution

Early on in the debates over environmental protection the European Greens began to refer to something called the *Vorsorgeprinzip* ('Foresight Principle'). This Principle probably began life in pre-war Germany, and was invoked later in the sixties as the blanket justification for state planning. Reissued in the seventies under the name of the Precautionary Principle, it is now being advocated at every level of European politics as a guide to regulation, legislation and the use of scientific research. Addressing the Royal Society in 2002, British prime minister Tony Blair told the assembled body of distinguished scientists that 'responsible science and responsible policy-making operate on the Precautionary Principle'. Yet nobody seems to know what the Principle says. Does it tell us to take no risks? Then surely it is merely irrational, since everything we do has a risk attached. Or does it tell us to balance the benefits of risk-taking against the costs? Then it is merely reminding us of a fundamental law of practical reasoning. Or is it adding some new axiom to decision theory that will enable us to deal with the hazards of modern technology in a way that will safeguard the future of mankind? Then we need a clear statement of what it says and clear grounds for believing it.

A footnote to the 1982 Stockholm environmental conference recommended the Precautionary Principle as the acceptable approach to scientific innovation – but did nothing to define it. Thereafter the Principle was repeatedly mentioned in European edicts, as authority for a creeping regime of regulation that ostensibly had the protection of the public as its rationale, but which also had the stifling of innovation as its consequence. In 1998 a gathering of lawyers, scientists, philosophers and Green activists in the USA produced the Wingspread Statement,[122] which defined the Principle thus: 'When an activity raises threats of harm to the environment or human health, precautionary measures should be taken even if some cause and effect relationships are not fully established scientifically' – which is a definition of nothing, since all activities raise some threat of harm, and the relevant science is never water-tight. Finally, in 2000, the European Commission published a twenty-nine-page communication on the Principle, purporting to clarify its use, but again answering the need for a definition with a fudge. The Principle, it said, may be applicable

122 Wingspread Statement on the Precautionary Principle, drafted and finalized at a conference at the Wingspread Conference Center, Racine, Wisconsin, 23–25 January 1998, www.gdrc.org/u-gov/precaution-3.html.

'where preliminary scientific evaluation indicates that there are reasonable grounds for concern that the potentially dangerous effects on the environment, human, animal or plant health may be inconsistent with the high level of protection chosen for the Community'.[123] The words 'preliminary', 'potentially' and 'may' betray the essential retreat from precision that this statement involves. And the reference to a 'high level of protection chosen for the Community' naturally leads to the question 'chosen by whom?' The statement is in fact a licence to forbid any activity that a bureaucrat judges, on whatever grounds, to have a possible cost attached to it.

Although there is little or no agreement as to what the Precautionary Principle says, it has now become a doctrine of European law. A recent decision of the European Court of Justice, having invoked the Precautionary Principle, concluded that the government of Italy is justified in preventing the sale of genetically modified food on the basis that 'no human technology should be used until it is proven harmless to humans and the environment'.[124] Taken literally that would forbid every innovation in food technology that we have recently witnessed. Personally I am in favour of a law that forbids non-biodegradable packaging or ensures its recapture, since I know that this is intensely damag-

---

123 Commission of the European Communities, 'Communication from the Commission on the Precautionary Principle', Brussels, 2.2.2000, COM (2000) 1 final.

124 ECJ, 9 September 2003, reported in *Official Journal of the European Union*, C 264, 01.11.2003, p. 10.

ing to the environment. But the ruling of the Court has not been applied to that case, since the attempt to apply it would bring our entire food economy to a standstill. Moreover, the ruling, because it forbids everything, permits everything too, since it compels us to construe everything that we do as an exception. The ruling can therefore be used arbitrarily to prevent whatever initiatives the bureaucrats momentarily take against, regardless of any serious study of the effects on health, on the environment or on the life of the planet. This is the inevitable result of making a meaningless nostrum into a rule of law.[125]

But there is an underlying issue here that needs to be addressed. When law becomes an instrument for regulating conduct, rather than adjudicating conflicts, it changes character. Instead of creating the framework in which human beings can take risks and assume responsibility for doing so, law becomes a universal obstacle to risk-taking – a way of siphoning responsibility from society and transferring it to the impersonal state, where it can be safely dissolved and forgotten. As soon as there is the faintest suspicion of risk, the legislators will produce an edict designed to eliminate it. In the case of the European Union, where the legislators are bureaucrats who can never be thrown out by the people who have to bear the burden of their edicts, the regulative machine is now running out of control. The

---

125 See also, for further illustrations, Gary E. Marchant and Kenneth L. Mossman, *Arbitrary and Capricious: The Precautionary Principle in the European Courts*, Washington DC, 2004.

Precautionary Principle justifies everything that the bureaucrats do, since they need nothing more than 'preliminary' scientific evaluation, giving 'grounds for concern' that the 'potential' effects 'may' be inconsistent with the 'high level of protection' that the bureaucrats themselves have chosen.

The result is illustrated by the directive banning the use of certain phthalates, which are PVC softeners used in making children's dummies, teats and so on. The 'preliminary' scientific evaluation consisted in slight evidence from one Danish researcher that phthalates may be carcinogenic. His research has never been confirmed by peer review and was rejected by the European Commission's own scientific committee.[126] However, the Precautionary Principle got to work on this non-evidence and converted it at once into conclusive grounds for panic. For what the Principle really says, when examined in the context of its use, is this: 'if you think there may be a risk, then there is a risk; and if there is a risk, forbid it'. Once again we are dealing with a principle that forbids and permits everything. Its effect is both arbitrary and absolute, silencing all counter-argument. It is, therefore, an extremely effective political weapon, and can be used not only by bureaucrats but also by all unrepresentative and unaccountable pressure groups, big business included, to enforce their point of view on the rest of us. Behind the edict forbidding

126 See Bill Durodié, 'Plastic Panics: European Risk Regulation in the Aftermath of BSE', in Julian Morris, ed., *Rethinking Risk and the Precautionary Principle*, Oxford, 2000.

phthalates there marches the regiment of self-appointed environmental guardians, who see the chemical industry as Public Enemy No. 1. Even if nobody gains from the edict, at least the industry that has invested so much in this product will suffer. And for the activists that result is a good in itself. Conversely manufacturers of safety devices constantly refer to the Precautionary Principle when lobbying for regulation that will lead to guaranteed sales throughout the European Union.

Even if what it says remains obscure, the Precautionary Principle clearly presents an obstacle to innovation and experiment, even in those circumstances (like ours, now, confronting unprecedented problems) where nothing is more needed than innovation and experiment. But there are deeper reasons for being troubled by it, reasons that bear on the very essence of human life, and on our ability to solve practical problems, in particular those problems of stewardship and management that are the theme of this book. First, there is the tendency of the Principle to encourage those who appeal to it to disaggregate risks, in ways that defeat the possibility of reasonable solutions. Risks are never single, nor do they come to us only from one direction or from one point of time. By not taking the risk of angering my child, I take the risk of dealing, at some later stage, with a spoiled and self-centred adolescent. All practical reasoning involves weighing risks against one another, estimating probabilities, ring-fencing uncertainties, taking account of relative benefits and costs. This mode of reasoning is instinctive to us and has ensured our extraordinary success as a species. The effect of the Pre-cautionary Principle is to isolate each risk as though it were entirely independent of every other. Risks, according to the Principle, come single-wrapped, and each demands the same response, namely – Don't! If, in obeying this command, you find yourself taking another risk, then the answer again is 'Don't!'

The Principle is therefore logically on a par with the command given by an American president to his senior civil servant: 'Don't just do something, stand there!'[127] But, as the president realized, standing there is not something that civil servants are very good at. Bureaucrats have an inveterate need to be seen to be doing something. The effect of the Principle, therefore, is to forbid the one identified risk, while removing all others from the equation. And in this the Principle makes explicit the main defect of top-down regulation. Even when there is no explicit forbidding of risk, of the kind ventured by the Precautionary Principle, bureau-cracies consider risks one by one, and strive to reduce each to zero, regardless of the cost. Normally you can reduce one risk to zero only by increasing risk elsewhere: and the risks that stand to be increased will be the concern of some other department, and thus removed from consideration. A European directive issued in response to the slight risk that meat from sick animals might enter the food chain insists that no abattoir can function without the

127 The story is related of Franklin D. Roosevelt among others, and is surely apocryphal. Chris DeMuth informs me that Thomas Schelling summarizes the Precautionary Principle in another way: 'Don't do anything for the first time!'

presence of a qualified vet. Qualified vets are expensive in Britain; hence all small abattoirs had to close. When Foot and Mouth disease broke out in 2001 it was not, as in the past, confined to the local source of the outbreak, but carried around the country by animals travelling a hundred miles or more to the nearest legal abattoir. Some 7 million animals were slaughtered in the attempt to confine the disease, and the cost to the economy was £8 billion.[128] Such was the short-term cost of an edict that considered only one fairly insignificant risk among the many that cohabit in the management of livestock.

Now, a responsible politician might have taken into account not only the small risk addressed by the directive, but also the huge risks posed to the farming community by the destruction of local abattoirs, the risks posed to animals by long journeys, the benefits of localized food production and local markets for meat, and so on. And he would have a motive for considering all those things, namely his desire to be re-elected, when the consequences of his decision had been felt. As a rational being, he would recognize that risks don't come in atomic particles, but are parts of complex organisms, shaped by the flow of events. And he would know in his heart that there is no more risky practice than that of disaggregating risks, so as one by one to forbid them.

Even bureaucrats, in their own private lives, will take the same

128 According to data contained in a Royal Society Report of 2002, and later reaffirmed in a 2004 report from the Department of the Environment, Farming and Rural Affairs. See the DEFRA website, FMD Data Archive.

line. They too are rational beings, and know that risks must be constantly taken, and constantly weighed against each other. However, when a bureaucrat legislates for others, and may suffer no cost should he get things wrong, he will inevitably look for a single and specific problem, and seize on a single and absolute principle in order to solve it. And if the costs of his regulatory zeal come under some other department, he barely needs to take note of them.

Nowhere is this truth more apparent than in the workings of the United States Environmental Protection Agency (EPA), whose daily task consists in forbidding things, but forbidding them one by one. It has been estimated that the cost of the EPA's vinyl chloride regulations, for example, is $4 million per life saved – as opposed to $10,000 per life saved for cancer screening programmes, and $80,000 per life saved for the use of car seat belts.[129] The costs of disaggregating risks and regulating them one by one have been recognized by the United States government, which established the Office of Information and Regulatory Affairs (OIRA) in 1980, with a view to evaluating regulations and making recommendations to the president when the costs are too high. The hope has been that cost-benefit analysis applied by an independent department would enable the political process to reassemble the complex bundles of risk that the bureaucrats take apart. Just how far the resulting regulation of the regulators has

129 See table, Aaron Wildavsky, *Searching for Safety*, New Brunswick, 1988, p. 89.

overcome their inherent arbitrariness is a moot point and one, interestingly enough, over which left and right are divided – the left arguing for more regulation and less costing, the right for more costing and less regulation.[130]

But the most important observation to be made, in the light of the attempts to regulate activities that pose a risk to the environment, is that those who live with the environment will spontaneously respond to threats, regardless of the direction that the threats are coming from, while bureaucrats will be in the grip of an agenda on which only a limited number of pre-identified threats are registered. The contrast here is illustrated by that between the gamekeeper and the animal rights activist. The game-keeper must protect an environment, and the creatures that flourish in it. He must control foxes and badgers if he is to protect ground-nesting birds; plant cover if he is to retain pheasants and partridge; ensure berries in winter and corn and kale in summer; take action against scavengers, dog-walkers and so on. If he eliminates the foxes he may be plagued by the moles and rats on which they feed, and if he alienates the neighbours who walk their dogs through his territory he will be without the support that he needs when the animal rights activists turn up to make his life hell.

130 For the left-wing argument here see Richard L. Revesz and Michael A. Livermore, *Retaking Rationality: How Cost-Benefit Analysis Can Better Protect the Environment and Our Health*, Oxford, 2008. For the right-wing response see the lengthy review of Revesz and Livermore by Christopher C. DeMuth and Douglas H. Ginsburg (both former administrators of the OIRA), 'Rationalism in Regulation', *Michigan Law Review*, 108.6, April 2010, pp. 877–912.

The animal rights activist, by contrast, has no need to balance risks or to work out the long-term cost of his activities. He is there to stop the killing, and the fact that the result is a mismanaged habitat, from which the game birds have fled, and in which the scavengers are taking over, is none of his concern. And of course it is people like animal rights activists, with their non-negotiable agendas and their 'passionate intensity', who are apt to put the most immediate and intelligible pressure on the regulatory process – either indirectly through lobbying of government, or directly through the bureaucratic machine. The gamekeeper, who is constantly assessing risks to one aspect of his managed environment, and balancing them against those to another, is unlikely to be well served by a regime of bureaucratic regulation. The animal rights activist, by contrast, can think of nothing better. And his preferred form of regulation will have an absolute character: an uncompromising 'no', in the face of his opponent's 'yes and no'. He is playing a zero-sum game; if he wins, his opponent loses, and compromise is out of the question.

The example points to a contrast that has been of considerable significance in environmental disputes. Local conflicts – for example, between polluting factories and those living downwind of them, between loggers and hunters, between weekenders and farmers – can often be resolved by discussion. But they will never be resolved if the parties believe themselves to be involved in a zero-sum game. They will be resolved by negotiation and compromise, and a shared willingness to give way for the sake of good relations. The big NGOs and absentee businesses, which lobby Parliament or Congress for the absolute edict that will advance their cause, see things differently. The Sierra Club, for example, which opposes all commercial logging in the national forests of America, could never have reached the agreement thrashed out in the Quincy Library, which finally ended the conflict between loggers, residents, farmers and environmentalists over a 2-million-acre patch. For this solution was a compromise, which allowed all parties to have some part of what they wanted.[131] Likewise the conflict between hunt-followers and the big animal rights NGOs in Britain was a zero-sum game, pursued to the end through Parliament, when it was obvious to most reasonable observers that the matter concerned local communities who should have sat down together and worked out a compromise acceptable to all. In the next chapter I return to this point, since it is so important in understanding the contours of a viable conservative policy.

The contrast just drawn suggests another and deeper irrationality in the regulatory process as this exists today. Legislators who wish to protect us from harms must assess the risks, but they should not automatically forbid them. We learn, as Aaron Wildavsky has emphasized, by trial and error. But the regulatory process wishes to replace that technique with one of 'trial and no

131 The fascinating story is related by Mark Sagoff, *op. cit.*, ch. 9.

error', from which we cannot conceivably learn.[132] This suggests further that there is an even greater risk attached to the habit of avoiding all risks – namely, that we will produce a society that has no ability to survive a real emergency, when risk-taking is the only recourse.

It is not absurd to think that this is a real danger. How many a soporific empire, secure in its long-standing abundance, has been swept away by barbarian hordes, simply because the basileus or caliph had spent his life in risk-free palaces? History is replete with warnings against the habit of heeding every warning. Yet this is the habit that regulation furthers. By anticipating and forbidding risk, it is courting the greatest risk of all, namely that we shall face our next collective emergency without the only thing that would enable us to survive it.

If von Clausewitz teaches us nothing else, he must surely persuade us that strategy in war proceeds according to principles of practical reasoning that are equally valid in peacetime.[133] Victory does not come through taking no risks, but through balancing risks against each other, and recognizing the limits to certainty. Strategic thinking in war is no different from strategic

---

132 See Aaron Wildavsky, *Searching for Safety*, *op. cit*. Learning from mistakes is one part of rationality; another part is learning to assess the cost of mistakes. If there is an acceptable version of the Precautionary Principle, therefore, it should be rewritten as ACE – assess the cost of error. So argues John Lucas in a little-known but important contribution to this debate: *Risk of Freedom Briefing*, 5, October 2000.

133 See Carl von Clausewitz, *On War*, 1832.

thinking in business. Moreover, if, during times of peace, we allow the capacity for rational choice to atrophy, then we shall feel the consequences in war. Recall the lesson of Pearl Harbor: unwilling to take the risk of fighting on terms that were not overwhelmingly favourable, President Roosevelt found himself forced to fight nevertheless, but without a Pacific fleet. This does not mean that a 'high risk' strategy is always the wisest one. It means only that risk is the premise of strategic thinking, and strategic thinking the *sine qua non* of success. In war the cost of failure is the loss of everything. In peace it is the loss of something. But in both cases rational decision-making means not avoiding risks, but choosing between them, and continuously adjusting in the face of new and unanticipated dangers.

Although the Eurocrats have made something they call the Precautionary Principle into the foundation of their legislative programme, we should not think that the invocation of the Principle is confined to Europe. Environmental NGOs have made repeated use of another non-definition, which occurs in the 1992 Rio Declaration on Environment and Development. According to Principle 15 of the Rio Declaration, the precautionary approach requires that, 'where there are threats of serious or irreversible damage, lack of full scientific certainty shall not be used as a reason for postponing cost-effective measures to prevent environmental degradation'.[134] Looked at in one way, that makes the

134 *Rio Declaration on Environment and Development*, UN Conference on Environment and Development, New York, 1992.

common-sense claim that, when taking a risk, we should protect
the environment from the adverse effects of failure, even if we are
not yet sure of the science. Looked at in another way, however, it
says merely 'Don't!' And it is in this second way that the Principle
is always interpreted by the activists, so that instead of contributing to the solution of our collective problems it merely prevents
us from addressing them. This has led many governments (in
particular those of Scandinavian countries) to abandon nuclear
energy programmes, even though they provide the best hope for
a comparatively clean source of energy capable of supplying
the enormous numbers of people who now inhabit the earth – at
least for the time being, and until we can master the science and
technology required to develop genuinely sustainable sources
of energy.[135] The case of nuclear energy has assumed an added
importance in the wake of the Japanese Tsunami of March 2011,
which caused serious and potentially catastrophic damage to
the Fukushima Daiichi nuclear power station. The immediate
response of the German Greens was to call on their government
to shut down nuclear facilities in Germany – a demand that
Chancellor Merkel promptly complied with. This panic reaction
typifies the 'precautionary' response. The true lesson of the
Japanese tragedy is that, in a country situated on a geological
fault-line, with a long history of earthquakes and tsunamis, there
is a high risk of unacceptable damage to nuclear facilities, especially when built on the shore. The Japanese took that risk and

135   See again the arguments in MacKay, *op. cit.*

paid the cost of it. They presumably will not take the risk again. Absolutely nothing follows from this concerning the wisdom of nuclear power stations built inland in a country that has not had a serious earthquake in recent history. Yet the habit of precautionary 'reasoning' has so dominated discussion in Germany, that only irrational responses are now available, so that purely hypothetical disasters eclipse all attempts to assess their real probability.

Nor should we assume that the Precautionary Principle is effective only where it has entered the official culture, as in Germany. American legislators are unlikely to invoke the Principle, since they recognize the extent to which it impinges upon entrenched civil freedoms. But American litigiousness has the same effect as the European nanny state. There are places in America where no doctor will take the risk of delivering a baby, for fear of a malpractice suit that will cost him all that he has. Scouting trips and adventure sports are now rapidly disappearing, as people acquire the habit of suing for every injury. And local legislatures try to forestall litigation by laws that have the same mad absolutism as the European edicts. We see this in the notorious case of asbestos. In the wake of unscrupulous and lawyer-driven litigation, which bankrupted a thousand innocent industries and storeowners across the United States, the federal government eventually introduced the Asbestos Hazard Emergency Response Act of 1986, which required the removal of asbestos from classrooms across the nation's 37,000 school districts. A symposium at Harvard University in 1988 concluded that the risk of dying from low-level exposure to asbestos was vanishingly small, and that the cost of the ban on asbestos had been $123 million per life saved, not to speak of the unseen costs in the destruction of attractive buildings and cherished environments.[136]

Manufacturers of children's playgrounds now predict that swings in public playgrounds will become a thing of the past, since safety regulations require prohibitively expensive padding beneath them. The regulations surrounding children's toys, clothes and activities are indeed now so strict, that it is no longer possible to have the kind of childhood that we read about with such longing and wonder in children's classics like *Huckleberry Finn* and *Swallows and Amazons*.

When assessing arguments proffered in the name of the Precautionary Principle, therefore, we should recognize that it is one aspect of a risk-denying and risk-averting culture. American litigation and European regulation both have the same effect – to increase the cost of risk to the point where risks really do become irrational. The cost is financial in America, penal in Europe, but the effect is the same. Rational beings, who are risk-takers by nature, no longer take the risks that they ought to be taking, since the cost has been artificially elevated by litigation and law. The

136 John D. Spengler *et al.*, *Summary of the Symposium on Health Aspects of Exposure to Asbestos in Buildings*, Harvard University Energy and Environmental Policy Center, John F. Kennedy School of Government, Cambridge, MA, 1989.

result does not damage adults only: it damages their children far more, threatening the very possibility of what was once considered a normal childhood. Boys used to join the Scouts, to go on camping holidays in which they learned the arts of survival, to take part in athletic sports that strengthened the body and also occasionally injured it, to expose themselves to hardships in order to enjoy the sense of overcoming them, and in all kinds of ways to surround themselves with character-forming dangers. Sometimes accidents happened, and sometimes bad things were suffered or done. Still, there was a widely shared sense not only that young people were strengthened by this kind of activity, but also that they enjoyed it, learned from it, and were better able as a result to cope with the stresses of adult life and the demands of ordinary decision-making.[137]

There is no evidence that people were wrong to think in that way. On the contrary, they were sensible of the truth, elaborately defended by Aristotle, that success in action requires virtuous habits, and virtuous habits must be acquired early if they are to be acquired at all. Young people brought up to think their way through practical difficulties acquire the art of survival. The risk-averse and timorous have no capacity to confront, still less to survive, a real emergency, nor are they likely to do well in ordinary competitive business. In love, as in war, they will be the losers,

---

137 It should be pointed out that 'education through risk' has also been targeted by certain forms of feminism. See Christina Hoff Sommers, *The War Against Boys*, New York, 2001.

and only where they can fall back on nanny state will they be sure of protection. Yet nanny state herself depends upon the risk-takers, since it is on their taxes that the whole structure of institutionalized timorousness is built.

This does not mean that we should dismiss the anxieties to which the Precautionary Principle is proposed as a solution. Rather we should make a clear effort to identify those anxieties, to state them precisely, and to see whether regulation of any kind could be an effective response to them. And it seems to me that the anxieties are of three kinds: first, those concerning our habit of transferring our costs; second, those concerning the problem of 'sinks and residues'; and third, anxieties concerning the non-negotiable nature of certain human goods, which we wish to rescue entirely from the process of deliberation. I deal with each in turn.

It is very clear that we must distinguish risks in which the cost falls on the person who takes them from risks in which the cost is exported to the rest of us. We can manage risks of the first kind by providing suitable warnings, such as the health warnings affixed to alcohol and tobacco, and which many might wish to affix also to junk food, televisions, mobile phones and all the other products that rot the minds or bodies of those who consume them. But risks whose cost is exported to others cannot easily be managed, since no individual may be wholly responsible for the damage, or solely able to repair it. Hence we need policies to reduce the cost of what we do, by distributing the power to repair it. That was the principle behind the old bottle-deposit habit, which rid the world of abandoned glass bottles. According to this principle, each person who enjoys the benefit of an innovation is made to pay a proportionate amount of the socially distributed cost. The innovation goes ahead, and the damage is rectified. This kind of solution has been generalized by Robert Costanza, an economist now at the University of Vermont, who has attempted to put something precise in place of the Precautionary Principle.[138]

The second source of anxiety to which the Precautionary Principle has been put forward as a cure is that concerning sinks and residues. The problem here is a special case of the problem of externalized costs. The environment has only a finite capacity to absorb our waste, and much that we release into it has unpredictable effects on ecosystems. Drugs, antibiotics, chemicals, pesticides, fertilizers – all flow through our drains into waterways and soils, there to accumulate and to be absorbed by plants, animals and, in due course, other humans. Every day we read of localized outbreaks of cancer in children, of premature menstruation, of hermaphrodites among fish and amphibians – and we naturally conclude that drugs and chemicals have entered the environment through careless and untested use. The fear of this underlies many people's anxieties about genetically modified

138 See Robert Costanza and Charles Perrings, 'A Flexible Assurance Bonding System for Improved Environmental Management', *Ecological Economics*, 2.1, April 1990, pp. 57–75.

crops, and is one cause of the movement for organic farming.

There is nothing irrational in these fears; the problem is that the Precautionary Principle does nothing to answer them. By forbidding everything it permits everything, and leaves us without clear instructions as to what we should do, to ensure that the risks attached to drugs and chemicals are properly confronted. Clearly drugs and chemicals must be subjected to *ecological* as well as medical testing, in order to ascertain their effect as *residues*, after their medical work has been done. But again absolute edicts will in the normal case be counter-productive. Regulations governing the treatment of sewage, for example, should be so formulated that local communities can comply with them, even if this means allowing a small amount of contamination to pass into rivers and streams. There is a clear case for regulation; but a regulation that is so strict that it cannot be complied with, or which cannot easily be altered when circumstances change, will normally be bypassed, to the common detriment.

Worse, in emergencies, when the state must perforce take charge, regulations may place an absolute impediment against the only available course of action. A pertinent example is presented by the 2010 Gulf of Mexico oil spill. Immediately after the catastrophe the Dutch government offered the use of ships equipped with devices for extracting oil from seawater and returning nearly pure seawater to the ocean – ships that have been used to great effect in managing spills and leaks from the oil platforms in the North Sea. The US government refused the offer, at least in part because the water being returned to the ocean would not comply with the strict EPA regulations forbidding oil-contamination of water released into the Gulf.[139] If water is not 99.9985 per cent pure, the regulations say, it may not be returned to the Gulf; and the Dutch equipment does not meet that impossible standard. Hence the Dutch equipment could not be used. This crazy decision exemplifies the worst effect of 'precautionary' reasoning: by aiming to avert disaster, strict precaution renders us powerless to deal with disaster when it comes.

I come now to the third kind of anxiety to which the Precautionary Principle is proposed as a solution. In reasoning about risk, many thinkers wish to make a distinction between those things that can, and those that cannot, be traded. The philosopher David Wiggins, for example, who has made the concept of need central to his account of moral thinking, introduces a version of the Precautionary Principle in the words of Pushkin's Herman (in *The Queen of Spades*): 'Cards interest me very much; but I am not in a position to risk the necessary in the hope of the superfluous'. It is irrational, Wiggins suggests, for us to risk the satisfaction of our vital needs in the pursuit of our other interests, however pressing those interests might seem to us.[140] Moreover, it is wicked for us so to risk the satisfaction of the

139 See Lawrence Solomon, 'Avertible Catastrophe', *National Post*, 25 June 2010.
140 David Wiggins, *Needs, Values, Truth: Essays in the Philosophy of Value*, Oxford, 1987. See especially 'An Idea We Cannot Do Without', in Soran Reader, ed., *The Philosophy of Need*, Cambridge, 2004.

vital needs of other human beings.[141] Care of the earth is required of us precisely because the earth is the source of all that we vitally need. In these claims Wiggins is at one with the German philosopher Hans Jonas, who has urged that humanity itself cannot be put at stake, so that a risk to the survival of our species is not one that can be weighed in the balance, however slight the risk may be.[142] Jonas has even proposed that, when deliberating over our collective future, we should adopt a 'heuristics of fear', always focusing on worst-case scenarios and the costs that we might endure, rather than the benefits, however great, that might otherwise cast them in shadow.

There is something plausible in those ideas, and I shall return to them in later chapters. But they do nothing for the Precautionary Principle as it is propounded by its normal advocates. Distinguishing needs from desires is simply one part of the process of weighing reasons. And we should be clear that we do, in our ordinary reasoning, bargain with both life and need, and that the attempt to prevent this is rarely successful. Human beings risk their lives in skiing, hunting, driving and competitive sport; they happily exchange health for whisky and safety for love; they leap to the defence of their family and their country and throw caution to the winds. And sometimes they are prepared to risk the

141 See David Wiggins, 'Solidarity and the Root of the Ethical', *Tijdschrift voor filosofie*, 2009.

142 Hans Jonas, *The Imperative of Responsibility*, 1984, English translation, Chicago, 1985.

end of everything, in defence of a way of life that they refuse to jettison. The prefect of a Roman city besieged by Vandals or Huns would often choose to resist rather than surrender, even though the cost of failure would be total destruction, and the cost of surrender a negotiable servitude. We do not regard the choice as irrational, or as an immoral imposition on the citizens for whom the prefect stood as guardian. Indeed, we look with suspicion on those who are unwilling to risk death in defence of a shared way of life, and we recognize sacrifice as a fundamental component in the resilience of human communities. The Roman Empire lasted because it schooled its citizens in sacrifice; and the principle that governed the beleaguered cities was not 'to save everything, risk nothing', but 'to save the best things, risk everything'. We should not, therefore, ring-fence our needs and our lives from the business of risk-taking. Whatever we do, the risk of death – our own death, but also the death of those who depend on us and whom we are duty-bound to protect – is real, however small. And to forbid us to bargain with this risk, as we bargain with all others, is to deprive us of our most important weapon in confronting it. Indeed, rational beings, it seems to me, can flourish only when they have risks to confront and responsibilities to assume. The risk-free life is not a life in which we are or can be fulfilled. Any pattern of thought that seeks to extinguish risk and to lift our responsibilities in the face of it is, therefore, one that threatens a primary human need.

Meanwhile, in all its putative forms, the Precautionary

Principle acts as a brake on the kind of research that we need to undertake, if we are to manage our growing environmental problems. In the circumstances in which we now find ourselves, there can be no riskier policy. If we are to apply the Precautionary Principle at all, therefore, we should apply it to itself. And the answer will be 'Don't!'

An important issue emerges from our discussion. Environmental problems involve managing risk. This means assessing what can and what cannot be changed, the likelihood of adverse and beneficial consequences, and the agencies best suited to manage risk on our behalf. The Precautionary Principle assumes that risk management concerns the environment only. From that assumption another is held to follow, namely that since the environment is everyone's concern it must be managed *on behalf of* everyone. For many environmentalists that means managed by the state. From that deduction a further deduction is made, namely that – because the risks are infinite and unknowable – it is best not to take them. The state exists to put a break on enterprise, on behalf of all who stand to lose from its side effects. Such a philosophy has been explicitly defended by the sociologist Ulrich Beck, who argues, in *The Risk Society*, that scientific and technological advance has created a new kind of society, in which the consciousness of risk dictates the first concerns of politics. According to Beck the democratic process must be devoted to tracking down and removing the risks that have been imposed on us without our consent. And, having discovered them, we can legislate to remove them.[143] Even if, in previous conditions, top-down regulation had the adverse effects that I have been outlining, those conditions no longer obtain. Regulation is now the leading solution to the problems of the new society, the way of returning to the people their stolen peace of mind.

This approach seems to me just as irrational as those typically advanced in the name of the Precautionary Principle. Estimating risk is an art that rational beings acquire by recognizing the indefinitely many ways in which safety in one area may spell danger in another. There is an objective measure of risk in terms of 'long-run frequency', and there is a calculus of probability that enables us to combine and abstract from risks once they have been measured. But this is not the concept that informs our everyday decision-making, nor is it the concept that appears in the 'risk management' exercises of government departments. Risk as normally understood is an inter-subjective matter – it involves estimating the likely or unlikely outcome of hypothetical actions whose effect depends also on the estimations made by others. In driving a car I spontaneously assess the risks of driving in one lane rather than another, and adjust my assessment according to my sense of how others too are assessing things. The art of combining and adjusting such assessments is not unlike the art of dealing in a market – responding to information that is altered by our response to it. Risk management, in short, is a homeostatic

---

143 Ulrich Beck, *Risk Society: Towards a New Modernity*, London, 1992.

process, which takes into account the results of its own perform-ance. In local and known environments we do this very well. But as the domain increases in size, and the risks begin to fall on unknown others and not on the person who is supposedly man-aging them, we are apt to take refuge in absolute rules like the Precautionary Principle. And such rules are insensitive to the risk involved in forbidding risk.

Moreover, we should question the assumption that risks can be managed only by altering the object that presents them. They can also be managed, and often better managed, by altering the subject who confronts them. When you bathe in the sea you run the risk of drowning. You manage that risk not by altering the sea but by altering yourself, learning how to swim, taking exercise for fitness and practising your strokes. Similarly we manage the risks that arise in our enterprises, sometimes by changing the objects from which they issue, sometimes by changing ourselves or our competences in order to cope better when things go wrong.

The point was expressed by Aaron Wildavsky, in his study of the subject, by applying C. S. Holling's distinction between resilience and interception.[144] The first prepares for adversity, the latter strives to avoid it. Increasingly, under pressure from lobby-ists, our governments have tried to manage risks by ensuring that they will not arise, usually assuming enormous and costly regula-

144 Aaron Wildavsky, *op. cit.* The contrast between resilience and interception was made central to ecology by C. S. Holling, 'Resilience and Stability of Ecological Systems', *Annual Review of Ecology and Systematics*, 4, 1973, pp. 1–23.

tory powers to take actions on behalf of 'health and safety'. This is the favoured strategy of the European Union, whose edicts include countless measures to ensure that normal risks, to which human beings are by nature adapted, simply cannot arise. Such edicts are both costly in themselves, and ways of activating the law of unintended consequences.

Nor is it only the EU machine that has adopted costly interceptive strategies. The American Food and Drug Administration insists that every drug must meet rigorous safety standards before it can be put on the market – standards so difficult to meet, and so costly to test against, that drugs reach the market many years after they might have been actively saving lives, and sometimes do not reach the market at all, since the delay shortens the patent life of the drug, making it not worthwhile to develop.[145] The Environmental Protection Agency's insistence on essentially riskless solutions has placed burdens on the American economy that vastly decrease the resources available for real emergencies.[146]

145 Sam Peltzman, 'An Evaluation of Consumer Protection Legislation: The 1962 Drug Amendments', *Journal of Political Economy*, 1973; 'Toward a More General Theory of Regulation', *Journal of Law and Economics*, 1976. A pertinent, and damning, examination of the effect of regulation on drug trials in the UK is given by Denis Mitchison, 'The Regulation of Clinical Trials', openDemocracy www.opendemocracy.net/author/denis-mitchison, 30 November 2009.

146 See, for example, the study of the EPA's continuing regulatory regime to control air quality: Joel M. Schwartz and Stephen F. Hayward, *Air Quality in America*, Washington DC, 2007. See also more generally John D. Graham and Jonathan Baert Wiener, *Risk vs. Risk: Tradeoffs in Protecting Health and the Environment*, Cambridge, MA, 1995.

And, as the oil-spill example shows, regulations forbidding risk may make it impossible to deal with emergencies in any case. Cases of the adverse effects of risk-free solutions are so familiar that there is little point in enumerating them, and they are all summarized in what one might call the paradox of hygiene. Playing with dirt involves the risk of disease; but by forbidding children to play with dirt we make them more vulnerable to disease. In short, by atomizing risks, and then forbidding them, we trade substantial long-term for insignificant short-term benefits. We also risk the atrophy of homeostatic systems that, like the human immune system, act of their own accord to maintain a viable environment.

Defenders of market solutions point out that no policy can work without incentives, and that the results of any policy will be the outcome of the incentives that it generates. And they have pointed out, argued at length, and roundly established that regulation by the state, applied by bureaucrats, has a nasty habit of producing the opposite results to those intended, precisely by changing people's incentives in ways that were not foreseen.[147] Since the early sixties there have been published, in such journals as *The Journal of Law and Economics* and *The Journal of Political Economy*, countless studies of the unintended consequences of regulation, showing the way in which minimum wages hurt those

147 See the famous account by Robert K. Merton, 'The Unanticipated Consequences of Purposive Social Action', *American Sociological Review*, 1.6, 1936, pp. 894–904.

whom they seek to help by causing them to be thrown out of employment, the way in which regulations governing employment for the disabled have led to increasing unemployment among the disabled, the way in which regulations to protect endangered species cause people to destroy habitats for fear of being burdened by the regulatory regime, and so on. These studies confirm the two seminal articles by Samuel Peltzman from the early seventies,[148] concerning drug and automobile safety regulation, which showed that in both cases the good results aimed at were in fact prevented, since the regulations destroyed the incentive that people otherwise would have had to produce those good results by their own initiative.

The rational response to risk and uncertainty is, therefore, not to devote all resources to reducing one risk to zero, but to balance costs and benefits, taking account of the relative likelihood of negative outcomes. That is how we reason in our own lives, and how generals reason in war, when things are serious. It is not how bureaucrats and legislators reason, since the incentive to make rational choices is less, in their case, than the incentive to show that a given problem has been 'solved'. Even if we follow Wiggins and Jonas in isolating and protecting those human goods that we cannot afford to risk, there is still a real question whether we could ever achieve this result by zero-risk regulation. Eliminating one risk, you open the way to another: protect drivers with seat belts and you threaten pedestrians. Stop people smoking

148 Peltzman, *op. cit.*

and they take to bingeing. Protect the farm from pests and you expose it to pesticides.

In all such cases top-down solutions have a tendency to confiscate problems from those whose problems they are. Gerald Wilde and John Adams have persuasively argued that rational beings possess a 'risk thermostat', which leads them to compensate for risks that have been confiscated by inventing new risks in their stead.[149] As Adams puts it, 'the greater the success of the safety regulators in removing uncertainty from our lives, the stronger will become the compulsion to reinstate it'. Compel people to wear safety belts when driving, and they will drive that much faster in order to recapture the risk to themselves – at the same time increasing the risk to others. Forbid children from climbing trees and they will canoe down the rapids or go tobogganing on precipitous slopes. Almost certainly the risk thermostat is an adaptation, whose advantages in Pleistocene conditions do not need spelling out. But top-down legislation seems incompetent to consider it. The best it can do is to transfer risk-taking from known to unknown areas, and the result of this is in the nature of the case unpredictable. (Thus, as Adams has shown, curing an 'accident black-spot' on a road is likely to lead to more accidents on other stretches of it, cancelling out the benefit.)[150]

149 Adams, *op. cit.*; Gerald J. S. Wilde, *Target Risk*, Toronto, 1994. The point is also sometimes referred to as the 'Peltzman effect', since Peltzman was the first to hit on the idea.

150 Adams, *op. cit.*

More importantly, Wildavsky argues, the worse our ability to predict, the less rational does a strategy of interception become. If the owner of a power plant knows that a particular part is going to burn out every 150 days, an interception strategy of replacing the part every 149 days is rational. But if a power plant has 8,000 critical pieces of equipment, each of which could create a fire upon failure, and the owner does not know the failure rate of each piece, then a strategy of interception becomes irrational. Instead a strategy of resilience, implementing a sophisticated fire-response system, and thereby preparing for adversity, is clearly the right one. Wildavsky argues that resilience systems build knowledge through research and build safety through the efficient use of resources. They optimize the use of local knowledge and the existing ways of confronting and adapting to disasters. He plausibly goes on to show that resilience is the way in which both natural systems and markets deal with adverse events – namely, by fast-acting negative feedback that leads to quick adjustments and the restoration of equilibrium. Homeostatic systems respond to negative inputs by countering them as they arise. We too are homeostatic systems, and our practical reasoning in terms of risk and uncertainty is one part of this.

So much is surely common sense. The implication is that, in confronting the day-to-day problems of stewardship, resilience may often be more reasonable than interception. It is true that, when the threat is clearly defined and easily averted, interception may be the most reasonable response to it. Thus all Western governments have adopted clean-air regulations that have effectively eliminated smog from cities. Here the threat was clear, its cause eliminable and its effects impossible to deal with by resilience strategies. But even where interception seems reasonable, preparing for the worst may involve resilience. Moreover, as we see from the case of the Gulf of Mexico oil spill, regulations designed to intercept a risk may destroy the resilience needed to manage it.

But it is at this point that the arguments of Wiggins and Jonas need to be considered. What if the threat is of a catastrophe so great that no amount of resilience could enable us to survive it? Surely, however uncertain we are that the catastrophe might arrive, we ought then to strive to prevent it. This is the thought that has motivated many of the more reasonable advocates of interceptive policies against climate change. Global warming is not something that produces fast-acting negative feedback. The bad effects of our current activities will be felt only when it is too late to rectify them. But the effects might be *really* bad. So we must do what we can to avert catastrophe, however uncertain it may be. This returns us to the deeper question: what motive can we call upon to ensure that people will accept the needed policies? Is rational self-interest sufficient, or must we call on some other, maybe less negotiable, source of action? Those questions will underlie the ensuing argument.

FIVE

Market Solutions
and Homeostasis

The two previous chapters have criticized tendencies within the environmental movements that are in direct opposition to each other. On the one hand, there is the tendency to describe environmental problems in hyperbolic terms, as posing a radical threat to humanity, and demanding some kind of comprehensive solution that requires a complete change of life and the exercise of far-reaching government powers. On the other hand, there is a deep distrust towards the exercise of economic and political power, a distrust so far-reaching as to cause those who feel it to put precaution ahead of all other values, so as to forbid every venture into the unknown. Change everything, but touch nothing, is a strange counsel. But in the end it is what we must expect from a philosophy that fails to address the real question, which is that of human motivation. What leads people to spoil their environment, and what leads them to protect it? By confiscating risk the modern regulatory state both diminishes human resilience and expels from our social experience the one factor that is needed if future generations are to be protected from our greed, and that is the sense of responsibility – the sense that I, here, now, am answerable to others, there, then. I begin the exploration of this motive by considering the market – the system of consensual transactions that, according to some people, is the primary cause of environmental problems, and according to others the only known solution to them. Markets, I shall suggest, are not the simplest, but certainly the clearest, forms of social network in which individual responsibility is the binding principle. They are the cause of some environmental problems, but also the solution to others. And they illustrate the way in which, when costs are borne by those who create them, human beings exercise responsible stewardship over the goods that they enjoy.

In opposition to that cheerful picture, however, there are many who say that environmental problems are the direct result of 'market failure' – in other words, of the failure of the market to generate an optimal distribution of benefits and costs. Sometimes this is put forward as part of a general critique of the free market approach to social problems, and as proof that we need to look on these problems in another way, perhaps assigning a larger role to the state than conservatives tend to favour, or drawing on some other motive in human beings than the self-interest that governs the market.

It is admitted on all sides that there are 'public goods' that, if not provided by the state, will simply not be provided: law, for example, without which contracts are unenforceable and markets either non-existent or sustained by mafia-style policing. And in all durable arrangements central authority may sometimes be necessary to overcome problems of the 'free rider' and the 'prisoner's dilemma' kind, which otherwise vitiate our attempts to find rational solutions to our shared predicaments. Such problems are not specific to environmental issues, and arise in connection with both radical and conservative policies. When considering the environment, however, one such problem is of particular importance, and that is the failure of collective rationality commented upon by Aristotle in the *Politics* and known, following an acclaimed article by Garrett Hardin, as 'the tragedy of the commons'.[151] Many of the earth's resources are either unowned or owned in common by some particular community – the fish in a lake, the grazing on common land, the air that we breathe, and so on. If we all have access to such commons, and if they are easily depleted by our use of them, then the situation can easily arise in which it is in the interest of each person to take as much as he can before others deprive him of the chance. Hence common land will be overgrazed to the point of sterility, and the lake will be fished to death. We see this happening today, with the very real tragedy

151   See 1261b in Aristotle, *The Politics*, Oxford, 1994; Garrett Hardin, 'The Tragedy of the Commons', *Science*, 162, 13 December 1968, pp. 1243–8. Hardin's original response to the tragedy was to call for government intervention to protect 'public assets'; he later moved in the direction of favouring privatization.

of our oceans, which are perhaps the most mismanaged of our many mismanaged resources.[152]

In the face of this one can naturally sympathize with those Greens who warn against the culture of greed, and who see the market as an expression of it. And one might be tempted to adopt some radical strategy that takes possession of common resources *on behalf of* the people, while safeguarding those resources from the people themselves. This is the root motive behind many of the moves towards state ownership of forests and fisheries in the twentieth century, and it underlies the Common Fisheries Policy of the European Union. Yet it is precisely the wrong response, not the least because it fails to take seriously what the tragedy of the commons shows. Even if people were not greedy, but merely wishing to obtain enough to satisfy their needs, a common resource would run the risk of being depleted to the point of disappearance. This is because no single person has the motive to maintain and replenish it, and because it needs only one greedy person to deplete a resource below the point where it can renew itself. The greatest defence that human beings have devised against the greedy person is the right of the others to resist him. This is the reason for thinking that it is not state control, but property rights, that are the real solution to the tragedy of the commons. And once property rights are in place they lead of their

152 The tragedy is described by Zac Goldsmith in *The Constant Economy*, London, 2009. For the particularly disturbing case of the cod, see Mark Kurlansky, *Cod: A Biography of a Fish That Changed the World*, London, 1999.

own accord to a market, as people transfer their rights to those most eager to acquire them and in return receive something preferable in exchange. The tragedy of the commons is not due to market failure, but to market absence.

Hence there have been very few vulnerable resources that have not been managed, by those who depended upon them, through a system of property rights, so giving each person an interest in maintaining his guaranteed share. This is in fact true of those lands designated 'commons' in medieval England, which were already being enclosed in the twelfth century.[153] And by the beginning of the thirteenth century territorial fishing rights in tidal waters existed in England, adjudicated in the common-law courts, and transferable from one owner to another.[154] These served to protect spawning grounds and to maintain a resource that endured until recent times – indeed, until the Common Fisheries Policy cancelled most of the customary sovereign rights in the coastal waters of Europe. Long before the arrival of the white man the Native Americans along the Columbia River had established a system of rights to salmon-fishing sites, sometimes residing in the tribe as a whole, sometimes in families, sometimes in individuals.[155] Such property rights can be easily established in coastal, tidal and river waters, allocated by places defined along

153 See Alan MacFarlane, *The Origins of English Individualism: The Family, Property and Social Transition*, Oxford, 1978.

154 Anderson and Leal, *op. cit.*

155 Anderson and Leal, *op. cit.*, p. 115.

the shoreline. Hence the tragedy initiated and managed by the European Union was avoided in Norway, where the Lofoten fishery was one of the largest commercial cod fisheries in the world. The Lofoten fishery was originally self-regulated, with no quotas, no licensing system and no participation from the Norwegian government. Regulation was entirely in the hands of the fishermen themselves, who operated a system of voluntary restraint and conflict resolution for over a hundred years.[156]

Such examples show that central control is not the only answer, nor the best answer, to the problem of the commons. Game theory tells us that, while the classical prisoner's dilemma has an equilibrium solution in which both parties are worse off than they might have been, this outcome results from a lack of information. The two prisoners are kept in isolation, so that neither has knowledge of the other's choice. In an iterated prisoner's dilemma, in which the game is played repeatedly, the partners will acquire knowledge of each other's strategy and adjust their decisions accordingly. The equilibrium solution to such a game is not 'always defect' but rather 'tit-for-tat', that is to say, co-operate at first, and then respond to whatever the other does by doing the same – defecting if the other defects, co-operating otherwise. This result has surprising consequences, first in showing that rational beings have a spontaneous disposition to

---

156 See Hollander, *op. cit.*, p. 62. The situation today is far less clear since regulation has been confiscated by the Socialist government, and the fishermen themselves no longer have a say in it.

evolve co-operative strategies in response to situations of potential conflict;[157] secondly, in suggesting that genes that produce
co-operative dispositions in their phenotypes will be selected for,
so that a spirit of 'altruism' will be the norm in social animals.[158]
Those results, put to fertile use by Robert Axelrod and John
Maynard Smith, have transformed both the social and the biological sciences in recent decades.

They have also been extended into the domain of 'common
pool resources' by Elinor Ostrom, in a striking book that backs
up a far-reaching *a priori* account of equilibrium solutions to
multi-player games with finely observed empirical studies of
successfully managed commons.[159] The sharing of water among
farmers in arid regions of Spain, for example, has been managed
over centuries by locally constituted rules and courts established
under local jurisdiction. Likewise the Alpine meadows of Switzerland are allocated by farmers under co-operative principles that
promote both fair shares and the renewal of the resource. Ostrom
shows that 'common pool resources' can be managed as a stable
asset, provided that: they are managed by a local community;
those with a right to them are clearly identified and others clearly
excluded; there is a system of sanctions in place to punish misap-
propriation and abuse; there is a collective decision-making

157 Robert Axelrod, *The Evolution of Co-operation*, New York, 1984.
158 John Maynard Smith, *Evolution and the Theory of Games*, Cambridge, 1982.
159 Elinor Ostrom, *Governing the Commons: The Evolution of Institutions for Collective Action*, Cambridge, 1990.

process with easily accessible procedures for resolving conflict; and the rights of the community are recognized by higher-level authorities. Ostrom's far-ranging examples are of great relevance to issues of planning and local government. For they show how, when sufficiently localized, a common resource can be managed from below, by the people who share it, and within a broader regime of private property. It is indeed in this way that planning decisions have been made in Switzerland, by a democratic vote among members of a defined local community with exclusive rights to take the relevant decisions.[160]

Those solutions to the tragedy of the commons depend on the rational self-interest of essentially co-operative people. Much of the antipathy to market solutions has come from those who see markets as *competitive* arrangements, in which dog eats dog and the biggest dog survives. But competition in a market depends on co-operation, and it is only co-operatively disposed beings that can make markets work. Markets, like the common pool arrangements discussed by Ostrom, depend on promise-keeping, conflict resolution and the punishment of cheats. They promote cheerful co-operation between their participants, who for the most part see themselves as engaged in a positive-sum game from which everyone can benefit. Ostrom's cases are not departures from market principles but ways of modifying them to cover institutional forms of property. These forms of property depend on localization of the common pool, procedures for defining those with a

160 I return to this case in Chapter 10.

right to it, and further procedures for punishing and excluding the rest. The larger the resource the less is it likely that it can be managed in such a way; though, as the Lofoten fishery demonstrates, even a large coastal fishery can be maintained over decades by co-operative strategies.

In the case of the wider ocean, the tragedy can be avoided by a central allocation of private rights. Thus there is the system adopted by Iceland and New Zealand of the 'individual transferable quota' (ITQ), which allows the individual holder to catch a specified share of the total allowable catch, and which can be transferred to those more interested in developing a fishing fleet, so that any individual's expansion of his catch will lead to a diminution elsewhere. This system has enjoyed considerable success in restoring those nations' once overfished territorial waters. True, the quota system creates a barrier to entry that limits competition to those already in the business. Hence the ITQ system moves of its own accord towards oligopoly, with damaging effects on the settlements in the north of Iceland, which are no longer communities of independent fishermen, and unable to offer employment to their young men. Nevertheless, the quasi-market established by the system achieves its primary goal, which is to protect the fish stocks and to prevent their over-exploitation.[161]

161 For other ways of managing the oceans through quasi-property rights, see the publications of Laura Jones for the Fraser Institute in Vancouver, available on the web. One example is *The Case for Individual Transferable Quotas in the Salmon Fishery of British Columbia*, Vancouver, 1997.

Centralization presents a danger, however. Rights allocated from a central authority destroy the local incentives to co-operation. A telling example is provided by the American treatment of communal grazing rights under the Taylor Grazing Act of 1934, an act that effectively established government control over grazing lands in the West. This assigned to qualifying ranchers a number of 'animal unit months' based on the carrying capacity of a given parcel of public pasture, the rancher paying a rent of about $1.35 per unit. In 1998 the Bureau of Land Management and the Forest Service took in $20 million in grazing fees. But these agencies spend annually between $75 million and $200 million to administer the programme. Meanwhile, the cattle trample the ground, break down riverbanks, foul the water and in general create a hostile environment for birds, fish and amphibians. Recognizing the folly of this, the Clinton administration introduced transferable property rights in the grazing units, comparable to the milk quota scheme familiar in Britain. Instead of campaigning against the ranchers, environmental groups can now buy up the grazing rights over large stretches of public land. Having done so they then come face to face with the business of restoring the land and accounting for its use. The result is responsible management, and an increase in the value of the land farmed by the ranchers.[162]

Solutions of that kind are legislated by an overarching sovereign power. They cannot be used to settle the question of fishing in international waters, or in those waters that have been brought

162 For the full story, see Sagoff, *op. cit.*, pp. 181–6.

under some transnational jurisdiction such as the one mismanaged under the Common Fisheries Policy by the European Union. International and transnational waters raise a question, raised also by climate change, which is whether the competition among nations for scarce resources can be subjected to the same kind of countervailing pressures that are exerted by a market on competition among individuals, and if so, whether these pressures will prevent the tragedy of the commons. But they also challenge us to find other forms of negative feedback than those associated with 'market forces'. Long before Ostrom put the study of common pool resources on a scientific footing, anthropologists argued that hunter-gatherer communities, whose members do not claim individual property rights over their common resources, nevertheless deploy effective codes of stewardship, in which stocks of game are protected by religious scruples or conventions limiting the chase.[163] The accounts of the Inuit given by Hugh Brody and others suggest that hunter-gatherers are every bit as concerned as we are that stocks should be renewed and the bounty of nature conserved.[164] Their resources achieve stability when territories are defined and protected, and governed by customs that distinguish free exchange from coercion, and rightful taking from theft. The result may not be a market economy as we know

163 See Calvin Martin, *Keepers of the Game: Indian–Animal Relationships and the Fur Trade*, Berkeley, 1978. R. N. Chakraborty, 'Sharing Culture and Resource Conservation in Hunter-Gatherer Societies', *Oxford Economic Papers*, 59.1, January 2007, pp. 63–88.

164 Hugh Brody, *The Other Side of Eden*, London, 2001.

it; but it is governed by comparable corrective practices. Individuals are held accountable for their takings, and must repair the cost of their misdeeds, and intruders are identified and repulsed.

At the same time, overexploitation is as much a possibility in a hunter-gatherer community as it is in a community of settled grazers or fishermen. Here as elsewhere, sources might run dry, or individuals may find ways to pass on their costs. Lewis and Clark recorded habitats hunted to near extinction, during their famous expedition through Native American territories in 1804.[165] And Keith Thomas has argued more generally that hunting to extinction has been the norm in many pre-pastoral communities, an argument that is given additional credibility by Jared Diamond's cases of total collapse.[166] On the other hand, fish, game, pasture, trees and other organic products are renewable resources, and will be renewed, just so long as good stewardship is in place. Good stewardship is that which distinguishes rightful taking and rightful use from theft and usurpation – in other words, which establishes some analogue of property rights, whether individual or communal. Any policy that abolishes rightful claims or refuses to identify and punish theft – such as socialist policies of state ownership, or the property vacuum that ensues when there is neither law nor enforceable custom – threatens

165 Meriwether Lewis and William Clark, journals, online at Project Gutenberg.

166 Keith Thomas, *Man and the Natural World: Changing Attitudes in England 1500–1800*, Harmondsworth, 1983, p. 23n, criticizing Martin, *op. cit.*; Diamond, *op. cit.*

stewardship, and is likely to lead to the kind of desertification that we witness in the failed states of North-east Africa, or to the irreversible degradation of the environment that we witness in Russia.

Minerals are not renewable, and rare minerals that are, or have become, vital to human wellbeing may be depleted at rates that threaten the long-term interests of our species. But what is the remedy? Dogmatists of the market will say that, in a free market, as resources are depleted their cost will rise, creating the incentive to look for other and cheaper ways of fulfilling the same need. That is why increasingly expensive copper wire gave way to cheap glass fibre, and why fossil fuels will give way in time to whatever can be discovered to replace them. Moreover, the argument goes, it is only in a free market that the incentive to make the necessary discoveries exists as a real and compulsive *individual* urge. The person who discovers the replacement for some dwindling resource will (given a regime of patents and copyright) make a fortune; hence in a market economy this discovery will occur long before it could be made by scientists working as servants of the state.

However, it has been suggested that without a well-articulated temporal plan, or a satisfactory set of forward markets, market prices may not provide the correct signals and incentives.[167] For

167 P. Dasgupta and G. Heal, 'The Optimal Depletion of Exhaustible Resources', *Review of Economic Studies*, 41, 1974, Symposium on the Economics of Exhaustible Resources, p. 4. See also the same authors' standard work on the subject: *Economic Theory and Exhaustible Resources*, Cambridge, 1979.

market prices are fixed by what is currently available and by current demand for it, and they will not prevent a resource from being exhausted before a substitute has been found. For all we know there was a thriving market in trees on Easter Island. Optimists tell us that things are better for us now than they were for the people on Easter Island. For we do not merely *find* substitutes for scarce resources; we *create* them. Thus John V. Krutilla has argued that in the modern economy it is rare to find a direct substitute for some depleted resource, and far more normal to find an alternative to the process that required it. Traditional concerns over the depletion of resources, Krutilla argues, are of less and less relevance as societies learn to dispense with them.[168]

The argument does not show that markets will survive the exhaustion of resources for which no substitute has been found. Nor does it imply that it is unwise to regulate the use of dwindling resources. Any such regulation should obey the ground-rules suggested in the last chapter. That is, even if designed to intercept a risk, it should be adjustable as circumstances change; and it should never confiscate the problem from those who have the job of solving it, or prevent them from acquiring the resilience that will be needed in a real emergency. Krutilla's argument is plausible, largely because the principal cause of human resilience is knowledge. When a resource is nearing depletion we do not, as

168 John V. Krutilla, 'Conservation Reconsidered', *American Economics Review*, 57, September 1967, pp. 787–96. The point has been taken up in the context of the so-called 'knowledge economy' by Peter Drucker, *Post-Capitalist Society*, New York, 1993.

a rule, search for a direct substitute: we develop the technology that enables us to dispense with it entirely. (As roads become congested, we try to enlarge them; recognizing that space is a dwindling resource, we now stay at home and use the Internet.) However, the argument assumes that consumers will immediately register the benefits from a discovery, and so switch their preferences. In considering environmental problems that assumption cannot be made, since we may be aiming for benefits to future generations that will not be directly felt by those living now.

Markets and quasi-markets may be good at producing substitutes for depleted resources, but they are far less good at disposing of waste. For waste is a cost that everyone tries to pass on. Our most important environmental problems have arisen because the sinks on which people have relied – the oceans, the atmosphere, the rivers and the soil – are filling up beyond their capacity to absorb and recycle our waste. There are no substitutes for these sinks. And at a certain point an over-full sink turns nasty – as the atmosphere is about to turn nasty, if the alarmists are to be believed.

At this point we need to explore the problem of externalities more generally. The classical defence of the market tells us that market transactions are positive-sum games in which parties benefit by exchanging something for another thing that they prefer – as when you buy something you want. The benefit that you acquire is yours, and the cost that you incur is also yours, and neither you nor the shopkeeper loses in the transaction. Suppose, however, that you manufacture funerary sculptures from marble that you quarry from a hillside that you own. To extract the marble you blow the cliffs open with dynamite, and in doing so send tremors through the earth that undermine the foundations of your neighbour's house. Here some of the costs of your economic activity are borne by your neighbour, and if you can get away with this you have effectively 'externalized' those costs.

The English common law of tort, which might reasonably be claimed to be among the greatest achievements of the English-speaking people, has adapted itself to this kind of circumstance from the very beginning of the manufacturing era, not only through the long-standing law of nuisance but through the creation, during the nineteenth century, of strict liability in tort. The leading case here is that of *Rylands v. Fletcher* of 1865.[169] The defendant was a mill-owner who had constructed a reservoir on his land. The water burst through old mine shafts into the mines of the plaintiff, which were thereby flooded and put out of use. No similar case had come before the courts, yet clearly there were questions of right and liability to be decided. The Court of Exchequer Chamber gave judgment in the following words of Mr Justice Blackburn: 'We think that the true rule of law is, that the person who for his own purposes brings on his lands and collects and keeps there anything likely to do mischief if it

169 [1868] UKHL 1.

escapes, must keep it in at his peril, and, if he does not do so, is prima facie answerable for all the damage which is the natural consequence of its escape'. This rule, the judge added, 'seems on principle just'.

Until *Rylands v. Fletcher*, however, no such rule had ever been formulated. The facts of the case arose in the context of new industrial activities, generating serious public anxiety concerning their environmental impact, along with conflicts that had not been tried at law. Did Mr Justice Blackburn merely invent the rule, therefore? If he did, then Mr Rylands (the appellant) was penalized by an act of retroactive legislation – in other words, by the invention of a law of which he could have had no prior knowledge. Surely that would be a flagrant injustice. But notice the judge's words: 'We think that the true rule of law is…'. In other words, in Blackburn's own eyes, he was not inventing the rule, but discovering it. And such was the opinion of the House of Lords, in upholding his judgment.

The attitude of the judges in this case is by no means unusual. The common law could hardly advance without the assumption that there *is* a law governing each judiciable conflict, and that its right application will provide a remedy to the person who is wronged, and a penalty to the person who has wronged him. The case shows clearly how the law may take the lead in forcing a manufacturer to internalize his costs – to ensure, in other words, that it is he, and not some innocent party, who bears the cost of his profit-making.

The case of *Rylands v. Fletcher* has been extensively discussed, and remains as controversial today as it has ever been[170] – not least because strict liability may make it risky to embark on an activity that everybody needs. Since the case was decided, however, strict liability has become embedded in common-law systems, being the simplest way to protect innocent parties from the negative side effects of enterprise. It is even called 'enterprise liability' in American law.[171] Moreover, the case illustrates an important principle, which is that an active law of torts can protect the environment more effectively and more rapidly than any normal action by the legislature, provided only that there are property holders to act as plaintiffs, who can legitimately claim that the costs of some damaging activity have been passed on to *them*. This was how the notorious case of the *Exxon-Valdez* oil spill on the Alaskan coast was resolved, with Exxon compelled to assume the costs of restoring a precious habitat to its previous condi-tion.[172] The comparable case of the 2010 BP spill in the Gulf of Mexico was dealt with similarly, with BP admitting liability, and preparing to meet costs that may very well exhaust its reserves. The contrast with the nuclear disasters in the Soviet Union, in

170 See the argument of Lord Hoffmann in *Transco plc v. Stockport Metropolitan Borough Council*, [2003] UKHL 61, qualifying the rule in *Rylands v. Fletcher*.

171 See George L. Priest, 'The Invention of Enterprise Liability: A Critical History of the Intellectual Foundations of Modern Tort Law', *Journal of Legal Studies*, 14.3, December 1985, pp. 461–528.

172 DeMuth and Ginsburg, *op. cit.*, p. 25.

which the state neither assumed liability nor even admitted that the disasters had occurred, is striking.

In a famous argument the economist Ronald Coase suggested that damages in tort and contract provide the feedback that, in the absence of transaction costs, overcomes of its own accord the problem posed by externalities.[173] Coase was opposing the widely accepted view of Arthur Cecil Pigou, that state action is necessary to ensure that the costs of market transactions are internalized by those who create them.[174] Pigou's suggestion was that pollution and similar externalities should be taxed, so restoring the incentive to assume the costs of market transactions along with the benefits. The burden of Coase's argument is that this misrepresents the underlying logic of the market, which is one of co-operation rather than antagonism. Thus if John's use of his land causes $5 of damage to his neighbour Bill, but brings in a profit of $6, then – assuming no transaction costs – it is worth John compensating Bill, since he can do so and still make a profit, and Bill is no worse off than he would have been had John ceased his business. In general, rational choosers, in a regime of frictionless compensation, will ensure that costs are internalized, and distributed in a way acceptable to all. Coase gives many examples to show how the spontaneous co-ordination of the market

173 See especially Ronald Coase, 'The Problem of Social Cost', *Journal of Law and Economics*, 3, October 1960.

174 A. C. Pigou, *The Economics of Welfare*, London, 1920, part 2. Pigou's solution was accepted by Garrett Hardin, in his original response to 'the tragedy of the commons'. Later he became more 'Coasey'.

through provisions to compensate loss will tend to an optimal social distribution and will rarely be improved upon by state regulation. In a striking 'theorem' Coase also argues that, when a commons is privatized, with property rights assigned to all those who might actively wish to make use of it, any preliminary assignment of private rights will lead, in the absence of transaction costs, to an optimal final distribution, by bargaining among the parties.

So far so good, but Coase's argument does not prove that regulation is unnecessary; only that it is unnecessary in certain special circumstances – where transaction costs are zero, and where the injured parties are identifiable. The situations discussed by Coase are like those researched by Ostrom: situations in which identifiable parties or local communities are being asked to bear the costs of a particular person's economic activity. Both Coase and Ostrom are exploring positive-sum solutions to many-player games. Even where injured parties can be identified, however, regulation might still be necessary, if transaction costs interfere with market solutions. And they do interfere. Seeking compensation is a costly process. Rarely does the party who causes the damage offer to pay in advance; and often the one who suffers cannot be identified until the damage has been done. He must then sue in a court of law, which costs time and money and is of uncertain outcome. And this action is rational only if the law is clear, the judge impartial and the matter clearly understood. Even in the best of jurisdictions the process is far from frictionless, and prior regulation to prevent externalities might be preferable by far to the painful attempt to rectify matters after the event.[175]

Such problems have become abundantly apparent in America, where the English law of tort has encountered a formidable accumulation of greed and vindictiveness, and lost out in the fight. In the American courts tort cases are decided by a jury – a right guaranteed by the seventh amendment of the US Constitution – and the jury also assesses damages. Predatory lawyers, taking advantage of 'class-action suits', and of the procedure whereby individual jury members can be 'challenged' and removed prior to the trial, have been able to ensure that the one who *can* pay is the one who *does* pay, regardless of fault. In the Exxon case just mentioned it is clear that Exxon and its agents were at fault and, therefore, were justly charged with the cost of the spill. But such carriages of justice are becoming less frequent, and it is worth noting what exactly has gone wrong with American tort law – namely, that a once homeostatic system has now been shorn of its principal feedback loop. The law of torts was designed to transfer the cost of damage to the one who causes it, following principles of accountability of a kind that are fundamental to the regulation of ordinary disputes. This means that those who cause harm also bear the cost of it, and the negative feedback provides

175 Coase's Theorem is also insensitive to the so-called 'endowment effect', according to which the receipt of property is in itself a value to the recipient. See Daniel Kahneman *et al.*, 'Experimental Test of the Endowment Effect and the Coase Theorem', in Cass Sunstein, ed., *Behavioural Law and Economics*, Cambridge, 2000.

a strong incentive to avoid tortious behaviour. The same is not true of American tort law today: the feedback loop from the damage to the cause has been severed, and the system proceeds out of control, amplifying the evil complained of by forcing innocent parties to pay for it, and augmenting the costs to match the capacity to cover them.[176]

The real cure for this – which is to restrict the capacity of juries to award punitive damages – is not the one considered. Instead the response of the American government has been to protect industries from malicious suits in tort by passing laws designed to prevent every tort before it happens. In other words, the government has adopted a strategy of interception, rather than encouraging the kind of resilience that issues from a regime of liability in tort. Interception is the task of the Environmental Protection Agency, whose absolutist regulations have been estimated to cost $7.6 million annually for each life saved. This cost is inflicted on municipal governments and businesses, and is one of the many painful and pointless burdens that make it difficult for enterprises to take a flexible and creative approach to environmental problems.[177] Once again we see the counter-productive nature of regulatory policies that confiscate risk and remove the incentive to prepare for it. Tort-law reform would restore a corrective device on which the market economy depends, by

176 Cass Sunstein *et al.*, *Punitive Damages: How Juries Decide*, Chicago, 2002.
177 Tammy Tengs, 'Optimizing Societal Investments in the Prevention of Premature Death', *Harvard School of Public Health*, 1994.

preventing wrongdoers and exploiters from exporting their costs. The EPA's regulatory regime, by contrast, both enhances the costs and transfers them to all of us, in the form of increased prices.

Ten years after the case of *Rylands v. Fletcher*, the British Parliament made its first attempt to deal with the problem of pollution, passing the Public Health Act in 1875 and the Rivers Pollution Prevention Acts between 1876 and 1893. These acts gave local authorities power to take criminal proceedings against polluters. However, the principal polluters were local authorities, which discharged sewage into the rivers without concern for the effect on the people and the fish downstream from them. Hence few prosecutions were initiated and the fines imposed were derisory. Subsequent Acts did nothing to rectify the principal weakness in the legislation, which was that it treated the rivers themselves as commons, in which no individual had an actionable right. In the years following the Second World War, when Britain was experiencing a socialist economy, with large-scale national-ized industries, compulsory purchases and massive privileges extended to any body that could be described as 'public', the rivers suffered severe pollution, and many of the most beautiful of them died.[178]

However, there was another way of proceeding. It had been

---

178 The case has been lucidly set out by Roger Bate, *Saving Our Streams: The Role of the Anglers' Conservation Association in Protecting English and Welsh Rivers*, London, 2001.

clear since the case of *Chasemere v. Richards* of 1859 that the common law recognizes a right of riparian owners to enjoy unpolluted water along their banks. Lord Wensleydale, giving judgment in that case, summarized the law in the following (not entirely pellucid) words: 'The landowner has the right to have water come to him in its natural state, in flow, quantity and quality, and to go from him without obstruction, upon the same principle that he is entitled to the support of his neighbour's soil for his own in its natural state.'[179] So defined, the quasi-property right gives riparian owners a cause of action in civil law against those who destroy the natural condition of the water flowing past their land.

It was a barrister and an angler, John Eastwood, who saw the opportunity that this presented to rescue the rivers from the state. While the criminal penalties created by the Acts against pollution were seldom so heavy as to stop the offences, and could be administered in any case only after the damage was done, a civil action could be used both to stop pollution entirely, and to prevent it before it occurred. This is because the common-law courts could grant the equitable remedy of injunction, which is issued prior to the offence, and which can lead to a severe charge of contempt of court against the one who disobeys it.

Civil action is expensive and the cost falls entirely on the one who loses. Few riparian owners were wealthy enough to take the risk of losing, and those with the greatest interest in the purity of

179 [1859] 7 H.L. Cas. 349.

the streams were anglers, most of whom had no ownership rights at all. Hence Eastwood encouraged anglers and angling clubs to buy land adjacent to the rivers so as to be entitled to actions in civil law against those who were destroying their sport. In 1948 he went on to form the Anglers' Co-operative Association, which was to become the Anglers' Conservation Association, designed to offer financial backing to those who were in a position to initiate legal proceedings.

This kind of civic initiative is facilitated by the law of trusts and the common law of associations, which enable clubs to appear as collective litigants in a court of law. Hence clubs need no act of incorporation and no kind of permission from the state. Within a few years anglers around the country had united in the protection of their sport, and the landmark 'Pride of Derby' case of 1952, in which three defendants – a private company, a nationalized industry and a local government – were compelled to cease from polluting the River Derwent, awoke both industry and the state to the need to change their behaviour.[180]

If the rivers of England are clean and stocked with fish today it is because the law recognizes riparian property rights and the right to associate of those who possess them. The rivers have been cleaned not by the state, but against the state, not by 'social ownership' but by the right of private property. It is to such

180 *Pride of Derby and Derbyshire Angling Association and Earl of Harrington v. British Celanese Ltd., the Derby Corporation and the British Electricity Authority*, [1952] 1 All ER 179.

examples that the defender of market solutions will refer, when arguing for their superiority over the state-imposed alternative, and in a patient and detailed survey Terry L. Anderson and Donald R. Leal give many comparable cases.[181] But it should also be recognized that the property rights that have cleaned our rivers are themselves common law creations, and that they are effective only because of the ancillary feedback loops established by a legal system in which free association, equitable remedies and the law of tort give power and standing to the individual litigant.

It should also be recognized that this exemplary civic initiative would not have occurred had it not been for the sport of angling, an activity that is condemned by the proponents of animal rights, and which is a frequent target of abuse.[182] The proper response to the attacks on fishing was articulated two centuries ago by Wordsworth, in a sonnet that he wrote on a blank leaf of Izaak Walton's *Compleat Angler*:

> While flowing rivers yield a blameless sport,
> Shall live the name of Walton: Sage benign!
> Whose pen, the mysteries of rod and line
> Unfolding, did not fruitlessly exhort

181 Anderson and Leal, *op. cit.*
182 Cf. PETA's campaign in America, at www.fishinghurts.com. I deal with some of the arguments in *Animal Rights and Wrongs*, London, 1995, Appendix on Fishing.

To reverend watching of each still report

That Nature utters from her rural shrine.

Meek, nobly versed in simple discipline,

He found the longest summer day too short,

To his loved pastime given by sedgy Lee,

Or down the tempting maze of Shawford brook –

Fairer than life itself, in this sweet Book,

The cowslip-bank and shady willow-tree;

And the fresh meads – where flowed, from every nook

Of his full bosom, gladsome Piety.

The 'reverend watching of each still report' is an apposite description of the oikophilia that I shall defend in Chapter 8, where I explain and justify the Wordsworthian concept of 'natural piety', attributed here to Walton, the Founding Father of English environmentalism, and by implication to his 'blameless sport'.

Stewardship is second nature to the sportsman. In Britain habitats and biodiversity have been protected not only by the Anglers' Conservation Association but also by the Game Conservancy Association, by the British Field Sports Society and by the Masters of Foxhounds Association during times when they have only been damaged by the state. Hunting, shooting and fishing create an interest in other species and a desire to conserve their habitats that is matched by virtually no other relation between man and animal – a point that needs no explaining to those who take part in these pursuits, and which can seldom be explained to anyone else.

The case of the Anglers' Conservation Association illustrates the general principle, which is that markets fail to satisfy the contending interests that animate them whenever parties can externalize their costs, and whenever transaction costs are too high for those injured to obtain a remedy. The big polluters assumed they were safe to pump effluent into the rivers, since there were no definable victims to whom they were passing their costs. They were proven wrong. Not only were the victims identifiable; they were capable of combining to protect their assets.

A problem remains, however. A business that externalizes its costs onto indefinitely many people and onto future generations may escape litigation. This is the problem of the 'sinks'; but it is by no means a recent problem. It was already apparent in the immediate post-war period, when Western governments and investors promoted industrial farming. Quite suddenly our ecosystems were confronted with a new kind of damage, with incalculable effects on the long-term interests of people. The use of pesticides had an immediate effect on wildlife, leading to the famous book by Rachel Carson – *Silent Spring* (1962) – that launched the environmental movement as we know it today. Environmentalists like Marion Shoard in Britain and Wendell Berry in America have since documented the catastrophe, and shown the way in which governments and agribusinesses have conspired to inflict lasting damage on the land and all that grows from it.[183]

As has been repeatedly shown, agricultural subsidies, of the kind we have seen in Europe and America, reward large-scale production, and proceed, like bureaucratic regulations, by disaggregating the many aspects of husbandry, so that their side effects are seldom corrected in time. Post-war British governments subsidized farmers to uproot the hedgerows, of which some 15,000 miles were lost. Perceiving too late the damage that this inflicted on wildlife and biodiversity, governments now subsidize the planting of hedgerows. By subsidizing the production of crops governments encourage their overproduction, which leads to dumping on the world market and the destruction of agriculture in the Third World. So now governments subsidize farmers *not* to produce, and fields are left fallow at the taxpayer's expense. In these and a hundred other ways the regime of subsidies destroys markets and the negative feedback that is their principal environmental benefit. Once the costs are externalized over undefined individuals, they cannot be returned to the one who causes them.

We should not blame the market for this, but rather the ease, in a modern economy, with which private gains can be combined with socialized costs. Thus manufacturers of soft drinks and similar consumables now rely on the plastic bottle as a cheap way

183 Marion Shoard, *The Theft of the Countryside*, London, 1980; Graham Harvey, *The Killing of the Countryside*, London, 1998; Wendell Berry, *The Unsettling of America*, San Francisco, 1977.

of transporting their products to the market in saleable portions. But these bottles, once used, enter the environment, so creating a cost to everyone. It is difficult to assign a monetary value to this cost, though nobody can doubt that the earth is being damaged by a product that threatens wildlife, blocks rivers and drainage systems, accumulates in the oceans, and – by destroying the beauty of the countryside – destroys also the motive to protect it. Plastic packaging is a form of immortal rubbish, which will accumulate for ever and cannot fail to be an ecological disaster if it is not either abolished or systematically recycled. It forms one small part of the 'sink' problem, and also reveals the structure of that problem, which arises because waste has not been priced, and is not immediately priced by the market. In such circumstances a price has to be invented and imposed – as in the bottle-deposit mechanism that worked so effectively in the days when bottles were made of glass.

I return later to the problem of plastic, which in my view is a problem that could be solved. But it is only one part of a larger problem. There is hardly an aspect of the modern economy that does not involve the transfer of costs to anonymous others by imposing them on our shared environment. And it does no good simply to invoke the state as the friend of the people against the predations of the market, since a great many of these predations are introduced and managed by the state. Health and safety regulations imposed by the state or the European Union are responsible for the vast amount of non-biodegradable wrapping

that festoons our food; state subsidies and inscrutable bureaucracies are responsible for our system of motorways; and it is the
unequal impact of state subsidies and regulatory burdens that has
enabled supermarkets to destroy the local food economy across
Europe and America. State-subsidized roads permit supermarkets
to operate on the edge of towns and to achieve enormous
economies of scale. State-imposed planning regulations compel
local shopkeepers to build in confined spaces, to maintain costly
façades and to serve customers who cannot park outside. State-
imposed regulations governing packaging and inspection can be
economically obeyed only through centralized processing and
distribution, of the kind that supermarkets can manage for themselves. And the economies of scale that supermarkets achieve
enable them to preside, from the edge of every town, over the
decay of its centre and its destruction as a self-sustaining human
habitat. This easy victory for the forces of environmental destruction would be impossible without the unequal burden of state
regulations and the unequal benefit of state subsidies, both of
which favour the edge-of-town retailer over the local store.
Although state action may be necessary to solve our environmental problems, therefore, we should not ignore the fact that state
action may also be the cause of them.

The externalization of costs exists in two forms – that which
sensibly affects people here and now, and that whose effect will be
apparent only to future generations. The motives that might lead
us to address the two problems will, therefore, be different, the

first being part of normal day-to-day housekeeping and account-ability to others, the second requiring the kind of stewardship that depends on identifying with people who are yet to be. This second motive will concern me in the chapters that follow. But how do we turn the world in the direction of day-to-day housekeeping?

There is no doubt that regulation could do something to block the routes whereby costs are passed to unidentifiable others. One of the great success stories of environmental management is that of smog – the curse of all major cities in the nineteenth and early twentieth centuries, now removed from Europe and America by laws governing household fuel. But the case also illustrates the dangers of regulation, which is apt to replace normal market fric-tion with a regime of zero tolerance. The costs of enforcing clean air regulation in America have been so amplified by the EPA as to produce price distortions that are a serious tax on consumers.[184] There are other reasons too for thinking that regulation alone will not prevent major polluters from externalizing their costs.

Firstly, governments have favourites. Those businesses that thrive by passing on their costs to the environment – the motor industry, the aircraft industry, the supermarkets, to name but three – are the ones that receive the most from government in hidden subsidies and the last ones to be called to account. A defender of market solutions would need to show, for example, how the

---

184 See Robert W. Hahn, 'The Politics and Religion of Clean Air', *Cato Review of Business and Government*, 1990. See also Robert W. Hahn, ed., *Risks, Costs and Lives Saved: Getting Better Results from Regulation*, Oxford, 1996.

hidden subsidies that maintain the supermarkets could be removed without destroying habits that have become second nature to modern people.

Secondly, top-down regulation disaggregates risk. Regulations designed to solve one problem are likely to create new problems of the same or a higher order. Thus regulations requiring the recycling of glass have removed one of the most important stabilizing factors from landfill sites, while health and safety regulations have promoted the poisoning of the entire world with plastic.

Thirdly, coherent regulation requires us to assemble problems in the order of their seriousness, and to price the solution accordingly. Incoherent regulation has, to date, been the major defect of the American EPA, which mandates vast expenditure to remove small risks, so diverting resources that could be used to protect people from the real disasters. Each year the money that would have served to update the levees of New Orleans, thereby protecting the city from the hurricane that was to destroy it in 2005, is spent on obeying the small print of the Clean Air Act, even though the air of America now presents no significant risk to those who breathe it.[185]

Fourthly, top-down regulation inevitably transfers both problems and solutions to a central decision-making body. It thereby lifts problems from their context and prevents them from being localized and solved by the kind of civic initiatives that are the

185 Schwartz and Hayward, *op. cit.*

real source of stewardship, including those discussed by Ostrom. In the England in which I grew up, when most wrappings were in any case biodegradable, someone who threw away a sweet-bag or a newspaper would be condemned as a 'litter-bug', and every now and then, in order to renew our concern for the world that we shared, we would get together as neighbours to clear up the small amounts of mess that fluttered across our lanes. Or if the neighbours did not do it, then the local Boy Scout troop would do it in their stead. Litter is now the concern of the council, and councils have bigger problems than litter. Worse, public spirit has been confiscated by government, national and local, and those volunteer groups have disappeared. An environmental problem that once was solved by the small-scale wisdom of the human heart now stands unsolved, and will soon be insoluble. By contrast, every lane and highway in Rappahannock County, Virginia, has been adopted by some group of volunteers. In a county with only a tiny local government, the environment is the concern of the citizens themselves. They don't manage it perfectly; but they manage it very much better than my local council in Wiltshire.

Volunteer groups proliferate when the state does not take charge. That is the experience of America, and it is one that made a lasting impression on Tocqueville nearly two centuries ago.[186] Left to themselves, people will try to rectify the damage, provided

---

186 Alexis de Tocqueville, *Democracy in America*, vol. 2, part 2, ch. 7. But see Chapter 10 below, where I discuss the work of Robert Putnam, documenting the decline of volunteers in America.

they believe that it is not some anonymous *they* that is responsible, but *we*. In the situations studied by Ostrom rational self-interest, acting in conjunction with the co-operative instinct, opens an escape route from the tragedy. In other situations, however, rational self-interest will not be enough, either because beneficiaries are indefinitely many and impossible to bring into the fold, or because the demands of identifiable players cannot all be met.[187] Here it is necessary to find another motive, a stronger motive than the instinct for co-operation, which will reach out to embrace absent generations and take their interests into account. The solution to the real environmental problems will always elude us, if we cast away the one human motive that is able to take over when markets fail, which is that of public spirit. But whence comes public spirit? It comes from patriotism, from love of country, from a sense of belonging and of a shared and inherited home. It comes from believing that this problem is *our* problem, and therefore *my* problem, as a member of the group. That belief disappears when anonymous bureaucracies confiscate our risks, and pretend that they can regulate them to extinction.

Those commonsensical observations are all but politically incorrect, in a culture that has surrendered so much to the state,

187 Such situations have been explored in the various 'impossibility theorems' in social choice theory, for example those of K. J. Arrow and Amartya Sen. For a brief summary see entries for Arrow's Theorem and Paretian Liberal in Roger Scruton, *The Palgrave Macmillan Dictionary of Political Thought*, London, 2007. For a full account of Arrow's Theorem see Kenneth Arrow, *Social Choice and Individual Values*, New Haven, 1990.

that it no longer trusts the ordinary human instincts. But it is only if we take such observations seriously that a solution to our every-day environmental problems can be found. It is not only property rights and the market that have helped to keep alive, in the English-speaking world, the tradition of civic initiatives such as that which saved the rivers of England. The law of trusts that protects charitable and public-spirited causes, the law of tort that returns costs to the one who produces them, the freedom of asso-ciation that forbids the state to intrude on our social initiatives – all such institutions combine with those of private property and the market to create a network of homeostatic systems, in which errors are corrected and risks compensated as they arise. All are liable to corruption, and all can be burdened by transaction costs that make them unserviceable. And all depend, in the last analy-sis, on the patriotic commitment that enables people to combine in their own defence and to extend their trust to strangers.

Here we reach what seems to me to be the crux of the disagreement between right and left. It does not reside in rival assessments of the problem – although, of course, a person's assessment of a problem is usually heavily influenced by his attitude towards it, and just as radical Greens are disposed to exaggerate environmental problems, so conservatives are dis-posed to belittle them. The real disagreement between them is existential, and corresponds to the deep psychological and spiritual distinctions that I explored in Chapter 3. The radical egalitarian is typically in rebellion against the ordinary world of 'getting and spending' that surrounds him. He finds his community not here and now, in the inherited and imperfect social order of those who are muddling along, but in an imagined society of kindred spirits, united around a shared and justifying goal. Where the conservative identifies with family, settlement and nation, the radical identifies with a *movement*, which will absorb and soothe the pain of his apartness.

We should see the plans and policies of the two kinds of person as issuing from their rival temperaments. Radical egalitarians are not satisfied with a policy that does not have a world-transforming character, and with which they cannot be caught up in a society of like-minded people, side by side in a 'struggle' against the 'powers that be'. Small-scale adjustments within the status quo have little appeal to them, and externalities and market failures seem, in their eyes, to call for some far-reaching policy that automatically invites the state to assume the leading role. Civic initiatives by local communities, sorting out among themselves the property-like principles that will enable them to solve their problem, simply awaken distrust: after all, these are the people who *caused* the problem. So how can they be relied upon to solve it? Contained within this view is the impetus towards bureaucratic and centralized solutions, and the expropriation of the moral space that might otherwise be occupied by volunteers.[188]

188 Hence the proliferation, under Labour governments in Britain, of quasi-autonomous non-government organizations (quangos), through which

The difference between that outlook and the typical conservative response is the difference between the 'movement' and Burke's 'little platoon'. In his criticism of the mass-movement politics of the French Revolution Burke repudiated what he saw as a false vision of social order – one in which people are conscripted by an 'armed doctrine' in pursuit of a common goal imposed by a central power. Against this he advocated a society of free association at the local level, acting within the constraints of law, custom and property rights, but resolving problems, in so far as it could, by compromise and negotiation. In the course of developing his argument Burke made a vitally important observation. The revolutionaries, he argued, were fierce advocates of Rousseau's social contract, hoping to establish a new conception of legitimacy, in which the consent of the citizen, rather than the inherited right of a monarch, would be the foundation of the political order. But who, Burke asked, are citizens, and how is their consent solicited and entered into the equation? If society is a contract, it is not a contract between the living only, but a contract that includes the dead, the living and the unborn – in short, not a contract at all, but a relation of trusteeship, in which the living have charge of assets inherited from the dead which they in turn must pass on to those unborn. Simply to waste in the lifetime of

government appointees expropriate one by one the affairs of self-regulating communities. As of 23 May 2010 it was reported that there were 1,162 such organizations, employing more than 100,000 people, some with salaries as high as £624,000, at a total cost to date of £64 billion. Article by Simon Walters, *Daily Mail*, 23 May 2010.

a nation's temporary tenants, the capital accumulated over centuries, is to breach the trust on which future generations depend. And of course, this is exactly the complaint, made in other terms, by environmentalists in our time – that we are destroying an asset that we hold in trust for future generations, and violating a fundamental duty of justice in doing so. This is true, but what motivates people to act in the way that Burke recommends? The answer to that question defines the difference between left and right. Burke is arguing that movements destroy social capital, little platoons preserve it. And the conservative will say that the same is true of environmental capital too.

Before leaving this topic it is important to address the issue of 'moral hazard' – the situation in which individuals or institutions are effectively insulated from the full costs of their choices, either by private insurance or by state support. Private insurance increases with the risk, and imposes a measure of self-discipline on the person who purchases it. Insurance offered by the state, however, is cost-free and open to exploitation. The state's presence in the economy lifts problems free from the situations that create them, overrides liabilities and transfers costs to the taxpayer, so jeopardizing the responsible use of resources. Consider the now notorious case of the American mortgage lenders Fannie Mae and Freddie Mac. Implicit in their lending policies was the assumption that, as state-sponsored enterprises with lower capital requirements than private institutions, they could look to the federal government for assistance if a high number of their clients defaulted. Hence they continued to lend money in obedience to unwise and politically motivated procedures until finally placed in federal conservatorship in 2008.[189]

The economic presence of the state has a comparable effect in many environmental problems. When Hurricane Katrina struck New Orleans in 2005, it caused over $150 billion worth of damage. Levees and sea walls were maintained by official bodies, rather than by those whom they were designed to protect, and nobody had troubled to reinforce them or to update their design. Many houses and businesses were not insured against flood damage.[190] People had continued to live in high-risk areas, confident that, when the disaster arrived, the Federal Emergency Management Agency would step in to compensate them. In similar manner, British people continue to build on flood plains, confident that any adverse consequences will be transferred to the state, and many don't bother with flood insurance, or take no heed when discovering that no insurance company will underwrite it. In all these ways government intervention increases the environmental risks by discouraging citizens from pricing them, and from acquiring, as a result, the resilience needed to adapt to them. Without suggesting that the market is the single all-purpose solution to environmental problems, we can at least see that our ability

189 The story of Freddie Mac and Fannie Mae, and their effect in precipitating the credit crisis of 2008–9, is told by Arthur Brooks, *The Battle: How the Fight between Free Enterprise and Big Government Will Shape America's Future*, New York, 2010.

190 See Charles Perrow, *The Next Catastrophe*, Princeton, 2007, pp. 37–8.

to cope with those problems is seriously damaged when the state helps to lift the cost of ignoring them.

The example of flooding points to the value of insurance in dealing with environmental threats. Those who rely on others to rescue them in a crisis are transferring the costs of their folly, and relying on systems that will inevitably break down if too many people do the same. Those who insure against risk are taking the cost of it on themselves, and also making a properly priced contribution to putting things right, should the risk materialize. Insurance is another aspect of the homeostasis on which durable communities depend, and its widespread existence in America is one reason why American communities recover so quickly from shocks and disasters. This is not to deny that insurance too is a source of moral hazard, tempting people to take risks that they should not be taking and shifting the cost of risk from the imprudent to the prudent. However, devices have evolved (such as incremental premiums and no-claims bonuses) that help to return the costs of foolishness to the fool.[191]

So far in this chapter I have been offering a qualified defence of the position normally identified with the 'right' in the discussion of environmental problems – the position according to which

191 There is also the problem of the extent to which insurance should be private, so as to shift the cost on to the individual, or social, so as to shift the cost on to the state. See Charles Murray, *Losing Ground*, New York, 1998, on the welfare trap, and, for a countervailing view, Peter Gosselin, *High Wire: The Precarious Financial Lives of American Families*, New York, 2008.

the market is not the problem but one part of the solution, with the state playing a subordinate role in the control of externalities. But it will be rightly said that this is to let big business off too easily. It is not as though the complaints from the left against the petroleum companies, the agribusinesses, the producers of GM crops, the developers, the supermarkets and the airlines were all based on fabrications, or as if these businesses can be run just as they are without any lasting environmental damage. In fact, the greatest weakness of the position that John Gray describes as 'neo-liberalism' – the ideological summoning of the market, as the sole remedy to all social and economic problems – is the refusal to make the distinction, apparent to all reasonable people, between big business and little business. When businesses are big enough they can cushion themselves against the negative side effects of their activity, and proceed as if all objections could be overcome by a consultant in 'Corporate Social Responsibility', without any change in the way things are done.[192]

The problem is as much one of institutional structure as one of size. No institutions have contributed more to the expansion of markets than limited liability and the joint stock company. Those two remarkable seventeenth-century inventions secured the pre-eminence of the Dutch and the British in international trade. They have done more to encourage free enterprise than virtually

---

192 See Roger Scruton, 'Virtue and Profit', in Samuel Gregg and James Stoner, eds., *Profit, Prudence and Virtue: Essays in Ethics, Business and Management*, St Andrews, 2009.

any other legal instruments by enabling small and vulnerable investors to risk their savings in business, without risking everything else. But they have also created moral hazards that seem fully to justify the anger and scorn that so many people (and not only those on the left) feel towards the unbridled capitalist economy. By separating ownership from control, and insulating both the shareholder and the director from the full costs of their mistakes, these legal devices encourage risk-taking beyond anything that the market would otherwise allow. In the words of Kenneth Arrow, 'the law steps in and forces a risk shifting not created in the market-place'.[193] Hence in the last two years we have seen bankers carelessly destroying the savings entrusted to them, and paying themselves vast bonuses at the very moment of doing so.

Whatever the adverse effects of limited liability and shareholding, however, we should not take them as a reason for welcoming the intrusion of the state. On the contrary, when the state steps in it is usually in order to put another cushion under the director's bum, reassuring him that the more irresponsible his behaviour, the more likely it is that the state will relieve him of the consequences.[194] When the Carter administration rescued Chrysler in 1980, this action conveyed a message to the Detroit-

---

193 Kenneth J. Arrow, *Essays in the Theory of Risk-Bearing*, Amsterdam, 1976.

194 See Martin Wolf, *Fixing Global Finance*, Baltimore, 2008. As Wolf puts it, the distortions introduced by government guarantees 'create an overwhelming incentive to privatize gains and socialize losses'.

based car manufacturers that they could go on producing cars that nobody wanted, that they could ignore the growing competition from Japan, and that they could give in to all the demands of the United Automobile Workers Union – in short, that they could relax, knowing that they would be rescued by the state when things got tough. In 2008 things got tough and they were duly rescued.

The latest CEO of General Motors, a business that is sustained in being as a Potemkin façade by the US government, paid himself a salary package of $9 million in 2010. In this example we see how limited liability and state subsidies can between them sustain a business that the market, left to itself, would long ago have killed. Moreover, not only is the business in question an environmental disaster; it also retains a vast amount of human capital that could be usefully deployed elsewhere in the economy – for example, in the development of clean energy. This last complaint is by no means trivial. For there is hardly an industry in the world today that contains such an accumulation of skill, knowledge and transferable expertise as the American motor industry. Indeed the human capital tied up in that industry, and maintained there in a state of futile quiescence, may very well be one of America's greatest economic assets, condemned to stagnation at the very moment when it is most needed elsewhere.

Nor would it be an improvement for the state to go one stage further and take over the business. Directors of state enterprises also enjoy limited liability, and are protected from any personal loss however foolish or malicious their decisions. Furthermore, state enterprises enjoy protections and buffers that shield them more fully from the effects of their mistakes than any private enterprise.[195] It seems, therefore, that the adverse effects of limited liability can never be overcome by state intervention, whatever form it might take – whether investment, subsidy or explicit control. The best we can hope for is a strict enforcement of bankruptcy laws, and the disqualification of directors of bankrupt industries from serving on other boards.

There is an important lesson to be drawn from the examples I have given in this chapter. Markets distribute costs to those who cause them and benefits to those who work for them, and make available to all participants the information about each other's wants that is otherwise irretrievably dispersed.[196] But they can solve the problems that they create only if the feedback loops are not severed. This severance occurs when agents within the market are able to externalize their costs, either by imposing them on indeterminate others through damage to the environment, by drawing on overt or hidden subsidies from the state or by buffering themselves against risk. In the first case the courts may step in

---

195 Hence, under the state socialist regimes of the Soviet Empire, it was impossible for firms to go bankrupt, all debts being redistributed across the economy as a whole by a process of 'economic arbitrage', which served to maintain useless industries indefinitely.

196 I refer to the Austrian School arguments concerning price and calculation, as presented by von Mises and Hayek. On the general importance of these arguments see Roger Scruton, 'Hayek and Conservatism', in Edward Feser, ed., *The Cambridge Companion to Hayek*, Cambridge, 2007.

to ensure that, through another homeostatic system (the law of torts), the costs are reassigned to the one who incurs them. But here too, as in the American courts today, the feedback loop can be severed. Then again the state may step in to reassign costs and benefits, and once again feedback loops may be severed, as when agents transfer the cost of insurance by depending on the state's emergency powers, or when risks are confiscated from those willing to take them and bequeathed against their will to future generations, as in the EU laws governing the packaging of food.

All the environmental problems with which we have to deal, climate change included, have this structure: they are problems that arise when agents can escape the costs of their transactions. So what is the solution? Clearly we must find the motives that cause people to internalize their costs, and the institutions through which those motives can be exercised to the common good. *That*, in my view, is the core aim of conservative politics, and it provides the theme of my subsequent discussion.

SIX

The Moral Economy

Markets can sustain a free and self-correcting economy. They do not merely produce consensual solutions. They assign responsibilities, and so help to maintain the close connection between free choice and individual accountability on which the moral order depends. But they function properly only in the context of other socially evolved systems, such as the laws of tort, contract and association. Even with the benefit of those institutions, markets may fail to give what is asked of them. If there is a purpose for regulation it should be to prevent that from happening. Regulations should be designed to return the costs of all transactions to those who incur them. Many people seem to let the matter rest at this point, arguing that the market, properly regulated, is the only known solution to economic problems, and that any attempt to interfere with its operation, beyond protecting participants from externalities, is bound to be counter-productive.

Here, however, we encounter a long-standing complaint from

the left. 'Market solutions', it is argued, subsume human motivation under the model of cost and benefit, and see all rationality in instrumental terms: the agent wants x, believes y is the means to x, and therefore pursues y; the agent prefers a to b and b to c, and therefore prefers a to c; and so on. Something seems absent from this picture, and even if the theory of preference and preference orderings can be developed to give a neat mathematics of practical reason,[197] the resulting picture of *homo economicus* seems to many people to be little better than a caricature of the human being.

It might be tempting to reply that economic theories were never designed to get inside the structure of human desire, so as to discriminate good and bad, deep and shallow, value and appetite, need and luxury, rational self-interest and momentary whim. Even if not all preferences are values, values show themselves in 'revealed preferences'. Environmental goods can, therefore, be assessed by asking what 'consumers' would be willing to pay to keep them, or what they would be willing to accept in compensation for their loss. Such computations have given rise to the discipline of 'environmental economics', which translates values into prices and prices into policies.[198] Why then do we need to 'get inside' our preferences, in order to solve the problems of co-ordination to which they give rise?

197 Something that is not easily achieved, given the conflicting constraints on preference orderings, and the paradoxes, from Condorcet to Arrow, that have caused such vexation. See Note 187.

198 See Eban S. Goodstein, *Economics and the Environment*, Hoboken, 2004.

That reply misses the point, however.[199] Human desires and projects arise from many different sources; some desires are more easily traded than others, and some are deeply bound up with the existential condition and self-identity of the subject. Unless we look into the sources of human motivation, we will find nothing that we can call upon, with which to correct the great fault in the scheme of things that markets can of their nature never remedy, namely the entirely reasonable habit among rational agents of escaping from their commitments and transferring their costs.

More simply put, environmental problems are problems of *morality*, not economics. Economic reasoning is all very well, so far as it goes, but it is one-dimensional, focusing on individual rational choice, and how rational choices can be summed to the common advantage. Game theory, the theory of the market, the theories of preference orderings and social choice – all have addressed the question encapsulated in the tragedy of the commons. And those disciplines have finely illustrated the difficulties that impede co-ordination when we try to adjust our choices to the sparse information that we might have about the choices of others. But they fall silent in the face of the larger question of future generations. Where should we look for the motive that will protect those who are not yet players in the collective game? Markets cannot register their choices, nor can game theory give them a seat at the table. Moreover, neither

199 The claims of environmental economics are subject to ruthless examination by Sagoff, *op. cit.*

approach can confront the fact that agents choose constantly in the face of circumstances that leave no room for the choices that they *really* want to have.

In the face of this many philosophers have argued that we need an 'environmental ethics', and that it should be a central task of philosophy to provide one.[200] Academic philosophers used to believe that their task is to clarify moral concepts and moral reasoning, but not to make substantial pronouncements about how we should live or what we should do. That belief has been decisively rejected in recent years, with many arguing that philosophy should repossess itself of its ancient credentials as the pursuit of wisdom and a guide to life. Hence we have seen the emergence of schools of 'applied' or 'practical ethics', offering to give cogent solutions to real-life problems. And practical ethics has made its presence felt in several fields – notably medicine, business and the environment – where people charged with life-changing decisions find themselves bereft of ready advice, and in need of the expert who will lift the burden of decision-making from their shoulders.

What I have read of 'practical ethics' has not persuaded me that professional philosophers today are any good at giving advice.[201] Wisdom, of the kind we learn from Aristotle, Epictetus,

200 See Holmes Rolston III, *Philosophy Gone Wild*, Buffalo, 1989, and David R. Keller, ed., *Environmental Ethics*, Chichester, 2010. For an elegant survey of views pertaining to the natural world, see Angelika Krebs, *Ethics of Nature: A Map*, Berlin, 1999.

201 See Peter Singer, ed., *Applied Ethics*, Oxford, 1986.

Confucius or Aquinas, does not consist in 'solutions' to everyday dilemmas, but rather in a comprehensive stance towards the world, through which we frail beings can make the best of our limited powers. In the place of wisdom, the exponents of 'practical ethics' offer a kind of casuistical expertise. And I doubt that there can be such a thing as a moral expert. However, I don't suppose the reader will take my word for it, so in this short chapter I want to suggest why the search for an 'environmental ethics' has not as yet led to a solution to the problems I have been discussing.

To date the main efforts of the practical ethicists have been devoted to two quite distinct enterprises. One is to extend utilitarian or consequentialist reasoning into the field of environmental protection and the needs of future generations.[202] The other is to argue for a 'new ethic', which will escape from the prison of our old ways of moral reasoning, judged insufficient either because they are unable to extend our duties beyond a concern with those living now, or because they are too 'anthropocentric', and therefore unable to embrace our duties to other animals and to the earth as a whole. In all versions the deliverances of practical ethics raise the question of motivation. What is the motive that others might have, should they agree that the 'expert' conclusions follow from the 'expert' premises, to do what

202 See, for example, Tim Mulgan, *Future People: A Moderate Consequentialist Account of Our Obligations to Future Generations*, Oxford, 2006. For earlier and less sophisticated work, see the collection by R. I. Sikora and Brian Barry, eds., *Obligations to Future Generations*, Philadelphia, 1978.

the 'experts' recommend? This question does not usually receive an answer.

The utilitarian approach is particularly vulnerable to this question, even though utilitarianism seems to have dominated practical ethics in all its most prominent manifestations. The utilitarian axiom enjoins us to maximize the good, and that means to consider the interests of all those who might be affected by our action. Now, either this utilitarian ethic is anthropocentric, taking into account the interests of humans only, or it is not, and extends its calculations to other creatures (perhaps to all creatures with 'interests', and to which we can therefore 'do good'). If anthropocentric, it is tantamount to an extension of economic reasoning, one in which the interests of future generations are entered into the equation. But then which interests, and how weighted? Most utilitarians distinguish interests that can, and those that cannot, be 'traded' in any cost-benefit calculation. For example, the interest that a person has in life and limb, in elementary freedoms, and in the basic needs of survival, cannot be entered into the equation. Ring-fencing those interests (which are thereby elevated into 'rights') is essential for the utilitarian goal, which is to produce a cost-benefit calculus that we can all accept. Yet, however sophisticated this amendment to the 'felicific calculus' may be, it has to confront the problem of numbers: future people are indefinitely many; and how can we even begin the great sums that will enable us to compare one endless future with another?

Normal practical reasoning concerning the future exhibits 'time preference', according to which future benefits are discounted in line with their distance in time. Economists employ a discount rate even when considering the costs and benefits of people who do not yet exist, discounting the interests of future people according to their distance from us in time.[203] In his report on the economics of climate change, however, Nicholas Stern argued strongly that, when it comes to environmental questions, the discount rate for 'time preference' should be zero, since there can be no solution that does not leave the earth intact for *all* our successors. This point has a ring of common sense, and recalls Locke's argument for the right of property, which permits people to take from the commons provided 'enough and as good' is left for those who have yet to receive a share.[204] (Stern added, however, that we are entitled to discount, at a low rate, to take account of assumed economic growth, which will ensure that future people are richer than we are, and more able to take action on their own behalf.)

The problem is that zero discount rates make utilitarian calculation impossible. Not only do we not know how future generations will manage their environment, or how many people they will include; we cannot know how their interests, their vision of the future, their sense of responsibility will evolve in time to match the unforeseeable circumstances that will prevail when they

203 For the theory here, see Pearce *et al.*, *Blueprint for a Green Economy*, op. cit.
204 John Locke, *Second Treatise of Civil Government*.

are around. Should we be planning for a future in which people are as selfish as they are today? Or should we be striving to arrange things so that better people are selected for – say, by creating an environment in which it pays to be unselfish?[205] Maybe we shouldn't measure our bequest to future generations in terms of *our* momentary preferences, but try to see what *their* preferences might be.[206] Maybe we could maximize the good of future generations if we ensured that there weren't so many of them, or that they had desires that were easier to satisfy. Maybe we should be thinking of Huxley's 'brave new world', in which desires and their fulfilment are manufactured so as to be in total harmony. Or maybe we should be working towards one of those 'transhuman' futures imagined by Raymond Kurzweil and others, in which desires and interests remain, but affixed to a new kind of creature that has escaped the limitations of human nature. And what do we say in response to Derek Parfit's 'repugnant conclusion' that a future in which a great many people scrape a miserable living might be better (i.e. might contain a larger sum of utility) than one in which a small number of people live fulfilled and mean-

---

205 Thus discount rates, according to one utilitarian, must take account not only of future preferences, but also of future second order preferences, including our present preferences for future preferences and future preferences for future preferences. Dieter Birnbacher, *Verantwortung für zukünftige Generationen*, Frankfurt, 1995, pp. 31–2.

206 See Robert Spaemann, 'Technische Eingriffe in die Natur als Problem der politischen Ethik', in Dieter Birnbacher, ed., *Ökologie und Ethik*, Stuttgart, 1988, p. 195.

ingful lives?[207] And, suppose we produce a solution that answers all those questions and describes the 'best' case that we can now aim for: who is to impose that solution, how and with what instruments of repression in the face of inevitable resistance from the losers?

I mention those points, since they bring home the deeper difficulty for utilitarianism in all its forms, which is, what motive do we have to think in this way or to act on the results? The confusions, contradictions and fantasies that immediately invade the human mind, when it tries to take charge of the entire future of our species, unable to decide whether it is permissible to reduce the population through carefully managed famines, to advance human interests by changing them to fit the environment, to plan for selfish or unselfish people – let alone how to reconcile conflicting needs and interests, or to begin the great sum of cost and benefit in which every member of society is to count as one (and why as one?) – these confusions and fantasies are so evident to those who have not been tempted by the utilitarian 'fix' that it is a source of unending wonder to them that the human race still contains people who issue advice based on utilitarian reasoning, and who claim that they are spokesmen for reason in a world of unreasoned desires. We should remember that the utilitarians have had plenty of opportunities to show what their philosophy amounts to. Lenin, Stalin and Hitler all justified their policies in

207 See Derek Parfit, *Reason and Persons*, Oxford, 1984, and 'Overpopulation and the Quality of Life', in Peter Singer, ed., *op. cit.*

utilitarian terms, arguing that short-term sacrifices were to bring long-term benefits. They were wrong in fact, and they happened not to believe that the utilitarian calculus could justify the belief in human rights; but this does not in any way impugn the judgement that their policies were the natural result of acting now for the sake of a future that none of us can really envisage.

We should not be surprised, therefore, if those utilitarians who take the calculation problems seriously should in the end retreat from their position, advocating, like Birnbacher, 'practical norms' instead of the ideal solutions to which we cannot calculate our way. Birnbacher's two norms – that we should act so as not to inflict irreversible damage (negative) and that we should cultivate our bequest to the future (positive) – are easy to agree with, since they merely restate the problem, and give no concrete guidance. You could accept them without any appeal to the utilitarian reasoning that they allegedly replace, and the elaborate calculations that precede them and which Birnbacher finally sets aside are shown in the end to be the calculations of spectres in an imaginary world.[208]

The non-anthropocentric version of utilitarianism is, if anything, worse placed to persuade us that it has anything reasonable to say. If we are to consider the interests of all future creatures then it is impossible to know how we should treat the environment at all. Suppose we spoil our existing resources, through anthropogenic climate change, plastic pollution, defor-

208 Birnbacher, *Verantwortung*, pp. 219–20.

estation and soil depletion, so that the human species dies out. But suppose that, in doing so, we create a new biosphere to which some future species adapts. Members of that future species would have cause to thank us, that we had provided the great plastic deposits which they mine for their favourite snacks; and they would react with distaste and horror on encountering the record of a previous world of lush vegetation, temperate climate and gentle breezes in which they could never have survived. Should we not take account of these creatures and their interests? Why does the discount rate suddenly rise to 100 per cent when we begin to contemplate their alien interests?

Even if we thought, as Peter Singer and his followers seem to think, that there is a class of uniquely reasonable people who will be both adept at utilitarian reasoning and inherently disposed to obey it, the futility of this belief is surely evident. If we are to solve our environmental problems through some piece of moral reasoning, it must be with an argument that motivates all normal people, and not one addressed solely to those armchair philosophers whose mastery of infinite moral space comes from being bounded in an academic nutshell.

It is of course true that human beings reason in means-ends ways when faced with practical problems – provided the problems are sufficiently local, the solution sufficiently near in time, and the goods affected (including the preferences and interests of those who need to be taken into account) sufficiently defined. We compare outcomes, judging one to be 'better than' another, and hoping to find the 'best'; and this form of reasoning is governed by *a priori* principles of rational choice that apply equally in the realm of economics. However, in real life this kind of reasoning is beset by thresholds that we cannot cross, since they define the rights and the sovereignty of others. And it is precisely because of its inherent tendency to crash through boundaries, sacrificing one person for the common good, or one population for another, that utilitarian reasoning, when lifted from the narrow context of private decision-making, strikes the ordinary conscience as morally pernicious.

If we retreat from the perspective of rational choice, and simply address the question of how creatures like us might have evolved – creatures able to settle their conflicts by discussion – we would surely conclude that utilitarian rationality, of the kind that aims to comprehend the widest possible picture of future costs and benefits, would have been (in our 'environment of evolutionary adaptedness') maladaptive, slowing all decisions to the point of stagnation, and giving a head start to failure. Our revulsion against utilitarianism is surely an adaptation – and also more than an adaptation, since it captures a fundamental truth about practical reasoning, namely that reasons are given from one person to another. It is by giving you reasons that I can try to secure your permission to be the thing that I am and to take the stand that I take. I return to this point below.

The general problem of motivating force comes to the fore too in considering the other strategy of environmental ethics, which is the attempt to develop a 'new ethic' in which the anthropo-centric reasoning that has hitherto held our species captive is somehow left behind, to be replaced by reasoning that is 'biocen-tric' (E. O. Wilson), 'geocentric' (James Lovelock), 'ecocentric' (Aldo Leopold, Holmes Rolston, Arne Naess) or even 'physio-centric' (Meyer-Abich). The literature here is vast; much of it is also tortured, and in a peculiar way private, like the literature of religious conversion, which tells the reader that the 'scales have fallen' from the writer's eyes. Naess identifies 'deep ecology' as a philosophy of Self-realization, understanding Self as *âtman*, the comprehensive force in which, according to Hindu belief, all living things participate. Warwick Fox advocates a 'transpersonal ecology' that will identify the self with all that is.[209] Not others, just the self – and writing Self with a capital S as Naess does fails to satisfy those who wonder whether this is anything better than a private crisis put on public display.

For what practical conclusions are we to draw and by what means are we to persuade ordinary people to go along with them? Arne Naess tells us that the earth will be restored to its true place in the scheme of things only in some future time, when the human population has dwindled and our trespasses have ceased. The fourth proposition of the Deep Ecology 'Platform', therefore, tells us that 'the flourishing of human life and cultures is

209 Arne Naess, 'The Shallow and Deep Ecology Movement', in Keller, ed., *op. cit*; Warwick Fox, *Toward a Transpersonal Ecology: Developing New Foundations for Environmentalism*, Boston, 1990.

compatible with a substantial decrease in human population. The flourishing of nonhuman life requires such a decrease'.[210] Of course, the commentators quickly reassure us that population reduction must not be achieved by cruel or wicked means. But the standard of cruelty and wickedness is our ordinary anthropocentric standard, and the pretence at a 'new ethic' is revealed for what it is – a pretence. If we are not to be what Richard Sylvan dismisses as 'species chauvinists', we should favour the hungry leopard as much as the child she is stalking; we should prefer habitats for wild animals over homes for people. Maybe we should also welcome the epidemics and malnutrition by which the population of sub-Saharan Africa has remained within the bounds of sustainability. Unsurprisingly, however, the 'new ethic' takes just the same attitude to those situations as the old one. If it did not, indeed, it would invite the charge of 'ecofascism' that has been levelled at Leopold and his disciple J. Baird Callicott.[211] The human perspective is implied in the very idea of a moral point of view.[212]

The call for a 'new ethic' first entered the philosophical litera-

---

210 See Andrew McLaughlin, 'The Heart of Deep Ecology', in Keller, ed., *op. cit.*

211 See J. Baird Callicott, ed., *Companion to a Sand County Almanac: Interpretative and Critical Essays*, Madison, 1987; for an illuminating discussion of this charge, see Krebs, *op. cit.*, p. 76.

212 See the argument for the inescapability of the human perspective given by Bernard Williams, *Ethics and the Limits of Philosophy*, London, 1985, pp. 118–19.

ture with a book by the Australian philosopher John Passmore, who argued that we must learn to look on nature and the environment in a new way, not for nature's sake, but for our sake.[213] Passmore was consciously anthropocentric, but believed that people had absorbed from our religious tradition the notion that man has been granted dominion over nature, that the plants, animals and ecosystems exist for us to *use* and therefore have only instrumental value. We should, he argued, replace dominion by stewardship, recognizing that we are here to care for the world and not simply to exploit it. Of course, stewardship is not opposed to dominion: it is merely the nicest form of it. But Passmore's point was a deeper one, namely that until we see nature as a source of *intrinsic* rather than instrumental values, we will not refrain from pillaging it, and present emergencies will continue to trump the claims of future people. Non-human things may have intrinsic value, even though it is only from the point of view of human interests that intrinsic value exists.

This emphasis on intrinsic value has an intuitive appeal. From the beginning of the environmental movement in America the wilderness has been regarded as something *valuable in itself*, and not by virtue of any use to which it might be put. It is precisely as *wilderness* – i.e. as a place removed from human uses – that the wilderness has a claim on us. At the same time it is humans, and humans alone, who appreciate such a claim. We alone among the

213 John Passmore, *Man's Responsibility for Nature: Ecological Problems and Western Traditions*, New York, 1974.

species can appreciate the useless. And this love of useless things has a use – not for the living only, but for future generations too. By respecting the intrinsic value of a wilderness we perpetuate its many instrumental values – its contribution to biodiversity, to the surrounding ecosystems, and to all who are downstream from its beneficence.

The point is well taken, and independent of the obsession with the wild that has prompted some philosophers to rank wilderness higher than all landscapes that result from the collusion of human beings with the forces of nature. But we still lack a description of the motive that leads people – that is to say, people in general, and not just moral 'experts' – to recognize intrinsic values and to set aside the energy needed to protect them. Nor do we have a procedure for settling, or even understanding, the conflicts that will inevitably arise when intrinsic and instrumental values collide. When our calculations come up against the threshold of individual sovereignty, telling us that a public good can be achieved only by denying someone's rights, we regard this as an obstacle, possibly an insuperable obstacle, to proceeding further – for example, when proceeding further involves judicial execution of the innocent, or sacrificing an innocent victim to a raging crowd. (Remember why Pilate, after accepting an impeccable utilitarian argument, washed his hands.) We have a clear sense here of the conflict between political expediency and moral right, and how the second cannot be extinguished by the first, even if it is sometimes overridden by it. But when it comes to the intrinsic values of the 'new ethic' we are on far less certain ground.

Only a few philosophers have gone so far as to assert that trees have rights, and I remain unconvinced that we should attribute 'rights' to animals, even if we must do what we can to safeguard their interests.[214] I recognize nevertheless that it is not permissible to build a road through a precious habitat just because it would be more useful to human beings to have the road than to have the habitat; and I recognize that most human uses, in leisure as in commerce, are insufficient grounds for driving a noble species to extinction. Yet was it wrong to exterminate the wolves and lions in Europe – wrong in the same way that it was wrong of the Vikings to destroy the lives and property of the Anglo-Saxons, of the French revolutionaries to commit genocide in La Vendée or Stalin to liquidate the kulaks? Or was it just wrong in the way that it might be wrong to use a canvas by Rembrandt to put out a dangerous fire, when there is nothing else to hand? Aldo Leopold famously declared, in 'The Land Ethic', that 'a thing is right when it tends to preserve the integrity, stability, and beauty of the biotic community. It is wrong when it tends otherwise.' Did he really mean that we should welcome a sustainable ecosystem in which

214 See Christopher D. Stone, 'Should Trees Have Standing? Toward Legal Rights for Natural Objects', *California Law Review*, 45, 1972, pp. 450–87; Scruton, *Animal Rights and Wrongs*. Interestingly Holmes Rolston III has distanced himself from the idea that animals, nature and the environment should be accorded rights and thereby protected from invasion. See Holmes Rolston III, 'Rights and Responsibilities on the Home Planet', *Yale Journal of International Law*, 18.1, 1993, pp. 251–79. Nature, Rolston argues, is protected not by its rights but by *our* rights to it.

leopards regularly dine on human children, and that we should oppose those who promote an unsustainable explosion of the human population by driving out the leopards? There is no knowing.[215]

It seems to me that we will have no clear answer to those questions until we connect the idea of intrinsic value more closely with the motives of people: that is what I propose to do in the chapters that follow. I shall conclude this brief venture into environmental ethics with some more general points about moral reasoning. We all of us (other than dogmatic utilitarians) recognize that morality is not concerned only with values, but also with rights and duties, and with the great question of what we rational beings 'owe to each other', as Tim Scanlon puts it.[216] We all recognize that human beings are not governed only by cost-benefit analysis, and that – even when costs and benefits enter their reflections – they take account of the costs and benefits to others. Human beings are capable of sacrifices, and they sometimes deny themselves the gratification of an appetite for the sake of something more important. They are also capable of renouncing what they want for the sake of what they value.

To the theorist of the market this behaviour amounts merely to a conflict of desires, in which the stronger prevails. But to the philosopher and the psychologist the conflict here is not simply a conflict of desire. It is a conflict between preferences that lie in

215 See Aldo Leopold, 'The Ecological Conscience', *Journal of Soil and Water Conservation*, 3, July 1948, pp. 109–12; Rolston, *Philosophy Gone Wild*.
216 Tim Scanlon, *What We Owe to Each Other*, Cambridge, MA, 2000.

the realm of individual choice, and needs that are too deeply implanted to be a matter of choice, and which can only superficially be described as preferences. The soldier who gives his life in battle does not 'prefer' to die, rather than to flee. His identity, his being, all that he is and values, are wrapped up in the decision to fight, and in the face of these things his 'preferences' are silenced. Likewise the mother who gives up all prospect of a career in order to nurse her disabled child is not just following a preference: she is realizing a conception of herself, and one that justifies her life as no self-interested project would justify it. To put it simply, moral reasoning is not economic reasoning. In moral reasoning we are not trading preferences, but safeguarding the things that cannot be traded. There are things on which we put a price, and things on which we *don't* put a price. Morality is primarily concerned with the second of those – the things that we withdraw from the market, like people, sex, community, justice and honour.

It is partly because morality is a realm of intrinsic and not instrumental value that philosophers have believed the moral motive to be of a completely different kind from desire and appetite. The moral motive is not a preference but the expression of a judgement; it is a motive of which only rational beings are capable, and is bound up with our sense of who we are. To defy morality is to be deeply conflicted, and emotions like guilt, remorse and self-accusation are the immediate effect of giving way to immoral desires. Kant took the extreme position that morality is the exercise of 'pure practical reason', arguing that reason alone can be a motive to action, and that it compels us to do what is right by a force comparable to the force of logic in compelling the conclusion to an argument. For Kant morality is founded upon a 'categorical imperative': an imperative of reason, which can be violated only by acting out a contradiction. The categorical imperative, which tells us to act on that maxim that we can will as a law for all rational beings, forbids us to lie, to cheat and to steal, since those actions cannot be willed as universal laws. Reason alone motivates us to avoid them.

This bold and brilliant theory of Kant's has not escaped the criticism that it is at best an idealization rather than a description of the moral motive. Nevertheless it should be respected as the purest and most systematic attempt yet embarked upon to distinguish moral judgement from empirical desire.[217] To take morality seriously, Kant argued, we must recognize that the moral agent is a very special kind of being, with a transcendental as well as an empirical aspect, a being who is free and obedient to reason, and also bound by natural laws and subject to the promptings of appetite. Kant's metaphysics of the person is controversial. But it points to an important truth that all must recognize, which is that people are not motivated only by self-interest; they are motivated by a conception of their place in the world, and by a habit of evaluation that situates them as objects of judgement among others, who can be praised and blamed. In short, people are governed by

217 And has been defended in these terms by Christine Korsgaard in *Creating the Kingdom of Ends*, Cambridge, 2000.

a sense of responsibility; it is precisely for this reason, and not because they are utilitarian calculating machines, that we can appeal to them on behalf of the common good.[218] Moreover, the Kantian morality represents rational beings as equal objects of respect, regardless of time, place or personal connections. It therefore invites past and future people into the moral equation, and for this reason has appealed to several philosophers – notably to Angelika Krebs – as the best foundation for a comprehensive environmental ethics.[219]

This is not the place to examine the intricate arguments for and against the Kantian conception of the moral life. Suffice it to say that Kant's attempt to prove that rational beings can be motivated by reason alone, and without reference to the sympathies that bind them to their fellows, has struck most commentators as flawed. More needs to be said about the roots of Kant's 'practical reason' in our social practices, if we are to understand the crucial Kantian claim that reason can stand in judgement over our desires and also defeat them. The point has been made in various ways and at various times.[220] In an important recent study Stephen Darwall has argued that the Kantian ethic of practical reason must be founded

218 *Ibid.*

219 Krebs, *op. cit.*

220 For example, by Max Scheler, in his discussion of the nature and genesis of sympathy (*The Nature of Sympathy*, English ed., London, 1979), and by certain proponents of 'discourse ethics', notably Karl-Otto Apel, 'The Ecological Crisis as a Problem for Discourse Ethics', in A. Øfsti, ed., *Ecology and Ethics*, Trondheim, 1992.

on the 'second-person standpoint'.[221] Reasons for action are not the impersonal evaluations that appeal to utilitarians nor the abstract and universal principles of the Kantian purists, but 'agent-relative reasons': reasons addressed from me to you and from you to me. Their force derives from the fact that we regard ourselves as *accountable* to others for what we do, and strive to act for reasons that they will find acceptable. Through moral reasoning we present ourselves as members of a community of accountable beings (a kingdom of ends). We address each other in the second person and adjust our conduct according to norms that we mutually recognize. The interpersonal nature of moral reasoning underlies both the motivating force and the rational justification of the Kantian moral law. The concept of a right derives from this second-person reasoning, and not from those imaginary thresholds that utilitarians introduce into their calculations.

Darwall's is one of several views of morality that have been described as 'contractarian'. Contractarians see the foundation of moral judgement and moral motivation in the mutual recognition of free and responsible agents. For them moral norms are not abstract principles on a par with the laws of logic, but the deposits, so to speak, laid down by the dialogue through which we express, justify and appease our interpersonal attitudes, such as resentment, gratitude, indignation, admiration and remorse. It is through such attitudes that we live out our lives as free and

221 Stephen Darwall, *The Second-Person Standpoint*, Cambridge, MA, 2006.

accountable beings.[222] Clearly if we see moral judgement as founded in this way, the far-reaching accountancy of the utilitarians and other consequentialists will have little appeal to us. But the feature of morality that is, or ought to be, of the first importance to environmentalists will be profiled in another way. This feature is responsibility, and it is the feature that was seized upon, in the context of the environmental debate, by Hans Jonas.

Jonas was not an analytical philosopher, and had his own way of expressing the intuitions that people like Darwall and Korsgaard have singled out as vital to the moral perspective. Jonas identifies responsibility (*Verantwortung*) as that which answers in us to the appeal of the good.[223] And he suggests that the 'feeling of responsibility' is the real motive of morality, and the true underpinning of the Kantian moral law. This motive arises from the recognition that it falls to *me* to achieve some good. In the context of environmental problems, good means the good of future generations. Hence, Jonas suggests, we should replace the Kantian categorical imperative, which enjoins us to will our maxims as laws for all mankind, with something more focused on the future. The first commandment is that we should act to preserve the existence of mankind; the second commandment is that we should so act that human beings who live in the future

222 A point made pivotal to the concept of freedom by P. F. Strawson, 'Freedom and Resentment', in *Freedom and Resentment and Other Essays*, London, 1974, but also central to the 'personalism' of Max Scheler and Karol Wojtyła.

223 Jonas, *op. cit.*, p. 84.

should be in a position to fulfil their nature.[224] As Jonas recognizes, these imperatives do not have the intrinsic motivating force that Kant thought he discerned in the moral law. The one who disobeys them is not in contradiction, nor even in conflict, with himself. He is simply lacking the 'feeling of responsibility' on which the good of others depends. Nevertheless, Jonas indicates, the sense of responsibility is deeply implanted in the human soul, and acquiring it is a necessary part of existing fully in time, as a being with a consciousness of past and future, and with a temporally extended life of his own.

All that is amiable and possibly true.[225] But it leaves us with a question. On Jonas's account the feeling of responsibility is as much a part of our empirical circumstances as the desires that conflict with it. Its force does not derive from reasoning, but from emotional sources that a rational being might lack, as indeed is the case with sociopaths and some severely autistic people. We must, therefore, ask whence comes this motive, how reasonable is it, and what form can it take in modern conditions? Those questions are real, whether or not we believe in intrinsic values, and whether or not we believe that environmental values are among them.

Other philosophers have tried to understand the claims of future generations through the concept of justice. Rawls, for example, argues that his contractarian theory of justice grounds a

---

224 *Ibid.*, pp. 99–100.

225 Krebs, however, denies that there is an obligation to *produce* future generations, only to provide for them if they actually arrive. *Op. cit.*, p. 126.

principle of 'just savings', according to which each generation must in justice leave to its descendants the equivalent of what it received.[226] Rawls's argument is part of a growing philosophical literature devoted to testing philosophical theories about justice between living people against the demands and needs of the unborn. Our way of thinking about future generations might one day be influenced by this literature and by the extremely interesting debates concerning 'intergenerational justice'.[227] But those debates are largely normative, concerned with what we *ought* to think, and what certain philosophers think that they already think. They do not tell us what ordinary people think, and rarely do they touch on the questions of motivation that should be considered by anyone who is looking for policies that would protect future people.

It is true that we have a concern for our successors: and it is true that we are motivated in this concern by arguments of justice, like the father who looks after his property *in justice to* the children who will inherit it. But – as that example shows – our concern for other generations does not arise from some abstract theory of just distribution. It arises from our attachment to others: it is our ancestors, our children, our successors in title who awaken our concern. And the claims of those people have weight

226 John Rawls, *A Theory of Justice*, Oxford, 1971, pp. 144–5; *Political Liberalism*, New York, 1993, p. 274.

227 For a well-informed presentation of some of these debates, see the article on 'Intergenerational Justice' by Lukas Meyer, in the online *Stanford Encyclopedia of Philosophy*. See also the contributions to Andrew Dobson, ed., *Fairness and Futurity: Essays on Environmental Sustainability*, Oxford, 1999.

for us because we belong to them and they to us. Moreover, if we take seriously the argument of Darwall, that moral reasoning is rooted in accountability, and that accountability arises between specific individuals by virtue of the relationship between them, we should expect exactly that result. Concern for past and future generations is created by attachment, and will wither when torn from that root.[228]

The moral motive reaches out to the world by anthropocentric bridges, but is founded in person-to-person reason-giving, and in sympathies that dwindle as distance increases. Responsibility may embrace the whole of nature and the whole of time, but only by spreading to the point of transparency the solid stuff of person-to-person sympathy. To evoke our responsibility for other generations in the abstract way of Jonas, or through some vision of intergenerational justice that takes no account of the distinction between *us* and *them*, *ours* and *theirs*, is to detach the idea of responsibility from the practice that gives it sense, which is that of holding each other to account. The elaborate apparatus of environmental ethics, therefore, ends where it began, with the problem of human motivation. What leads us to care for those who are not yet born?

228 My argument in this chapter parallels that of *Outlines of the Philosophy of Right*, in which Hegel argues that the ethical life (*Sittlichkeit*) is not comprehended by the 'abstract right' of Kant's universal principles, but requires a synthesis between abstract right on the one hand, and concrete and historically rooted obligations (*Moralität*) on the other.

SEVEN

Heimat and Habitat

For many decades sociologists and anthropologists, influenced by such observers as Clifford Geertz and Ruth Benedict, and by the tradition of social thought that began with Émile Durkheim, explained sacrificial and altruistic motives in terms of culture. They saw the raw material of human nature as entirely transformed by the influence of social structures that generate motives of their own accord. These structures arise through the interaction over generations of people who otherwise would be merely self-motivated and self-seeking animals.[229] This cultural theory of the human person seems to account for the many different ways in which people address the critical moments of human life, and the many different customs, rituals and self-conceptions that we observe around the globe. It has also emphasized the systematic differences in people's attitude to risk that I explored in

229 See especially Clifford Geertz, *The Interpretation of Cultures*, New York, 1973; Ruth Benedict, *Patterns of Culture*, London and New York, 1934.

Chapter 3 – though whether these differences are really cultural rather than genetic is not established by the cultural model. In any case, cultural theory creates an explanatory vacuum in its wake: for what generates culture, and what endows culture with the power to implant in us motives deeper and more compelling than our individual preferences, including the all-important motive to sacrifice what we want for what we value – in other words, to cast off the yoke of preference and don the armour of identity instead?

Recently, therefore, evolutionary psychologists have begun to doubt what John Tooby and Leda Cosmides call the 'standard social science model' of the human condition, arguing that culture is generated by people, not people by culture, and generated from impulses that are common to our species. These impulses emerged as adaptations in our hunter-gatherer childhood.[230] Just as we are adapted by evolution to acquire language, so are we adapted to acquire culture, and culture, like language, is organized by a universal grammar. Hence we should not be surprised to find a shared emotional repertoire around the globe, displayed in such arrangements as marriage, family, religion, rites of passage, territorial warfare, sexual jealousy, incest taboos and child-rearing. Nor should we be surprised to discover that the care for the home, and grief over its violation, are human universals.[231]

230 John Tooby and Leda Cosmides, Introduction to Jerome Berkow, Leda Cosmides and John Tooby, *The Adapted Mind: Evolutionary Psychology and the Generation of Culture*, New York and Oxford, 1995.

231 The Australian philosopher Glenn Albrecht has coined the term 'solastalgia'

This is not to say that all our deepest motives are simply adaptations, acquired during the Pleistocene age, in circumstances that we have long ago left behind. Nevertheless, these adaptations predispose us to develop in a particular way. They also set limits to our social and cultural variation. Subsequent cultural development can modify or amplify our genetic endowment but not extinguish its traces, and a feature that we imagine to be peculiar to our cultural inheritance may be the local form taken by the species-wide solution to a vanished evolutionary problem. Putting things that way brings us into the centre of the controversy between those who assimilate our customs and states of mind to adaptations that we could conceivably share with other species, and those who emphasize what is distinctive in the human condition, and who believe that there is a radical break in the scheme of things, represented by the transition from causality to freedom, or (less contentiously) from animal to person. The controversy here goes back to that between Darwin and Wallace over 'the descent of man'.[232] In whatever way human beings *became* what they are, *what* they are involves their conception of what they ought to be. As a result human beings describe each

to denote the pain that human beings seem to feel when their place of comfort is destroyed. See G. Albrecht, 'Solastalgia, a new concept in human health and identity', *Philosophy Activism Nature*, 3, 2005, pp. 41–55.

232 Wallace proposed a theory of evolution by natural selection before Darwin published *On the Origin of Species* but believed human faculties were too advanced from those of other animals not to have a spiritual dimension. Darwin published *The Descent of Man* largely as a rebuttal to Wallace's spiritualism.

other and respond to each other as though they were not fully a part of the causal order, and that indeed is what the 'feeling of responsibility' demands of them.

As I argued, morality is rooted in the fact that we hold each other accountable for what we do. Our world contains rights, obligations and duties; it is a world of self-conscious subjects, in which events are divided into the free and the unfree, those that have reasons and those that are merely caused, those that stem from a rational subject and those that erupt into the stream of things without conscious design. Thinking of the world in this way, we respond to it with emotions that lie beyond the repertoire of other animals: indignation, resentment and envy; admiration, commitment and praise – all of which involve the thought of others as accountable subjects, with rights and duties and a self-conscious vision of their future and their past. Only responsible beings can feel these emotions and, in feeling them, they situate themselves in some way outside the natural order, standing back from it in judgement. The attempt to fit this aspect of the human condition into a scheme of preference orderings, or a cost-benefit calculus based on 'willingness to pay', leads to a repugnant caricature of the moral life – though one that some philosophers find acceptable.[233]

It does not follow from this that we *are* outside the natural order, or that no causal explanation could be devised that would show how beings that think of themselves in this Kantian way

233 See, for example, John Broome, *Weighing Lives*, Oxford, 2004.

could emerge through natural selection. But it suggests that there might be a two-fold explanation of the deeper human motives, such as the motive to sacrifice. There might be an explanation at the evolutionary level, which sees the motive as an adaptation promoting reproductive fitness in the harsh conditions of the Pleistocene age. There might also be an explanation at the rational level, which sees the motive as emerging from the reasoned dialogue between self-conscious beings, who address each other I to I. Clearly the explanations are so different that we might hesitate to say that they are explanations of the same thing, and those who adhere to the 'radical break' thesis will suggest that it is *only* at the level of self-consciousness that the moral motive fully emerges. For such thinkers our feeling of responsibility and willingness to make the sacrifices that responsibility requires are grounded in reason. They belong with freedom, shame, pride and the sense of honour, as part of the repertoire of interpersonal dialogue. Indeed, one theory of the radical break takes sacrifice as the crucial moment – the moment of 'hominization', in which the anthropoid tribe reshapes itself as a community of persons.[234]

Those controversies bring sharply into focus the issue that concerns us. *Homo economicus*, as described by theories of the market, is a one-dimensional creature, rational certainly, but with no conception of the ends of life, no idea that desires can be

234 I refer here to the 'sacrificial victim' theory of René Girard, *La Violence et le sacré*, Paris, 1972, and *Des choses cachées depuis la fondation du monde*, Paris, 1978. See also Karl Rahner, *Hominization: The Evolutionary Origin of Man as a Theological Problem*, New York, 1965.

judged and found wanting, no ability to renounce what he wants for the sake of what he values. It is precisely those defects that render him useful as a scientific device, since they permit economists to model complex situations in terms of a unitary idea of rational choice. However, real human beings are more complex than the models that we use to make sense of them. We are subject to motives that we do not necessarily understand, and which can be displayed in terms of utilities and preference orderings only by misrepresenting them. These motives make war on our circumstantial desires. Some of them – the fear of the dark, the revulsion towards incest, the impulse to cling to the mother – are adaptations that lie deeper than reason. Others – guilt, shame, the love of beauty, the sense of justice – arise from reason itself, and reflect the web of interpersonal relations and understandings through which we situate ourselves as free subjects, in a community of others like ourselves. At both levels – the instinctive and the personal – the capacity for sacrifice arises, in the one case as a blind attachment, in the other case as a sense of responsibility to others, to the gods or to the moral law. It is in these areas, it seems to me, that we must search for the motive that will rectify our lamentable disposition, as rational beings, to inflict the costs of our pursuits on those who have not incurred them. The motive that emerges with full persuasive force at both levels is that of oikophilia, the love of home, a motive that comprehends all our deepest attachments, and which spills out in the moral, aesthetic and spiritual emotions that transfigure our world, creating in the midst of our emergencies a shelter that future generations also may enjoy.

In sketching the conservative approach to environmental problems I have several times mentioned Edmund Burke's celebrated argument against the 'geometrical' politics, as he called it, of the French revolutionaries – a politics that proposed a rational goal, and a collective procedure for achieving it, and which mobilized the whole of society behind the resulting programme. In the course of his argument Burke developed three ideas that, it seems to me, were then and ought to be now the core of conservative thinking: respect for the dead, the 'little platoon' and the voice of tradition. Those ideas arouse smirks and even guffaws from people who see politics in terms of goals, movements and global agendas. But those smirks and guffaws, in my view, are the outward signs of moral emptiness. Rightly understood, Burke's ideas remain as relevant to us today as they were in alerting his contemporaries to the dangers of the revolutionary consciousness.

Burke was one of the first major political thinkers to place future generations at the heart of politics. The revolutionaries claimed the gratitude of unborn generations who would benefit from their violence. But in no sense could their actions be interpreted as expressions of the *care* that unborn people ought always to inspire in us. Nor did they offer more than a perfunctory glance towards the future that they promised. Burke's view of society, as an association of the dead, the living and the unborn, carries a precious hint as to how the responsibility for future generations arises. It arises from love, and love directed towards what is unknown must arise from what is *known*. The future is not known, nor are the people who will inhabit it. But the past is known, and the dead, our dead, are still the objects of love and veneration. It is by expending on them some part of our care, Burke believed, that we care also for the unborn. For we plant in our hearts the transgenerational view of society that is the best guarantee that we will moderate our present appetites in the interests of those who are yet to be.

This point is very obvious in family life. The dead and our gratitude towards them are woven into the narrative of domestic love. Tender feelings towards ancestors and those of whom family stories are told prepare us to make room in our hearts for our successors, whose affection we wish to earn. We learn to circumscribe our demands, to see our own place in things as part of a continuous chain of giving and receiving, and to recognize that the good things we inherit are not ours to spoil, but ours to use wisely and pass on. Utilitarianism overlooks the fundamental fact about our concern for future generations, which is that we are concerned for them as *ours*. There is a line of obligation that connects us to those who gave us what we have; and our concern for the future is an extension of that line. A coherent environmental ethics must recognize that we take the future into account not by fictitious cost-benefit calculations, but more concretely, by seeing ourselves as inheriting benefits and passing them on. Concern for future generations is a non-specific outgrowth of gratitude. It does not calculate, because it shouldn't and can't.

Burke's complaint against the revolutionaries was that they assumed the right to spend all trusts and endowments on their own self-made emergency. Schools, church foundations, hospitals – all institutions that had been founded by people, now dead, for the benefit of their successors – were expropriated or destroyed, the result being the total waste of accumulated savings, leading to massive inflation, the collapse of education and the loss of the traditional forms of social and medical relief. In this way contempt for the dead leads to the disenfranchisement of the unborn, and although that result is not, perhaps, inevitable, it has been repeated by all subsequent revolutions. Through their contempt for the intentions and emotions of those who had laid things by, revolutions have systematically destroyed the stock of social capital, and always revolutionaries justify this by impeccable utilitarian reasoning.

Trusts provide another example of the kind of homeostasis that the conservative environmentalist is seeking. A trust imposes on trustees an indefinite burden of responsibility. They must discharge the terms of the trust in the interests of the beneficiaries, and they are accountable for any mismanagement. They are constrained on every side by negative feedback, and future beneficiaries have the same standing in their deliberations as those currently living. The English law of trusts steps in to protect the beneficiaries against abuse by the trustees, even though it is the trustees and not the beneficiaries who have legal ownership.

Trustees have all the duties of ownership without the rights. No more effective device has ever been discovered for ensuring the proper maintenance and durability of a bequest, and it is not surprising that Maitland singled out the trust concept as the greatest legal achievement of the English-speaking peoples.[235]

As important for Burke as the concept of trusteeship was that of the 'little platoon'. Society, he believed, depends upon relations of affection and loyalty, and these can be built only from below, through face-to-face interaction. It is in the family, in local clubs and societies, in school, church, team, regiment and university that people learn to interact as free beings, each taking responsibility for his actions and accounting to his neighbour. When society is organized from above, either by the top-down government of a revolutionary dictatorship, or by the impersonal edicts of an inscrutable bureaucracy, then accountability rapidly disappears from the political order, and from society too. Top-down government breeds irresponsible individuals, and the confiscation of civil society by the state leads to a widespread refusal among the citizens to act for themselves. Against the society of conscripts Burke wished to propose a society of volunteers; and in my view one of the greatest causes of environmental degradation in the modern world is the decline in volunteers. Wherever the socialist project and statist solutions have taken precedence over civic initiatives, as in the former Soviet Empire, we witness the neglect

235 F. W. Maitland, 'Trust and Corporation', in David Runciman and Magnus Ryan, eds., *State, Trust and Corporation*, Cambridge, 2003.

of public assets and the erosion of commons. Wherever the volunteer spirit remains strong, as in America, Switzerland and Australia today, people take charge of their environmental problems and get together to clean up the park, to fence in the river, to adopt a highway or to set up a market for local food.[236]

Such little platoons are the places where traditions form. Social traditions, Burke pointed out, are forms of knowledge. They contain the residues of many trials and errors, and the inherited solutions to problems that we all encounter. Like those cognitive abilities that pre-date civilization they are *adaptations*, but adaptations of the community rather than of the individual organism. Social traditions exist because they enable a society to reproduce itself. Destroy them heedlessly and you remove the guarantee offered by one generation to the next. Burke's argument parallels the argument given by the Austrian economists for the market economy. Only in a free market, argued Mises and Hayek, does the information exist that enables each individual player to dispense his budget rationally. For only in a free market do prices provide a guide to the economic needs of others. Prices distil information about the indefinitely many strangers living now.[237] In

236 Though whether the volunteer spirit is now weakening is a question to which I return in Chapter 10.

237 The argument that I have here condensed is spelled out in detail in Ludwig von Mises, *Socialism: An Economic and Sociological Analysis*, London, 1951 (first published 1922 as *Die Gemeinwirtschaft: Untersuchungen über den Sozialismus*), and in the essays in Hayek's *Individualism and Economic Order*, Chicago, 1948, especially the three essays on 'Socialist Calculation' there reprinted.

a similar way, for Burke, traditions and customs distil information about the indefinitely many strangers living *then*, information that we need if we are to accommodate our conduct to the needs of those who precede and succeed us. Moreover, in discussing tradition, we are not discussing arbitrary rules and conventions. We are discussing *answers* that have been discovered to enduring *questions*. These answers are tacit, shared, embodied in social practices and inarticulate expectations. Those who adopt them are not necessarily able to explain them, still less to justify them. Hence Burke described them as 'prejudices', and defended them on the ground that, though the stock of reason in each individual is small, there is an accumulation of reason in society that we question and reject at our peril. Reason shows itself in that about which we do not, and maybe cannot, reason – and this is what we see in our traditions, including those traditions that contain sacrifice at the heart of them, such as military honour, family giving and the worship of the gods.

Another way of putting the point is to say that tradition is a form of *knowledge*. Not theoretical knowledge, of course, concerning facts and truths; and not ordinary know-how either. There is another kind of knowledge, which is neither knowledge *that* nor knowledge *how*, which involves the mastery of situations – knowing *what to do*, in order to accomplish a task successfully, where success is not measured in any exact or fore-envisaged goal, but in the harmony of the result with our human needs and interests. Good manners form an excellent illustration of what I have in mind. Knowing what to do in company, what to say, what to feel – these are assets we acquire by immersion in society. They cannot be taught by spelling them out but only by osmosis, yet the person who has not acquired these things is rightly described as ignorant. The common law too is such a tradition – and I have already given examples of the way in which tort law and equity have enabled common law governed societies to cope with environmental problems, by finding rational and consensual solutions long before the state has discovered how to legislate about them.

Undeniably those ideas – respect for the dead, the little platoon and tradition – are difficult to invoke in the modern climate of opinion, partly because progressively minded people have done their best to marginalize them, recognizing them as obstacles to radical solutions and as the foundations of the ordinary civil society that they seek to change. But conservatism means nothing as a political idea if it does not support and amplify the reach of those three ideas, since they form the primary *motives* on which enduring societies are built, and it is in terms of them that any believable solution to problems of environmental management must be expressed. The emphasis on future people, when detached from the past and the continuities that it has bequeathed to us, merely cuts us off from the only motives that we have to regard those future people as *ours*.

Burke was not a philosopher, and if he was a psychologist it was only in the way that Jane Austen and George Crabbe were psychologists – namely, through the accurate observation of people as they are, and the sympathetic response to what frustrates and fulfils them. It is worth pointing out, however, that the ideas that I have briefly sketched correspond to powerful arguments advanced by both philosophers and psychologists concerning the origin and nature of love. I give two such arguments – that of the philosopher Hegel, and that of the psychologist John Bowlby, the one attempting to make sense of self-conscious political life, the other reflecting on a pre-rational adaptation. And I go on to connect their arguments with important considerations raised by philosophy in the phenomenological tradition.

Political philosophers of the Enlightenment, from Hobbes and Locke, reaching down to John Rawls and his followers today, have found the roots of political order and the motive of political obligation in a social contract – an agreement, overt or implied, to be bound by procedures and principles to which all reasonable citizens can assent. Although the social contract exists in many forms, its ruling principle was announced by Hobbes with the assertion that there can be 'no obligation on any man which ariseth not from some act of his own'.[238] My obligations are my own creation, binding because freely chosen. When you and I exchange promises, the resulting contract is freely undertaken, and any breach does violence not merely to the other but also to the self, since it is a repudiation of a well-grounded rational choice. If we could construe our obligation to the state on the

238 Thomas Hobbes, *Leviathan*, part 2, ch. 21.

model of a contract, therefore, we would have justified it in terms that all rational beings must accept. Contracts are the paradigms of self-chosen obligations – obligations that are not imposed, commanded or coerced but freely undertaken. When law is founded in a social contract, therefore, obedience to the law is simply the other side of free choice. Freedom and obedience are one and the same.

From Hobbes to Rawls social contract philosophers have relied on principles whose validity they believe to be universal, and therefore acceptable to all people, whatever their history and condition. However, human societies are not composed of all people everywhere, and are indeed by their nature exclusive, establishing privileges and benefits that are offered only to the insider, and which cannot be freely bestowed on all-comers without sacrificing the trust on which social harmony depends. The social contract begins from a thought-experiment, in which a group of people gather together to decide on their common future. But if they are in a position to decide on their common future, it is because they already have one: because they recognize their mutual togetherness and reciprocal dependence, which makes it incumbent upon them to settle how they might be governed under a common jurisdiction in a common territory. In short, the social contract requires a relation of membership, and one, moreover, which makes it plausible for the individual members to conceive the relation between them in contractual terms. Theorists of the social contract write as though it presupposes only the first-person singular of free rational choice. In fact, it presupposes a first-person plural, in which the burdens of belonging have already been assumed.

Furthermore, people are not born with the capacity to make choices of this kind. Only in certain circumstances will human beings develop into rational choosers, capable of undertaking obligations and honouring promises, and oriented towards one another in a posture of responsibility. In the course of acquiring the 'second-person standpoint', so as to live by the calculus of rights and duties, people acquire obligations of quite another kind – obligations to parents, to family, to place and community, upon all of which they have depended for the nurture without which the human animal cannot develop into the human person. These obligations are not obligations of justice, such as arise from the free dealings of human adults. The Romans knew them as obligations of piety (*pietas*), meaning that they stem from the natural gratitude towards what is *given*, a gratitude that we spontaneously direct to the gods. Today we are reluctant to provide these obligations with such a theological backing, though it is important to see that, for religious believers, unchosen obligations are not only vital to the building from below of a durable social order, but also properly owed to God. There is not a religion in the world today that does not see family life as its central concern, and the presence of God or his avatars in marriage, sex and child-rearing as a necessary part of getting things right.

Hegel, who was perhaps the first systematic political philosopher in modern times to put the concept of piety at the centre of his thinking, emphasized the role of the family, and the obligations of family life, in the development of the free citizen.[239] Civil society, he argued, is not based on a contract: it is the *sphere* of contract, in which people create through their free agreements the institutions, corporations and social networks that form the stuff of communal life. But these institutions and networks depend on two things – the trust that grows between citizens, and the law that regulates their conduct. The trustworthy citizen is produced by the family, and the law is imposed by the state. Yet neither the state nor the family is founded on a contract: both precede the individual, and both are presupposed by the free association through which individuals come together in an enduring political order. Both depend upon unchosen obligations, and both will collapse if people lose the instinctive gratitude and piety that enable them to identify kin and country as personal assets, to be cherished and protected in return for what they give.

Hegel's account is philosophical – providing *a priori* reasons, rather than empirical causes, for seeing the attachment to home and country as presupposed by any free political order. There is no shortage of psychological explanations of the attachment to home – explanations that trace the mental origins of an attitude that is, on any reasonable account of the human condition, an adaptation that benefits our genes. And evolutionary explanations have no difficulty coping with piety, or with the 'ethic of pollu-

239 Hegel, *Outlines of the Philosophy of Right.*

tion and taboo' that seems everywhere to have grown around the need for home.[240] True, such explanations sometimes proceed by ignoring the contribution made to piety and purity by our rational and interpersonal understanding, but this does not refute the claim of evolutionary psychologists that the need for home is an adaptation, which generates motives that can be witnessed in every aspect of a settled life.

Perhaps no contribution to our understanding of this need has been more important, both in pointing to its fundamental character and in warning against the consequences of ignoring it, than the work of John Bowlby.[241] In his three great studies of children – *Attachment*, *Separation* and *Loss* – Bowlby gives overwhelming evidence for the view that interpersonal love and relational competence are rooted in an original experience of attachment, that children deprived of that experience are disturbed and often profoundly asocial, and that both normal adult relations and the capacity for love are critically dependent on finding that core experience of home. Sociological research has confirmed that broken homes and out-of-wedlock births, which communicate the absence of commitment to the child, are indicators for later depression and delinquency,[242] and the evidence abounds that home

---

240 See Haidt, *op. cit.*, and Haidt and Graham, *op. cit.*

241 John Bowlby, *Attachment*, London, 1969; *Separation*, London, 1972; *Loss*, London, 1980.

242 James Q. Wilson, *The Moral Sense*, New York, 1993; Charles Murray, *Losing Ground: American Social Policy 1950–1980*, New York, 1984.

is not merely 'where we start from', but the place of sacred memory, to which our longings return. It has this status in our self-conscious feelings, which feed upon those primeval adaptations, but it grows in time to embrace all our projects, as Hegel shows.

Those observations establish, to my mind without question, that human beings, in their settled condition, are animated by an attitude of oikophilia: the love of the *oikos*, which means not only the home but the people contained in it, and the surrounding settlements that endow that home with lasting contours and an enduring smile. The *oikos* is the place that is not just mine and yours but *ours*. It is the stage-set for the first-person plural of politics, the locus, both real and imagined, where 'it all takes place'. The depth of this attitude is not necessarily apparent from the surveys of sociologists. But we don't need those surveys in any case: we have *David Copperfield, Great Expectations, Swann's Way, The Portrait of the Artist as a Young Man* and *Intimations of Immortality*. We have the unforgettable narrative of a home brutally smashed and then incestuously rediscovered in Wagner's *Die Walküre*; the idyllic invocation of Granny in Božena Němcová's *Babička*; the raw, needy mother-love of *Sons and Lovers*. We have that great founding narrative of Western literature, the *Odyssey* of Homer, in which a hero gives up immortality and life with a goddess in order to journey through every kind of danger to his home. We have our Western tradition of landscape painting, ranging from the landscapes of Constable and Crome, to the glades of Corot, and the summer resorts of Cézanne, Seurat and Monet. We have musical evocations of home and settlement like the Fifth Symphony and 'London' Symphony of Vaughan Williams, the symphonies of Sibelius, and the beautiful tribute to life on the porch in Samuel Barber's setting of James Agee, *Knoxville: Summer of 1915*. Throughout the long tradition of Western art and literature, from Hesiod and Theocritus to Jean Giono and Ingmar Bergman, poets, painters, film-makers and composers have traced over and over again the picture of that home from which we started, which remains in our affections, the measure and the goal of all that we embark on, and from which our subsequent homes spill out in those long trails of hope and regret, so impressively captured by Edgar Reitz in his cinematic trilogy, *Heimat*.

The same story is told by recent philosophy, and above all by those writing in the phenomenological tradition founded by Edmund Husserl. Husserl reminds us that our experience and our concepts are interwoven, and that the way the world appears to us will be affected by the way in which we interact with it. Human beings live in the world of nature, and seek to explain it through scientific categories and causal laws. But they also live in the 'natural world' to which their primary attitude is not one of explaining, but of belonging. This natural world is a 'surrounding world' (*Umwelt*) and a 'world of life' (*Lebenswelt*). It is known through appearances, which we conceptualize in terms of our interests and needs, rather than in terms that would enable us to explain how it functions.[243]

Our motives are not governed by the way the world is but by the way it appears; and the way the world appears depends upon the way we interact with it. The concepts that are vital to us, and on which we build our social life, are not scientific concepts, embodying incipient theories of natural kinds. They are concepts of functional, moral, aesthetic and spiritual kinds, which have no place in the 'laws of nature'. For example, the concepts of house, tool, friend, home, music; the noble, the majestic, the sacred; legality, politeness, justice. To imagine reasoning beings who lived without such concepts, who never divided the world into friend and foe, sacred and profane, just and unjust, home and not home, is to imagine a race of inhuman creatures, to whom we could not relate as we relate to each other, I to I.

Husserl's students and followers developed this line of thought, each in some favoured direction, with groundbreaking studies of shame and sympathy from Max Scheler, of empathy from St Edith Stein, and of building and dwelling from Heidegger.[244] For Max Scheler it was clear that the ways in which human beings relate to each other – in love and hatred, forgiveness and anger, remorse, shame and desire – depend upon seeing themselves and others as freely acting persons, and that neither

243 Edmund Husserl, *Die Krisis der europäischen Wissenschaften und die transzendentale Phänomenologie*, The Hague, 1954.

244 Max Scheler, *The Nature of Sympathy*, New Haven, 1954; Edith Stein, *On the Problem of Empathy*, The Hague, 1917; Martin Heidegger, 'Building Dwelling Thinking', in *Poetry, Language, Thought*, New York, 1971.

the concept of freedom nor that of the person can be incorporated into a natural science of the human condition. Such concepts are not biological concepts, nor are they anchored in the physical qualities of the things to which they apply. They reach for what is subjective, what belongs to 'how things seem', whether to self or other, and in using them we are attempting to establish another mode of relation than that which exists between objects in the physical world. Martin Buber described this relation of subjects as the 'I–Thou' relation, as opposed to the 'I–It' relation that binds us to material things.[245] And, as I argued in the last chapter, it is precisely this relation that lies at the foundation of the moral life, and which provides the concepts and principles whereby the sense of responsibility is nurtured and applied.

For Scheler one of the tasks of philosophy was to study the structure of personal relations, and to explore the way in which they nourish and fulfil us. We can understand personal relations only if we also understand the concepts upon which they are built. Concepts of personality, freedom, responsibility and embodiment are essential to us, and one source of the disharmony and dis-equilibrium of technological societies is that these concepts are being displaced in favour of scientific, or rather pseudo-scientific, ways of describing human beings, so undermining the relations on which we depend for our happiness. Sciences and pseudo-

---

245 Martin Buber, *I and Thou*, Edinburgh, 1923. The argument has been filled out in two contrasting ways by Darwall, *op. cit.*, and Robert Spaemann, *Persons: The Difference between Someone and Something*, Oxford, 2006.

sciences, from Freudian psychoanalysis to the 'neurononsense' that influences psychology today, encourage us to see each other as automata, by-products of processes that we do not control. We are tempted by these theories because they simplify our commitments, void the world of responsibility, and enable us to drift without guilt on the current of our present appetites. And when people give way to this temptation, then do they waste both themselves and their world. Here, we might add, is a deep explanation of our environmental problems: under the influence of depersonalizing views of the human condition people can no longer orient themselves easily towards the natural world, no longer find their ecological niche, which is not a biological niche but a spiritual niche, decked out by the personality and freedom of the one who occupies it.

Virtues like thrift and cleanliness, the habit of offering and receiving respect, the orientation towards others that Jonas called the 'feeling of responsibility' – all those aspects of the human condition that feed into oikophilia and shape us as stewards and guardians of our common settlement – arise through our growth as persons, by creating islands of value in the sea of price. To acquire these virtues we must circumscribe the 'instrumental reasoning' that governs the life of *homo economicus*. We must vest our love and desire in things to which we assign an intrinsic, rather than an instrumental worth, so that the pursuit of means can come to rest, for us, in a place of ends. That is what we mean by settlement.

Heidegger took Husserl's phenomenological way of thinking much further, developing technical categories to describe all the distinctions, real and imaginary, with which we experience the *Lebenswelt* in our thought and action, and stealing from physics even the concepts of space and time, as though they owed their content to the self-consciousness of people. I don't go along with Heidegger's method, or the outrageous claims that he makes in *Being and Time* for his kind of armchair philosophy. This is not the place to debate the point, however. Heidegger is important for my argument because he illustrates the centrality of the concepts of home and care in shaping the phenomenology of attachment, and because his otherwise unaccountable popularity is derived almost entirely from this fact. Heidegger's philosophy is a philosophy of settlement, a set of mystical instructions for being at home in a godless world, a liturgical spell for changing solitude and alienation into the comforted fullness of being *here* and *now*.[246]

For Heidegger care (*Sorge*) is a kind of redemptive relation to the world, a taking responsibility that is also a settling down. Three ideas became central to his later thought – *techne*, dwelling and building. According to Heidegger technology has ceased to be a way of relating to the natural world and has instead become a *challenge* to nature.[247] Modern agriculture has been *set upon* nature, and we too are submitting to the challenge, ceasing to be

246 See especially the lectures on Hölderlin's 'Ister' poem in Martin Heidegger, *Hölderlin's Hymn 'The Ister'*, Bloomington, 1996.

247 Martin Heidegger, *The Question Concerning Technology*, New York, 1977, p. 296.

people and becoming 'human resources' instead. And, in language that suffers from a notorious deficit of concrete words, Heidegger exhorts us to turn back from this false way of seeing our predicament, so as to rediscover the path that leads to dwelling and building. Dwelling and building denote ways in which we human beings fix ourselves to the world and make it our own. And they are the end-point of that 'turning for home' or *Heimkehr* that is the underlying theme of Hölderlin's poetry. The point has recently been put more simply by Karen Joisten: man, unlike other animals, is a home-ish being: *der Mensch ist ein heimatliches Wesen*.[248] Not just *heimlich* but *heimatlich*, in need of, in search of, and fulfilled through an *oikos*, which he sees not simply as mine or yours, but as *ours*. As Joisten points out, the security (*Geborgenheit*) of the home is also a 'hiding', and we live with an internalized divide between the revealed and the hidden – a divide that is fundamental to the experience of intimacy, when all barriers between us are finally pulled away.

Those writers remind us that settlement is a deep experience and a deep concept too. The settled person and the nomad differ not only in their experience of space and place, but also in their experience of time. The time of home belongs to what Henri Bergson called *la durée*, the flow that we inwardly experience and which connects past to future through the lived present.[249]

248 Karen Joisten, *Philosophie der Heimat: Heimat der Philosophie*, Berlin, 2003, p. 24.

249 Henri Bergson, *Essai sur les données immédiates de la conscience*, Paris, 1889.

Duration is a feature of the *Lebenswelt*, and how we receive it is an important part of what we are. To be fully in time, aware of our identity from past to future, we must live according to the regime of responsibility: so Jonas argues. And time, experienced in that way, connects us to worlds before and after us. The time for which we yearn and to which we gravitate is one that stretches beyond this moment, this person and this life. It is a time in which the dead and the unborn are also present, and its mysterious oneness is captured in the famous opening lines of T. S. Eliot's 'Burnt Norton':

> Time present and time past
> Are both perhaps present in time future,
> And time future contained in time past

That is why oikophilia leans naturally in the direction of history and the conservation of the past: not from nostalgia, but from a desire to live as an enduring consciousness among things that endure. The true spirit of conservation sees the past not as a commercialized 'heritage', but as a living inheritance, something that lasts because it lives in me. To exist fully in time is to be aware of loss and to be working always to repair it. It is to listen as

> Footfalls echo in the memory
> Down the passage which we did not take
> Towards the door we never opened
> Into the rose-garden.

The past lives in us as a place of untaken pathways, of decisions and commitments, and it is by experiencing the world thus that we acquire the sense of stewardship. We come to see that this present moment is also past, but the past of someone else, who has yet to be.

The radical environmental movement seems to neglect those fundamental experiences, and what they mean both socially and politically, and this is why it is so counter-productive. Defining itself through global agendas, internationalist initiatives and worldwide mobilization of the enlightened, it uproots the very cause that it claims to serve – namely, the search for roots. Its only effect is to bind the world in top-down edicts, some issued by transnational bureaucracies, others imposed by treaty, all unaccountable, unresponsive to local conditions and rotten with unintended consequences. In so far as it despises the motives that attach ordinary people to their home and inspire in them a small but genuine feeling for stewardship, the movement merely undoes what hopes we have of ecological balance.

There is a partial explanation for the neglect of *Heimatlichkeit* in the environmentalist literature. With its roots in German-language philosophy, and in particular in the phenomenological movement and the personalist philosophies of Scheler and Jonas, this literature has found itself deeply conflicted by recent German history, and by the moral impossibility of identifying with the conception of the 'homeland' that had fed into Nazi propaganda. Hence for a long time following the Second World War the proliferation of philosophical reflections in German on our obligations to future generations went with a marked reluctance to explore the root of those obligations in our respect for the dead.[250] What has been called *die Unfähigkeit zu trauern* – the impossibility of mourning – infected post-war German culture, so that a vital recourse for any environmental thinking that will engage with ordinary human sentiment was removed from the picture.[251] This explains, in my view, the intellectual and emotional sterility of the German Greens during the sixties and seventies, and their constant need to identify themselves as 'on the left', lest they should be thought to be endorsing the homeland in its years of disgrace. Since that time, however, there has been a widespread revival of the *Heimat* idea, and philosophers like Angelika Krebs and Karen Joisten have made the idea central to the discussion of environmental ethics.[252]

I earlier referred to an important essay by the judge and novelist Bernhard Schlink, in which he points to the utopian character of the invocation of home in all its ideological or political forms. Precisely because the home lies in the past, a place of unrecover-

250 See, for example, Birnbacher, *Verantwortung*, and the symposium collected in Roswitha Kirsch-Stracke and Julia Wiche, eds., *Der Heimatbegriff in der nachhaltigen Entwicklung: Inhalte, Chancen und Risiken*, Weikersheim, Margraf, 2005. Also Reinhard Piechocki, *Landschaft-Heimat-Wildnis: Schutz der Natur – aber welcher und warum?* Munich, Beck, 2010.

251 Alexander and Margarete Mitscherlich, *Die Unfähigkeit zu trauern: Grundlagen kollektiven Verhaltens*, Munich, 1967.

252 Joisten, *op. cit*; Krebs, *op. cit.*, and 'Naturethik im Überblick', in Krebs, ed., *Naturethik*, Frankfurt, 1977.

able safety and protection, the yearning for it can never be fulfilled, and the image of it serves as a magic talisman, with which available compromises can be waved away and condemned.[253] The home, treated in this way, becomes the place where one is not, and the only real *Heimatgefühl* is *Heimweh*, the longing for home that Novalis describes as the perennial theme of philosophy.[254]

Schlink's own response to those thoughts is ambivalent and tentative, not allowing the unqualified pursuit of global ambitions, and not denying the force of our local attachments. My response is to say, yes, there is this backward-looking invocation of a fictitious refuge, the place where everything is mine and nothing demands an explanation. But it is precisely the message of Burke and Hegel that the home is to be *rediscovered* by moving forward and creating it anew. It is created, not as a shrine or a memorial, but as a place where *life goes on*, and where love, affection and mutual obligations are renewed. Moreover – and this is the most important fact from the point of view of my argument – it is created as a *place*, an *Umwelt*, somewhere to be cared for both as a refuge and as a thing of intrinsic value.

The reflections of the phenomenologists suggest that the human psyche is, in this sense, intrinsically *concerned with home*.

253 Schlink, *op. cit.*

254 *Philosophie ist eigentlich Heimweh, ein Trieb überall ʒu Hause ʒu sein* – 'Philosophy is indeed homesickness, a longing above all to be at home'. *Das allgemeine Brouillon, Materialien ʒur Enʒyklopädistik*, 1798/99, No. 857.

What we know of personality, love and freedom we learn through attachment to the others who first protected us, and to the place that was theirs. We move away from them, but take with us the need for attachment, wandering like free radicals until fixed to some other spot. Our posture might remain in that wandering condition: such, I believe, characterizes the left-wing mentality. Or it might be turned always towards home and settlement, searching and finding the place that is ours: such is the conservative way. But both postures are *heimatlich* – addressing the world with a question: 'Do I belong? And if so, is it here?'

We find this 'concern with home' in the Torah, in the story of Israel's wanderings. We find it in the *Odyssey*, which relates the *nostos*, the homecoming, from the Trojan war. It is taken up by the new religion of Jesus and St Paul, to find sublime expression in the words of St Augustine: 'our hearts are restless, until they rest in You'. And the *Baghavad Gita* tells us that 'even as the mighty winds rest in the vastness of ethereal space, all beings have their rest in me.' The self-consciousness of America, which has chosen Thanksgiving as its national feast, returning to that first apologetic attempt of the Pilgrim Fathers to find acceptance among the Native Americans from whom their descendants were to steal the land, has its roots in the concern with home. Just what it means in practice is something that we can know through history, through works of the imagination, and through our own attempts to live through days 'bound each to each in natural piety'. We know it too through the evolution of settled communities, in which individuals take a measure of responsibility for a collective fate.

If that is true then it surely identifies a motive that could be called upon in the service of the environment. Home is not just any place. It is the place that contains the ones you love and need; it is the place that you share, the place that you defend, the place for which you might still be commanded to fight and die. Oikophilia is the source of many of our most generous and self-sacrificing gestures. It helps soldiers in battle to give their lives for the benefit of their 'homeland'; it animates the place where children are raised, and in which parents make a gift of what they have been given; and it enables neighbours to overlook differences of religion and culture for the sake of their common home.

In a democracy governments make decisions and impose laws on people who are duty-bound to accept them. Democracy means living with strangers on terms that may be, in the short term, disadvantageous; it means being prepared to fight battles and suffer losses on behalf of people whom one neither knows nor particularly wants to know; it means appropriating the policies that are made in one's name and endorsing them as 'ours', even when one disagrees with them. Only where people have a strong sense of who 'we' are, why 'we' are acting in this way or that, why 'we' have behaved rightly in one respect, wrongly in another, will they be so involved in the collective decisions as to adopt them as their own. This first-person plural is the precondition of a political as opposed to a sacred order, and must be safeguarded at all costs, since the price of losing it is either social disintegration or priest-haunted tyranny – the default position of human communities.

Nationality is not the only kind of social membership, nor is it an exclusive tie. However, it is the only form of membership that has shown itself able to sustain a democratic process and a liberal rule of law. Tribal societies define themselves through kinship. In such a society individuals see themselves as members of an extended family, and even if they are strangers, this fact is only superficial, to be instantly put aside on discovery of the common ancestor and the common web of kin. Tribal societies tend to be hierarchical, with accountability running one way – from subject to chief – but not from chief to subject. The idea of an impartial rule of law, sustained in being by the very government that it sustains, has no place in the world of kinship ties, and when it comes to outsiders – the 'strangers and sojourners' in the land of the tribe – they are regarded either as outside the law altogether and not entitled to its protection, or as protected by treaty, like the *dhimmi* in Islamic law. Nor can outsiders easily become insiders, since that which divides them from the tribe is an incurable genetic fault.

It is in contrast with tribal and religious forms of membership that the nation should be understood. By a nation I mean a people settled in a certain territory, who share language, institutions, customs and a sense of history and who regard themselves as equally committed both to their place of residence and to the legal and political process that governs it. Members of tribes see each other as a family; members of religious communities see each other as the faithful; members of nations see each other as neighbours. All these forms of self-identity are rooted in belonging and attachment. But only the sense of nationhood makes territory central and, in doing so, provides the first-person plural adapted to the society of strangers, and to the peaceful coexistence of people who share no family loyalties or religious creed. First and foremost the nation is a common territory, in which we are all settled, and to which we are all entitled as our home.

People who share a territory share a history; they may also share a language and a religion. It is evident that nations also stand in need of a territorial jurisdiction. Territorial jurisdictions require legislation, and therefore a political process. This process transforms shared territory into a shared identity, and that identity is the nation state. There you have a brief summary of American history: people settling together, solving their conflicts by law, making that law for themselves, and in the course of this process defining themselves as a 'we', whose shared assets are the land and its law.

To put the matter simply: nations are defined not by kinship or religion but by a homeland. Europe owes some of its greatness to the fact that the primary loyalties of the European people have been detached from religion and reattached to the land. Those who believe that the division of Europe into nations has been the primary cause of European wars should recall the devastating wars of religion that national loyalties finally brought to an end. They should also study our art and literature, which is an art and literature not of war but of peace, an invocation of home and the routines of home, of everydayness and enduring settlement. Its quarrels are domestic quarrels, its protests are pleas for neighbours, its goal is homecoming and contentment with the place that is ours. Even the popular culture of the modern world is a covert reaffirmation of a territorial form of loyalty. *The Archers*, *Neighbours*, *EastEnders*: such mirrors of ordinary existence show settlement and neighbourhood, rather than tribe or religion, as the primary social legacies.

This is not the place to defend national loyalties as the root of a settled and tolerant politics – I have undertaken this task elsewhere.[255] My sole concern here is to emphasize that, in so far as there is a pre-political loyalty that lends itself to exploitation in the environmental cause, this is it – a loyalty defined through home, land and settlement, in which the 'feeling of responsibility' is rooted. The love of nation does not extinguish the feeling for our other homes – on the contrary, it subsumes them and endorses them. In Chapter 10 I give an extended illustration of the way in which the oikophilia of the English and the Americans has enabled them to overcome the worst of their environmental problems – not through legislation, but through civic initiatives that summon legislation in the wake of their success. In general environments are best maintained where oikophilia is strong, as it is in

255 See *The West and the Rest* and *The Need for Nations*.

the Scandinavian countries, in Switzerland, and in the English-speaking world. They are most degraded where oikophilia has been deliberately destroyed or neutralized, as under communism.

To what extent, however, can we rely on the motive of national oikophilia today? The modern environmental movement began with the writings of Wordsworth, Cobbett and Ruskin in England, with those of Rousseau, Jean Paul and the Schlegels on the Continent, and with those of Cooper, Muir, Thoreau and Emerson in America, all of whom urgently wished to convey their sense of being blessed by the land and by its spirit of renewal. But surely things have moved on, and moved in the direction of doubt and hesitation? For it is undeniable that momentous forces have since transformed our world. I briefly consider two of them: technology and oikophobia.

I earlier referred to Heidegger's discussion of *techne*, and his view that modern technology has been 'set upon' nature so as to transform its significance for us. This thought should be rescued from the convoluted jargon of its author. For it corresponds to a widely held intuition, that the human psyche has changed under the impact of its own discoveries. The myth of Prometheus suggests that human beings have never been wholly at ease with their technological competence and have always suspected it to be an offence against the gods. But something new entered the world in the wake of industrialism – a radical fracture in the scheme of things that divided people from each other and each from himself. On the one hand we find the cult of human competence, the pursuit of 'mastery over nature' and the belief that all our problems can be solved by more technology. On the other hand we witness a growing alienation from the world of instruments, a sense that the machines are taking over, and that we, like the rest of nature, are being ground into dust. The anxiety here is never more clearly brought into prominence than in the writings of those latter-day followers of Marx, like Adorno, Horkheimer and Marcuse, who accept the master's condemnation of the capitalist machine, while despairing of the world that he promised, in which mastery would be the cure of 'alienation' and not the cause of it.[256] For thinkers of the Frankfurt School the mastery and the alienation belong together, and the more we possess ourselves of the one the more we succumb to the other, finding ourselves in a world of mechanism and commodities, in which nothing is valued as an end in itself and everything has been reduced to a means.

The sense of living in a fractured world is a recurring theme in modern literature, and often the cause is identified by one route or another as the triumph of technology, and the corresponding ease with which human appetites can be satisfied and the world placed in their service. Anxieties over consumerism and the globalized marketplace have their origins here, and while they to some extent replicate the Judaeo-Christian tradition of religious guilt, they also correspond to a new experience of the environment.

256 See, for example, Theodor W. Adorno, *Minima Moralia*, Berlin, 1951; Adorno and Max Horkheimer, *Dialectic of Enlightenment*, London, reprinted 2008; Herbert Marcuse, *One-Dimensional Man*, London, 1964.

The *Lebenswelt* of the modern person has been 'instrumentalized'. All around him he encounters buttons, switches and gadgets; alone at his desk he confronts a machine into which all his relationships are squeezed: faces, messages and emotions that have their home in hidden circuits, and thoughts that seem hardly to belong to him since they were long ago stolen by the mouse and stored in its nest behind the screen. The world divides into those for whom this realm of instrumentality is an escape from life and its demands, and those for whom it is a vacant and hollow thing in which they are blown restlessly from place to place, with no hope of a refuge. Technophilia dominates popular culture, but it is also a culture of homelessness and transgression, and its by-products, in the form of gadgets and machines discarded in favour of more exciting or efficient versions, lie everywhere about us, along the verges of our roads, in dumps and landfill sites, or even set up deliberately in city streets like the computer-designed architecture that now giggles facetiously between discountenanced façades.

It is one thing to describe a problem, another thing to solve it. The greatest writers of recent times have devoted their efforts to describing the alienation of man in the man-made world, and my brief sketch is the merest summary of things that have been better said by others, even if not by Heidegger. But what do we do about it? In this transformed world, where things all around us are 'to be used', 'to be consumed', or 'to be jettisoned', can we ever be at home? And if so, how, and with whom? Heidegger himself was uncertain that we could recapture the ability to dwell in a world that is everywhere framed by our devices and regarded as a resource to be pillaged rather than a home to be loved. But still, the effort must be made. We must both resist the destruction of our settlements and constantly resettle them. We can do this through cultivating the love of beauty and the sense of piety. It is not easy to move in this direction. The technological fix is addictive, and many people now hang for a lifetime at the breast of gadgetry. Such people prefer the undemanding nowhere of the consumer society to a settled life, since settlement means sacrifice. In the journey from the home we start from, to the home we start, they fall by the wayside into the ditch of addictive pleasures. If everyone were to live like that, the cause of the environment would be lost.

Not everyone does live like that, however, and even those most tempted by technological addiction know in their hearts that it is something to be overcome. I remain persuaded that the cause of oikophilia can still win out against the life of fabricated pleasures, and that it will do so, just as soon as the case for it is properly made. If the addictive culture seems to be so resistant to opposition, this is partly because of the reluctance of conservatives to condemn it – seeing consumerism and technophilia as integral to the 'market solutions' that must be protected from the socialist state. In fact, it is precisely in the fight against consumerism that left and right should be united, establishing an alliance on behalf of the environment that would also heal the rift in our civilization. When critics of the environmental movement dismiss it as 'nostalgia', or 'technophobia', they are right – it is just that these descriptions are not *criticisms* but true identifications of the thing for which all of us yearn and which is there, ready to be recuperated, if we do but take heart. That thing is oikophilia.

This leads me to the second countervailing force with which the green conservative must contend, and that is oikophobia. Nobody brought up in the West since the end of the Second World War can fail to be aware of the educated derision that has been directed towards historical loyalties by our intellectual elites, who have tended to dismiss all the ordinary forms of patriotism and local attachment as forms of racism, imperialism or xenophobia. I coin the term oikophobia to denote this attitude, on the analogy of the xenophobia of which it accuses the world. I do not mean *fear* of home, however, but the repudiation of home – the turning away from the claims and attachments that identify an inherited first-person plural.

Oikophobia is a stage through which the adolescent mind normally passes, and a partial explanation of this can be gleaned from the theories of attachment that I referred to earlier. But oikophobia is also a stage in which some people – intellectuals especially – tend to become arrested. As George Orwell pointed out, intellectuals on the left are especially prone to it, and this has often made them willing agents of foreign powers.[257]

257 See 'The Lion and the Unicorn', in *My Country Right or Left 1940–1943: Collected Essays, Journalism and Letters of George Orwell*, vol. 2, New York, 1968.

Nor is oikophobia a specifically English-speaking tendency. When Sartre and Foucault draw their picture of the 'bourgeois' mentality, the mentality of the Other in his Otherness, they are describing the ordinary decent Frenchman, and expressing their contempt for his national culture. This contempt is the dominant theme of French intellectual life, to be found in all the fashionable nonsense, from Iragaray to Cixous, and from Deleuze to Kristeva, that has spread from the *rive gauche* to humanities departments around the world.[258] A chronic form of oikophobia has also spread through the American universities, and is encapsulated in the speeches and writings of Noam Chomsky and Howard Zinn. What is normally meant by 'political correctness' is the repudiation of rooted American values, and a pronounced tendency to blame America and its success for all that is wrong with the world. In all its versions oikophobia gives rise to what I call a 'culture of repudiation', which spreads through school and academy all but unresisted by the guardians of traditional knowledge.[259]

The roots of oikophobia lie deeper than reason, and it is unlikely that any argument will eradicate it or do anything more, in the eyes of the oikophobe, than to discredit the person who presents it. Moreover, it will always be an influence on the political decisions that are made on our behalf, and it is one reason – indeed the primary reason – why environmental problems have

258 See Alan D. Sokal and Jean Bricmont, *Fashionable Nonsense*, London, 2003.
259 See Roger Scruton, *Modern Culture*, London, 2004.

become so intractable. For oikophobia cancels out the only motive that has been known to solve them.

Oikophobes define their goals and ideals *against* some cherished form of membership – against the home, the family, the nation.[260] In the political arena, therefore, they are apt to promote transnational institutions over national governments, accepting and endorsing laws and regulations that are imposed on us from on high by the EU or by the institutions of the UN, and defining their political vision in terms of universal values that have been purged of all reference to the particular attachments of real historical communities. In their own eyes, oikophobes are defenders of enlightened universalism against local chauvinism. And it is the rise of the oikophobe that has led to the growing crisis of legitimacy in the nation states of Europe. Oikophobes seek a fulcrum outside their society by which all its foundations might be overturned. Hence we are seeing a massive expansion of the legislative burden on the people of Europe, and a relentless assault on the only loyalties that would enable them voluntarily to bear it.

As I show in Chapter 10, the love of the English people for the place that is theirs, for the landscape, the way of life and the institutions that hallowed it, has been the greatest single cause of environmental stewardship whereby an overcrowded island has been maintained as a viable habitat for its population. A thousand

260 Against the home and the family, Foucault, Laing, Esterson; against the nation, Pilger, Chomsky, Zinn.

civic initiatives and private charities have drawn on the great fund of public spirit in England. These initiatives derive from, and aim at, the possession of the land as a common home. They are patriotic, peaceable and imbued with the spirit of settlement, and it is thanks to them that governments are often defeated in their insane plans to build roads, airports and business parks in every corner of the landscape. None of that appeals to the oikophobes who, if they have a scheme for environmental protection at all, will conceive it as the agenda of some activist NGO, campaigning for top-down solutions in which ordinary people have no say. They will dismiss the efforts of the Campaign for the Protection of Rural England, the National Trust, the Women's Institute, the Countryside Restoration Trust and all the other civic initiatives as 'nimbyism', and will in all probability welcome the roads and concrete plazas that plough through the backyards of comfortable people.

Oikophobia does not mean indifference: on the contrary, it is a form of intimate repudiation, such as young people direct towards their parents in the crisis of growing apart. Damage done by oikophobes is, therefore, strictly incomparable to that done by negligent spoilers and exploiters. All over Eastern Europe the big developers, agribusinesses and supermarket chains are taking advantage of the legal vacuum and the inherent political corruption to install themselves, spoiling the habitats of people and animals, and indifferent to the long-term price that they themselves won't pay. This is not oikophobia, but business. If we deplore the result, at least we should see that it does not issue from the dark side of the human psyche, but from motives that could in principle be corrected, were the legal instruments and political procedures in place with which to force these predators to internalize their costs. Oikophobia is far more dangerous. For it is relentless, implacable, giving no quarter to the thing that it hates.

Conservatism is the voice of people who find their social needs and aspirations in a familiar and loved environment, a place that is home to them and which they strive to improve, if at all, by small adjustments and the efforts of volunteers. Underlying many left environmental movements is the desire for another *kind* of society, one organized around a cause rather than a rooted loyalty – that is the real meaning of the campaigning NGO, as opposed to the 'little platoon'. The NGO is something that fills you with purpose; it is what Oakeshott called an 'enterprise association', organized around a goal, rather than a 'civil association' that exists primarily as a form of membership. The big NGO typically becomes a pressure group, pursuing a change in the law. Radical pressure groups hold a natural appeal for oikophobes, who seek to eject the household gods from their polluted thrones. But the normal result of victory for such a pressure group is a set of regulations, and a bureaucracy established to enforce them, and the law of unintended consequences at once kicks in to ensure that the goal is defeated. When it comes to environmental policy, therefore, the worst thing that can happen is that the left-wing movements and their mobilized spokesmen should prevail. The best thing is that ordinary people, motivated by old-fashioned oikophilia, should volunteer to localize the problem, and then try to solve it. If they are losing the habit of doing this, it is in part because governments, responding to pressure groups and activists, have progressively confiscated the duties of the citizen, and poured them down the drain of regulation.

But what, in practice, does oikophilia amount to? What initiatives, institutions and policies spring from this motive, and how might they be bent in the direction that we require – so as to encourage people to make the sacrifices needed by the planet?

EIGHT

Beauty, Piety and Desecration

Oikophilia originates in our need for nurture and safety, but it spreads out across our surroundings in more mysterious and less self-serving ways. It is a call to responsibility, and a rebuke to calculation. It tells us to love, and not to use; to respect, and not to exploit. It invites us to look on things in our 'homescape' as we look on persons, not as means only, but as ends in themselves. It absorbs and transforms many subsidiary motives, two of which deserve our attention, since they have inspired almost all the major conservation movements of recent times: love of beauty and respect for the sacred. Since the Enlightenment, aesthetic taste and natural piety have stood vigil over our surroundings, and held back the hand that was raised to destroy them. In recent times the beautiful has been exalted above the sacred. But we should bear in mind that, for thinkers like Burke, Kant, Rousseau, Schiller and Wordsworth, the beautiful and the sacred were connected, to be rescued together from the human urge to exploit and destroy.

There is a special reason for putting beauty first, other than its ascendancy in the thinking of modern people. It is a long-standing thesis of philosophy that beauty is an intrinsic value.[261] To look on a thing as beautiful is to value it for what it is, not for what it does or for the purposes it serves. It does not follow from this that beauty is useless. On the contrary, it is the intrinsic value of beautiful things that renders them useful. The case may be compared to that of friendship. Your friend is valuable to you as the thing that he is. To treat him as a means – to use him for your purposes – is to undo the friendship. And yet friends are useful: they provide help in times of need, and they amplify the joys of daily living. Friendship is supremely useful, so long as we do not think of it as useful.[262]

Many people treat their surroundings as having only instrumental worth. They recognize future generations among its users; but, for such calculating people, the environment is still no more than a tool.[263] That attitude, which would be regarded as impious by many more primitive people, seems to be embedded in political thinking, and it erodes the barrier between use and misuse.

261 Kant, *Critique of Judgement*, Oxford, 2008; Roger Scruton, *Beauty*, Oxford, 2009.

262 For more on this point, and on the concept of intrinsic value generally, see John O'Neill, 'The Varieties of Intrinsic Value', *The Monist*, 1992, in Keller, ed., *op. cit.*, and also Krebs, *Ethics of Nature*, which explores the many ways in which we might discover and enjoy intrinsic values in nature.

263 This approach to value is second nature to economists, and 'environmental economics' has been subjected to severe criticism for this very reason by Sagoff, *op. cit.*

The instrumental treatment of nature, which puts a price on everything, has led to a deep disgust in many of the younger generation, whose sense of sacrilege has been awakened by the exploitative habits of their fellows. They have wanted to find some other way to be on the side of the earth than being on the side of future humans. Lovelock's Gaia hypothesis may be scientific nonsense, but it appeals to many people because it reformulates the environmental question as one about the earth and its needs, rather than people and their appetites. Thinkers like Lovelock and Aldo Leopold offer a geocentric perspective, in place of the anthropocentric perspective of the environmental economists. They appeal both to those in search of sacred things, and to those for whom humanity is little better than a disease on the face of the earth.[264]

The example of friendship suggests a clearer and less challenging way to discard the instrumental approach to environmental questions. It would be enough to focus on an intrinsic value that has utility not as a goal but as a by-product. And there is such a value, namely beauty. By seeing something as beautiful, you lift it out of the practical arena and endow it with a worth that cannot be surrendered or exchanged. And the case resembles friendship. The intrinsic value of beauty confers a long-term utility on beautiful things, a utility that comes only when you do not pursue it.[265]

264 For some of the tendencies here see Krebs, *Ethics of Nature*.
265 See Martin Seel, *Eine Ästhetik der Natur*, Frankfurt, 1991.

Oikophilia works in that way, which is hardly surprising, since it shares the moral roots of friendship. It comprehends all those ways in which things around us are regarded as intrinsically meaningful and irreplaceable: not to be valued in terms of their substitutes, but to be seen as persons are seen, I to I. Things seen in the light of oikophilia are not to be exploited, surrendered or exchanged. It is fair to say that, seeing the environment in this way, we are far more likely to be of service to future people than if we regard it merely as a means, even if as a means to *their* ends rather than ours.

The histories of the national parks in America, and of conservation movements in Britain, America, Australia and Africa, show clearly that the love of beauty has been a far stronger motive than any utilitarian or scientific interest, in preserving land and landscape for future generations, and in protecting the habitats of other species. Beauty has an even more important role in preserving the habitat of civilized people. It seems to me that many of the worst environmental depredations of recent times have come about because beauty has been displaced from the agenda, and utility elevated in its place. The trashing of human habitats by throughways, megaliths and bypasses is always conducted in the name of utility, and the opposition dismissed as 'merely aesthetic' and, therefore, 'just a matter of taste'.

The turn away from beauty has been encouraged by two erroneous assumptions.[266] The first is that beauty is an entirely

266 See Scruton, *Beauty*.

subjective matter, about which there can be no reasoned argument and concerning which it is futile to search for a consensus. The second is that beauty in any case doesn't matter, that it is a value without economic reality, and which cannot be allowed to place any independent constraint on economic growth. Those two assumptions between them have led to what Milan Kundera has called the 'uglification' of our world: to the wrecked downtown areas of American cities and to the trash scattered all around them, to the contaminated monotowns of the former Soviet Union, to the concrete war-zones of the Parisian *banlieux*, to the destroyed landscape of Arabia and to the grim wasteland of the British Midlands.[267] It is important, therefore, to refute them, and to make clear that no cogent environmental policy can be developed that does not, in the contest between beauty and utility, put beauty first.

The assumption that beauty is subjective has a certain function in a democratic culture. It helps you to avoid giving offence to the one whose taste differs from yours. Your neighbour likes garden gnomes, illuminated Christmas displays, Bing Crosby singing 'White Christmas' and a thousand other things that give you the creeps, but that's his taste, and he is entitled to it. Leave him to enjoy it and he will leave you to get on with listening to Beethoven quartets, collecting antiques and designing your house in the style of Palladio, which he in turn finds weird. Both of you are motivated by oikophilia: both are building a home, a place of comfort

267 Milan Kundera, *The Unbearable Lightness of Being*, New York, 1984.

and nurture. But somehow the critical feature of the home – its identity as a place of sharing and hospitality – has failed to materialize. Each year his illuminated Christmas display increases in size, gets brighter and more obtrusive, and lasts longer. Eventually his house is a year-round Christmas tree, with Santa protruding from the chimney and glowing reindeer on the lawn. The sight entirely spoils the view from your window. You retaliate by playing Wagner late at night, only to receive blasts of Bing in the early hours. Here is the democratic culture at work – on its way to atomization.

This kind of thing has been felt strongly in Europe, and it is one of the reasons for the reaction against American multinationals like McDonald's, which assume a right to display their logos in every place where they take their trade. Interestingly it is the aesthetic indignation of Europeans against McDonald's that has launched two of the most significant recent initiatives on behalf of the environment: the movement in defence of the local food culture in France, led by the farmer José Bové, and the Slow Food Movement in Italy, which arose from protests against a proposal to establish a McDonald's in the Piazza di Spagna in Rome – an aesthetic crime the prospect of which awoke the Roman people to the downside of the global economy.[268] While everyone has a right to advertise his wares, Europeans assume that the advertisement

---

268 See José Bové and François Dufour, *The World is Not for Sale: Farmers Against Junk Food*, London, 2001, and the websites of Slow Food International and Slow Food UK.

must not spoil the place on which it shines. American adverts seem invariably designed to do just that. By drawing attention to themselves they overwhelm their surroundings. Maybe they don't have that effect in America: after all, it is hard to see how the average American main street can be spoiled by an illuminated sign or by anything else. The ordinary American main street is an instrumentalized environment – more, an environment that has been, as Heidegger might put it, *set upon*. It is not surprising, therefore, if nobody lives there. But the main streets of European cities are the result of meticulous aesthetic decisions over centuries, in which the details aim to harmonize and nothing willingly obtrudes. Do we really want the double yellow arches competing with the arches of a classical *cortile* or breaking the string course of a Renaissance façade? The answer is obvious, and the city of Salzburg has recently responded by denying the use of logos and fascias. Businesses wishing for customers in Salzburg must respect the façades behind which they operate as things more important than their sales. Since this disadvantage is imposed equally on all of them, none of them really suffers.

The conflict here goes deep. Aesthetic revulsion against adverts and logos is not a new thing, nor will it be overcome by habituation. Indeed, it is one aspect of the negative response to *techne* described in the last chapter: one aspect of our alienation from a world in which everything is an instrument and nothing stands proud. From Vance Packard's *The Hidden Persuaders* to Naomi Klein's *No Logo* writers have drawn attention to the fact that we are not just distracted by these things, but *invaded* by them. They seek possession of the human soul, and they do this by colonizing the human habitat. We experience them as ugly because they are the avatars of the thing that is destroying us – the habit of remaking the world and everything in it as an object of consumption. The aesthetic attitude is one refuge against consumerism, one all-important way of restoring the world to a sphere of intrinsic values, and therefore a place where we are spiritually and morally at home. It is a prophylactic against the desire to pillage, and the environment's greatest friend.

That observation might prompt us to revise the assumption that beauty is subjective. Aesthetic judgements may look subjective when you are wandering in downtown Houston or Las Vegas. In the old cities of Europe, however, you discover what happens when people are guided by a shared tradition that makes aesthetic judgement central, and which lays down standards that constrain what everybody does. Indeed, the old cities of Europe are popular. Residents make considerable sacrifices in order to settle in Paris, Rome, Florence, Bath or Prague. Such cities are renewable habitats, with their own oikophilia, and they remind us that there is all the difference in the world between aesthetic judgement treated as an expression of individual taste, and aesthetic judgement treated in the opposite way, as the expression of a community. Maybe we see beauty as subjective only because we have given the wrong place to aesthetic judgement in our lives – seeing it as a way of affirming ourselves by standing out, rather than denying ourselves by fitting in. The atomization to which I earlier referred comes not from the aesthetic attitude to home-building, but from a failure to see what home-building requires.

I earlier referred to manners as an important example of a self-correcting tradition, and manners are continuous with aesthetic choices. Even if Americans feel entitled to build as they wish, they don't feel entitled to behave as they wish towards their neigh-bours. On the contrary, America's is a culture in which manners are of supreme importance, and recognized as the ultimate guar-antee of peaceful coexistence. Americans greet their neighbours, speak politely, are always smiling. If someone bumps into them in the street they apologize; they cannot take leave of anyone, not even a stranger, without wishing him a wonderful day. In short, American manners exhibit a kind of self-denial. They are ways in which individuality is suppressed, and a *lingua franca* of conform-ist gestures adopted in its stead. This has a function, namely to protect the private from the public, to ensure that each person is secure within his space, and that the public realm is minimally threatening.

Beauty should be seen in a similar way – as a co-ordinating device, whereby individuals can adjust to each other and live on terms. Even if artists can sometimes shine an outsider's light on our conformist habits, they do this by drawing on the normal place of beauty in our feelings. The *ésthetique du mal* of Baudelaire makes sense because the language and imagery of the verse touch our sympathies, and bring us into a conceding relation with the poet's subversive posture. By offering his senti-ments in beautiful verse, the poet softens them, since he is now addressing them to others, and granting to others a greater import-ance than himself. Beauty stands above the artist in an attitude of judgement. We have been habituated by the self-advertising art of recent times to see beauty as a form of self-expression; but true beauty is equally a form of self-denial. It is a tribute that we pay to our common habitat, and the way in which we achieve a right to display ourselves in a world that we share. But if that is so, then the assumption that beauty is merely subjective begins to fall away. Beauty begins to take on another character, as one of the instruments in our consensus-building strategies, one of the values through which we construct and belong to a mutually consoling world. In short, it is part of building a home.

We can understand this from the rituals and customs of family life. Consider what happens when you lay the table for a meal. This is not just a utilitarian event. If you treat it as such, the ritual will disintegrate, and the family members will end up grab-bing individual portions to eat on their own. The table is laid according to rules of symmetry, choosing the right cutlery, the right plates, the right jugs and glasses. Everything is controlled by aesthetic norms, and those norms, freely obeyed and freely varied, convey some of the *meaning* of family life. The design on a willow-pattern plate has been fixed over centuries, and imports into the ordinary bourgeois home the ancient oikophilia of China. It relates a sad, forgotten story; but to its modern users it speaks not of sadness but of tranquillity, gentleness and things that remain forever the same. Ordinary objects on the table have been, as it were, polished by domestic affection. Their edges have been rubbed off, and they speak in subdued, unpretentious tones of belonging. Serving the food is also ritualized, and you witness in the family meal the continuity of manners and aesthetic values. You notice another continuity too, between aesthetic values and piety, which is the recognition that the world is in other hands than ours. Hence the gods are present at mealtimes. Religious people precede their eating with a grace, inviting God to sit down among them before they sit down themselves. This is a use of religion that is very far from the crusading passions of the spiritually needy – religion as an outgrowth of oikophilia, and a standing invitation to the gods to dwell among us. Such, in a word, is piety.

That example shows the centrality of beauty to home-building, and therefore to establishing a *shared* environment. When the motive of sharing arises, we look for norms and conventions that we can all accept. We leave behind our private appetites and subjective preferences in order to achieve a consensus that will provide a public background to what we are and what we do. In such circumstances aesthetic disagreements are not comfortable disagreements like disagreements over taste in food (which are not so much disagreements as differences). When it comes to the built environment we should not be surprised that aesthetic disagreements are the subjects of fierce litigation and legislative enforcement – even in America, where each person is sovereign in his land.

We can reject the assumption that beauty is merely subjective without embracing the view that it is objective. The distinction between subjective and objective is neither clear nor exhaustive. I prefer to say that our judgements of beauty are bids for a socially recognized *presence*. They do not express simple preferences, to be traded in the market of desire. They are bound up with the social identity of those who express them, and who wish others to acknowledge and endorse the choices that they make. They are not so very different, in those respects, from moral judgements, and often concern similar themes – as when we criticize works of art for their obscenity, cruelty or sentimentality.[269] Just how far we can go down the path of rational discussion depends upon what we think of the second assumption, namely that beauty doesn't matter.

Consider again the case of my neighbour's house, with its kitsch decorations and illuminated tableaux. These things matter to him; and they matter to me. My desire to get rid of them is as great as his desire to retain them – maybe even greater, given that my taste, unlike his, is rooted in a desire to fit in with (rather than stand out from) my surroundings. So here is one proof that beauty matters – and also that the attempt to co-ordinate our tastes is vital to sharing our home, our town and our community, in other words vital to creating a habitat. Of course, we may not

269 I defend this view in *Art and Imagination*, London, 1974, and *Beauty*.

succeed in achieving a consensus, and different communities, in different places, will arrive at aesthetic co-ordination in different ways. The Italian hilltop town of stone and tile is very unlike the Zulu village with its huts of mud and grass and its church of corrugated iron, but they both obey aesthetic constraints, in which individual differences are softened and made acceptable by a common style.

Hence there has to be a place for aesthetic judgement in the creation of every human habitat, and most of all in the planning and building of cities. In a fêted work, *The Death and Life of Great American Cities*, published in 1961, Jane Jacobs argued that cities should develop spontaneously and organically, so as to enshrine in their contours the unintended results of the consensual transactions between their residents. Only then will they facilitate the peaceful evolution of urban life. A true city results from what uncountably many residents have wanted, rather than something that a few self-appointed experts have planned. That is the aspect of old Rome, Siena or Istanbul that most appeals to the modern traveller. Some urbanists interpret Jacobs's argument as showing that aesthetic values can be left to look after themselves; others, on the contrary, have insisted that her examples really derive their force from the aesthetic values that she smuggles in as side-constraints.[270]

270 Jane Jacobs, *The Death and Life of Great American Cities*, New York, 1961; Nicolai Oroussoff, 'Outgrowing Jane Jacobs and Her New York', *New York Times*, 30 April 2006.

We should certainly recognize that the old cities whose organic complexity Jacobs admired show the mark of planning: not comprehensive planning, certainly, of the kind executed by L'Enfant in Washington or by the Adam brothers in Bath, but the insertion, into the fabric of the city, of localized forms of symmetry and order, like the Piazza Navona in Rome, or the Süleymaniye mosque and its precincts in Istanbul. And those are projects constrained and controlled by aesthetic values. The concern of the architects was to *fit in* to an existing urban fabric, to achieve local symmetry within the context of an historically given settlement. No greater aesthetic catastrophe has struck our cities – European just as much as American – than the modernist idea that a building should *stand out* from its surroundings, to become a declaration of its own originality. As much as the home, cities depend upon good manners; and good manners require the accommodation to neighbours rather than the assertion of apartness. Of course, *some* buildings should stand out – as do the Capitol in Washington, the Houses of Parliament in London and St Peter's Basilica in Rome. But those buildings draw attention to themselves not as violations of the urban texture, but as completions of it. They are affirmations, rather than denials, of the ordinary life around them, symbols of the political and spiritual authority on which everyday existence depends.

Jane Jacobs's target was not the stylistic offences of high modernism but functionalism, according to which buildings are dictated by their purposes, so as to remain wedded to those purposes for ever. Since there is, in economic life, no such thing as 'for ever', the result is buildings that stand derelict after twenty years, and indeed whole cities that are abandoned as wasteland when the local industry dies. This effect is exacerbated in America by the zoning laws, which banish industry to one part of town, offices to another part and shopping to another, leaving the residential areas deserted in the daytime, and without the principal hubs of social communication. A city governed by zoning laws dies at the first economic shock – and we have seen this effect from Buffalo to Tampa, as areas of the city first lose their function, then become vandalized, and finally provide the sordid background to scenes of violence and decay. By clearing the city centre of residents, American zoning laws leave it unguarded, prey to every kind of nomadism and occupied by buildings that can never adapt to social and economic change. The law of ethology, which tells us that maladaptation is the prelude to extinction, applies also to the American city. Some fine examples remain – self-renewing, street-dominated habitats like downtown Chicago, San Francisco and New York – but far too many have declined to wastelands, offices and parking lots, and almost everywhere the solid skyscrapers with their stone shoes firmly in the street are giving way to insubstantial dreams of glass.

Furthermore, functionalist building styles, which appropriate whole blocks or thrust jagged corners in the way of pedestrians, prevent the emergence of the principal public space, which is the street. Streets, with doors that open on to them from houses that smile at them, are the arteries and veins, the lungs and digestive tracts of the city – the channels through which all communication flows. A street in which people live, work and worship renews itself as life renews itself; it has eyes to watch over it, and shared forms of life to fill it. Nothing is more important than the defence of the street against expressways and throughways, against block development, and against zoning provisions that forbid genuine settlement. Recent research suggests that a city loses 18 per cent of its population for every expressway that is driven through it – and that is only one of the many social costs of planning and building codes that favour cars over people.[271]

Jacobs's ideas have shared the fate of every prophecy in recorded history, which is to be ignored until it is too late to act on them. However, her message has been taken up and refined in recent years by James Howard Kunstler, who, in *The Geography of Nowhere*, describes what he believes to be the aesthetic and moral disaster of American urbanization, as the zoning laws drive people constantly further from their places of work and recreation, leaving the abandoned wreckage of fleeting businesses in their wake. Kunstler has gone on to argue (in *The Long Emergency*) that suburbanization – which is the only consensual solution to the disaster – is unsustainable, and that America is

---

271 Nathaniel Baum-Snow, 'Changes in Transportation Infrastructure and Commuting Patterns in US Metropolitan Areas, 1960–2000', *American Economic Review: Papers and Proceedings*, May 2010.

preparing an extended emergency for itself when the oil runs out.[272]

Jacobs and Kunstler belong to a tradition of urban thinking that began in Europe with Pugin's *Contrasts* and the Gothic revival and which culminated in America with Lewis Mumford's acclaimed work of 1937, *The City in History*. Mumford takes the tightly packed and field-surrounded medieval city as his ideal. What made the medieval city so compact, however, was not the aesthetic of the street and the square, so much as the need to wall every community against its enemies. The aesthetic of the European city is as much a response to war and pillage as to the demands of settlement and trade. America's one experience of civil war was understood by both sides as a unique tragedy; nothing was further from the thoughts of those who survived it than to plan for a repeat. The external circumstance of military threat has, therefore, exerted no constraint on the American city. The result has been another kind of aesthetic, not scorning the suburb in the manner of Jacobs and Kunstler but on the contrary embracing it, and accepting both the centrifugal force of domestic settlement and the centripetal movement of industry and business.

Writers like Joel Kotkin have, therefore, argued that in North America suburbanization is all but irresistible, and indeed the only

272 James Howard Kunstler, *The Geography of Nowhere: The Rise and Decline of America's Man-Made Landscape*, New York, 1993, and *The Long Emergency: Surviving the Converging Catastrophes of the Twenty-First Century*, New York, 2005.

way to satisfy the legitimate demands of a growing population, estimated to add another 100 million to its number over the next forty years.[273] Moreover, the move to the suburbs is the true moment of settlement for aspiring Americans, the moment when their membership of the community is finally established and unashamedly declared to the world, and the moment when they can choose home, school and neighbourhood for the family's sake, and not for the sake of schemes dreamed up by social engineers. Hence suburban houses in America are not conceived on the model of the uniform European 'housing estate', but rather on the model of the country retreat, a collection of mansions rather than streets, and the whole designed as a garden, in which fairy castles can be glimpsed through the trees. Nor has it only been in America that this aesthetic has acquired its adherents. The idea of the park as a nature reserve in the heart of the city – magnificently realized by Frederick Law Olmsted in his design for New York's Central Park – has had a long line of European adherents, spawning the 'garden city' movement of Ebenezer Howard in England, and the recent 'greening the city' movement in Britain, Scandinavia and Germany.

Kotkin's argument has been backed up recently by Robert Bruegmann in America and Paul Barker in Britain, both defending the suburbs as *chosen* environments, even as places of deep settlement, in which ordinary people achieve a freedom and security that are not easily available to them elsewhere. Their case has

273 Joel Kotkin, *The Next Hundred Million: America in 2050*, New York, 2010.

been amplified by Joel Garreau's striking advocacy of 'edge city' – of the temporary focus on the edge of things, moving always outwards across the land, and largely indifferent to the chaos that it leaves in its wake.[274]

The conflict between the two visions of urbanization – the centripetal and the centrifugal – has come to a head with the emergence of the New Urbanist movement, with the work of Léon Krier, adviser to the Prince of Wales's model new town of Poundbury in Dorset, and with the writings of Christopher Alexander and Nikos Salingaros.[275] The New Urbanists have forcefully argued that aesthetic choices are not ecologically neutral but, on the contrary, internally connected to the whole enterprise of settlement. The aesthetic of the American suburb embodies an environmental policy as much as does the rival

274 Robert Bruegmann, *Sprawl*, Chicago, 2005. Joel Garreau, *Edge City: Life on the New Frontier*, New York, 1991; Paul Barker, *The Freedoms of Suburbia*, London, 2009. See also Paul Krugman, *The Self-Organizing Economy*, Cambridge, MA, 1998, on edge cities as issuing from the dialectic of centripetal and centrifugal forces. Howard Kunstler's response to Bruegmann is well worth reading, and appears in *Salmagundi*, 152, Fall 2006.

275 The Congress for New Urbanism is an American voluntary association, whose current president is John Norquist, and which is beginning to recruit a following among architects, planners and schools of architecture across the country. For the intellectual reaction against modernist architecture and planning see Christopher Alexander, *The Nature of Order*, Berkeley, 2002, and Nikos Salingaros, *A Theory of Architecture*, Solingen, 2006. My own contribution to the New Urbanist movement is contained in two books: *The Aesthetics of Architecture*, Princeton, 1979, and *The Classical Vernacular*, Manchester, 1992. See also Léon Krier, *Architecture: Choice or Fate*, London, 1998.

aesthetic of the city street – even if, in both cases, the policy is one that arose 'by an invisible hand'. It is by attending to aesthetic requirements that the suburb becomes a shared habitat: one in which a residual delight in nature is punctuated by the desire to present an agreeable façade in a community of neighbours.

Whether that aesthetic succeeds is a question that cannot be separated from the question whether the result is sustainable – the question whether people can live in this way from generation to generation. To that question the answer, according to Léon Krier (who in this agrees with Kunstler) is no. We must follow another design for building, which is also another design for living. We should replace the 'downtown plus suburbs' idea with that of the polycentric settlement. If people move out, then let it be to new urban centres, with their own public spaces, public buildings, places of work and leisure: let the new settlements grow, as Poundbury has grown next to Dorchester, not as suburbs but as towns. For then they will recapture the true goal of settlement, which is the human community in a place that is 'ours', rather than individual plots scattered over a place that is no one's. They will create a collection of somewheres in place of the ever expanding nowhere.

This solution has a precedent in London, where the original city of London grew next to the city of Westminster in friendly competition, and where the residential areas of Chelsea, Kensington, Bloomsbury and Whitechapel grew as autonomous villages rather than overspills from the existing centres. All that is needed to achieve this effect, Léon Krier has argued, is a master plan.[276] By this he does not mean one of those comprehensive experiments in social engineering that appealed to the modernists, but a set of aesthetic constraints, within which people can make the choices best suited to their needs.

Whether or not you go along with Kunstler's doom-scenario, with Kotkin's celebration of the suburbs, or with Krier's defence of the polycentric city, the question that Jacobs has bequeathed to us remains: how do we return from the wasted cities of today to an ecologically durable form of settlement? If the problem is planning, how can we plan to avoid it? And is there no distinction between a good plan and a bad plan? Was not Venice planned, after all, and Ephesus, and Bath, and a thousand other triumphs of urbanization? Perhaps the wisest response to Jacobs's argument, therefore, is to point to the distinction between goal-directed plans and civil side-constraints. Although a free economy is needed if we are to solve the problem of economic co-ordination, a free economy depends on the rule of law. Legal side-constraints ensure that cheats will not prosper and that agreements are upheld. But the law does not dictate our economic goals or take the lead in entrepreneurship. Likewise with the city: there must be planning; but it should be envisaged negatively, as a system of side-constraints, rather than positively, as a way of 'taking charge' of what happens and where. This, it seems to me, is the core insight of both Jacobs and Krier.

276 Léon Krier et al., *The Architecture of Community*, Washington DC, 2009.

For side-constraints to work there has to be some life to constrain. Many American downtowns are animated by day, without being habitats. Such areas become uninhabitats: places from which habitation is excluded. With the arrival of universal motor transport and modern building techniques, they were rapidly turned from cities to blocks of glass and concrete over which a few concierges and cleaners stand vigil, but in which no one takes an interest, except as a communal tool for business. After a while people cease to care how they look, and value only what they do. Kotkin notwithstanding, it is hard to think that this result can be anything but negative from the environmental point of view. Yet it would go against the whole tradition of settlement in America to believe that the process of suburbanization could be reversed. The answer to the problem of the American downtown and its decay must be to find a way of incorporating the downtown area as a proper part of the settlement, even for those who have pitched their mansions in the suburbs.

Here, it seems to me, is where beauty matters and how. Over time people establish styles, patterns and vocabularies that perform, in the building of cities, the same function as good manners between neighbours. Like manners, aesthetic conventions should operate as side-constraints: dictating not what we do but the way we do it, so that whatever our goals we advance towards them gracefully and considerately. A 'neighbour', according to the Anglo-Saxon etymology, is one who 'builds nearby'. The buildings that go up in our neighbourhood matter to us, in just the way that our neighbours matter. They demand our attention, and shape our lives. They can overwhelm us or soothe us; they can be an alien presence or a home. And the function of aesthetic values in the practice of architecture is to ensure that the primary requirement of every building is served – namely, that it should be a fitting member of a community of neighbours. Buildings need to fit in, to stand appropriately side by side; they are subject to the rule of good manners just as much as people are. This is the real reason for the importance of tradition in architecture – that it conveys the kind of practical knowledge that is required by neighbourliness. The American downtown too can be a neighbour, even if it is only a part-time neighbour, visited in working hours. Indeed, the more neighbourly it is, the more people will move into the centre and begin to settle there.

Architecture is not like poetry, music or painting – an art that belongs in the world of leisure and luxury. It survives regardless of its aesthetic merit, and is only rarely the expression of creative genius. There are great works of architecture and often, like the churches of Mansart or Borromini, they are the work of a single person. But most works of architecture are not great and should not aspire to be so, any more than ordinary people should lay claim to the privileges of genius when conversing with their neighbours. What matters in architecture is the emergence of a learnable vernacular style – a common language that enables buildings to stand side by side without offending each other.[277]

The original American towns were built using standard parts derived from the 3,000-year-old tradition that we know as 'classicism'. The old pattern-books (such as those published by Asher Benjamin in Boston in 1797 and 1806, and which are responsible for the once agreeable nature of the New England towns, Boston included) offered precedents to builders, forms that had pleased and harmonized, and could be relied upon not to spoil or degrade the streets in which they were placed. That is what we see in the streets of the old European cities: not the imposition of some overall proportion or outline, but the organic growth of a street from the repetition of matching details. The failure of modernism lies not in the fact that it has produced no great or beautiful buildings – Le Corbusier's Chapel at Ronchamp, and the houses of Frank Lloyd-Wright abundantly prove the opposite. The failure of modernism lies in the absence of any reliable patterns or types that can be used in awkward or novel situations so as spontaneously to harmonize with the existing urban decor, and so as to retain the essence of the street as a common home. The degradation of so many downtown areas is the result of a 'modernist vernacular', whose principal device is the stack of horizontal layers, with jutting and obtrusive corners, built without consideration for the street, without a coherent façade, and without intelligible relation to its neighbours.

277 I have defended this approach in *The Classical Vernacular*. See also John Silber, *Architecture of the Absurd*, New York, 2007.

Offence is compounded by the new kind of postmodern 'gadget' architecture, designed at the computer, using the patterns established by coffee machines, hairdryers and desk-top gizmos. Such buildings are without faces, and show the triumph of utility, their 'gadget' character being an attempt to borrow the aesthetic of the domestic utensil. Their effect is to remake the exterior space of the city as a place of discarded interiors – of household junk thrown out in the street. Such buildings cannot fit into the street or stand happily next to other buildings, for the simple reason that they do not stand at all. They are designed as waste – throwaway architecture involving vast quantities of energy-intensive materials, which will be demolished within twenty years. Townscapes built from such architecture resemble landfill sites – scattered heaps of plastic junk which will always look like discarded waste.

Aesthetic side-constraints disappeared for another reason than changes in the materials and forms that architects employed. They disappeared also because a new kind of planning took over the cities of Europe and America – a kind of planning that grew from the socialist and communist experiments in politics, and which was absorbed by the early modernists as part of the air they breathed. The Bauhaus under Hannes Meyer was an explicitly socialist establishment, influenced by the 'democratic centralism' of Lenin; its contribution to urbanization was the comprehensive plan, involving the demolition of streets and settlements and their replacement by tower blocks of workers' flats. Urban planning was henceforth seen as an integral feature of the architect's task, which was no longer concerned with fitting in but with replacing whole neighbourhoods and even cities. The modernist styles emerged from the spirit of the top-down plan, which replaced that of the side-constraint all across the Western world at the same time, and with the same force, as the spirit of socialism. Like socialism it spelled ecological disaster. Typical was Le Corbusier's plan to demolish all of Paris north of the Seine.[278] Frustrated in this project the architect turned his attention to Algiers, which, as a French protectorate, was less able to resist demolition. Although only one section of Le Corbusier's plan was ever built, the plan itself is nevertheless studied assiduously in schools of architecture as one of the great 'solutions' to a problem that, prior to Le Corbusier, no one had ever perceived. The 'problem' is that of packing people into a city while allowing free movement across it.

Corbusier's solution was to put highways in the air, with the people shovelled into apartment blocks beneath them. Ancient homes and corridor streets were to be demolished, and huge tower blocks were to front the ocean, dwarfing mosques and churches. The plans were opposed by the elected mayor of the city, which led Le Corbusier to approach the unelected French governor of the protectorate, asking him to overrule the mayor. 'The plan must rule,' he wrote. 'It is the plan which is right. It proclaims

278 On Le Corbusier see Theodor Dalrymple, 'The Architect as Totalitarian', *City Journal*, 19.4, 2009.

indubitable realities.' When he led the Vichy government's commission on national building in 1941, Le Corbusier insisted on putting his plans for Algiers at the top of the agenda.[279] The very idea of the city, as a human habitat that grows organically from the needs of neighbours, and in conformity with moral and aesthetic values that constrain what is done without dictating it, was alien to Le Corbusier's idea of the architect's mission.

The planning mentality took root in Britain in the years of socialist government that followed the Second World War. Central government, local authorities and architects cheerfully combined to sweep away the crowded and insalubrious slums, and to gather up their populations into hygienic towers above open spaces filled with light and air. This recipe for improving the conditions of the urban working class was more influenced by the Russian constructivists and the Bauhaus than by Le Corbusier. But at the time all architects seemed to endorse it, and the fact that it coincided with the socialist programme, according to which housing is really the responsibility of the state, meant that it had an insuperable advantage over the old recipe of private houses along a public street, which was in any case more a by-product of freedom than a conscious choice.

The opposition to the modernist housing project has come less from critics than from the people that the projects were designed

279 See Silber, *op. cit.*

to serve. To the surprise of the planners, people began to resist the attempt to demolish their streets and to sweep away the familiar backyards. The workers made it clear that they don't like living in the air: nor do they like to stand at a window and stare at nothing. They want the life of the street; they want to feel life around them and at the same time to know that they can shut it out and let it in at will. They want neighbours beside them, not above them or below. They want to sit in cosy rooms with old-fashioned windows that open and close, and listen to the noise of passers-by. And most of them want a home of their own, rather than property that belongs to the local council and which they can never pass on to their children. The Bauhausing of the working class was, therefore, rejected by the workers who, in this as in so many other ways, refused to do as the socialists told them until coerced by the state.

The history of the tower block estate illustrates the way in which the defiance of aesthetic norms leads to ecological disaster. The costly demolition of the old streets and the costly building of the new blocks led in a matter of a few years to the even more costly demolition of those new constructions and the desperate, but in the end futile, attempt to replace them by something more humane. The attempt was futile since by now the communities on which the buildings depended for what patina of human life they might acquire had been destroyed, irretrievably scattered by the plan that nanny state had dreamed up for their greater happiness. The result has been the loss of a self-sustaining habitat, and the planting in the centre of our cities of environments for which nobody cares.

Nor have downtown developments fared any better. The glass and steel-frame blocks, built without façades and indifferent to alignment with their neighbours, have proved to be entirely unable to adapt. Traditional architecture concentrates on the *generality* of form, on details that embody the tacit knowledge of how to live with a building and adapt to it. Hence traditional architecture in turn adapts to us. It fits to our uses, and shelters whatever we do. Hence it survives – in the way that Rome, Paris and Helsinki have survived, or in the way that Georgetown, Greenwich Village and Old Town Alexandria have survived, despite zoning laws that reduce their ability to adjust to modern needs. Modernist architecture cannot as a rule change its use, so architects assume that their buildings will have a lifespan of twenty years. By building with that thought in mind you are not building a settlement, still less a neighbourhood. You are constructing an extremely expensive and ecologically destructive tent. The environmental impact of its demolition is enormous, and the energy that goes into building it must be spent again on demolishing it and yet again on replacing it. The ecological disaster is compounded by the use of carbon-intensive materials like concrete and alloys as the core structural components.

It is worth recalling that great human discovery, the window. The windows of traditional pattern-book houses form agreeable, humanizing details; they are the eyes of the house. In hot weather they can be opened to let in the breezes, and ensure a circulation of air. In cold weather they can be closed. They are adorned with simple mouldings and often crowned with architrave and keystone that emphasize their proportions. They are integrated into the implicit order of the façade, so that it is easy to find the matching door or attic window that will look right beside them. In all this we see an accumulation of practical knowledge that issues from the aesthetic side-constraints in something like the way in which deals and market transactions issue from good manners.

This knowledge of the window, its beauty and its function, has been preserved in the American suburb, but it has not survived in the American city. The windows of modern downtown buildings are not eyes; they do not humanize the façade; they suggest no form or pattern that could be repeated, and lay no constraints on what can and cannot be placed beside, above and beneath them. They cannot be opened in hot weather, and they forbid the circulation of air from outside the building. The building is, therefore, dependent on a year-round consumption of energy, in the winter to heat it, in the summer to cool it, and the stale air that circulates inside captures and perpetuates the diseases of the inmates – producing the well-known 'sick building syndrome'. The result is not just an aesthetic disaster: it is an ecological disaster too. And it exemplifies an important feature of the modern world, which is the hard work that is being constantly expended on losing knowledge. The modernist vernacular, which conceives buildings as curtains of tinted glass raised on invisible scaffolds of concrete and steel, represents both an unusual advance for ignorance and a giant ecological threat, and architects and their theorists devoted an immense amount of intellectual labour to achieving this result.

The example of architecture is especially vivid, since it is obvious to everyone that the way we build determines the nature of our home and the attitude that we take towards its conservation. But beauty guides us in all the other ways that we humans strive to adapt ourselves to the world and the world to ourselves. It motivates our love of nature and species, our reverence towards the earth and the oceans, and our concern for lakes and waterways. It is at the heart of oikophilia, and illustrates the deep distinction between prices in a market and the priceless things of home. As Mark Sagoff has shown, environmental values are misrepresented by the attempt to subsume them under the willingness of consumers to pay. In caring for the environment we are trying to guarantee the persistence of features like beauty, whose value cannot be priced.[280]

The sense of beauty puts a brake upon destruction by representing its object as irreplaceable. It is not the whole of oikophilia, nor is it confined to those who are content with the place in which they find themselves: it is simply one of several motives through which *heimatlich* creatures endow their world with an air of permanence. A comparable motive is piety – an ancient feature

280 Sagoff, *op. cit.*

of the human condition, mentioned here and there by Jonas, but not often invoked by contemporary environmentalists. Readers of Pausanias, the second-century Greek geographer and traveller, will notice that the temples of the gods, the sacred groves and the tombs of heroes were still intact when Pausanias visited them, even though they might have been around for centuries.[281] The sacred places, with their woods and streams, were maintained as public assets by priests and devotees of the old religion, in those last years before Christianity swept everything away. Piety forbad their destruction, and it is piety that animated Pausanias in visiting them and recording their charms.

This motive is a human universal, and as Simon Schama has argued, in his beautiful tribute to landscape art and to the myths and mysteries of settlement, land and landscape have been portrayed as sacred in all our human attempts to belong in the world.[282] This experience of sanctity is deeply tied to memory. We all carry within us the after-image of primeval attachment. Memory corrects and straightens our recollections, and shapes the remembered *oikos* in terms that are as much imagined as real. We see the process whereby a lost home becomes sacred, and purged of all its irritating ordinariness, in Mickiewicz's invocation of old Lithuania in *Pan Tadeusz*, and Proust's invocation of Combray. The American environmental movement began from a powerful sense of the sacredness of the American landscape. Thoreau and

281 Pausanias, *Description of Greece*, New York, 2007.
282 Simon Schama, *Landscape and Memory*, New York, 1994.

Emerson, Muir and the Hudson River painters made hymns in word and pigment to the awe-inspiring landscapes that surrounded them, and were determined to awaken in their audience a sense of piety sufficiently strong to counteract the rapine that was being visited on the God-given wilderness.

This motive has not disappeared: we see it recorded in contemporary American art, from the poetry of Wendell Berry to the stories of Eudora Welty, and from the photography of Ansel Adams to the music of his namesake John. It is central to the poetry of Seamus Heaney, to the music of David Matthews, to the paintings of David Inshaw in Britain. It dominates the music of Messiaen and Dutilleux in France. And whenever ordinary people strive to protect the places and environments they love we see the workings of natural piety. Recent contests over the environment in Britain vividly illustrate the point. When government ministries and planners propose to drive a bypass through some scenic region, to expand an airport or to give permission for a shopping mall, people do not merely protest that the development is unnecessary, unsightly or socially disruptive. They refer to it as a 'violation', and often prepare themselves for acts of sacrifice, lying down in front of bulldozers, chaining themselves to trees and abusing the vandals and iconoclasts who trample on the things they love. Those who protested at the building of a bypass across Twyford Down, and those who formed the Bath Preservation Society in order to resist what was called 'the sack of Bath', described the developments that they deplored as 'desecrations'.[283] You can only desecrate what is sacred; and the widespread desire to describe environmental vandalism in this way is surely proof that people still share the sentiments that animated Pausanias.

Nor is the idea of a sacred place merely a product of settlement and civilization. The sense of the land, the quarry and the habitat as sacred is a well-known feature of hunter-gatherer societies, touchingly described by Hugh Brody in his account of the Inuit of Northern Canada, and clearly serving a vital ecological function in the Pleistocene conditions from which we all emerged.[284] Sacred things have a peculiar status, being both removed from us and deeply connected to our wellbeing. That which is sacred cannot be touched by profane hands. But on special occasions, marked out by ritual and acts of purification, it can be bent to our uses. The priest, the acolyte and the initiate can participate in the communion and drink the Eucharistic wine. The uninitiated and the unbelievers commit sacrilege by doing the same. The hunter-gatherer, surveying the land in which he habitually searches for food, knows that there is a right and a wrong way to treat it, that the right way is a 'communion' with the tribe, that other tribes are to be excluded, and that there is a consecrated method to the hunt – a method that ensures the renewal of the quarry from season to season. When the outsider intrudes into the landscape, and wipes away the quarry with weapons that show no

283 Adam Fergusson, *The Sack of Bath*, Salisbury, 1973.
284 Brody, *op. cit.*

respect, the tribesman views him with a sense of outrage and pollution. In just such a way John Ruskin, who had established a right to the Lakelands by walking in them, caring for every detail of what he saw, viewed the encroaching railways as an offence against the things he held most holy.[285]

Ruskin is an interesting case, not only as a major figure in the nineteenth-century conservation movement, but as someone motivated in all his thinking by the concept of the sacred, while hesitating to attach that concept to any precisely held religious faith. The burden of *Seven Lamps of Architecture* is to impress on the reader that to build beautifully is to build for ever, which means building in a posture of obedience towards the Eternal. The builder must detach himself from earthly interests and calculations, set aside material goals, and offer instead a gift to all creation, one that will outlast each fleeting function that it serves. Ruskin's defence of the Gothic stems from this source, and his love of nature and landscape likewise. We may dissent from the narrow aesthetic that Ruskin advocated, but we cannot deny that his writings and campaigns exhibit oikophilia in its most passionate and contagious form, and show that the beautiful and the sacred are contiguous objects of ecological concern. His enormous influence is due primarily to his ability to awaken in his readers the sense that they live among precious and consecrated

285 John Ruskin, *Railways in the Lake District* (1876), in *The Works of John Ruskin*, eds. E. T. Cook and Alexander Wedderburn, London, 1903–12, vol. 34, p. 141.

things, and that the new world of industry and energy and progress tempts us and empowers us at every point to desecration. Hence Ruskin illustrates one of the most important features of modern conservation movements, which is the way in which the idea of the sacred survives the fading of religious belief, and takes on a new and more earth-bound force, as people strive to care for a world that can no longer rely on God as its protector.

We must recognize the difference between a religion directed towards salvation, and a religion that is focused on the immediate presence of the sacred, as this is revealed in the here and now. The two may be combined in a single faith; but they are surely very different as motives. And while the hunger for salvation may spill over into the environmental movement with damaging effect, the love and care for sacred places is a real obstacle to destruction. This care for sacred places is part of the *domestication* of religion – a process that has for two millennia worked on the Christian faith, attaching it to local saints and shrines, to towns and civic ceremonies, even (as in the case of the Anglican Church) to a nation and its law.

It is not only religious believers who respond to sacred things. There is something left out of every scientific account of our rela-tion to our surroundings, and that is the I–Thou encounter, and the sense of responsibility that stems from it. The I–Thou rela-tionship is also present in our response to the world. And I suspect that those who are attracted to the Gaia hypothesis, or to the call of 'deep ecology', are really attempting to rediscover a way of personalizing our connection to the environment, so that the It that surrounds us on every side becomes an I. The earth, they feel, can be protected only if it can in some way appeal to me as persons do. As a mere 'it' the earth stands undefended from our predations.

Rilke, in the ninth of the *Duino Elegies*, writes of the earth's 'dream to be some day invisible'. This extraordinary poem invites us into a wholly new relation to the world, and one that engages immediately with the crisis through which we have been living. For Rilke the earth must no longer be treated as an object among objects, a thing of purely instrumental value, which has no claim on our commitments. It must enter the world of thinking, naming and loving, so as to exist in another way, as lovers exist in each other's feelings, as the past lives in memory, and as the future is contained like a seed in our most reflective states of mind. The earth must become part of each of us, not an object but a subject, which addresses me I to I. This is the great *Verwandlung* – the transformation – which is the earth's 'insistent demand'. And to accomplish it we must live in another way, with a kind of tenderness towards places and their history, towards the things that we see and name, and which are 'refashioned by age after age', until they 'live in our hands and eyes as part of ourselves'. The transformation of the earth is a transformation of ourselves. We must discard the habit of using things and learn instead to praise them; the *Elegies* are a kind of 'praiser's manual' for those who love the earth.

Rilke's attempt was one of several in recent times, to re-consecrate the earth, without the help of any god. The poet repudiated every kind of transcendental faith and believed that there is no afterlife, but only this one life on earth, which we can waste or fulfil as we choose. But he also believed that life is sacred, as are all the beings that we encounter in the course of it. Rilke's purpose in the *Duino Elegies* was to draw on the raw material from which every experience of the sacred is derived – namely, the first-person experience of embodiment – and to use it to build a path away from nihilism. The earth is not just a heap of objects; it has its own subjectivity, and it achieves this subjectivity in me.

My argument has taken us to a critical juncture. The last two chapters have attempted to discover and explore a deeply rooted family of motives in the human psyche, motives that belong to us by nature, and which spill out in many ways – through ideas of home, beauty and consecration, through the sense of responsibility and tradition, through the care for absent generations and the love of kin. But these motives are intensely localized. They distinguish what is ours from what is theirs, home from alien territory, that which belongs to me from that which does not. They can be relied upon, perhaps, to ensure the good government of small communities and the management of local amenities cut off from the surrounding disorder. But our environmental problems today are global, not local; the disorder that causes them cannot be cured by small-scale homeostatic systems, or addressed by the motives that teach us to care for our home. Only large-scale solutions can address the problems of pollution, depletion of resources and global warming. And these solutions, like the problems, must be defined internationally, and pursued through global treaties and new forms of global governance, in which the interests of nation states are set aside for the benefit of the planet as a whole.

Such, at any rate, is the urgent call of the radical environmentalists. In the next chapter I attempt to answer it, and to show that, in fact, it is oikophilia that offers us the best hope, on the global as much as the local level.

NINE

Getting Nowhere

Not all people who identify themselves as on the left are oiko-phobes. In America a kind of liberal patriotism has arisen, centred around journals like *The New Republic*, and writers like John Schaar, who, while claiming left-liberal credentials, writes thus in defence of patriotism:

> At its core, patriotism means love of one's homeplace, and of the familiar things and scenes associated with the home-place. In this sense, patriotism is one of the basic human sentiments. If not a natural tendency in the species, it is at least a proclivity produced by realities basic to human life, for territoriality, along with family, has always been a pri-mary associative bond. We become devoted to the people, places and ways that nurture us, and what is familiar and nurturing seems also natural and right. This is the root of patriotism. Furthermore, we are all subject to the immense

power of habit, and patriotism has habit in its service.[286]

There is a kind of left patriotism that brands itself as the true spirit of the American settlement, and the defender of the Constitution against its reactionary foes. The influence of this left patriotism can be felt in some of the defenders of the 'civic environmentalism' that I discuss in the next chapter.

It was George Orwell's wish that a British patriotic left would displace the traitors whose principal loyalty was to the Communist International, a wish that some think was granted in the post-war Attlee government.[287] Those defenders of the 'unofficial countryside', the plotlands and settlement by 'mutual aid' are left-wing oikophiles, people who strive to reconcile a deep love of history and rootedness with a belief that history and home are created as much by the common labourer as by the aristocrat and the industrial magnate. From Richard Jefferies and George Sturt to Ken Worpole and Paul Kingsnorth, left-wing oikophilia has profoundly influenced the environmental movement in Britain, defending the local, the rooted and the characterful against the global, the uprooted and the bland, and affirming the real attachments on which communities depend for their duration.[288]

286 John H. Schaar, 'The Case for Patriotism', *American Review*, 17, May 1973, pp. 62–3.

287 See 'The Lion and the Unicorn', in Orwell, *op. cit.*

288 Richard Jefferies, *The Amateur Poacher*, 1879, and *The Story of My Heart*, 1883; George Sturt (George Bourne), *Change in the Village*, 1912; Worpole, *op. cit.*, and *Last Landscapes*, London, 2003.

My father was such a left-wing oikophile. He identified entirely with the Labour Party, was a class warrior in politics and had little time for the Monarchy, the established church, or the House of Lords. But he loved England, loved the countryside, and loved the old settlements of the Home Counties. He subscribed to *The Countryman*, read the works of Hugh Massingham and Richard Jefferies, established a centre for the study of the environment in the primary school where he was a teacher, and founded the High Wycombe Protection Society in order to save his town and its public spaces from tower blocks and throughways. He was an avid guardian of protected species, a vigilant opponent of all who laid waste and polluted. He belonged to clubs and societies devoted to local history, nature study and the conservation of woodlands, and at the sight of food in plastic, he would utter a heartfelt groan of despair.

Left-wing oikophiles today tend to see themselves as pitted against the ever-expanding entropy of fast food, shopping malls, solipsistic entertainment and multinational brands – things that belong to Kunstler's 'geography of nowhere', and which are part of a worldwide uprooting of attachments. But my father's oikophilia belonged to another time, when multinational branding had hardly begun, and when the most ominous threat to locality came from the left. Nothing was more antipathetic to him than the internationalism of the Communist Party. More than the ruling classes, more than the lords, knights and squires who filled all local offices, more than the privileged bureaucrats who controlled the teaching profession and kept him (a working-class boy from the industrial north) from advancing, my father hated the Communist Party. And he hated it precisely because it sought to divert the loyalty of the British people away from their nation, their history and their island future towards its own timeless, placeless and (in my father's view) loveless cause. The moral bankruptcy of communism has long been apparent to the world. But the internationalism on which it fed remains in altered form, as a resource to radical causes, and a point of view outside national politics from which national politics can be influenced and even controlled. This has been especially influential in the politics of the environment, precisely because environmental problems leak across national boundaries, cannot always be solved at the local level, and concern the one physical thing in which every human being has a stake, namely the planet.

Because of this leakage there can be no long-term environmental policy that does not at least *attempt* to conclude treaties among the nations affected by each other's conduct. The problem, as I see it, is that treaties are only as effective as the ability and willingness of governments to be bound by them, and this ability varies from place to place around the globe. This is particularly pertinent when considering the problem of global warming, now that an increasing proportion of greenhouse gas emissions come from states in which there is no rule of law, or in which privileged groups and their clients are above the law and able to evade it.

Consider China. Prior to the Communist takeover the

majority of the Chinese people, appallingly governed though they were, strived to live according to the precepts of Confucianism, surely the most oikophile of all worldviews, whose central requirement is piety (*Li*). For the Confucian, nothing is more important than respect for the dead, and the honour bestowed on ancestors. Places of settlement are sacred, as are the home and the family table. The literature, art and ceramics of old China speak as clearly and tenderly as any in the world of the *oikos* and its eternal meaning.

If any readers doubt what I earlier wrote about the prevalence of oikophobia and its destructive effect, then let them consider the Cultural Revolution of Chairman Mao – that rage against the past, and against the given reality of Chinese society. And let them study the incredible assault not only on human habitats, but on the entire environment of China, that was carried out in the revolution's name.[289] Under Mao's regime it was unclear whether there was any law at all in China – the book purporting to describe that law was tiny, its edicts were vague, and there were no reports from the courts that would enable anyone to guess what it meant. Every act of destruction was authorized in any case, provided it was China, its culture and its people that suffered.

Since the death of Mao many observers have looked forward

---

289 See Roderick MacFarquhar and Michael Schoenhals, *Mao's Last Revolution*, Cambridge, MA, 2006; Jung Chang and Jon Halliday, *Mao: The Unknown Story*, London, 2004.

to a return of Confucian peacableness, as some slight compensation for the 60 million dead. And no one can doubt that, economically and also politically, things have changed for the better. A growing system of commercial and contract law has been developed under the influence of international trade, and the extensive use of Hong Kong law, which remains part of the English common-law system, has made contracts secure. But nobody today supposes that the local elites of the Chinese Communist Party, or the business interests that support them and which they support, would allow anything so flimsy as a law, still less a treaty, to compromise their material and social dominance. This does not mean that we should not try to establish a treaty with the Chinese government, and to exert what pressure we can to ensure obedience to it. But it does mean that, in negotiating such a treaty, we are not dealing with a normal corporate agent, nor are we aiming at a change in the law that governs it. We are dealing with a massively powerful cartel of wealthy people, who control the law that purports to control them, and who cannot tolerate any erosion of their privileged status. Power is no longer centralized as it was under Mao Zedong; but the government must buy support from the rent-seeking elites in industry and local administration, and can do nothing that will undermine their privileges.[290] Even if something of the Confucian spirit has returned, therefore, it is impossible to assume that the elites will respond to it.

290 See Minxin Pei, *China's Trapped Transition*, Cambridge, MA, 2006.

The point is developed in different terms by Douglass C. North, John Joseph Wallis and Barry R. Weingast in a series of publications designed to explain both how the rule of law emerged in Western states and why it has not emerged elsewhere.[291] North, Wallis and Weingast contrast what they call 'natural states', in which powerful individuals and groups impose themselves through violence or the threat of it, with 'open access orders' in which people are equal before the law and violence is a state monopoly.[292] In natural states the powerful individuals and groups have an incentive not to employ violence only if they are granted rents on the social product and privileges consonant with their expectations. In Europe and America, however, and perhaps also in certain countries on the Pacific Rim, 'open access orders' have emerged. In orders of this kind the rule of law commands the consent and submission of the people; elsewhere people are aware of the great danger of withholding privileges from those who can threaten violence. What we see as 'corruption' is, according to North et al., something rather different: a necessary part of the bargains that must be concluded if a state is not to crumble to anarchy.

Although I am not persuaded that the 'open access order' can

291 Douglass C. North, John Joseph Wallis and Barry R. Weingast, *Violence and Social Orders*, Cambridge, 2009. See also the very pertinent reflections in Barry R. Weingast, 'Why Developing Countries Prove So Resistant to the Rule of Law', in James J. Heckman *et al.*, eds., *Global Perspectives on the Rule of Law*, London, 2010.

292 This Weberian way of expressing the point is my addition.

be characterized so simply as the authors maintain, their negative thesis is surely plausible, and contains a vital message for foreign policy today.[293] Democracy, free markets and the rule of law do not, as recent American foreign policy has seemed to assume, define the default position of human societies. They are rare achievements, and what stands in the way of them is not corruption or the intrusion of some arbitrary force that the people would willingly overthrow. What stands in the way is fear – fear of the violence that will follow, when powerful individuals, clans and groups can claim no rents on the social product. The elites may represent their interests through the Communist Party as in China, through the 'Alawite sect as in Syria, or through the state itself as in Mugabe's Zimbabwe. But they demand their price, and one price is that they are above the law and not bound by any deals to which they were not themselves party. Hence states of the kind that North *et al.* call 'natural' are without perpetuity. No agreement made by one set of officials can bind their successors: whoever gains power gains it for his own uses, and regards agreements undertaken by his predecessors as null and void until proven to be useful. In such states, therefore, all property rights are insecure, and all international treaties liable to evasion.

Those observations are especially pertinent when it comes to considering the problems of the environment and climate change.

293 I give another account of the distinction that North *et al.* are attempting to locate in *The West and the Rest*, where I distinguish states that are genuine corporate persons, from states that maintain only a threadbare mask of personality.

Two of the developing countries currently most responsible for greenhouse gas emissions are India and China, both of whose highly inefficient and polluting energy industries are under the control of the state and its privileged clients. India may be on the way to becoming an 'open access order'; but China is neither on the way nor desirous of getting there. In China it is difficult for citizens to influence the government. There are no democratic procedures and there is no real public opinion; hence there is no way in which the ordinary citizen can influence the government and we should not be surprised to learn that riots, protests and strikes occur at the rate of around 90,000 a year.[294] The Party elite is well aware of what happens when free opinion and control from below are granted to the people, and is quite clear that no such thing is going to happen in China. Hence there can be no *internal* pressure that will influence the Chinese government to abide by its treaties. This is very different from the situation in Western democracies, in which treaties become law (though sometimes, as in the USA, only by a subsequent enactment), and where they can be invoked as law by the citizen and enforced against the state. When the US Senate ratifies a treaty this represents a huge and lasting cost to the United States and its people. When the Chinese president signs a treaty it is very unclear who will pay the cost of it or how.

In such a state, incentives for efficient energy use arise not

294 See Minxin Pei, 'Will the Chinese Communist Party Survive the Crisis?', post on *Foreign Affairs*, 12 March 2009.

from market forces but from political pressures and the muscling for power of rival elites. It is entirely credible, therefore, that the technology embodied in the installed base of capital equipment in China produces emissions (as recent estimates claim) at about four times the rate of technology in use in the United States.[295] Energy production remains under the control of the state, which is under the control of the Communist Party, which is in turn a vehicle for exercising the power of elite families and factions. Furthermore, since the Chinese state, for all its monumental appearance, is not a 'perpetual state', bound by lasting agreements, the present elite has neither the ability nor the desire to commit its successors. This does not mean that there are no incentives for clean energy creation in China. The governing elites as well as the ordinary people have to breathe the notorious smogs of Beijing. Moreover, the government is very conscious of its image, and sees the demand for clean energy as a valuable export opportunity. China is rapidly becoming the world's leading producer of wind turbines and solar panels, and the government has invited foreign manufacturers of these things to set up shop in China with a view to exporting the product. The government has also embarked on well-publicized projects to replace the polluting coal-fired power plants that provide most of the country's electricity.[296] Perhaps these developments are signs of

295 David Montgomery, quoted in Lee Lane, *Strategic Options for Bush Administration Climate Policy*, Washington DC, 2006, pp. 20–21.
296 Report in *New York Times*, 31 January 2010.

the hoped-for return to Confucian oikophilia. But the massive and forced destruction of renewable human habitats and low-impact housing in Beijing and Shanghai, and their replacement by megalopolis architecture that will never survive a change of use, cast doubt on that conclusion. It is difficult to gauge the sincerity of China's new image as a purveyor of clean energy, when the country continues to build coal-fired plants at the rate of two a week, meanwhile signing an unprecedented $69 billion deal with an Australian mining firm to supply coal for the next twenty years.[297]

We should not be surprised, therefore, that conferences on climate change and environmental protection tend to end as the Copenhagen Conference ended, with no binding agreement, general reproaches against the USA and China as having 'sabotaged' an agreement that was in fact never on the cards, and an attempt by the politicians and the NGOs to pretend that the whole thing was nevertheless worthwhile, and that the world is moving in 'the right direction'. At the same time, it is recognized on every side that a treaty addressing the problem of greenhouse gas emissions will be worthless if it does not include China and India, if it does not secure the conditional acceptance of developing nations generally, and if the Western powers are not fully committed to it. The failure of the Kyoto Treaty was due in part to American

---

297 *BBC News*, 6 February 2010. The vast size of China's carbon dioxide emissions is revealed in Ning Zeng *et al.*, 'Climate Change – the Chinese Challenge', *Science*, 8 February 2008, pp. 730–31.

recognition that China and India could comply with it only with symbolic gestures and had no intention of implementing the institutional changes that would make it possible to hold them to any agreement that did not suit their current interests.[298] The United States government tried to mitigate the adverse international publicity generated by its failure to sign up to the Kyoto accords by sponsoring the Asia-Pacific Partnership for Clean Development and Climate, to include Australia, China, India, Japan, South Korea and the United States. This, rather than pursuing a policy of 'cap and trade', which allows nations effectively to set their own limits for carbon emissions, is directed towards technological innovation. The Kyoto Clean Development Mechanism was intended to establish an incentive structure that would encourage either private firms or governments to devote the resources needed to develop a genuinely renewable source of clean energy.[299] However, the system of carbon credits proposed, besides opening the way to corrupt deals and evasions, would have inflicted a cost on the United States that the Senate was not prepared to underwrite.

The history of post-colonial Africa suggests that, should the continent overcome its stagnation and experience the industrial revolution that has occurred elsewhere, the chances of controlling the resulting emissions by treaty are next to zero. Or rather, they are more than zero only if Western governments and

298 See the analysis in Lee Lane, *op. cit.*
299 See the next chapter.

entrepreneurs have discovered a form of energy that is both clean and affordable and are willing to make this discovery available around the world, offering incentives to introduce it. Meanwhile, we must recognize that negotiations to reduce emissions have been proceeding for twenty years with no result other than diverting attention from the possibilities of action that might be achieved by 'coalitions of the willing'.

Even if a treaty were in place, there is still a further question of the incentive to abide by it. Sanctions are effective against democratic states, which respond to burdens imposed on their people, but they are not effective against tyrannies and party-monopolies, in which the power of ruling groups is only enhanced by sanctions that weaken the people over whom they exercise their power. (Witness the cases of North Korea, of Saddam Hussein's Iraq, and of Iran today.) Moreover, even among law-abiding states, the need to keep the ghost of an agreement in place militates against the imposition of serious penalties. As Thomas Schelling has put it, 'there is no historical example of any international regime that could impose penalties on a scale commensurate with the magnitude of global warming', and he cites, in illustration, the inability of the EU to impose the severe penalties threatened under its treaties against member states that defect from crucial obligations.[300] In other words, the greater the fault, the less the incentive for avoiding it.

300 Schelling, 'What Makes Greenhouse Sense?', *Foreign Affairs*, 81.3, May/June 2002, pp. 2–9.

That observation points to a general weakness in international treaties, which is that they rarely create the motive for obeying them when it is in the interest of one of the parties to defect. If incentives exist, it is usually because parties are obtaining a real and present benefit that could be easily withdrawn in response to defection. Thus nations have willingly signed up to the WTO, recognizing the economic benefits, and also the ease with which those benefits might be taken away. (The fact that, in signing up, they also surrender a slice of their sovereignty to multinational business interests is usually ignored.) The nations have also willingly signed up to the Montreal Protocol on Ozone Depleting Substances since the benefits were immediate, and not delayed for decades (as would be the case for any agreement over greenhouse gas emissions). Moreover, the technology to replace the harmful emissions was already being developed in the private sector, and, in accepting the agreement, no nation incurred large costs or had to disrupt the way of life of its citizens.[301] None of those things could conceivably obtain when it comes to a treaty to combat greenhouse gas emissions. When considering international action to limit atmospheric pollution we should, therefore, regard the Montreal Protocol as an exception, rather than a model.

On the other hand it is an important exception, since it helps us to understand the distinction between useful and useless treaty negotiations. The Montreal Protocol concerned the elimination of products that could be removed from the environment without

301 Lee Lane, *op. cit.*, p. 48.

seriously disturbing the economy or the way of life of any signatory nation. The incentives to sign were sufficiently strong, and the cost of doing so sufficiently weak, that an agreement was reached. Greenhouse gases are not like CFC gases. As things stand they can be eliminated only at great economic and even greater social cost, and few nations are prepared to pay that cost. By devoting their sparse supply of global goodwill to negotiating futile treaties against emissions, the nations are wasting assets that could be spent on co-operative research into renewable energy. They are also losing sight of environmental problems that can be solved in the Montreal way.

One such problem is plastic. It is possible to eliminate non-biodegradable plastic from a modern economy without causing the kind of social upheaval that would come from interfering with energy production. The initial cost would be great, but adaptation would be rapid. Just as nations accepted the moratorium on CFC gases, so they could accept a moratorium on non-biodegradable plastic (provided exceptions were permitted, to be justified case by case). Technological progress has made it possible to use biodegradable materials in all normal packaging, and there is no insuperable cost in imposing a substantial deposit on plastic bottles and containers. Such measures would quickly remove plastic from the environment of any nation that introduced them. If adopted by the United States, which is the largest recipient of plastic trash from China, the measures would create the incentive for the Chinese to begin making biodegradable trash instead, so lessening the cost of complying with any international treaty. Bit by bit the trade in plastic would come to an end, and the nations could then get together to clean up the Great Pacific Garbage Patch.

Such a process requires an initiative from two or three strong-willed, law-abiding states, and would lead in a relatively short time to a situation in which the amount of plastic in the environment is constantly declining. If all the effort devoted to futile treaties like Kyoto were devoted to this task it would lead assuredly to a positive result. If the task is not undertaken the earth will one day cease to be a viable human habitat, whatever its temperature.

It is partly in recognition of the weakness of treaties that many people, and not only those on the left of the political spectrum, have advocated systems of transnational government, whether on the model of the European Union, in which nation states renounce some of their sovereignty to a centralized administrative and legislative power, or whether on the model of the United Nations subordinate bodies, such as the ILO, WHO and UNCTAD which have quasi-legislative powers under the UN treaty. This tendency towards transnational governance is sometimes put forward as the inevitable consequence of globalization, of the growing interconnectedness of decisions around the world as markets and migration break down traditional barriers, and of the growth of power structures outside the control of any single nation state – including multinational corporations, international organizations like the IMF and the World Bank, transnational NGOs like Greenpeace and IFAW, and the emerging 'virtual communities' that span the globe.[302]

When we look at the facts, however, the idea of transnational governance begins to lose credibility. Such transnational institutions as have emerged from globalization are either dependent on the nation states for their legitimacy and motivating power, or else seen as symptoms of disorder rather than the cure for it. Multinational corporations and NGOs exist within the institutional space created by the nation states, and it is a fantasy to think that any form of governance could be produced that would not overtly or covertly rely, in the end, on the territorial jurisdictions that those states have established.

It is surely obvious that law does not exist merely because some code of law has been written down by a bureaucrat or pinned up in an office. Law exists only if it is enforced; and only if it is enforced *as law*. This means that those charged with making, disputing, applying or enforcing the law cannot themselves be exempt from it. An intricate and interlocking system of institutions is required if law is to be enforced as law, and not as

302 See, for example, the well-known argument of Thomas Friedman in *Lexus and the Olive Tree*, New York, 1999, and the writings of the global governance advocates: David Held, Anthony McGrew, David Goldblatt and Jonathan Perraton, *Global Transformations: Politics, Economics and Culture*, Cambridge, 1998; and Robert O. Keohane and Joseph S. Nye Jr, in Nye and John D. Donahue, eds., *Governance in a Globalizing World*, Washington DC, 2000. Also Monbiot, *op. cit.*

arbitrary violence. To cut a long story short, there can be law only where those charged with administering and enforcing the law have a deep-down respect for procedure and a sense of the law's authority. How is this feeling – which the Germans call *Rechtsgefühl* – engendered? Law-abiding people, it seems to me, come into being because obedience to the law is *expected* of them. They are living up to a standard. But expected by whom? And a standard laid down by whom? Kant believed that reason lays down and upholds the standard. But even if that were so, the evidence of history is that reason does not in itself produce obedience. There has to be a public expectation of law-abidingness, and a desire to live up to what others expect. This returns us again to the question: which others?

The obvious answer is this: I desire to live up to the expectations of *those with whom I belong*. I make a distinction between people who are mine and people who are not mine, and part of what is involved in this distinction is that the opinions of those who are mine *matter* to me. Now intellectuals, businessmen and aristocrats have no difficulty in belonging to a multinational group. They compare and compete across national boundaries, since that is precisely what their status or metier requires. The same is not true of ordinary people. Their sense of belonging is tied down to a locality, a language, a set of customs, and family affections. Ordinary people are the majority, and their law-abidingness is therefore of the greatest importance. Hence some element of national loyalty is a necessary precondition of law –

and also of the international law that is built precariously on domestic foundations.

This is not to deny that there can be transnational jurisdictions, but it is worth considering what, in the past, they have involved. There are four salient examples: Roman law, English law, Canon law and the shariah. In Roman law and English law a system of law was spread far and wide across the globe, by people who were attached to it as a symbol of their superior civilization and a justification for their imperial power. Neither system could have succeeded in bringing peace to the world were it not for two vital facts: first, that citizens loyal to the metropolitan centre were put in charge of it, and secondly, that each system left room for local laws adapted to local loyalties. The Romans and the British upheld the overarching law precisely because they identified themselves as Roman and British – i.e. apart from, and in a measure superior to, those over whom they ruled. Their international jurisdiction was made possible by a version of national loyalty, and when the empires collapsed then the law collapsed along with them.

The Canon law and the shariah are more truly universal. The first borrowed extensively from Roman law and was very quickly pushed into a subordinate position by the secular law of European states. The second has claimed sovereignty in many Islamic countries, and is the nearest we have to a truly international jurisdiction that depends on no equivalent of national loyalty. However, the shariah owes its authority to loyalty of another kind: to God, and to the word of God as spoken through the Prophet Muhammad. It gives us no grounds for thinking that there could be such a thing as an international and secular rule of law, which did not depend, at the deeper level, on national or quasi-national loyalties. From the very beginning the shariah has been fraught with conflict fomented by the four rival schools of jurisprudence, and since the Ash'arite ascendancy in the eleventh century of our era has (in the Sunni, but not the Shi'ite, interpretation) expressly excluded innovation or *ijtihad*. It applies only to Muslims and deals with non-believers under a 'treaty' or *dhimmah*, which leaves their rights only partially defined.[303] Old Turkish law, which tried to respect the shariah, was, therefore, compelled to distinguish the religious part of the law from the separate jurisdictions of the various communities, or *milletler*, that refused to submit to Muslim commandments. The fate of the shariah today, when it is invoked all over the world as a source of absolute edicts by people who cannot agree among themselves as to what it says, is surely a warning against any attempt to divorce law so radically from the territorial sovereignty that is needed to apply it.

Systems of law applied transnationally, and without regard for territorial jurisdiction, should be distinguished from what we know today as 'international law', which comprises conventions

---

303 See Antoine Fattal, *Le Statut légal des non-musulmans en pays d'Islam*, Beirut, 1958; Robert Reilly, *The Closing of the Muslim Mind*, Wilmington, 2010.

developed through treaties, designed to facilitate the relations among sovereign nation states. And both should be distinguished from the new form of multinational jurisdiction that has emerged in Europe, in which the sovereignty of the member states of the European Union is both recognized, and also subordinated to a system of top-down governance that makes no overt appeal to nationality.

In the EU there is no imperial power, and therefore no law-enforcers with a sense of their civilizing mission, who would remain bound to each other as the Romans were bound to the Romans and the British to the British under their respective empires. There are only bureaucrats, based in a country (Belgium) notorious for its failure to produce a sentiment of national unity and now on the verge of disintegration.[304] The edicts of these bureaucrats are propagated without respect for national differences or existing sentiments of legitimacy, and with no real expectation that anyone will be motivated to obey them. The result is a gradual erosion of respect for law and the growth of a new kind of corruption – a bureaucratized mafia that shields its actions by passing laws that no one is really expected to comply with.

Defenders of the EU often argue that it provides a model for addressing environmental questions, since it avoids the incentive and defection problems that bedevil international treaties.

304 See Paul Belien, *A Throne in Brussels: Britain, the Saxe-Coburgs and the Belgianization of Europe*, London, 2005.

However, because the only motive to obey European legislation is created at the national level, the legal instruments of the European Union have become battlegrounds for national interests. Consider again the example of fisheries. As a condition of admitting Britain and Denmark to the Community (as it was then called), it was required that every member sign up to a Common Fisheries Policy, which was hastily cobbled together as Britain and Denmark entered into negotiations for membership. This was not in order to conserve European fish stocks as a common asset, but in order to remove British and Danish coastal waters, the best-supplied in Europe, from the national jurisdictions that had protected them from the fishing fleets of other countries. A system of national property rights, which had been effective in conserving fish stocks in the North Sea and the English Channel, was destroyed, and a new tragedy of the commons created in its place. The result has been a major ecological disaster, with stocks in the North Sea continuing to decline at an alarming rate.[305]

The EU is now encumbered by 180,000 pages of regulations and directives, with no guarantee that they further the common good, since the law of unintended consequences is never considered by the bureaucracies responsible. This *acquis communautaire* is always increasing in size, and no procedure exists whereby those who suffer the burden of regulation can eject the people

305 See Ruth Lea, 'The Common Fisheries Policy and the Wreckage of an Industry', *Institute of Directors Policy Study*, December 2002.

who impose it. Two examples will help us to see the problem. First, there is the EU's response to the problem of carbon emissions. As in the ineffectual Kyoto agreement, the EU has opted for a cap and trade scheme, under which firms must purchase from governments the right to carbon emissions, and can trade their rights with other firms across the Union. While Britain and Spain have chosen tough targets, other member states (notably Italy) have set targets higher than existing emissions. The price of carbon, therefore, rises in Britain and Spain, giving firms an incentive to buy emission permits in laxer jurisdictions, in particular those whose governments have printed a glut of permits, as an asset to be sold on the open market. As a result of the policy, carbon emissions have continued to rise across the European Union, with no incentive to develop the new technologies that might replace the major sources of greenhouse gas. In addition technical problems have made the Emissions Trading Scheme extremely untransparent and costly to operate. All in all an expensive failure, that imposes no control on emissions, while adding a pointless layer of bureaucracy to policies devoted to national, rather than transnational, goals.[306] Like all such imaginary solutions, including the massive investment in wind power that has also been promoted by the European Union, the scheme diverts

306 See Open Europe blog post of 15 December 2009 at www. openeuropeblog.blogspot.com, and work back from there. The lessons of the European experience are well rehearsed by Ben Lieberman, 'The European Experience with Cap and Trade', congressional testimony delivered 8 July 2009, and available on the Heritage Foundation's website.

resources away from the only thing that could possibly produce a long-term solution, which is research into alternative sources of energy.

Secondly, regulations are seldom if ever corrected or reversed, regardless of their environmental cost. Consider the other most damaging by-product of modern prosperity: packaging. All over Europe fields, rivers, lakes and hedgerows are filling with plastic bottles and bags, and the per capita production of packaging waste ranges from 100 kilograms a year in Finland to more than double that amount in France.[307] Yet what is the reaction of the EU? To require all food to be packaged before it can leave the farm; to lay down stringent health and safety regulations that cannot be met by small local shops, so that food must be centrally processed and packaged in plastic; to oblige manufacturers to wrap detailed instructions in ten languages along with all their products; and in general to force upon producers and consumers across the Union a culture of litter and waste. No national government that wished, now, to get rid of non-biodegradable packaging, to return to the benign regime of sweets in paper bags, fish in newspaper or pickled beets in barrels, could adopt such a policy. All governments throughout the Union have been locked into policies concerning the production and distribution of food which, though they may enhance the health of present consumers,

307 *New Scientist* Environment blog, 29 March 2007, www.newscientist. com/blog/environment/2007/03/packaging-waste-facts-and-figures. html.

have a long-term environmental cost that will far outweigh the short-term benefits.

Those are just two examples: but they are symptomatic. Transnational government on the European model leads to regulations that cannot be corrected, which are presented in zero-tolerance packets, and which are subject to lobbying so as to become the instruments of national and commercial rivalry. The French government is currently lobbying for extensive central controls to be imposed on financial institutions throughout the Union, aware that this will eliminate the competitive advantage hitherto enjoyed by the City of London, which has for three centuries regulated itself under the English law of trusts and corporations.[308] The result will not be a more honest or accountable banking system in London, which continues to attract global finance because the English laws of contract, tort and trusts provide a reliable guarantee of transnational agreements. But it will destroy a British trading advantage that has been a long-standing provocation to the French.

The laws and regulations of the European Union originate in bureaucracies whose members are never subject to election, or in a court whose judges are appointed from national jurisdictions for fixed terms and without accountability to any particular government. Hence these laws and regulations proliferate without control, and without any assessment of the cost of complying with them. Moreover, the legislative process is subject to lobbying

308 Tim Congdon, *The City of London Under Threat*, London, 2009.

from businesses, national governments and individual politicians, who do not face, in Brussels, the kind of feedback that the members of National Assemblies face at home. Added to this there is the effect of the European Court of Human Rights, which arbitrarily converts one side of a conflict of interests into a right, and so unsettles long-standing customs on which oikophilia depends.[309] In such circumstances it is surely unlikely that transnational government on the European model will provide the kind of sensitive instrument that will enable us to co-ordinate our attempts at environmental protection.

To this kind of objection the convinced internationalist will argue that time is needed before the practice of transnational government can lodge in the public mind. It takes time to get used to new institutions, but there is no reason why the process that united the known world under Roman jurisdiction two millennia ago should not begin again under the Treaty of Rome. A new public spirit will arise, they will say, in which people support the judgements of transnational courts against the domestic law of nations, and in which individual citizens appeal above the heads of their governments for a justice that makes no distinctions around the world.

Can there be such a public spirit – a public spirit whose foundation is the internationalist idea? Some of the most public-spirited movements of our times have been expressly internationalist in their aims: the Olympic movement, the Red Cross,

309 I give an example of this in the next chapter.

the United Nations and the aptly named Medecins sans frontières. But I do not think that any of these movements could have succeeded without the fund of national sentiment on which they drew. The Olympic movement seeks to bring about international cooperation through enhancing, rather than diminishing, national pride: for that is what competitive international sport requires. And, as the Berlin Olympics demonstrated, the result may enhance nationalist belligerence too.

Public spirit is an attribute of local communities. It grows, as Burke argued, from the 'little platoon', and it can grow to become the conscience of a nation. Not all people possess it in equal degrees. Indeed, there is a notorious difference between those people for whom family is the source and object of social loyalty, and those people who recognize the web of obligations to strangers. The Sicilians, being of the first kind, have wrought havoc in America, where they have found themselves among people of the second kind, who are without effective defences against them. And in the new international jurisdiction in Europe we find an interesting dividing line, which separates the *Langue d'oc* from the *Langue d'oïl* and the German-speaking from the Latin- and Greek-speaking peoples. Above this line corruption is minimal; below it corruption is the normal state of affairs: hence the present crisis with the common currency, which has not been honestly maintained by Italy, Portugal, Greece or Spain. Ponder those facts, and the history of public spirit in those countries – Britain, Switzerland, Scandinavia, the USA – that have most

evidently displayed it, and you will surely conclude that internationalism is very unlikely to produce public spirit without help
from a more local source of moral sentiment. Public spirit is, in
origin, a domestic product, the manufacture of which is greatly
stimulated by Protestant habits of self-accusation and the inheritance of common law.

It is fairly obvious that empires diminish sovereignty, but they
do so by enhancing the sovereignty of the central power. Can
there be a shared diminution of sovereignty that will be agreed to
by all those who join the system, but which will not transfer
sovereignty to some central body? The answer is that there can
be, but only if such a central body owes all its powers to the
ongoing agreement of member states, and only if those member
states retain their freedom to withdraw from the agreement at
every stage. Such a body is the WTO, which is itself not without
adverse effects on the ability of its poorer members to protect
perceived national interests from aggressive global trade.[310]
Although, as I pointed out above, membership of the WTO
involves surrendering a slice of sovereignty to multinational
interests, the surrender is reversible (at a cost), and its benefits
tangible to each individual member. But as soon as sovereignty is
pooled, and membership entangled in irreversible agreements,

---

310 Thus multinationals are constantly campaigning for a WTO agreement
that will allow them investment rights on equal terms with local competi-
tors around the globe. The dangers of this were pointed out by Paul
Kingsnorth, in 'Cancun: Why You Should Care', *Ecologist*, 33.5, June
2003.

there results a central executive and legislative power. As the experience of the United States confirms, sovereignty relinquished to a federal body is also transferred to it: the States of the Union lost powers, which the federal government gained, and once transferred they could not be recaptured. The result, at a certain point, was civil war, after which the States of the Union retained only nominal sovereignty.

The European Commission tries to pretend that this need not happen. The Maastricht Treaty deploys a peculiar principle, called 'subsidiarity', in order to explain the point. The term seems to derive from a papal encyclical of Pius XI of 1929, in which the Pope argued that all political decisions should be taken at the lowest possible level – i.e. by those whose decision in the matter can be regarded with indifference by everyone else. The problem is that subsidiarity, so defined, has no clear legal meaning. Which matters affect *us* but not *them*? What exactly is the 'lowest' level? Why speak of low and high levels, if we do not wish to imply the existence of a supreme and sovereign apex? Moreover, who is to decide whether 'subsidiarity' applies? Only, it seems, the European Commission – the central body in which true sovereignty accumulates. If we are free to make decisions in a matter only if the Commission decides that we are free, then we are not really free, since it is the Commission that is deciding. Subsidiarity is not sovereignty at all, but a kind of soothing myth with which we habituate ourselves to our subjection.

I don't think this question of sovereignty has ever been

properly addressed, or that it could be resolved in the way that internationalists desire – namely, so as to grant sovereignty to the people who want it, while binding them to international rules. This points to one of the greatest dangers in internationalism: that people will be drawn into a transnational web, believing that they enhance their power and their choice, only to discover that both power and choice have been confiscated. At a certain point they will discover that they are subject to a power to which they have, and can have, no instinctive loyalty – since loyalty is a local and historical phenomenon, and cannot be conscripted.

All that ought to make us wary of the internationalist idea. Even if we think that the new forms of internationalism have little in common with the insolent dealings of the Communist Party, we must ask ourselves seriously what the real interests are that advance, in the postmodern world, behind internationalist projects and ideas. It helps, in confronting that question, to distinguish between cosmopolitanism and internationalism. Cosmopolitans are at home in any city; they appreciate human life in all its peaceful forms, and are emotionally in touch with the customs, languages and cultures of many different people. They are patriots of one country, but nationalists of many. Internationalists, by contrast, wish to break down the distinctions between people; they do not feel at home in any city since they are aliens in all. They see the world as one vast system in which everyone is equally a customer, a consumer, a creature of wants and needs. They are happy to transplant people from place to place, to abolish local attachments, to shift boundaries and customs in accordance with the inexorable tide of political need or economic progress.

Those who first dreamed up the European Union, and who promoted it through political and cultural activities into which they put their heartfelt emotions and ideals, were cosmopolitans. Those who are now exploiting it and shaping it are internationalists, who have no affection whatsoever for the identities on which it has been built. Behind the EU, pressing always for its expansion, hoping to use its legislative powers to turn the market in their favour, are the big businesses of Europe, Japan, China and America – and in particular the supermarket chains, the fast-food franchises, the pharmaceutical companies, the car manufacturers, the purveyors of global goods and global entertainments, who wish to make everywhere identical in order to secure a 'level playing field' that gives maximum custom to their goods. Do we really want to go in this direction, to lose everything that was distinctive of our histories and traditions, and to lose the loyalties that made Europe and America possible in the first place? This direction too leads to Nowhere, and this Nowhere is the very same threat against which the left-wing oikophiles mobilize in defence of local communities and rooted ways of doing things.

In the light of all this, it seems to me that we must consider the possibility that, in the end, we can defend our environment only by unilateral action on the part of a competent and law-abiding state. Our model should be the kind of intervention that was made by the British Navy in ending the transnational market in slaves, or that made (against Britain) by Iceland, in protecting the breeding grounds of the Atlantic cod. All such interventions have their dangers, and could be taken (as almost in the latter case) as a *casus belli*. In the case of climate change, however, there may well be no alternative. Advances in climatology and the theory and practice of geo-engineering could well put within the power of a law-abiding nation state – and evidently the USA is the likely example – the means of initiating global cooling to counteract the effect of greenhouse gases in the atmosphere. If we are at the point where this alone is feasible, then this alone must be done. It seems to me that the only way to prepare ourselves for this contingency is by ceasing to put our trust in punitive treaties that no nation has a lasting motive to honour, or in transnational governance that merely erodes the obedience on which it depends, and instead reinforcing our attachment to the nation state, and to the kinds of policy that I have been advocating in this book, which put research and enterprise before regulation and control. The USA has already proposed a series of Research and Development Treaties – such as the Carbon Sequestration Leadership Forum – that will be 'coalitions of the willing', and which impose no penalties on their signatories.[311] If treaties are to be effective at all they must surely be of this kind – treaties that offer only benefits, which minimize the incentives to defect, and which compensate for the principal failure of markets in the matter of global

311 See www.cslforum.org/aboutus/index.html.

environmental problems, namely that they do not invest sufficiently in the needed research. But the energy required to make
such treaties work must be generated within the nation states that
sign up to them, by the oikophilia of their citizens.

TEN

Begetting Somewhere

My intention in this book has been to argue the case for an approach to environmental problems in which local affections are made central to policy, and in which homeostasis and resilience, rather than social reordering and central control, are the primary outcomes. My argument has been both philosophical and psychological, concerning the nature of practical reasoning and the motives on which we can rely in the effort to protect others from our waste, and future generations from ourselves. But the argument has abutted at every point on historical and political facts, and raised questions of policy that must surely be addressed if the conservative approach to ecology is to be plausible. In these two final chapters, therefore, I consider practicalities: first by studying some examples; then by making modest proposals concerning the guidelines that a conservative environmental policy should follow.

I begin from the example that I most intimately know, namely that of the British Isles, and specifically of my own corner of it, which is England. My intention is to give a brief account of the conservation movements that have emerged in England, to show that, where successful, they grow from oikophilia, and that, where unsuccessful, it is largely because they have been neutralized or overridden by centralizing projects, initiated by state planning, by lobbying from business interests or by the imposition of some internationalist scheme.

Julien Sorel, the hero of Stendhal's *Le Rouge et le noir*, is at a certain stage obliged to visit England; he disparages the gross manners and crude conceptions of the people, finds nothing in the cities that would remotely interest a person of refined sensibility, and yet is taken aback by the 'indescribable sweetness' of the countryside, which surpasses anything that he had known in France. Visitors to England today report the same impression, and are often at a loss to understand how such a delicate fabric could have stayed in place despite industrialization, a tenfold increase in population since the eighteenth century, aerial bombardment by the Luftwaffe and the ever-accelerating impact of commerce. The impression is all the more striking, given that England is the most densely populated country in Europe, with 395 people for every square kilometre – over three times the European average. To compare England as it is today with the Netherlands (which has 392 people for every square kilometre) is to find vivid proof that there is such a thing as successful environmental management.

Like many other European countries, England has a narrative

of national renewal.[312] Poets and storytellers have evoked the dark surrounding forest, from which the clearing of civilization has been painfully extracted, and to which men and animals return in order to refresh themselves from the fount of life. This picture, which is not unique to English literature, is traced over and again in medieval narratives, in the stories of Arthur and the Knights of the Round Table, in *Sir Gawain and the Green Knight*, in the legends of Tristan, Parsifal and Lancelot. And no doubt Jessie Weston is right to discern in such stories the survival of an ancient vegetation cult, which blended roughly but firmly with the Gospel narrative of the risen Christ.[313] Whatever its origins, following Malory's *Morte d'Arthur* and the popularization of the legend of Robin Hood, a myth of the Greenwood became firmly anchored in the national consciousness. The myth tells of a place outside conventional society where a primeval restitution is sought and granted. It provides the backcloth to Shakespeare plays, to the poetry and songs of the Tudor court, to many popular stories and to the Robin Hood poem, *The Greenwood Tree*, published around 1600.

It is possible to discern in the Greenwood idea the first stirrings of environmental consciousness among the English people.[314] Laments over the violation of the forests and pleas to replant them occur from the earliest years of the printing press.

312 On the pre-history of the environmental movement in Britain see Keith Thomas, *op. cit.*

313 Jessie L. Weston, *From Ritual to Romance*, Cambridge, 1920.

314 See Schama, *op. cit.*, pp. 153–74.

By the time of the Restoration, following a civil war in which Charles II had established his mystical identity with the English settlement by hiding in an oak tree, the Greenwood myth had become a core element of national consciousness. John Evelyn's *Silva, or A Discourse on Forestation* appeared in 1664 and was immediately popular, marking the beginning of a movement to conserve and replant the woodlands, and inspiring Acts of Parliament to plant the Forest of Dean, 1668, and the New Forest, 1698. Parliament was influenced by the need to provide timber for the Royal Navy; however, as Sir Keith Thomas has shown, aesthetic values also had an important part to play.[315] The republication of Evelyn's book in 1776 by the public-spirited doctor and conservationist Dr Alexander Hunter led to similar civic initiatives. It also brought about a revival of the Greenwood legend, when Joseph Ritson published, in 1795, *Robin Hood: A Collection of all the Ancient Poems, Songs and Ballads*, illustrated by Thomas Bewick. This collection was the inspiration for Sir Walter Scott's enormously influential novel *Ivanhoe*.

The Enlightenment cult of natural beauty had by then become part of the culture. Under the influence of Milton, Shaftesbury, Addison and Knight, the landscape painters, landscape gardeners and nature poets of the eighteenth century set about to create the image of England as Eden.[316] This image has survived into our

315 Keith Thomas, *op. cit.*, pp. 203 ff.

316 3rd Earl of Shaftesbury, *Characteristics*, 1711; Joseph Addison, *The Pleasures of the Imagination*, 1711–12; Richard Payne Knight, *An Analytical Inquiry into the Principles of Taste*, London, 1805.

days as a moral resource on which the nation draws in every crisis. It was evoked in the last war to great effect by the films from Ealing Studios (notably those of the Czech refugee Alexander Korda) and by the landscape paintings of the Nash brothers. During that great twentieth century crisis the 'countryside' was represented as a place of tranquillity, the heart of England, and the birthright of Everyman. In the eighteenth century, however, the Edenic image was associated with the aristocracy, with private sovereignty, and with the fashion for the 'picturesque'. For the aristocrat the landscape was not a wilderness but a garden. It could be owned like a picture, and shaped by its owner in accordance with aesthetic values and nostalgic whims. This search for the picturesque did not detract from the deeper significance of the landscape as land. Polishing the landscape was part of emphasising its permanence, and therefore maintaining it as a renewable resource.[317]

However, the privileged ownership of the landscape was already being put in question, not only in the realm of politics, but also in the realm of art. Painters were beginning to take an interest in scenes shaped as much by work and need as by leisure. The English landscape tradition – which came to fruition in the work of Constable, Cotman and Crome – was devoted to images of a home in which the common people also had a stake, and in which labour and leisure coexisted in mutual dependence. Taking inspiration from the soft climate and changing skies of Southern

317 On the picturesque see Knight, *op. cit.*

329

England, the tradition showed a community that had grown from the landscape and shaped itself to its contours. Hogarth apart, the painters ignored the city, and sought in the lanes and fields of Old England an image of a society moving in ancient rhythms, as yet untouched by the manufacturing industries and the population movements that were beginning to turn the world upside down.

In 1752 Burke published his *Philosophical Enquiry into the Origin of our Ideas of the Sublime and the Beautiful*, a work that opened the eyes of the thinking public to another and more troubling view of aesthetic taste and judgement than the one revealed in the horses of Stubbs or the lakes and valleys of Richard Wilson. Beauty, Burke suggested, is not the only aesthetic value: gentleness and harmony occur in nature side by side with violence, vastness and the eerie vacancy of the oceans and the moors. These overwhelming things are less beautiful than sublime. They are reminders that, after all, nothing is truly stable or durable, and that our human habitats may be at any moment swept away by forces that we cannot control.

The cult of the 'sublime' was a conscious attempt to situate human activity amid powers that surpass us. This cult gave rise to a passionate interest in 'wild nature', in the highlands and moors, in the poems of 'Ossian' and the Border ballads. It also inspired the novels of Scott and the rise of the 'Gothick' in art, literature and architecture – a fashion adroitly satirized by Jane Austen in *Northanger Abbey*. The interest in the sublime went hand in hand with an awareness that the wilderness was retreating, not because it was being civilized, but because it was being destroyed. The Industrial Revolution was releasing new forces into the world, and the landscape could survive only if people were prepared to protect it. People learn to appreciate the wild only when they have tamed it, and what we know as wilderness is invariably over-looked and policed from civilized shelters that it does not threaten.[318] The art that celebrated the untamed forces of nature issued from the knowledge that nature had been tamed, and made vulnerable to human abuse. Moreover, there was a dark side to the emerging England, and the smiling landscape had been drawn over it like a veil. Paintings like those of Constable and Crome were icons of remembrance, reminders of what is at stake in the new economic order, and pleas to those with power and influence to do what they could to save things.[319] The beauty of the English Eden was tied to an old order of things, and that order was a remembered order, idealized and therefore falsified by those who sought to cling to it.

Izaak Walton's *The Compleat Angler* appeared in 1653, shortly before John Evelyn's *Silva*, and grew from the same search for peace and solace in nature, following the ravages of civil war. It inaugurated a literary genre that was to enjoy three centuries of success – the nature documentary, simultaneously user's manual, dreamer's rhapsody, and a plea to respect the ways of nature and

318 See Keith Thomas, *op. cit.*, pp. 263–5.
319 John Barrell, *The Dark Side of the Landscape: The Rural Poor in English Landscape Painting 1730–1840*, Cambridge, 1980.

to leave her undefiled. James Thomson's long poem *The Seasons*, which appeared in 1730, describes in loving detail the Scottish border country where the poet was raised, and its idiom was adapted by William Somerville in his poem *The Chase*, of 1735, the work that began the abundant literature of hunting in English.[320] Perhaps the most important aspect of English landscape literature is the awareness of the need to protect the natural world from human mismanagement. The laments over woodfelling continued from Evelyn to the present day: in Pope's *Epistle to Burlington*, in Anne Winchilsea's 'The Tree', in the lyrics of Cowper, Clare, Campbell and Tennyson, down to 'Binsley Poplars' by Gerard Manley Hopkins, and the landscape poetry of Basil Bunting, R. S. Thomas and Ted Hughes.

Nature literature entered a new phase towards the end of the eighteenth century, when people began to feel the impact of the Industrial Revolution. Few books about the countryside have been more influential than *The Natural History and Antiquities of Selborne*, by the Reverend Gilbert White, vicar of Selborne in Hampshire, which has been reissued in every year since its first publication in 1788, and which inspired the founding in 1885 of the Selborne Society, a private trust that now manages a nature reserve at Perivale Wood. The concern for habitats was to some extent in conflict with a growing interest in agricultural science,

---

320 I say something about this literature in 'The Sacred Pursuit', in Nathan Kowalsky, ed., *Hunting – Philosophy for Everyone: In Search of the Wild Life*, London, 2010.

and the desire to place agriculture on a footing that would counteract the loss of population to the towns. Arthur Young began
publishing the monthly *Annals of Agriculture* in 1784, and counted
among his contributors Jeremy Bentham, the pioneering Coke of
Holkham and King George III (who adopted Ralph Richardson,
the name of his shepherd, as his *nom de plume*).

At the end of the eighteenth century began to appear Thomas
Malthus's *Essay on the Principle of Population*, which sounded the
first of many alarm-bells about growth – in this case the growth
of population, made apparent by the flight to the towns and the
sudden visibility of the ordinary people. The plight of the land
and of those who were employed on it was a leading concern of
William Cobbett, the farmer and pamphleteer whose *Rural Rides*
(summarizing two decades of environmental activism between
bouts of hare coursing and fox hunting) appeared in 1830.
Although Cobbett's principal cause was parliamentary reform, his
activism was infectious, and fed the desire of people to take action
against the social and environmental damage that had become
visible in the wake of the Industrial Revolution.

Just when the conservation movement began in earnest is a
moot point, and perhaps it never would have begun or taken the
form that it took, had it not been for two fundamental British
institutions: the dispersal of property rights and the place of
equity in the law. Ownership of land and natural resources was
not, in Britain, centralized in the monarch; the owners of estates
tended to live on them, spending much time, energy and money

in improvements devoted to environmentally positive ends, such as landscape gardening, model villages and field sports; and the rural economy had since the Middle Ages made substantial room for the yeoman farmer, who instinctively maintained the land as a renewable home, the place marked out by his own entitlement.[321] Ancient common-law rights – notably rights of way, green lanes and rights of commons – ensured that the countryside remained open, so that even the enclosed portions could usually be crossed at will. Hence the owner's desire to maintain and embellish did not undermine the experience of collective settlement.[322]

The English law provided the concept that was used both to preserve the aristocratic estates and, when they were broken up, to organize the resistance to spoliation. The law of trusts enabled owners of land to create settlements that were passed from generation to generation under terms that forbad their sale or destruction. The advance of the Industrial Revolution created opportunities for mining and other forms of industrial exploitation that were denied to the 'tenant for life' by the trust that compelled him to relinquish the estate to his successor in the condition in which he had inherited it, he meanwhile enjoying the rents attached to the land. In a series of measures, culminating in the Settled Land Act of 1882, the government freed the hereditary estates from the trusts that encumbered them, permitting the tenant for life to sell, so that any trust would become attached to

321 See MacFarlane, *op. cit.*

322 Michael Turner, *Enclosures in Britain, 1750–1830*, London, 1984.

the monetary proceeds, rather than to the land itself. This de-feudalizing of the rural economy accelerated the growth of industrial and mining operations in rural areas, and fed into the collective concern for the land and the landscape that is one of the most striking features of Victorian culture.

The Settled Land Act was a top-down decree of Parliament, intended to annul the provisions of certain trusts. But the trust concept had by then begun to fight back, as the oikophiles combined to protect their country from destruction. Over the many centuries of its operation, the law of trusts has helped English-speaking people to combine without putting themselves under the power of anything but themselves. It has offered protection to the 'little platoon' against the state and the intruder; it has safeguarded charitable funds and the private educational and medical establishments that depend on them; it has made it possible to start a civil association just as soon as the decision to do so has been taken, so reacting at once to the perceived need for action. It places a feedback loop in the path of every innovation, by giving opposition the right to combine immediately against it and to raise the funds needed for success.[323]

Public anxiety came to a head, as it had come to a head in the early seventeenth century, with the destruction of the forests, cut down for timber by owners who saw no need to harvest and replant. By 1851 the conservation societies were forming, as local people rose in protest against the desecration and began to raise

323 See F. W. Maitland, *Equity*, Cambridge, 1909.

money to purchase threatened sites, to campaign for legislative protection and to petition Parliament to take the matter in hand. The immediate cause was an Act of Parliament of 1851, permitting the enclosure of Hainault Forest, previously governed by 'forest law' as a Crown property. The destruction caused such public outrage that local people joined together in an attempt to save the forest as a commons. Their efforts culminated in the foundation by George Shaw-Lefevre of the Commons, Open Spaces and Footpaths Preservation Society in 1865, and the foundation in the same year of the Society for the Preservation of the Commons of London. These societies were able to make use of old common-law rights and easements both to protect places from destructive development and to keep the ancient rights of way unobstructed. The existence of these rights of way proved, in the long run, to be one of the most powerful weapons in preventing large-scale invasions of the landscape, since it was a weapon that anyone could wield in the courts, regardless of social status or ownership. The remaining segment of Hainault Forest was eventually saved in 1906, when local councils and private individuals put up the money required to purchase it as a recreational amenity. The oikophiles had better luck with Epping Forest, obtaining an injunction against enclosures, and eventually an Act of Parliament – the Epping Forest Act of 1878 – that protected the forest henceforth as common land.

Laws to protect wildlife are of ancient provenance, being originally designed to reserve game for the sport of monarchs and aristocrats. The notorious Black Act of 1723, which made it a felony (i.e. a hanging offence) to poach wild deer was of course not designed to conserve a threatened commons. However, its repeal in 1827 was followed quickly by the Ground Game Act of 1831, intended to conserve game by imposing closed seasons. The Seabirds Protection Acts of 1869 extended closed seasons to coastal shooting, and other Acts followed, under pressure from the general public, to ensure that populations were preserved and threatened species given proper protection. Wildlife enthusiasts founded the Selborne Society in 1885; this was followed in 1889 by what was to become the Royal Society for the Protection of Birds. This Society was established in part as a reaction against the habit among society ladies of sporting the feathers of rare birds in their clothing, but it soon recruited naturalists and birdwatchers to become, during the twentieth century, one of the most vigilant of pressure groups in defence of wildlife – and one that has often been in conflict with rival organizations on account of its inevitable favouritism.[324] Today it has 1,500 employees and over a million members, making it the largest wildlife charity in Europe. Equally important have been the local wildlife trusts and the Game Conservancy Association, a private charity that began life in 1931, in response to the concerns of game-shooters over the decline of quarry species. This has had an effect on wildlife

324 Thus the RSPB finds itself in conflict today with another private association, the Countryside Alliance, which represents sporting interests, the RSPB seeking to protect birds of prey like the hen harrier, the CA wishing to protect the game birds (notably grouse) on which they feed.

habitats comparable to that of the Anglers' Conservation Association on the waterways.

Concern for the habitats of other species was matched by a concern for the habitat of human beings. Robert Owen, appalled by the squalor of the industrial slums, took the initiative by founding the Scottish industrial village of New Lanark in 1800 – now a World Heritage Site – which was followed forty years later by Saltaire, designed and founded by Titus Salt. These new communities showed how industrial and residential architecture could stand side by side, how beauty could be combined with productivity, and how the new economic realities could be integrated into the rural environment. Augustus Pugin and John Ruskin, equally appalled at the destruction of London and the neglect of our architectural heritage, campaigned not only for the preservation of old buildings, but also for the development of a new style suited to the industrial age, which would be continuous with the medieval idioms that were being swept away. Thus was born the Gothic revival, which coexisted with the Classical revival for a century or more, enabling the English to design and build the new towns required by the industrial process as genuine habitats for their residents, places to which ordinary people could relate as their home.

Thanks to Wordsworth, Coleridge and the *Lyrical Ballads*, the Lake District became a symbol of England, the place that must be conserved if our island is to retain its identity. A proposal by the Kendall and Windermere Railway Company to build a railway around Lake Windermere was put forward in the 1840s: the successful campaign to oppose it was led by Wordsworth himself. Subsequent plans to build a railway across the district, so as to join Scotland to England along the West Coast, led to Ruskin's influential pamphlet attacking the idea as sacrilege, a surrendering of the slow life in which man is at home in the world, to the new gods of steam and locomotion.[325] Ruskin was not alone in this attitude. Indeed, many of the British literati had taken a stand against railways, on behalf of the old life that they seemed to threaten. Matthew Arnold and Thomas Carlyle had written contemptuously of the new cult of steam, and 'little platoons' and civic initiatives like the Guild of St George (founded by Ruskin in 1870) grew up in time to endorse their efforts. But the Lakeland railway elicited a particular fervour of denunciation from Ruskin, since it seemed like a blow aimed at the heart of England.

The railway was built at last, and stands today as a monument to Victorian engineering and architectural skill. Its architecture is influenced through and through by the Gothic that Ruskin had championed, and its viaducts and stations are widely admired for their beauty and for the way in which they slot into the landscape. But why did the railway company pay such attention to detail, and work so hard to respect the landscape through which its trains were to pass? The answer is surely obvious: it too was constrained by oikophilia; it saw the Lakelands as Ruskin saw them, part of a

325 Ruskin, *op. cit.*

shared home, and its own work as an improvement to that home. Today we look on the railway as an environmentally friendly form of transport, and one that leaves habitats and farmlands largely undisturbed. Its presence in the landscape, now that we are used to it, does not violate, but on the contrary intensifies, our attachment. Indeed, one of the most famous invocations of rural tranquillity in English poetry – Edward Thomas's 'Adlestrop' – describes a country railway station, viewed from a train.

The work of conservation did not bypass Parliament, but was nurtured outside it, and arose from the ordinary public spirit of ordinary citizens. It received some endorsement from people who considered themselves left of centre, like William Morris, the Pre-Raphaelite Brotherhood, Richard Jefferies and (later) Hugh Massingham. But it was nothing like the kind of mass movement for which socialists were hoping, and indeed, in so far as left-wing movements existed at the time, they were dedicated to the cause of revolutionary transformation, often associated with large-scale futuristic schemes like those of the Socialist Internationals.

The conservationist spirit in England ran through all the institutions of civil society, and showed itself in a hundred local initiatives. The work of the local Naturalists' Trusts in preserving habitats and woodlands has been partly documented by Oliver Rackham, in a striking book that shows the way in which the homeostasis of the English countryside was maintained through 200 years of economic and social transformation, by initiatives that owed everything to people and little or nothing to the state.[326]

These initiatives culminated in 1895 with the foundation of the National Trust by three Victorian philanthropists, Miss Octavia Hill (a long-standing environmental campaigner and disciple of Ruskin), Sir Robert Hunter and Canon Hardwicke Rawnsley. They established the Trust as a 'guardian of the nation', in order to acquire and protect coastline and countryside that was under threat from uncontrolled development and industrialization. The National Trust was not then and has not been since a government organization, and to call it an NGO is to misrepresent its moral character. It is a civil association, granting privileges to its members, of whom there are now 2 million, and devoted to setting an example of stewardship to the nation as a whole. Its members are not mobilized behind a campaign, but settled around a common interest, and they refresh that interest by visiting the places that the Trust maintains. No longer a little platoon, it is nevertheless a civil institution, an expression of the *Heimatgefühl* of a people and a place.

In the famous 'people's budget' of 1909, Lloyd George, then chancellor of the exchequer, introduced substantial death duties. Many landed families – providers of the vulnerable officer class in the First World War – were repeatedly taxed on their whole estate on the death in battle of their head. By the end of the war many of the settled estates that had survived into the twentieth century were in a state of bankruptcy. Death taxes are controversial,

326 Rackham, *op. cit.*

with many economists arguing that they have a negative effect on savings and small businesses, while favouring ownership by corporations over ownership by individuals, so contributing to the 'corporatization' of modern societies.[327] Without taking sides in this controversy, it is reasonable to suggest that Lloyd George's policy squandered one of the most important stores of social and cultural capital that had been invested in the environment. Nevertheless, civic initiatives stepped in to save what could be saved. The National Trust, which had already preserved the coastline from destruction, now set about preserving the country estates. To the Trust and its members the estate was a symbol of settlement. Notwithstanding its aristocratic associations, the country estate had inspired the British people over centuries with the thought of their landscape as a stable resource, in which the tranquillity of nature and the tranquillity of good government are synthesized and put side by side on display. Thus was institution-alized a sentiment that had been dominant in British public life for two centuries: the sentiment of the land as a 'manscape', simulta-neously nature and civilization, commons and enclosure, a place of freedom and a symbol of law.

The National Trust's initiative is one reason why the country-side of England still exists, but it is not the only reason. In 1915 the Women's Institute was founded, with the aim of revitalizing rural communities and encouraging women to become involved

327 See Antony Davies and Pavel Yakolev, 'Myths and Realities Surrounding the Estate Tax', on the American Family Business Association website.

in producing food during the war. It was followed in 1929 by the Youth Hostel Association, established in order to encourage young people to walk and cycle in the countryside, and to acquire a commitment to conserving it. The National Council of Ramblers' Federations followed in 1931 – though with a more political agenda, which was to draw attention to, and to challenge, the exclusionary rights still exerted over parts of the land by its aristocratic owners.

The proliferation of initiatives to conserve the rural environment was matched by similar initiatives to conserve the historic centres of towns. Agitation on behalf of old buildings was well under way by the time of Pugin's influential record of the damage to medieval London in *Contrasts*, self-published in 1836. In 1849 Ruskin issued his great classic, *The Seven Lamps of Architecture*, in which he wrote that 'it is no question of expediency of feeling whether we should preserve the buildings of past times or not. We have no right whatever to touch them. They are not our own. They belong partly to those who built them, and partly to all generations of mankind who are to follow us'. Naturally Ruskin's Burkean advocacy of the inherited townscape would have sounded less plausible if the buildings in question had been those inherited today by the residents of the Moscow suburbs. Still, the point was taken. The Society for the Protection of Ancient Buildings was founded by William Morris and Philip Webb in 1877, inspiring people around the country to resist the demolition of organic townscapes, and to restore the churches and public buildings that had fallen into disrepair. In 1882 Sir John Lubbock obtained an Act of Parliament for the Protection of Ancient Monuments, which led to the founding of the Royal Commission for Historical Monuments in 1908.

Meanwhile, partly as a result of influences spreading from post-revolutionary France, town planning had become a major issue of public concern. In 1899 Sir Ebenezer Howard formed the Garden City Association, in order to advocate a new kind of conurbation, free from the overcrowding and pollution of the Victorian slum, and reviving an idea that had been first entertained by John Evelyn in 1661.[328] This institution was eventually to become the Town and Country Planning Association in 1941, joining forces with other civic associations to press for planning laws that would constrain development in both town and country. Today it is one of the most important campaigners for 'eco-towns' and sustainable development. The Campaign for the Preservation (subsequently Protection) of Rural England (CPRE) was launched in 1925, and now has branches all over the country, doing what they can in the cause of the 'beauty, tranquillity and diversity of the countryside'.

The efforts of the CPRE were boosted by the historian G. M. Trevelyan, whose book *Must England's Beauty Perish?*, published in 1926, awoke the reading public to the threats posed by urban sprawl and the growing network of roads. Trevelyan's warning was amplified in 1928, when the architect Clough Williams-Ellis,

328 See Keith Thomas, *op. cit.*, p. 206.

founder of the model town of Port Merion in Wales, published *England and the Octopus*, describing the danger for both town and country of ribbon development – sprawl along the roads between conurbations. Williams-Ellis's concerns, like Trevelyan's, were primarily aesthetic, but the book provides an eloquent illustration of the role of aesthetic values in environmental protection. Sustainable farming, wildlife habitats and energy conservation are all threatened by ribbon development, and Williams-Ellis's initiative was one of the most fruitful of all the pre-war attempts to conserve the many managed environments of England. In 1938, when the situation was worsening, he gathered together some of the most eminent authors of the day, including E. M. Forster, A. G. Street, G. M. Trevelyan and H. J. Massingham, to produce *Britain and the Beast*, a book that profoundly influenced government thinking, and which was eventually to lead to the Town and Country Planning Act of 1946, establishing Green Belts, forbidding ribbon development and laying down nationwide constraints on building in rural areas. Comparing England as it is today with Holland or Belgium gives a pronounced sense of the ecological benefits that have flowed from the 1946 Act. And it is hardly surprising if its provisions have been eroded by a government hostile both to the so-called 'nimbyism' of the middle class and to a landscape that bears the imprint of the privileged people who have had the time and the foresight to maintain it.

When my father saw the damage that was being inflicted on his town and its surroundings by outside developers and motorway-mad politicians he formed the High Wycombe Society, with the aim of saving what he could of his home. Within a year the Society had 500 members, regular meetings and a programme of action that was successfully pursued through a petition to Parliament. He did not save everything; but he saved enough to ensure that High Wycombe is still home to those who live there, with the Society actively continuing its work in protecting both the town and the surrounding countryside. Likewise when Robin Page, the television presenter and old-fashioned farmer, decided to protect what he could of his village near Cambridge, he founded the Countryside Restoration Trust, devoted to bio-diverse and wildlife-friendly farming practices, and serving as a model for farmers across the country. The Countryside Restoration Trust has continued to acquire land, and is now one of the most important symbols of what can be done by ordinary citizens, regardless of government policy.

The reaction against top-down planning and modernist urban-ization recently took heart from an important private initiative – that of the Prince of Wales at Poundbury, a new town built on land belonging to the Duchy of Cornwall. Until this initiative the new towns that sprang up after the war had been built by edict from central government, with massive compulsory purchases, and plans imposed from above by specially constituted develop-ment corporations. The architectural modernists – who think of people as numbers and so are favoured by bureaucrats who think in the same way – were invariably entrusted with the task of providing boxes for the proles, and the town centres were construed as bleak promenades among the glass and concrete cliffs, where the luxuries of the consumer culture could be put on display. The paradigm was Milton Keynes, begun in 1967, and influenced by the centrifugal concept of the city developed in California by Melvin M. Webber. The resulting sprawl houses a population only two-thirds the size of Florence (a city you can walk across) spread over eighty-eight square miles of aesthetic pollution, absorbing and extinguishing villages, towns and farms in a tangle of throughways and roundabouts, with the population trapped in little globules between the streams of fast-flowing cars. Dependent in every particular on fossil fuels and with a centre that is recognizable as a centre only from its supererogatory ugliness, the 'city' is an ecological disaster of the first order, and a monument to state planning. Poundbury, by contrast, is small, compact, with a centripetal plan that leaves each landowner free to build within aesthetic side-constraints. There is no zoning, and residential accommodation stands side by side with businesses and warehouses, just as it does in Florence. Immensely popular with its residents and also with tourists, Poundbury has been attacked with every weapon to hand by the architectural establishment, since it is a living proof that the monumental and high-paying schemes from which modern achitects live in such splendour are neither wanted nor required. Compare Poundbury and Milton Keynes and you see vividly how civil initiatives motivated by oiko-philia differ from state projects in the grip of powerful lobbies.

During the twentieth century roads came to occupy the place in conservationists' thinking that had been occupied in the nineteenth century by the railways. Now the fight was to save the railway services, many of which had been condemned by two short-sighted reports of 1963 and 1965. These had been prepared by Richard Beeching, then chairman of the nationalized company through which the state exercised its monopoly control over the railways. The fight to save the branch lines went hand in hand with another, which was to prevent the building of motorways, or at any rate to ensure that they did not destroy valuable habitats and beautiful countryside. Neither fight succeeded; both the Conservative government that commissioned Beeching's reports, and the Labour government that acted on them, were too heavily in league with the road-building lobbies to listen to any other interests. But the fights again illustrate the nature of environmental contests in England: on one side the 'little platoons' and civic associations; on the other side government planning, compulsory purchase and ministerial decisions taken without consultation, and often under heavy pressure from big business (Conservative) or big trades unions (Labour).

In almost all the controversies in which the environment of England has been at stake, homes and habitats have been as much threatened by the top-down plans of government as by the megalithic ambitions of the developers, while the work of conservation has been initiated by civil associations, which have enjoyed the endorsement of government only *after* they have changed public perception. To say this is not to take sides against the government. It is the duty of government to cater for and if possible to reconcile competing interests, of which a loved environment is only one. Nevertheless, it is to offer confirmation of the thesis of this book, which is that environmental protection comes from the oikophilia of people, and not from those who use money, influence and political power to impose large-scale projects from on high.

The efforts of civil associations are sometimes dismissed as the work of middle-class 'nimbys' and hobby farmers, and we need to bear that sceptical attitude in mind. It resonates in many people today and there is a truth contained in it. It is part of living properly that one should love one's surroundings; and it is part of love to resist unprecedented change. But we cannot base our policy towards the past on mere resistance. We need a philosophy of conservation, one that will make the distinction between policies that conserve the life of a nation, and those that merely pickle what is dead. After all, no conservation makes sense if it is directed *only* to the past. It is for the sake of future generations that we do these things. Such is Burke's message, and it is the message of this book. But the history of conservation in England suggests that this philosophy will not be shaped by government or government agencies. It will arise as all other successful environmental movements have arisen, through free association of the citizens, working to restore the homeostatic systems that are destroyed or disturbed by the wrong kind of government.

That this is so is suggested by recent history. Early in the Second World War the Luftwaffe took aerial photographs of the entire island, in preparation for invasion. As Oliver Rackham has shown, the fields, hedgerows, woods and copses captured on these photographs correspond to those marked on the oldest maps in our possession.[329] Despite enclosures, transfers and changes in agricultural practices, the countryside of England remained largely unchanged right up to the start of the war, threatened by roads, motor transport and ribbon development, but retaining its traditional form as a habitat in which hedges and copses provided cover for native species, and in which woods and fields were harvested in sustainable ways. Although urban development proceeded during the nineteenth and twentieth centuries at an ever-increasing rate, it is generally agreed that the destruction of nature did not begin in earnest until the arrival of modern agriculture, and the state's determination to impose it by a regime of subsidies and zero-tolerance controls.

The post-war transformation has been surveyed and deplored by many authors, of every political persuasion. To mention only the most prominent among them: W. G. Hoskins, *The Making of the English Landscape*, 1955; Richard Mabey, *The Common Ground: The Place for Nature in Britain's Future*, 1980; Marion Shoard, *The Theft of the Countryside*, 1980; Sir Richard Body, *Agriculture: The Triumph and the Shame*, 1982; Graham Harvey, *The Killing of the Countryside*, 1998. Those authors all forcefully present the case

329 Rackham, *op. cit.*

that modern agriculture has been far more destructive of the land and its history – of habitats, biodiversity, archaeology and native species – than urban development. But it should not go unmentioned that the destruction of urban fabric in the immediate post-war period was just as great as the destruction of landscape. These were the glory days of oikophobia – of government-sponsored sneering at a repudiated past. City councils and central government connived with the developers to desecrate our ancient cities, and to place the working class on Bauhaus perches above the ruins. Coventry, one of the greatest medieval cities in Europe, lost 30 per cent of its timber-frame houses as a result of bombing; the city council got rid of the rest; and the example is by no means untypical.[330] Unfortunately, although the Town and Country Planning Act of 1946 put a stop to urban sprawl, it could not save the cities themselves, many of which were in the hands of corrupt councillors and vengeful oikophobes.

The destruction of agriculture had begun in the wake of the First World War, with the introduction of large-scale mechanized farming and the purchase of the bankrupt holdings by absentee investors. These changes had met even then with strong reactions – leading to the movement for 'bio-dynamic' farming initiated in the twenties by Rudolf Steiner. But the destruction accelerated after the Second World War, when the government subsidized

330 Oliver Marriott, *Property Boom*, New York, 1989. See Simon Jenkins, 'Urban Landscape', in Jennifer Jenkins, *op. cit.*, pp. 110–11, in which he documents the effect of socialist-style planning at the local level, and the massive revenge taken on our historic settlements.

practices judged to produce a more efficient agriculture, which would make the best use of the land as a food factory. The aim was to ensure that the country would never again suffer the privations inflicted by the war; the result has been that the country now imports 50 per cent of its food requirements, and could not possibly survive a blockade.

Subsidies did not merely direct farmers to plant crops without regard for proven ways of soil management; they also rewarded farmers for uprooting hedgerows and coverts and in general for turning the farm from a shared habitat to an industrial precinct. Moreover, they increased the value of the land, so that the rents paid by the small farmer ceased to be affordable and the large agribusinesses were given an incentive to take over. The British countryside began to be managed by absentees – people whose oikophilia, however genuine, could not be relied upon to protect an environment in which they did not live. Hand in hand with the regime of subsidies came the new species of 'scientific' food production, using artificial fertilizers and pesticides. The catastrophic decline in the insect and bird population that immediately ensued – made famous by Rachel Carson in the book (*Silent Spring*, 1962) that launched the environmental movement as we know it today – was only one consequence of a style of agriculture that broke the long-standing connection between farming the fields and dwelling in them.

The provisions of the Agriculture Act 1947 removed self-correcting devices from the path of what was then seen as 'progress', by ensuring that those who profited would not encounter the adverse effects of their pillaging. They would be absentee agribusinesses, which would neither see the damage nor be uprooted by it. Interestingly enough, however, civil associations expanded to meet the emergency and to restore homeostasis. The most famous of them – the Soil Association, founded by Lady Eve Balfour and others in 1946 – was viewed by many people at the time as a society of nostalgic cranks. It now occupies a position as adviser to governments, in their efforts to undo the damage inflicted by their predecessors, and has the right (conferred by national and European law) to authorize organic producers. The example offers vivid proof of the rival merits of civil associations and top-down edicts in securing environmental goals.

Post-war governments have treated farming as a vast experiment in land management, with laws prohibiting one thing, and subsidies offered to another, in order to produce outcomes that nobody could predict or guarantee. Equally damaging has been the Common Agricultural Policy (CAP) of the European Union, which purportedly absorbs a budget of €50 billion a year, in order to achieve goals that seem to recede further, the more money that is spent on them. The CAP was initially defended as a scheme with two purposes: to make Europe self-sufficient in food, and to support the small farmer, whose status as a symbol of European peace, stability and beneficence had been the constant theme of wartime propaganda. Self-sufficiency was achieved, largely on account of worldwide (though in all probability unsustainable) changes in the methods of farming; but the first victim of this was the small farmer, who has been more disadvantaged than helped by the CAP.

As I remarked above, farm subsidies push up the price, and therefore the rental value, of land, so penalizing the small producer who rents his fields, while favouring large landowners and absentee agribusiness. Hence, while the EU makes payments to over 100,000 different farms and agribusinesses, the top one hundred recipients receive over 23 per cent of the total, while the bottom 50 per cent take only 2.6 per cent – which means that the policy has served to marginalize small farmers and is rapidly leading to their extinction. Furthermore, the CAP has maintained food prices at an artificially high level throughout Europe, costing the average family an extra €1,500 a year. It has also produced surpluses which it has dumped on international markets, further alienating food-producing countries elsewhere; and it has destroyed local food economies across the Continent by imposing finicky standards that only the supermarket chains and the agribusinesses can easily comply with – for example, the requirements for animal slaughter, for packaging, and for storage of fruit and vegetables that cannot be complied with by the small farmers of Poland, Romania or Hungary, and which are therefore destroying what have hitherto been environmentally friendly peasant lifestyles, conserved against the odds in the shadow of the massively damaging collective farms.

Interestingly the policy of regulating farming through subsidizing production has been followed all over the world, even though the environmental costs are now apparent to everyone: the loss of small farms and local food economies, the creation of surpluses, dumping and waste, soil erosion and depletion, the destruction of habitats and wildlife corridors, the decline in biodiversity – in short the scraping away of the earth's living surface, and its replacement by a chemical veneer.[331] In addition to the explicit subsidies that favour the big producer and the regulations that only big producers can afford, there are the hidden subsidies offered to the centralized distributors in terms of free roads, planning exemptions and packaging requirements. The result is the terminal decline of the local food economy, and of the arts of stewardship that it promotes.

This decline has been so well documented by Mabey, Shoard, Harvey and others that it is not necessary to review it here. Briefly, an environment that had remained in homeostatic equilibrium over the two centuries of population growth and industrial expansion was all but destroyed in fifty years of well-meaning comprehensive plans. Nor is the example of England unique. A similar catastrophe has been documented in America by Wendell Berry and others.[332] In a striking article drawing on a technical report of Charles Ricq, Tony Curzon Price has compared the

---

331 Jules Pretty *et al.*, 'Farm Costs and Food Miles', *Food Policy*, 30.1, February 2005, pp. 1–19.

332 Berry, *The Unsettling of America*.

effect on the Alpine landscape of two distinct forms of management in two adjacent valleys — that of French top-down administration and that of Swiss participatory democracy, in which the people are involved at every stage in planning their environment.[333] Curzon Price shows in detail how the tragedy of the commons is enacted under the regime that operates in France, while it is avoided for the most part in Switzerland, as people come to agree among themselves on solutions that would benefit them all.

In effect, beauty is treated by the Swiss community as a commons, and administered under a regime close to those studied by Elinor Ostrom. Beauty is treated in France as a resource to be pillaged by those who can get their hands on it, and who can secure the protection of the political structures. While the Swiss valley is still beautiful and popular with tourists, the French valley is a rapidly decaying eyesore. The positive environmental effect of local initiatives and neighbourhood coalitions in Denmark is the subject of a similar study by the late Paul Hirst.[334] The remarkable story of the Quincy Library Group, as told by Mark Sagoff, shows how an environmental problem made intractable by lobbying for top-down policies was solved by a civic initiative leading to a consensual solution.[335]

333 Tony Curzon Price, 'How Beauty Can Survive', in Barnett and Scruton, eds., *op. cit.*

334 Paul Hirst, 'Can Rutland learn from Jutland?', in Barnett and Scruton, eds., *op. cit.*

335 Sagoff, *op. cit.*, ch. 9.

Sagoff's example should be seen as one episode in another long story of oikophilia, and one that is rather different from the story of England. Nobody witnessing what Jefferson built at Monticello would doubt that the third president of the United States was an oikophile, and one who left a permanent mark on the landscape of Virginia. However, the Jeffersonian landscape is a European import, and far from what has been most distinctive of the American love of nature. From the expedition of Lewis and Clark in 1805 to the founding of the National Trails system in 1968, nature has been associated in American feelings with the frontier experience – the experience of standing at a threshold, civilization behind you, the wilderness before. 'In wildness is the preservation of the world' wrote Thoreau, and although *Walden* describes a domesticated place, the writer sees it as a place that dwarfs his humanity, returning him to his proper and subordinate place in the scheme of things. That is the sentiment taken up by John Muir in his religious panegyric to the Yosemite Valley, and which led to the foundation of the Yellowstone National Park in 1872, the National Park Service in 1916 and the Wilderness Society in 1935.

This sentiment is readily explained when we remember that the American landscape was being taken over by the settlers from hunter-gatherers and subsistence croppers just when the new industrial methods of production were growing in the towns, and spreading along the railroads to the remotest frontiers of the country. There were few settlements, and those that existed were not under threat from the communications on which they depended – on the contrary, the goods and knowledge that came to them along the railroad amplified the oikophilia of their residents and overcame their sense of isolation. The thing most under threat was the 'wilderness', that partly mythical residue of the interaction between tribal man and hunted animal, into which the white man had come uninvited. This wilderness was lovingly described by James Fenimore Cooper in *The Last of the Mohicans*, and lovingly painted by the artists of the Hudson River School. It was invoked by Muir, Emerson and Thoreau as a sacred background to the American adventure, and their sentiments were absorbed by educated Americans during the latter half of the nineteenth century in the same way that Ruskin's very different sentiments about the Lakelands and the cities of old Europe were absorbed by their British contemporaries.

The Sierra Club was founded by John Muir and others in 1892, and at first had a role comparable to that of the English National Trust, founded three years later. Today the Sierra Club has 1.3 million members. Unlike the National Trust, however, which has remained a civil association without campaigning goals, the Sierra Club has become an active campaigning NGO, devoting itself to the defence of wild places and threatened landscapes. The pastoral valleys and ancestral homes kept up in England by the National Trust for the benefit of its members have their likenesses in America, and especially in Jefferson's Virginia; but for the most part they find private protectors and are seldom the subject matter of campaigns. Rather than attend to those small-scale ecospheres, the Sierra Club identifies with the large environmental 'causes'. The Club was the publisher of Paul Ehrlich's book, *The Population Bomb* (1969), which initiated one of the panics that I described in Chapter 2, and today is in the forefront of the battles over logging, ranching and urban sprawl. But it has a more pacific aspect too, as educator of the American public. The great photographer Ansel Adams, whose images of the American landscape have been every bit as influential as those of the Hudson River painters, served for thirty-five years on its board, and through his work, and the work of those associated with him, the Club has played a major part in familiarizing ordinary Americans with the astonishing treasures of landscape and wildlife to which they are heirs.

Given the difference in history and geography we should not be surprised that American environmentalists rarely share the English predilection for country houses and garden-like farms, and devote themselves instead to the wilderness.[336] Crucial in defining the issues was George Perkins Marsh, whose *Man and Nature*, published in 1864, spoke out for the forests against the loggers. Marsh was active in promoting the movement for national parks. He was also a highly learned man, whose book *The Earth, as Modified by Human Action* (1874, revised ed.

---

336 See, for example, David Brower, *Wilderness: America's Living Heritage*, San Francisco, 1961. On the contrast with the English case see Richard D. North, *op. cit.*, p. 217.

1885) made a strong case for government intervention to protect the environment from the predators and to ensure the renewal of natural resources. Since then the issue of logging and deforestation has been a major preoccupation of American environmentalists, with campaigning groups making extensive use of the Endangered Species Act to protect areas of forest that provide unique forms of habitat.

As in England, however, the US environmental movement has been led by civil society, with the state stepping in only later, in response to demands that had been shaped by groups of volunteers. The Environmental Protection Agency was established only in 1970, and although its regulatory regime has provided guarantees against the worst forms of pollution it has done as much to confiscate as to support the oikophilia of ordinary Americans, by issuing regulations that leave little or no room for compromises.[337] Some of the civic initiatives have had a decidedly political bent, and in the seventies, Earth First!, the brainchild of the mountaineer David Foreman, declared war on the established order, and set out to remove the loggers and the cattle-ranchers from the land that they were allegedly despoiling. Foreman was strongly influenced by Edward Abbey's novel *The Monkey Wrench Gang*, in which Abbey exalted violent resistance on behalf of trees and wilderness. In 1985 Foreman published *Ecodefense: A Field Guide to Monkeywrenching*, containing advice of a dubious and barely legal kind for those who wished to make trouble for loggers

337 See the argument of Chapter 4.

and ranchers. Earth First! was also one of several environmental organizations that fed upon the beatnik and counter-cultural sentiments that flourished in America in the wake of the sixties. Such activist movements should not mislead us, however. They are the exception and not the rule. For the most part environmental protection in America has been the work of peaceable middle-class volunteers, animated by romantic 'wilderness' sentiments, but working tirelessly to clean and conserve, to plant and maintain, and to open the landscape to sensitive wanderers in search of their souls. The Wilderness Society was founded in 1935 and today has 350,000 members, devoted to visiting and protecting the unspoiled hinterlands and to defending wildlife from the adverse effects of civilization. Among the founders of the Society were Aldo Leopold, whose writings in defence of 'ecocentrism' inspired a whole generation of environmentalists after the Second World War, and Benton MacKaye, originator of the Appalachian Trail in 1921, and the first dedicated campaigner against urban sprawl.

This wilderness-obsessed approach to conservation is, on the surface, contradictory. As Bernard Williams once put it, 'a natural park is not nature, but a park; a wilderness that is preserved is a definite, delimited, wilderness. The paradox is that we have to use our power to preserve a sense of what is not in our power.'[338]

338 Bernard Williams, 'Must a Concern for the Environment be Centred on Human Beings?', in Bernard Williams, *Making Sense of Humanity*, Cambridge, 1995, p. 68.

Maybe we can live with that paradox, just as a man may live with the image of the innocent and unspoiled girl he married, and treat his wife all the better because he sees her through a veil of his own devising. However, there are real downsides to the wilderness obsession, other than its epistemological frailty. The old disease of favouritism can give rise to ecological imbalance – as in the case of the northern spotted owl, protected under the Endangered Species Act, whose occasional presence has made it impossible to carry out logging operations in large tracts of the Pacific Northwest, so preventing harvesting and replanting. The financial cost of this is enormous: the ecological cost hardly less so.[339] Likewise the National Park Service suffers from all the negative effects of top-down control, and complaints are repeatedly made that the Yellowstone National Park, for example, is no longer a wilderness, but a man-made landscape, deprived of necessary predators such as wolves, one species of which, the grey wolf, has been driven to extinction, with woodlands protected from natural fires and therefore unable to regenerate, and with invasive species moving into every feebly defended ecological niche.[340] On the other hand, it is one consequence of the volunteer-led approach to public assets in America that these complaints, once made, become the subject matter of some new civil initiative. Hence, in addition to the federal programme, there is now a private

339 See Richard D. North, *op. cit.*, p. 219.
340 See Alston Chase, *Playing God in Yellowstone: The Destruction of America's First National Park*, New York, 1986.

Yellowstone Park Foundation introducing new measures to conserve the Park's fragile ecosystem.

A more important downside to the wilderness obsession is the comparative neglect of the human habitat. The environment is seen not as the place where we are, and where we settle, but as the *other* place – the untamed place where we go, like Thoreau, in search of our soul. For wilderness lovers the true *oikos* is a place of solitude where they commune with a non-human nature. This is the sentiment invoked by Leopold and affirmed in the comfort of the suburbs by the National Geographic culture that governs the coffee table and the video screen. Yet real oikophilia, like charity, begins at home, and it is precisely in this respect that American environmentalism has been deficient. Urban sprawl is only part of the problem; far more serious, as I suggested, is the collapse of the inner city, under the impact of zoning laws, inhuman building styles and ghettoization.

Again, however, we should recognize that the problem is no sooner brought into prominence than the civic initiatives begin that promise to mitigate it. In reaction to the wilderness culture there has arisen an agrarian culture represented by writers like Wendell Berry and Allen Carlson, and by associations like the National Family Farm Coalition and the Food Family Farming Foundation.[341] In reaction to the devastation of the cities there has

341 Berry, *The Gift of Good Land, op. cit.*; Allen Carlson, *The New Agrarian Mind: The Movement Towards Decentralist Thought in Twentieth Century America*, New Brunswick, 2000.

arisen the New Urbanism movement I discussed earlier, itself anticipated by the seminal Country Club House development of J. C. Nichols in Kansas City. In 1912, shortly after the skyscraper idiom had established itself, Nichols gave a pivotal speech to the National Association of Realtors, of which he was president, advocating low-rise buildings with connected façades, walkable streets, classical details, mouldings, cornices and decorated skylines. He rightly described this as 'planning for permanence', anticipating that ordinary people would not want to demolish the result (though he reckoned without his fellow realtors). Nichols's small-scale but enduring influence is one that depended neither on government support nor legal authority, but on his position as an upstanding member of a more or less unregulated business.[342] Small-scale civil initiatives continue to evolve in response to local problems – some of them described by William Shutkin in a book devoted to the cause of 'civic environmentalism'.[343] A brief search of the internet delivered the details of eighty-four American non-profit institutions organized nationally for the study, protection and enjoyment of the environment – compared with thirty in Britain, three in France, one (under government control) in Germany and none in Russia. Of course a quick internet search

342 See William S. Worley, *J. C. Nichols and the Shaping of Kansas City*, Columbia, 1990. Nichols's ideal was celebrated in the popular 1946 novel by Eric Hodgins, *Mr Blandings Builds His Dream House*, the basis of a movie starring Cary Grant and Myrna Loy.

343 William A. Shutkin, *The Land That Could Be: Environmentalism and Democracy in the Twenty-First Century*, Cambridge, MA, 2001.

is no definitive guide to the reality: but it confirms what all impartial observers know to be true of America, which is that the 'little platoons' still flourish, and tackle the problems that are often amplified by governments and in any case seldom sensitively solved by them.

But for how long? My argument inevitably abuts against that question, which goes to the heart of environmental politics not only in America but also in those less fortunate places where the volunteer culture has either failed to arise or been destroyed by political oppression. In a much-admired book the sociologist Robert Putnam – taking up the observations first put before us by Burke and Tocqueville – argues that the social capital on which we draw for the solution of our collective problems is built up through the autonomous associations of civil society.[344] He expressly excludes the politicized campaigning groups, which (he plausibly suggests) are as likely to waste social capital as to enhance it. The associations he has in mind are the 'little platoons': clubs, societies, sports leagues, churches, reading circles, pubs – places and groups that bring people together for no other purpose than themselves. Documenting organizations like the Red Cross, Lions, Elks, League of Women Voters, Boy Scouts and bowling leagues, Putnam finds that, despite steady increases throughout the twentieth century, all such 'secondary associations' have recently experienced sudden and substantial declines

344 Robert Putnam, *Bowling Alone: The Collapse and Revival of American Community*, New York, 2000.

in membership. He suggests various causes – such as women entering the workforce, home entertainment, social and geographical mobility – but whatever the causes it is certain that oikophilia is likely to be the first victim of those institutions' decline.

The value of 'little platoons' is perhaps never better appreciated than when visiting a place where they have been crushed. One such place is Romania – a country that has enjoyed only fitfully the experience of nationhood, which has been combined and disjoined according to the whims of foreign powers, and which suffered under the Communist Party for four decades, pillaged by the ruling elite, and brutalized at last by the megalomaniac Nicolae Ceauşescu. As in other communist countries, civil associations and private charities were forbidden in communist Romania. The country's environment was subject to ruthless assault from collectivization, forced industrialization, and finally Ceauşescu's radical oikophobic plan to raze the villages to the ground and tear out the heart of Bucharest.

The destruction of Bucharest was begun but never completed, since Ceauşescu was toppled by the Securitate, and a kind of democracy was built on the ruins. What is interesting to the visitor today, however, is that the ecological catastrophe continues. Rubbish is not collected but thrown into rivers or piled up by the roads. Multinationals, exploiting the legal vacuum, have covered the buildings of Bucharest with animated digital advertisements that fidget and flicker through day and night, entirely

destroying the city's character as a human habitat. The old factories lie abandoned on poisoned land, and new factories, roads and
infrastructure are being dumped in the countryside with only
perfunctory environmental controls and without regard for
aesthetic values. Resistance to this is slight or non-existent, since
the habit of civic initiative and the identification of the land as
home have been eradicated by the brutalities of recent history.
True, there are one or two private initiatives that are doing
what they can to protect and restore the rural economy. But the
principal such initiative, and the one that took the lead even before
the collapse of communism, is the Mihai Eminescu Trust,
founded and led by an English woman (Jessica Douglas-Home),
and largely financed by the Packard Foundation in America.

Visiting this sparsely populated country, with its legacy of
wildlife and low-impact agriculture, and encountering the rivers
and streams clotted with rafts of plastic bottles, the waste piled
up in every field, the vast tracts of poisoned land and the gush-
ing chimneys of the factories, is a sobering proof that, without
civil associations animated by oikophilia, no environment can
really be saved. For all this pollution and disorder is overseen by
the regulative structure of the European Union, which offers no
motive to ordinary Romanians to do anything for their country,
but simply reminds them that the whole problem has been confiscated by bureaucrats from elsewhere. Hence the regulations
are systematically evaded. Those empowered to enforce them –
government officials, local politicians and the like – are easily

bribed, and often have a commercial interest in evading the law.

The case of Romania raises the question – raised also by many other devastated regions of the planet, not least Russia and China – of how oikophilia can be restored in a place where it has been deliberately crushed. This, to my mind, is the most important of all our environmental problems – namely, the extinction in large parts of the world of the only motive that people have for solving them. Without a concerted effort of education and leadership I doubt that a place that has lost the face of home can easily regain it. If there is to be a coherent international politics of the environment, however, it must address this question. What can settled nations, with patriotic citizens and healthy little platoons, do to encourage oikophilia in the places where it is most needed, like the Amazon rainforest, the heartlands of Russia, and the desert kingdoms of Arabia and the Persian Gulf? And if Putnam is right, then the settled nations must also put their own houses in order, by making the space in which the 'little platoons' can once again grow and recruit their membership.

I return to the case of England, so as to consider the impact of internationalism on a locally managed environment in which oikophiles have – on the whole – held their own against the vandals. One instrument that greatly assisted the environmental cause has been the Town and Country Planning Act of 1946. Although it did not enable the oikophiles to save our cities, it proved effective in the defence of the smaller towns and villages, and also in securing the boundary between town and country. The cause of this is that the Act was not designed to control planning decisions from the centre, but rather to place them in the hands of local government. At the same time the Act conferred extensive rights on citizens both to object to schemes that will impact on their amenities, and to participate in the planning process. Recent Labour governments have removed this particular corrective device and invented regional planning bodies that have neither democratic nor traditional legitimacy, while conferring on them the right to control decisions affecting places that their members will never visit.

Of all the many resources that benefit the environment, the most easily acquired and the most easily renewed is oikophilia, but it is renewed only if passed on by education that amplifies the love for place, for community, for tradition and for country. The old school curriculum was shaped with that in mind, and its deliberate destruction by the advocates of multiculturalism (which is oikophobia of a vociferous and self-righteous kind) has been the most significant of all the acts of vandalism that occurred in the late twentieth century. It is not possible to blame the Labour Party for all that happened, but it is certainly possible to blame it for rejoicing in the result.

Oikophobia threatens a national culture from within, but some forms of internationalism also threaten it from without, by striving to impose from an external vantage point decisions that would never be adopted by the local community or its elected representatives. Thus, in addition to the threat posed to the Town and

Country Planning Act by the Labour Party's confiscation of local powers, a new threat has come from the Court of Human Rights in Strasbourg. The case is an interesting one, which illustrates another way in which homeostatic systems are destroyed by external controls.

Whatever the faults of legislative decisions to social conflicts, they have one insuperable advantage over decisions taken in the courts, which is that they can aim at a compromise. The Town and Country Planning Act was an attempt to legislate on the basis of an emerging consensus. The intention was to take many competing interests into consideration and to arrive at a solution broadly acceptable to the nation as a whole. The Act provided a set of rules that achieved the most reliable way of reconciling the conflicts generic to building: in this case the conflict between the one who wishes to develop land, and the neighbor who will thereby suffer a loss of amenity, and a loss in the value of his property. All in all, it is one of the reasons for preferring legislation to adjudication, as a source of law, that a legislature can take the widest possible view of the many interests that need to be addressed and if possible reconciled. Human rights legislation, however, returns conflicts of interest to the courts, and enables judges to override decisions of the legislature on behalf of individual plaintiffs.

The Town and Country Planning Act protected the countryside from abuse through half a century following its introduction. Then, however, Irish travellers (that is to say, people who move from place to place, taking with them a mobile home) began to take advantage of the EU's freedom of movement provisions, so as to settle in the English countryside, buying fields from farmers at agricultural rates, and developing them as sites for mobile homes. The farmer cannot sell these fields for agricultural use, since agriculture is in a state of crisis. Nor can he obtain planning permission for any other use, and specifically for development as houses. So the deal offered by the travellers is the best he can get. Their practice is to scrape away the topsoil and replace it with concrete, then install mobile homes, and gradually change the mobile homes to stationary prefabs. Why, you ask, is this permitted? Well, it is not. However, since the incorporation of the European Convention on Human Rights into UK law, the travellers have argued that they have a right to pursue their traditional way of life, a right on which they can sue in a court of law, and to which they are entitled as an ethnic minority. To deny this right would be tantamount to 'discrimination' as forbidden by the European Convention, and this right entitles them to move freely about the country, settling where they will. Judgements of this kind, with their arbitrary invention of 'group rights' that trample on the individuals who cannot claim them lead one to sympathize with Bentham's original attack on the idea of human rights, as 'nonsense upon stilts'.[345] For Bentham 'human rights', even if introduced by legislation, involve a fatal transfer of power from

345 Jeremy Bentham, 'A Critical Examination of the Declaration of Rights', in *Anarchical Fallacies*, London, 1843.

the legislature to the courts. Rights are interests for which the individual can *sue*, so obtaining a legally binding decision that has not been debated by a legislature and which may be counter to the interests of everybody save the victorious party. Nevertheless, the courts have upheld the argument of the Irish travellers, and therefore granted a right that effectively nullifies one of the most carefully considered and expensive pieces of UK legislation, and one that represents an enormous investment on the part of the whole community.

Thus in the Wiltshire village of Minety the development of farming land as a travellers' camp has led to the collapse of property values all around, causing enormous social tensions between residents in the camp and those whose savings they have wiped out. It has also led to anger among villagers who have had planning permission for this or that comparatively innocent addition refused, and who now refuse to obey the law, causing huge problems of enforcement. So far there have been no murders – which distinguishes the Minety case from a similar case in Cambridgeshire – but there is also no sign that people are or ever will be reconciled to the decision of the court.

The case illustrates four very important matters. The first is that, as Ronald Dworkin puts it, 'rights are trumps'.[346] That is, in a court of law, if you can show that your interest in the matter is also protected as a right, then you win the case against anyone

346 Ronald Dworkin, 'Taking Rights Seriously', in *Taking Rights Seriously*, London, 1977.

whose interests, however great, are not so protected. (Rights provide 'exclusionary reasons', in Raz's plausible way of putting it.)[347] The huge interest of the Minety residents in retaining the value and amenity of their properties (which represent, for most of them, their life's savings) counted for nothing in the case I am considering, since – although protected by planning law – that interest was not protected as a right, but only as an interest.

The second important point is that, unlike the solutions issued by a legislature, those issued by a court are not compromises: they are not attempts to reconcile the many interests involved in a situation, and the court does not see itself as formulating a policy for the good government of a community – that is the task of a legislature, not a court. The court sees itself as resolving a conflict in favour of one or other of the parties. In normal circumstances, a case before a civil court is a zero-sum game, in which one party wins everything, and the other loses everything. There are no consolation prizes. Moreover, the doctrine of precedent ensures that the court's decision will punch a hole in any legislation designed to solve issues of the kind that come before it. The decision could do irreparable damage to a delicate piece of legislation. And it is a very good illustration of the dangers inherent in 'human rights' legislation – namely, that it places in the hands of the ordinary citizen a tool with which even the most vital piece of public policy can be overturned, and overturned in favour of the individual, regardless of the common interest and the common

347 Joseph Raz, *The Authority of Law*, Oxford, 1979.

good. The fulcrum on which our law has been overturned is situ-ated outside the country, in a court dominated by judges who have no real interest in preserving what our ancestors fought to save. Increasingly, in Europe, the idea of human rights is being used in this way to cancel national traditions and undermine managed environments, in the interest of internationalist ideals that are imposed without counting the cost to those who must conform to them.

That returns me, in conclusion, to the subject of climate change, which appeals partly because it seems to internationalize the environmental question. It neutralizes the kind of argument that I have been presenting in this chapter, by presenting a calamity so great that none of our ordinary devices can be adapted to cope with it. In my view this is the most poisonous aspect of the campaign to put global warming at the top of the environmental agenda. For it removes attention from the fact that good stewardship begins at home, and can never be guaranteed by treaty. The only feasible response to the threat of global warming is to devote our resources to discovering how we might produce energy cheaply and renewably, and then making those discoveries available around the world. Local initiatives, under a regime of private property, in which the incentives of the market are amplified by those of oikophilia, will guide research and develop-ment towards our goal – first locally, by way of protecting our home, and then globally, when others make use of our discover-ies. No other solution is, in my view, remotely possible. If there is a role for the state in all this it is in stimulating and funding the much-needed research.

Those who believe that the feeling for home and habitat that I have praised in this chapter is a form of meanness or xenophobia should reflect on the argument of that paragraph. Just as children brought up through attachment become better and more responsible adults than those from broken homes and randomized relationships, so do nations that conduct their affairs in a spirit of stewardship, cherishing their identity as a home, and encouraging the *Heimatgefühl* of their citizens, become better and more responsible members of the international community. It is they who will make the useful discoveries, take the necessary risks, share their advances and – when necessary – submit to international jurisdiction. And it is they who will promote the free discussion of the threats, and of the ways and means to counter them, of which we are now so much in need. The solution to our environmental problems lies here or nowhere: either we turn for home, and learn to care for it, or we drift on the tumultuous sea of causes, agendas and panics, pursuing vast goals with meagre means, and never knowing whether we are fulfilling or frustrating our purpose. That, it seems to me, is why Greens should be conservatives.

ELEVEN

Modest Proposals

A conservative environmental policy does not aim at a healthy environment but at other things, which have a healthy environment as their effect. It is addressed to the oikophilia of the citizen, and its products include all of the following: human resilience, autonomous associations, market solutions, effective tort law, aesthetic side-constraints emerging from open discussions among the citizens, biodiversity, natural beauty, local autonomy, serious research, and a regime of pricing and feedback loops that return environmental costs to those who create them. The aim is to establish the conditions under which people manage their own environment in a spirit of stewardship, and in such a way as to facilitate the political actions that may be necessary to accomplish what the 'little platoons' cannot embark on. What I have written so far concerns the raw material for such a policy and the philosophy behind it. It is no easy matter to translate philosophy into policy, and the suggestions I make in this chapter are only provisional and subject to discussion and refinement. But I am encouraged by the appearance of Zac Goldsmith's *The Constant Economy*, an explicitly Burkean account of policies that address the major environmental needs of our society.[348] Over-optimistic though Goldsmith certainly is, and not a little blind to the oiko-phobia that has gripped our communities, he nevertheless gives a clear and upbeat account of what can be done by you and me to put the earth back into its orbit.

The first principle of any conservative policy must be to prevent the state from undertaking tasks that can be better performed by the citizens. The policy must be one of permitting and freeing private initiatives, enabling and encouraging volun-teers, deferring to local solutions and deregulating whenever regulation is part of the problem. This does not mean laissez-faire, but rather the informed division of labour. There are environmental problems so great that *only* the state can success-fully address them, and it is one aspect of a conservative policy to identify those problems and to leave civil society to look after the rest. I begin by addressing the large problems, and then say some-thing about the small ones.

In 1972 the Club of Rome commissioned a celebrated book, *The Limits to Growth*, which revived the thesis for which the Reverend Thomas Robert Malthus is so well known, namely that human demand constantly rises while resources diminish as they

348 Goldsmith, *op. cit.*, 2009.

are used, so that eventually resources must fail.[349] The book has been profoundly controversial, and its worst predictions have allegedly been refuted.[350] International negotiations today – notably those concerning climate change – do not propose any cessation of growth, but assume that current growth rates are desirable or at least inevitable.[351] It is often pointed out that it is the *absence* of growth that leads to depletion, as people fail to find substitutes for dwindling resources. Growth in the Western countries and Japan, for example, has been accompanied by a per capita fall in energy consumption, and a rise in the efficient use of scarce resources.[352]

The 'limits to growth' thesis nevertheless keeps returning in altered form. In a study published in 1976, Fred Hirsch argued that, as wealth increases and markets expand, intimacy and

349 Donella H. Meadows *et al.*, *The Limits to Growth*, London, 1972; Rev. T. R. Malthus, *Essay on the Principle of Population*, London, 1798.

350 See H. S. D. Cole *et al.*, eds., *op. cit.* See also Matt Ridley, *The Rational Optimist: How Prosperity Evolves*, London, 2010, ch. 4.

351 Thus Kyoto, the Stern Report, etc.

352 See Michael Brower, *Cool Energy: Renewable Solutions to Environmental Problems*, Cambridge, MA, 1992. See also the US Energy Information Administration chart for US energy consumption, expenditures and emissions indicators from 1949 to 2009: www.eia.gov/emeu/aer/txt/ptb0105.html. It shows that per capita energy consumption increased fairly steadily, peaked around 1979, and then started decreasing steadily from there. In 2009 it was back to around the 1968 level. Moreover, energy consumption per real dollar of GDP has decreased steadily from 1949 to 2009 (a total decrease of 58%). The same is true for GHG emissions per real dollar of GDP (although there is only data available for 1990–2008) and carbon dioxide emissions per real dollar of GDP (decreased 65% from 1949 to 2009).

commitment decline; affluence breeds alienation, which in turn sets 'social limits to growth'.[353] In an influential article published in 1986, Peter Vitousek, Paul and Anne Ehrlich and Pamela Matson introduced the idea of the 'net primary production' of terrestrial ecosystems, to suggest that the photosynthetic capacity of the planet sets limits to the production of economic value.[354] The argument overlooks the fact that human beings augment the photosynthetic capacity of the land they occupy, and constantly find new ways of doing so. But, even if it fails, the argument serves to illustrate the variety of the finite resources that sustain us: the proof that we will not run out of one vital thing will never show that we won't run out of another.

The point is often made that GDP – the economist's measure of growth – says nothing about the real wellbeing of a society.[355] An oil spill from a tanker at sea is part of the economy, so is the attempt to clean up the mess: oil spills are a boost to GDP. But they destroy what we value.[356] Growth is good only if it does not fill the sinks. In this sense much of the growth that we have seen since the Second World War has been not a gain but a loss – a vast appropriation from the future of assets that are being used up and not replaced. Hence, although growth, as measured by GDP, will

353 Fred Hirsch, *Social Limits to Growth*, Cambridge, MA, 1976.

354 P. M. Vitousek, *et al.*, 'Human Appropriation of the Products of Photosynthesis', *BioScience*, 36.6, June 1986, pp. 368–73. See the discussion of this article in Sagoff, *op. cit.*, pp. 169–74.

355 See Arthur Brooks, *Gross National Happiness*, New York, 2008.

356 The point is vigorously made in Goldsmith, *op. cit.*

continue, the argument of *The Limits to Growth* seems self-evidently true. Demand grows, activity increases, and the sinks fill up. Then, in the words of William Empson, 'slowly the poison the whole bloodstream fills: It is the waste, the waste remains and kills.'

Malthus was not alone among the great pioneers of social thought in believing that humans will surpass the capacity of the earth to maintain them. John Stuart Mill also recognized the danger, and introduced the idea of a 'steady-state economy' as a response to it.[357] Only if we can achieve a constant rate of consumption, Mill believed, can we ensure a constant supply of goods. Without this 'stationary state' we will be subject to continual emergencies, and our panic-stricken raids upon the stock of natural resources will leave them irreparably depleted. Mill's thought has been developed in our time by Herman Daly, who has argued that true environmental protection requires an economy maintained at 'the lowest feasible flows of matter and energy from the first stage of production to the last stage of consumption'.[358] The cause of Mill and Daly has been taken up by environmentalists, and there is today a Center for the Advancement of the Steady State Economy, a non-profit organization based in Arlington, Virginia. Daly continues to argue that economic life must be seen as occurring *within* the wider ecosystem, and as

357 J. S. Mill, *Principles of Political Economy*, book 4, ch. 6, 'Of the Stationary State', London, 1848.

358 Herman Daly, *Steady-State Economics*, San Francisco, 1977; *Beyond Growth*, Boston, 1996.

subordinate to its broader needs. Pursued as an end in itself, growth is bound to be a threat to the resources on which it feeds.

Not everyone is persuaded by the 'steady state' idea.[359] In 1987 the World Commission on Environment and Development, under the chairmanship of Norwegian prime minister Gro Harlem Bruntland, issued its report entitled *Our Common Future*. This report was a response to the 'limits to growth' debate, and argued that growth is necessary – especially in developing countries – if environmental problems are to be addressed. The report introduced the rival concept of 'sustainable development', which instantly became the rallying cry of another school of environmentalists. Not growth, but development – in other words, the proper use of resources to improve the quality of human life. Not exploitation but sustainability – using resources in a way that leaves 'enough and as good' for future generations.

All sides to the 'limits to growth' controversy accept that economic activity must be exercised in a sustainable way; but there is considerable controversy as to what the word 'sustainable' means. Some radicals have built as much as they can of the old leftist agenda into the new slogan, arguing with David Orr that hedonism, individualism and conspicuous consumption must now be discarded, along with financial and technological complexity, exclusive allegiances, whether ideological or ethnic, and the

359 Ridley, *op. cit.*, p. 249, dismisses it as 'Pareto piffle'. In all its forms it is hard to reconcile the steady-state economy with models of economic growth (such as that developed by Robert Solow) in which the expansion of technological knowledge is seen as the principal growth factor.

ongoing militarization of the planet.[360] Whether or not those causes are good, one can at least anticipate that to wrap them up in the goal of environmental protection is to jeopardize the consensus on which any successful policy will depend. Things are not helped by the proliferation of definitions in the wake of the Bruntland report, with distinctions between 'weak' and 'strong', 'deep' and 'shallow' sustainability that threaten to open again all those internecine quarrels among environmentalists that hold up the business of action.[361] Without entering those controversies I shall simply assume that a process is 'sustainable' if it can go on for the foreseeable future without irreversible harm. I don't know whether a steady-state economy is achievable or desirable, but I can make good guesses as to what is or is not sustainable. For example, it is not sustainable to treat waste and spoliation as cost-free externalities. The first step in any environmental policy, therefore, must be to devise a scheme for pricing pollution and waste, so that consumers and producers have an incentive to avoid or contain them. This lies at the root of the 'Polluter Pays Principle' formulated and recommended by the OECD in 1975.[362]

Development is not sustainable if it relies on unclean energy,

---

360 David W. Orr, 'Four Challenges of Sustainability', *Conservation Biology*, 16.6, 2002, pp. 1457–60. And see Orr's influential book *Earth in Mind: On Education, Environment, and the Human Prospect*, Washington DC, 1993.

361 See the discussion by Daniel Bonevac, 'Is Sustainability Sustainable?', *Academic Questions*, 23.1, March 2010, pp. 84–101.

362 OECD, *The Polluter Pays Principle: Definition, Analysis, Implementation*, Paris, 1975.

and as yet there are no proposals for the worldwide provision of clean energy that have the remotest chance of being adopted. Whatever we think about climate change, it is surely common sense to suggest that clean energy means energy that can be obtained without adding greenhouse gases to the atmosphere. Advocates of nuclear power are right to emphasize its virtues. However, the energy needed to extract uranium imposes an environmental cost that is not always taken into account by its advocates. Besides, anxieties over accidents and terrorist attacks have made nuclear power controversial in a way that militates against its widespread deployment.

Wind power likewise is at best a partial solution, since it can produce only a small fraction of the energy needed. The variable speed of the wind means that energy supplies fluctuate dangerously, so that windmills must always be backed up by some other and generally more polluting source, while surges threaten to overload the grid.[363] Even in Denmark, therefore, which has expanded its wind farms to the maximum possible, only 20 per cent of energy derives from wind. There are other environmental costs too. The arms of the turbines seem to us to move fairly slowly; at the tip, however, they approach the speed of sound. Birds and bats are unable to take avoiding action and are frequently killed. Wind farms require a vast acreage if they are to

363 This problem is discussed, and the solution of 'pumped storage' offered, in MacKay, *op. cit.*, pp. 190–201. The evidence is summarized in Booker and North, *Scared to Death, op. cit.*, pp. 369–72.

produce a significant contribution to the grid, and the tangle of cables and pylons needed to gather their meagre product hugely increases the territorial outlay. On these and other grounds the case against land-based wind farms has been argued to considerable effect by John Etherington and Matt Ridley.[364]

Moreover, unless situated offshore, the aesthetic cost of wind farms counters their marginal ecological benefit. The turbines intrude on the horizon like an army of visiting insects, their sails agitating the skyline, their raw structures negating the contours of the land. Wherever these eerie visitors settle, people are unsettled, and the motive of stewardship receives a damaging blow. There are people who claim to like the look of them. Thus Yes2Wind, a campaigning group that has the support of WWF, Friends of the Earth and Greenpeace, argues on its website that 'while some people express concern about the effect wind turbines have on the beauty of our landscape, others see them as elegant and beautiful'. But one can confidently say that the authors of that statement do not live within sight of a wind farm.

Aesthetic pollution is not a cost that all environmental activists are in the habit of counting. Many of those who advocate these visually intrusive devices rejoice in the blow struck against the nostalgic 'nimbys' who had invested so much in their viewshed. Wind turbines, for many of their advocates, are symbols of progress and the redistribution of resources. They are the

364 John Etherington, *The Wind Farm Scam*, London, 2009. See especially ch. 6 on landscape degradation and wildlife. Ridley, *op. cit.*, pp. 239, 343–5.

vanguard of social justice, claiming all beneath them for a more equal future. The turbines recall Lenin's definition of communism as 'soviet power plus electrification'. And the giant pylons that gather the product and march with it across the moors give rise to just as much protest as the turbines themselves. The British government's latest plan to erect a line of giant pylons across the Highlands of Scotland has led to a rash of civic initiatives equal to those that sprang up in defence of the Lakelands in the nineteenth century. The National Trust of Scotland has now joined the volunteer groups such as Highlands before Pylons and Cairngorms Revolt Against Pylons in an attempt to stop what is widely regarded as an impious violation.

The search for clean energy is discredited by such controversial solutions. What is needed is a costing of alternatives, together with serious research into the harnessing of solar energy and into the ways whereby carbon emissions can be recaptured. Any solutions proposed must be such that ordinary people willingly accept them and do not, as with wind farms, campaign actively to prevent their use. The issue has been explored by David MacKay in a book to which I have referred several times, and which carefully costs all the current solutions while pointing to the areas where research is likely to be most fruitful.[365] MacKay's plausible conclusion is that the energy needs of Britain (the only country he considers in detail) cannot be met from renewables, such as wind power and solar-thermal heating, and that the British people

365 MacKay, *op. cit.*

must reduce their demand, electrify their transport system (cars included), and explore the options of nuclear power and 'clean coal' (that is, coal burning combined with the capture and sequestration of the resulting carbon dioxide). The alternative is to continue emitting greenhouse gases at an unacceptable rate. One important point that emerges from MacKay's detailed and erudite discussion is that it is already within the power of ordinary people to reduce their energy consumption, and that this can be done with only a small outlay, through lowering thermostats, deploying solar panels, using efficient stand-by systems and low energy light bulbs.

There is a financial incentive to take these steps, since they reduce household energy bills. There is also an incentive to those who manufacture solar panels, geo-thermal heating systems and low energy devices to reduce the cost of them, to the point where they represent a genuine saving for ordinary people. In this area the market is working, since nobody has an easy way to externalize the trading cost of domestic energy.

But what about those who produce energy? The cost of what they do, in terms of global warming, is almost impossible to estimate, and is in any case transferred to future generations. How can such a cost be internalized? Surely only some top-down solution can make any difference to what such people do. Yet top-down solutions have a nasty habit of making things worse. We must take the arguments of Peltzman and others seriously,[366] and

366 See Chapter 4.

recognize the danger of trying to guarantee environmental outcomes by regulations that interfere with the incentives that we might already have for producing them.

One step in a cogent energy policy might, therefore, be to follow the Danish example and decentralize the production of energy. The result would be a pylon-less landscape, with industries producing their own energy from local sources, such as solar panels or geo-thermal processors. This makes economic sense – the maintenance of the national grid is costly, and one third of all electricity flows away as leakage from the power lines. Moreover, such a policy will create incentives to produce energy economically and with minimum emissions, since the most polluting forms of energy production will not be tolerated by neighbours.

The production of energy should be subject to regulations that conform to the general requirements suggested by Chapters 4 and 5. We should not set legal limits to the emissions of new cars or factories, since that will simply encourage people to keep using their old cars or factories. We should not allocate rights to emit greenhouse gases industry by industry, and in response to special interests and lobbying from environmental groups and industries – since this will destroy the incentives for research and development that might lead to emission-free production. Instead of all such regulatory initiatives, we should introduce a flat-rate carbon tax. The more you emit, the more you pay. Moreover, this tax should be imposed on products regardless of their origin. Carbon-intensive products should be taxed at a rate that reflects the amount of carbon exhaled in their production, regardless of whether they are made in Britain, America or China, and the government should use the tax to finance research. This way some of the cost of climate change will be internalized by those who contribute most to producing it – and that means everyone, since the cost is passed on at the end to the consumer, who is the one ultimately responsible. The feedback loop will finally be in place.

That Pigovian solution is not the only one.[367] Instead of taxing pollution it is possible to control it by setting a limit to the permitted amount and then issuing tradeable permits – so adopting a more Coasean approach (see the argument of Chapter 5). This solution has been actively promoted in the United States, both by government and by the Environmental Protection Agency. The 1990 Clean Air Act, devoted to the control of acid rain, establishes a regime for trading sulphur dioxide emissions. And cap and trade, as it is commonly known, forms the basis of carbon trading regimes, such as those established by the Kyoto Treaty and the European Union's Emissions Trading Scheme. Such schemes are attempts to create a market that will assign a price to emissions by the logic of supply and demand. A properly functioning cap and trade scheme would have the advantage that it works as a market works, towards the optimal distribution of a scarce resource.[368]

However, as the European experience illustrates, cap and trade

367 Pigovian in honour of Arthur Cecil Pigou's solution to the problem of externalities, which is to allow 'goods' and to tax 'bads'.

368 See the eloquent defence of trading schemes in Pearce et al., *Blueprint for a Green Economy*, op. cit.

schemes are expensive to operate, not very transparent, and wide open to corruption. Moreover, because they target the producers of energy rather than the consumers, they misrepresent the burden of responsibility. It is the consumers who are ultimately responsible for greenhouse gas emissions, and who have hitherto escaped having to pay the cost of their habits, so by taxing consumption we create the best incentive to reduce production. Since consumption is greatest in the rich countries of the West, where taxes are relatively transparent and people disposed to pay them, this would have an immediate effect.

Such a policy would, I believe, have the intuitive support of ordinary people, and by raising the cost of energy it would provide them with an incentive to economize in the use of it. It does not directly internalize the cost of energy production – since that is not a cost that can be calculated and in any case the people to be compensated do not yet exist. But it gives a role to the state of a kind that people are schooled to accept. Taxes may be burdensome; but people are willing to pay them, provided they are not misused (as in eighteenth-century France, or in twenty-first-century Greece) to maintain a parasite class.

This last point raises a question that is often put out of mind by the defenders of market solutions, which is the question of research. In certain circumstances competition in a market will stimulate research – provided discoveries are protected by patents that will justify the research expenditure. But there is a downside to this. It must be possible to translate the discoveries into profit, and that means into something for which consumers are currently prepared to pay. In the case of clean energy the benefits are conferred not on present consumers but on their descendants. So the market will not generate the incentive to carry out the very expensive research that is required.

As Paul David has argued, the scientific revolution of the seventeenth century occurred largely because knowledge had ceased to be hermetic, hidden like a spell and used to gain power over adversaries, and instead had become a public asset, which conferred honour and status on those who acquired it and also on the patrons who supported them.[369] The open science regime encouraged the publication and sharing of results, and the exploitation of each new discovery by those best able to make use of it. The result was the scientific revolution.

I doubt that an open science regime can endure without substantial public funding. Already universities are attempting to earn extra money by patenting their scientific results, a move that threatens the collegiate nature of scientific enquiry. Without publicly funded research projects this practice will increase. The

369 Paul A. David, 'The Historical Origins of "Open Science": An essay on Patronage, Reputation and Common Agency Contracting in the Scientific Revolution', *Capitalism and Society*, November 2008. See www.bepress. com/cas/vol3/iss2/art5 for download of the full article, and www. bepress.com/cas/announce/20081103 for the whole issue that contains Kenneth Arrow's 'Discussion' of this article. See also Richard R. Nelson, 'The Market Economy, and the Scientific Commons', working paper to the Laboratory of Economics and Management at Sant'Anna School of Advanced Studies in Pisa, www.lem.sssup.it/WPLem/2003-24.html.

research needed to overcome the clean energy problem will be extensive, will involve scientists around the world, and will assuredly not be sufficiently funded by private companies.[370] Nor will it be funded by states governed by tightly knit and self-interested elites, like those that govern China. A sensible environmental policy must, therefore, concede an important role to the state: taxing carbon emissions, and funding the research needed to reduce them. But if the funding is supplied by the taxing, the research will be jeopardized by its own success.

Here is one of those policy knots that are difficult to untie – like the knot made by tobacco taxes, which fund government campaigns against the habit that funds them. Indeed, Pigovian solutions are subject to a general criticism. By lifting tax from good things (such as employment) and imposing it on bad things (such as gambling or pollution) Pigovian solutions make the solvency of government depend on the bad behaviour of the governed. Their success as policy is their failure as taxation, and vice versa; and an insolvent government cannot succeed in carrying out its policies. Pigovian solutions are therefore at best stopgaps, designed to hold things steady while civil society adjusts to take charge of the problem.

The aim of a conservative policy must, therefore, be to achieve a managed environment, in which good results arise

370 See Lee Lane *et al.*, 'Institutions for Developing New Climate Solutions', Proceedings of the International Seminars on Planetary Emergencies, 42nd Session, 19 August 2010.

spontaneously from what ordinary people do. This means main-taining or creating the feedback loops that cause people to bear the cost of their own activities, and to prevent them from passing that cost to future generations. As I have argued, this will involve reforming the law of tort so that it penalizes the one who causes the environmental problem, rather than the one who is able to pay for it. It will involve a regime of regulation designed to rectify externalities – though not the kind of zero-tolerance regulation that we are used to in Europe, where unaccountable bureaucrats have a free hand to disaggregate our problems and to attempt to solve them one by one. Regulations should be imposed by elected politicians, in consultation with experts, and in a manner subject to constant revision at the political level in the light of conse-quences. Where feasible it should be possible for regulation to be replaced by warning notices, so as to return risks to the consumer. This policy is a necessary part of putting resilience before inter-ception, and responsibility before dependence, in the management of risk.

Population increases do not, of themselves, disrupt the ability of ordinary people to manage their environments: witness the largely successful urbanization of the 'Five Towns' during the nineteenth century, and the rapid growth of public-spirited local communities in America. However, there is a great difference between population growth by natural increase and internal trans-fer, and population growth by immigration. It is surely evident that ordinary people are less liable to accept sacrifices for the sake of their environment when the attachment to locality is being replaced by competition between self-identifying tribes, families and religions. It is difficult to write of these matters, so great has been the intimidation of those who have defended immigration controls or who have warned against the fragmenting effect of multiculturalism. Nevertheless, it is surely evident that a conservative environmental policy that did not set limits to immigration, and which did not work to assimilate newcomers into the oikophilia on which the nation state depends, would have no chance of success.

Clearly Europe and America have different policy constraints when it comes to immigration. In America second-generation immigrants settle down, to become American oikophiles, with their eyes on the 'little house in Alabama' of which Brecht writes so sneeringly in *The Seven Deadly Sins*. This does not happen automatically in Europe; and recent events have made it clear that the 'multicultural society' is not a solution but a problem to be solved. It should be part of the work of schools, universities and community initiatives to integrate minorities into the national culture, and not to foster a spirit of apartness.

There is a growing weight of evidence that population growth slows down or goes into reverse when people reach a certain level of comfort, and when the loss is not made up by immigration. The environmental benefit of this is offset by the enormous social cost of maintaining an ageing population on the labour and the taxes of a declining workforce. To make the most of this environmental gain, therefore, policy should be directed to raising the retirement age, privatizing pensions and generally encouraging older people to keep working and to refrain from transferring the cost of their lives to the young. An environmental policy that did not see ageing as part of the problem would in my view fail to make contact with realities.

Population growth is one problem: mobility growth another. Fossil fuels have permitted people to amplify the distances travelled to such an extent that traditional settlement patterns have been blown apart. Some countries (notably Britain and Switzerland) have adopted planning regulations that strive to contain settlements within traditional boundaries and to protect downtown areas from destruction. Other countries – notably America and Canada – have allowed settlements to expand to the furthest reach of the motorists who reside in them, as well as enforcing out-of-town shopping malls and industrial precincts through zoning laws that amplify the need for transportation. Even in Britain the subsidized expansion of roads and out-of-town developments, together with regulations governing the packaging of food, have enabled supermarkets to achieve economies of scale by passing on fossil-fuel by-products, non-degradable packaging, and aesthetic pollution to future generations.

The cost of the energy consumed in transport does not, at present, fall on the consumer. By explicit and hidden subsidies, it is dispersed across the whole of society, the unborn included.

Returning the cost to the consumer should be the first priority of any government. To some extent this can be achieved through mileage taxes on the use of roads, and the carbon tax on fossil fuels. In the end, however, nothing will solve the problem of transport that does not redress the balance in favour of the local economy, not least the local food economy, which has been damaged by the hidden subsidies enjoyed by the supermarket chains and by the heavy hand of the state on the practice of agriculture.

The global food economy brings benefits to Third World farmers, and is not necessarily as destructive as its opponents argue. However, it is distorted by farm subsidies, and especially by those granted to large producers in Europe and the USA. It is distorted by lobbying of the WTO from global producers like Monsanto, and by the unscrupulous use of Trade-Related Intellectual Property Rights to confiscate the social capital of peasant economies.[371] It reflects central regulations and subsidies, rather than the free trade of goods whose cost has been assumed by the producer. It is of course true that, thanks to global trade, popular tastes have changed; tandoori chicken is now the favourite dish of the British, and hamburgers are gaining ground even in France. But cosmopolitan tastes are compatible with a local food economy. For nearly two centuries the British have

371 Cf. the notorious patenting of basmati rice by RiceTec. See Matthew Clement, 'Rice Imperialism: The Agribusiness Threat to Third World Rice Production', in www.bulatlat.com, 8–14 February 2004.

made chutney, a relish brought from India, with local apples and pears, while the North African cuisine enjoyed in Marseilles is supplied with couscous and peppers grown locally and merguez made from local lamb.

There is no social reason, therefore, why small farmers and their products should not occupy the place in the economy that once they occupied. To achieve this would require the steady elimination of those zero-tolerance regulations that only the big producers can comply with. It should be permissible to sell food at the farm gate or in the local market without packaging, just as it is sold all over Africa. It should be permissible to sell products like unpasteurized milk and cheese, properly labelled, but nevertheless with the risk passed to the purchaser. It should be permissible to slaughter animals on the farm, provided humane methods are used. Get rid of the raft of regulations that impede those healthy practices and the small farmer and the farmers' market will be able to compete with the large producer and the supermarket. Impose on supermarkets the planning controls that are appropriate to town centres, so that building on the edge of town ceases to be an option preferable to slotting into the centre. Begin the process of charging proper tolls for roads, so that transport is to be priced according to its real cost. Do all those things and the local food economy will again be competitive, and some part of the mad motion that currently fills the globe will be quietened.

In the short term it will be impossible to remove all subsidies from the agricultural sector. But it is possible – and both the European Union and the United States government have recognized and acted on the possibility – to turn subsidies in another direction, away from crops towards biodiversity, habitats and natural beauty. These were *by-products* of the old way of farming. But that way was destroyed. Hence they must become *products* of a new way of farming that should take seriously the economic costs of the regime of fertilizer- and pesticide-governed agribusiness. Research carried out by Jules Pretty and others has been taken to suggest that the annual external costs of the current British food and farming economy are well over £1 billion greater than the costs of the properly localized and organically managed alternative.[372]

Growing public awareness of the damage done to ecosystems by modern farming techniques has sparked off a large number of civic initiatives, the first influential one – Rudolf Steiner's movement for 'biodynamics' – having set the pattern nearly a century ago. Already in Britain the Countryside Restoration Trust and the Family Farmers Association are advocating a subsidy-free agriculture, which will remove the advantages enjoyed by the big polluters and the agribusinesses. Small farms run by hobby farmers and organic producers as yet account for only 3 per cent

---

372 Jules Pretty et al., *op. cit.* As things stand, however, organic production is just as dependent on fossil fuels as other methods of farming, and needs extra land to supply the nitrogen-fixing crops that are required in the absence of artificial fertilizers. See Alex Avery, *The Truth About Organic Foods*, London, 2006.

of farm produce in the USA, but the proportion is growing; journals and clubs catering for hobby farmers are springing up across the country, and the local food movement is gathering momentum.[373] There is a new interest in 'permaculture', with a Permaculture Association providing courses and a Permaculture Magazine with an increasing number of subscribers. It is of course unrealistic to expect to feed the entire population without the large farms that currently provide such staples as potatoes and corn, but the rebirth of local markets will change the ways that those farms produce and distribute what they grow.

The pastures, hedgerows, copses, coverts and streams of England were not preserved simply because people loved them. They were created and preserved by the self-interest of those who farmed and owned the land. They arose by an invisible hand from pasture farming, from historic rights of way and the maintenance of boundaries, from field sports, and from the local food economy in which milk and cheese were sold in the markets. This local food economy survived intact until recent years, as did the other economic interests that maintained the landscape. The replacement of local food economies by the global supermarket is not the result of free and fair competition. It is the result of hidden subsidies and intrusive regulations – in particular regulations concerning 'health and safety' – with which only centralized businesses can comply. It is government, not civil society, that has

373 Visit the website of Local Harvest for up-to-date information about local food, and Farm Aid for the efforts made to save the small family farm.

398

destroyed the local economy; and if we see the local food economy as part of sustainability we must do what we can to counter the regulative machine, and to remove or redirect the regime of subsidies.

Localization is not merely the best hope for a sustainable agriculture and food economy. It also creates a strong disincentive to the externalization of costs. In a local environment, in which people know each other and observe each other's delinquencies, social pressures internalize costs. At this local level a conservative environmental policy is not one in which the government strives to secure environmental benefits; it is one in which the government enables people to secure those benefits for themselves. The decline of civil associations documented by Robert Putnam has many causes, by no means the least important of which has been the confiscation of the citizen's powers by the state. Many farmers would like to sell their food at local markets: health and safety regulations prevent them. Many communities would combine successfully against government plans to dump airports on top of them or drive motorways through them if these matters were – as in Switzerland – put to a local vote. Planning decisions would accord with the requirements of beauty and adaptability if they were in the hands of neighbours, and not imposed by a central machine. In general a conservative policy returns decisions and risks to the people who are most affected by them. It sees the state as the friend of civil society, and civil society as a self-regulating organism, in which resilience and inventiveness, rather than regulation and dependence, are the instruments of survival. Is it utopian to demand a return to such conservative ways of thinking? I do not think so. Indeed, people are moving of their own accord in this direction. In Britain there is now a movement towards Transition Towns – places in which the citizens are combining in order to live in a more sustainable way. Simon Fairlie's prescriptions for 'low impact development' are beginning to be listened to,[374] while advocates of carbon-neutral lifestyles and farmers' markets are gaining recognition. Although the regulative machine continues to expand, and the externalities continue to multiply, we see people increasingly hostile to intrusive regulations, and looking for ways to circumvent them. This is happening in rural areas already. It is beginning to be obvious to all decent people that we must repossess ourselves of the risks that are ours: that it is up to us to make headway in cleaning the earth. And if oikophilia remains, that is what we shall do, through the civic initiatives that are the natural resource of all people who are settled and who love the place where they are. The greatest danger to the environment, it seems to me, comes from the growing tendency of governments to confiscate the powers and freedoms of autonomous associations, and to centralize all powers in their own hands. If the people can combine, they can win.

One last word about global warming. The question in every-

374 Fairlie, *Low Impact Development: Planning and People in a Sustainable Countryside*, Charlbury, 1996. See also the work of Locality, under Steve Wyler: an organisation devoted to encouraging local civic iniatives in response to local problems. (locality.org.uk)

one's mind is, what do we do if the worst-case scenarios are true? The activists' answer is simple: we get together at international conferences and forge a treaty that will bring our bad behaviour to an end. That answer is based on a misconception of international politics, and a failure to observe the difference between states that can bind themselves by treaties and states that cannot. Of course, if we are threatened, we must do something. But who are we? There is only one answer: we are those who are capable of collective action, who have the resources, the will and the mutual concern to act as one. In other words, we are communities with the capacity for corporate action, who can take collective responsibility for what we do. In the context of international politics this means that we are the nation – the law-governed body of people whose destinies are linked by a shared political process. The only answer to global warming is action by individual nation states – those rich enough to conduct research and to act on the scale required, responsible enough to answer to the need to do so, and with a public opinion shaped by open discussion. In the circumstances that means first the United States of America, and secondly all those nation states in which law, democracy and free opinion serve to arouse in the citizen a sense of collective responsibility. It does not mean China, Russia, or any of the kleptocracies of Africa and the Middle East.

When such a 'we' takes action it can do two things: it can set an example, as the Scandinavians have done. And it can take an initiative that will tackle the global problem directly, through research into clean energy, carbon sequestration and the benefits and costs of geo-engineering. It could be that all those actions are required. But one thing is certain: none can be achieved through international conferences and treaties alone, and all depend on the sense that each of us has, of being responsible for his home. The only conceivable solutions to the global problem emerge from the motive that I have outlined in this book.

To emphasize this motive is not to advocate anarchy or to deny the need for legislation. It is to set the goal at which legislation must aim. There are many environmental problems that require the power of the state if they are to be addressed, but they must be addressed in such a way that oikophilia is amplified and not extinguished by the attempt to solve them. A regime to price roads, waste and packaging so that the cost falls on the user will hurt everyone, and will be useless if not imposed uniformly by the state. But such a regime will encourage ways of living that amplify the feelings of neighbourhood, and the state will gain in legitimacy as a result, since it will be seen as the expression of a vital civil society, able to take action on behalf of the nation as a whole. By acting always to enhance oikophilia and not to confiscate its sphere of legitimate action, the state will prepare the people for the sacrifices that are now unavoidable, if the earth is to be a home to us, and not a place of exile.

APPENDIX I

Global Justice

The average emission of carbon dioxide into the atmosphere is around five tonnes per capita per annum. For Americans it is twenty tonnes, for sub-Saharan Africans one tonne or less.[375] Moreover, the Western world generally, and the industrial parts of it in particular, have a head start over all the others, since Western countries have been emitting greenhouse gases for two centuries. In justice, therefore, not only should Western countries reduce their emissions substantially now, they should also compensate less developed countries for having taken advantage of an opportunity that their conduct has destroyed – the opportunity to pour out greenhouse gases into the atmosphere without counting the cost. In this, as in so many other things, the West has taken more than its share of the commons.

375 Ross Garnaut *et al.*, 'The Implications of Rapid Development for Emissions and Climate-change Mitigation', in Helm and Hepburn, eds., *op. cit.*

That argument crops up repeatedly at international negotiations on climate change. You also find it in the more influential attempts to cost the targets set by the Kyoto Protocol or by the IPCC.[376] What should we make of it? First, terms like 'country', 'Western countries' and 'developing countries' are vague. Questions of justice do not arise between geographical entities but between *agents*, with rights that they may claim and duties that they must fulfil. Justice and injustice are qualities of acts, and of the agents who perform them. And while there can be collective agents that inflict and suffer injustice, 'countries' are not among them. Only a collective that can identify itself in the first-person plural can act and be accountable. Talk of global justice, therefore, presupposes the 'we' of collective action – the very 'we' that has been the subject of this book. No government can conceivably respond to demands of global justice if it does not regard itself as representative of a nation, liable for the bad, and taking credit for the good that 'we', as a nation, have done.

Hence the demand for global justice requires us to acknowledge the nation state as the primary vehicle of political responsibility. Moreover, demands for justice are founded not on states of affairs but on the liabilities that they crystallize. Proof of liability requires us to determine how present generations inherit the faults of their predecessors, when bound to those predecessors

376 Nicholas Stern, *The Economics of Climate Change*; Helm and Hepburn, eds., *op. cit.*; Henry D. Jacoby *et al.*, 'Sharing the Burden of GHG Reductions', MIT Joint Program on the Science and Policy of Climate Change, report no. 167, 2008.

in the first-person plural of a nation state. Vague terms like 'country' may be used to make emotionally satisfying accusations of collective guilt, but the accusations can be turned into definite demands only if we settle questions of agency, personality and transgenerational accountability.

The problem here is partly philosophical, partly political. Contractarian theories of justice, such as that famously developed by John Rawls, assign benefits and costs to the members of a 'society', which is the subject matter of the contract. They are not global theories, since those outside the contract are not considered. Hence such theories do not yield a clear answer, either to questions of intergenerational justice, or to questions of the just distribution across the world of the benefits and costs of economic growth. In an effort to rectify this deficiency Amartya Sen has proposed an idea of justice as 'impartiality', in the spirit of Adam Smith's discussion of the impartial spectator.[377] I 'do justice' to others when I look on them with impartial concern, according to them the same consideration as I would expect to be accorded in turn. I must discount differences of nationality, and the web of contractual and historical contingencies that bind the other but don't bind me. It is this attitude – which, Sen insists, is directed towards raising questions rather than giving formulaic answers – that should be adopted when considering global justice.

The power of Adam Smith's heuristic device is undeniable. Impartiality and justice sit together in the human mind, and form

377 Amartya Sen, *The Idea of Justice*, London, 2009.

the necessary balance to the relations of interpersonal account-ability that I discussed in Chapter 6. Impartiality tells me not to discount the situation of the impoverished Indian just because he lives in India, or of the Sudanese mother just because her strug-gle to survive occurs in distant Sudan. However, it also tells me not to discount their local attachments just because they are exclu-sive, or to pay no respect to their tribal, national and religious loyalties just because they are at odds with mine. Although Sen wishes to advance from impartiality to a kind of Enlightenment universalism, maybe even to a consistently global view of polit-ical decision-making, this step does not follow. An impartial view of the human condition must surely recognize that, while oikophilia is a human universal, its manifestation is essentially particular, local, national and territorial. And it is in this way that transgenerational loyalty must be understood. I can do justice to my antecedents by respecting their endowments and carrying out their wills. I can do justice to my descendants by good steward-ship of the assets that I hold in trust for them. And we can do justice to ancestors and descendants as a group. But no human being is able to globalize this natural sentiment, and the attempt to do so will always spill over into those exultant acts of repudia-tion after which no obligations survive.

Undeniably the British have benefited from the prosperity brought to them by 200 years of greenhouse gas emissions, and in this may have narrowed the options now available to the people of Africa. Morally speaking we have inherited a benefit that we should do our best to pay for. But what are the political consequences? Should the British people, or the United Kingdom as their representative, be held strictly liable for the damage that this has inflicted on sub-Saharan Africa, as Mr Rylands was held strictly liable for the flooding of Mr Fletcher's mines? Just where would such reasoning end? How can we conceivably count the cost to Africa? And what about the benefits? The energy consumed by the British enabled them to spread the rule of law and a plethora of technical accomplishments all over Africa. Should that benefit be entered into the final account? Or should it be discounted, because it has been squandered by the kleptocrats who subsequently acquired it? Maybe the twenty tonnes per capita enjoyed by Americans today are part of the cost of the *pax Americana*, without which the world would (in John's view, but not in Mary's) be far more dangerous than it is.

Clearly we don't know where the argument is going. Rather than indulge in speculations that have no end and upon which no politician could conceivably act, we should look for a clear principle that will enable self-defining nations to assess their liabilities and compensate the victims, without undermining their freedom to act. The massive transfers of resources from the West to the rest that are often advocated by the radical Greens would destroy the capacity of the Western powers to take the measures that we all need, and which the Western powers alone can encompass. Such self-destructive behaviour would be of no benefit to anyone, and is surely not what global justice requires.

Global justice can only mean allocating sacrifices fairly among all the agents who must make them. A fair allocation is not an equal one. It is an allocation that acknowledges the unequal responsibility for the damage, and the unequal power to repair it. Those to be assessed include nation states like Britain, France and the United States. But they also include corporations, both national and multinational, as well as entities like Gazprom, which are corporate masks worn by political forces and partly criminal elites. Fairness requires that the bigger polluters should commit more of the resources needed. These resources should be devoted to subsidizing research into clean energy, and subsidizing the transfer of this energy to the 'developing countries'. That in turn means providing clean energy to the people in developing parts of the world, whether or not they have the benefit of a government that can say 'we' on their behalf. This forward-looking approach to the compensation problem presupposes the concepts that I have been defending in this book: national identity, transgenerational responsibility and a preference for decentralized initiatives over radical goals. How easy it will be to take such a forward-looking approach is a moot point. But the alternative – Western breast-beating, followed by yet more transfers to the kleptocrats of Africa – will leave the earth in the same parlous condition as it is today.

How Should We Live?

Our tradition of moral philosophy is the product of thinkers who lived in conditions of scarcity, without the awareness that they were using up the finite resources on which their successors would depend. In so far as their writings signal any tensions in the practice of moral judgement, they are tensions between the pursuit of happiness and the sense of duty. For the Kantian, duty is all-encompassing, and the pursuit of happiness subordinate to it. For the Aristotelian, happiness is the ultimate good, and virtue the means to it: conduct towards others should be governed by the circumstantial requirements of friendship and justice. No clear rules are likely to emerge from an Aristotelian morality, just as only a cold and forbidding account of human virtue is likely to emerge from the followers of Kant. Hence, even before the environmental crisis through which we are living, philosophers did not speak with one voice as to how we should live. The hope was nevertheless that the life of virtue and the life of duty would, in normal circumstances, coincide, and that both would receive the support of our pious sentiments.

During the times of those philosophers the uneasy equilibrium between man and nature was kept in being by conflict and disease. The equilibrium has been fatally disturbed by medical science, and the usual way back to it, through some devastating epidemic, is not one that we should aim at or hope for. It was then considered a part of virtue to sacrifice oneself for one's children. Family life, respect for parents and the love of offspring were considered the fertile ground of the moral life, and to avoid them was something shameful. Overpopulation was not on the agenda, and the finitude of resources was understood only as a parable of human mortality, and not as a near and pressing disaster. But one way of understanding that first bleak cry of the modern era – Zarathustra's announcement of the *Übermensch* who is both artist and acrobat, but neither father nor king – is as a call to remake humanity. We are to be the species that turns its back on reproduction, the species that brings itself to an end.[378]

Charity asks us to help the poor and the sick, so increasing the earth's burden. Our duties to both intimates and strangers require the use of modern medicine, which invites us to consume resources that we are powerless to replenish. The cardinal virtue of temperance has a positive ecological spin-off. But the virtue of justice forbids us to impose temperance on populations that have only recently begun to enjoy the wealth and freedom that we and

378 On the ecological significance of Nietzsche see Sloterdijk, *op. cit.*

our forebears have known for a century or more. Compassion for the needs of those living now can prompt us to develop, exploit, and even destroy natural resources, while piety points in the opposite direction, forbidding us to touch beloved landscapes or to disturb delicate ecosystems however much we damage existing interests and needs. In the wake of Rachel Carson's *Silent Spring*, there was a campaign against DDT, which had killed insects and with them the whole food chain of which they were a part. The campaign was successful; as a result the mosquito population in Africa has soared and many millions of children who might otherwise have survived have died of malaria.[379]

In the light of those and other conflicts, actual or incipient, it might be supposed that morality has to be entirely rethought, so as to reconcile, if we can, personal duty and ecological piety. Does not the earth have a claim on us?[380] Should we not strive to leave the smallest possible carbon footprint; to treat the earth as a vulnerable mother to whom gratitude and love are owed; to respect the works of nature, and to eat only those things that have been properly sown and harvested – maybe not to eat animals at all, and meanwhile to live frugally and quietly like a Tibetan monk?

When I read the 'wholier than thou' moralizing of the eco-crusaders I confess that the spirit of the hunter rises within me.

379 Donald Roberts *et al.*, *The Excellent Powder: DDT's Political and Scientific History*, Indianapolis, 2010, chs. 4 and 5.

380 Stephen Clark, 'Gaia and the Forms of Life', in R. Elliot and A. Gare, eds., *Environmental Philosophy*, New York, 1983; Meyer-Abich, *op. cit.*; etc.

I hear the voice of Aristotle, extolling the virtues of liberality and magnanimity, reminding me that justice without friendship is only half a virtue, and that friendship means the shared pursuit of the good, in which giving and taking, courage and danger are all part of the deal. Eco-puritans fit uncomfortably into that picture, and are apt to cast a pall over convivial company, conscious as they are of the comet-tail of waste that follows all our festivals. I would like to think that environmental rectitude does not require me to renounce the joys of life, and especially not the joy that comes from membership of a privileged species, able to eat any other that stands in its way.

The solution, it seems to me, is to care for one's home, meanwhile living not frugally but temperately, not stingily but with a prudent generosity, so as to embellish and renew the plot of earth, and the community, to which one is attached. Of course it matters what we eat – we should be careful not to buy products that have reached us by the route of destruction. Hence we should not shop in the supermarket; we should eat meat only from animals that have been cared for or hunted in humane and sustainable ways; we should avoid packaged products and seek out local food. And maybe we should take our holidays at home, or at any rate in some familiar and constantly revisited place that we can reach without burning up the planet. We should not keep environmentally destructive and carnivorous pets like cats and dogs. And we should live in families, sharing resources, not in order to make use of each other's body heat (though that too is good) but in order to generate the spiritual resource on which the earth depends, which is home and our attachment to it.

Those precepts are predicated upon wealth and freedom that we could renounce only at a cost that most of us are not willing to pay. They are small adjustments – good for the soul, and reinforcing the best of our motives. But they are essentially conscience-soothing devices: they require little of us, and nothing that we find hard to bear, except perhaps the injunction to live in families. The difficult part is that of putting oikophilia into practice. For it means combining with others in order to live the civic life; it means resisting entropy, whether it comes from below in the form of social nihilism, or from above in the form of oikophobic edicts; it means creating and sustaining neighbourhoods. It means actively handing on to the next generation all that we have by way of knowledge and competence, and imbuing our successors with a spirit of stewardship that we also, in our own actions, display. This is hard work, requiring patience and sacrifice. But 'better a dish of herbs where love is, than a stalled ox and hatred withal'.

Bibliography

Abbey, Edward, *The Monkey Wrench Gang*, Salt Lake City, Dream Garden Press, 1975.

Adams, John, *Risk*, London, Routledge, 1995.

Adorno, Theodor W., *Minima Moralia: Reflections on a Damaged Life*, Berlin, Suhrkamp, 1951.

Adorno, Theodor W., and Horkheimer, Max, *Dialectic of Enlightenment*, London, Verso, 2008.

Albrecht, G., 'Solastalgia, A New Concept in Human Health and Identity', *Philosophy Activism Nature*, 3, 2005, pp. 41–55.

Alexander, Christopher, *The Nature of Order*, 4 vols., Berkeley, Center for Environmental Structure, 2002.

Anderson, Terry, and Leal, Donald, *Free Market Environmentalism*, London, Palgrave Macmillan, 2001.

Apel, Karl-Otto, 'The Ecological Crisis as a Problem for Discourse Ethics', in *Ecology and Ethics*, ed. A. Øfsti, Trondheim, Tapir-Trykk, 1992.

Aristotle, ed. Sir Ernest Barker and Stalley, R. F., *The Politics*, Oxford University Press, 1994.

Aron, Leon, 'Russia's "Monotowns" Time-Bomb', *AEI Russian Outlook*, October 2009, www.aei.org/outlook/100080.

Arrow, Kenneth, *Social Choice and Individual Values*, New Haven, Yale University Press, 1990.

Arrow, Kenneth J., *Essays in the Theory of Risk-Bearing*, Amsterdam, North-Holland Publishing Company, 1976.

Avery, Alex, *The Truth About Organic Foods*, London, Henderson Communications, 2006.

Axelrod, Robert, *The Evolution of Co-operation*, rev. ed., New York, Basic Books, 2006.

Baird, Callicott, ed., *Companion to a Sand County Almanac: Interpretative and Critical Essays*, Madison, University of Wisconsin Press, 1987.

Balfour, Eve, *The Living Soil*, London, Faber & Faber, 1943.

Barker, Paul, *The Freedoms of Suburbia*, London, Frances Lincoln, 2009.

Barnett, Anthony, and Scruton, Roger, eds., *Town and Country*, London, Vintage, 1999.

Barrell, John, *The Dark Side of the Landscape: The Rural Poor in English Landscape Painting 1730–1840*, Cambridge University Press, 1980.

Bate, Roger, *Saving Our Streams: The Role of the Anglers' Conservation Association in Protecting English and Welsh Rivers*, London, Institute of Economic Affairs, 2001.

Baum-Snow, Nathaniel, 'Changes in Transportation Infrastructure and Commuting Patterns in US Metropolitan Areas, 1960–2000', *American Economic Review: Papers and Proceedings*, May 2010.

Beck, Ulrich, *Risk Society: Towards a New Modernity*, London, Sage, 1992.

Beckel, Eric J., 'The Climate Engineering Option: Economics and Policy Implications', Center for International Energy and Environmental Policy, University of Texas at Austin, 2010.

Beckerman, Wilfred, *In Defence of Economic Growth*, London, Jonathan Cape, 1974.

Belien, Paul, *A Throne in Brussels: Britain, the Saxe-Coburgs and the Belgianization of Europe*, London, Imprint Academic, 2005.

Benedict, Ruth, *Patterns of Culture*, Boston, Houghton Mifflin, 1934.

Bentham, Jeremy, 'Anarchical Fallacies; being an Examination of the Declaration of Rights Issued during the French Revolution', *The Works of Jeremy Bentham*, vol. 2, London, Elibron Classics, 2005.

Bergsten, C. Fred, Freeman, Charles, Lardy, Nicholas R., and Mitchell, Derek J., *China's Rise: Challenges and Opportunities*, Washington DC, Peterson Institute for International Economics, 2008.

Bergson, Henri, *Essai sur les données immédiates de la conscience*, Paris, Libr. Felix Alcan, 1889.

Berkow, Jerome, Cosmides, Leda, and Tooby, John, *The Adapted Mind: Evolutionary Psychology and the Generation of Culture*, New York, Oxford University Press, 1995.

Berry, Wendell, *The Unsettling of America*, San Francisco, Sierra Club Books, 1977.

Berry, Wendell, *The Gift of Good Land: Further Essays Cultural and Agricultural*, San Francisco, North Point, 1981.

Birnbacher, Dieter, *Verantwortung für zukünftige Generationen*, Frankfurt am Main, Reclam, 1995.

Birnbacher, Dieter, ed., *Ökologie und Ethik*, Stuttgart, Reclam, 1988.

Body, Sir Richard, *Agriculture, the Triumph and the Shame*, London, Temple Smith, 1982.

Bonevac, Daniel, 'Is Sustainability Sustainable?', *Academic Questions*, 23.1, March 2010, pp. 84–101.

Booker, Christopher, and North, Richard D., *The Mad Officials*, London, Constable, 1994.

Booker, Christopher, and North, Richard D., *Scared to Death. From BSE to Global Warming: Why Scares are Costing Us the Earth*, London, Continuum, 2009.

Bové, José, and Dufour, François, *The World Is Not for Sale: Farmers Against Junk Food*, London, Verso, 2001.

Bowlby, John, *Attachment*, 2nd ed., New York, Basic Books, 1999.

Bowlby, John, *Separation*, New York, Basic Books, 2000.

Bowlby, John, *Loss*, London, Pimlico, 1998.

Bradsher, Keith, 'China Leading Global Race to Make Clean Energy', *New York Times*, 31 January 2010.

Brahic, Catherine, 'Packaging Waste: Facts and Figures', *New Scientist Environmental Blog*, www.newscientist.com/blog/environment/2 007_03_01_archive, 2007.

Bramwell, Anna, *Ecology in the 20th Century: A History*, New Haven, Yale University Press, 1989.

Brent Spar Dossier, Shell Oil website: www-static.shell.com/static/ gbr/downloads/e_and_p/brent_spar_dossier.pdf, 2008.

Brody, Hugh, *The Other Side of Eden*, London, North Point Press, 2001.

Brooks, Arthur C., *Gross National Happiness*, New York, Basic Books, 2008.

Brooks, Arthur C., *The Battle: How the Fight Between Free Enterprise and Big Government Will Shape America's Future*, New York, Basic Books, 2010.

Broome, John, *Weighing Lives*, London and New York, Oxford University Press, 2004.

Brower, David, *Wilderness: America's Living Heritage*, San Francisco, Sierra Club Books, 1961.

Brower, Michael, *Cool Energy: Renewable Solutions to Environmental Problems*, rev. ed., Cambridge, MA, MIT Press, 1992.

Bruegmann, Robert, *Sprawl: A Compact History*, University of Chicago Press, 2005.

Brundtland, Gro Harlem, *et al.*, *Our Common Future*, World Commission on Environment and Development, Oxford University Press, 1987.

Buber, Martin, tr. Ronald G. Smith, *I and Thou*, Edinburgh, T. & T. Clark, 1923.

Buchanan, James, 'Rent-seeking, Non-compensated Transfers, and Laws of Succession', *Journal of Law and Economics*, 26, April 1983, pp. 71–85.

Buchanan, James, *Cost and Choice: An Inquiry in Economic Theory*, Indianapolis, Liberty Fund, 1999.

Buchanan, James, and Tullock, Gordon, *The Calculus of Consent: Logical Foundations of Constitutional Democracy*, Ann Arbor, University of Michigan Press, 1962.

Burke, Edmund, *Philosophical Enquiry into the Origin of Our Ideas of the Sublime and the Beautiful*, Oxford University Press, 2008.

Burke, Edmund , *Reflections on the French Revolution*, London, J. M. Dent, 1935.

Calder, Nigel, see Svensmark.

Canadian Fisheries and Oceans website: www.dfo-mpo.gc.ca/fm-gp/seal-phoque/index-eng.htm.

Carbon Sequestration Leadership Forum website: www.cslforum.org.

Carlson, Allan, *The New Agrarian Mind: The Movement Toward Decentralist Thought in Twentieth-Century America*, New Brunswick, Transaction Publishers, 2000.

Carson, Rachel, *Silent Spring*, London, Hamish Hamilton, 1963.

Chakraborty, R. N., 'Sharing Culture and Resource Conservation in Hunter-Gatherer Societies', *Oxford Economic Papers*, 59.1, January 2007, pp. 63–88.

Chang, Jung, and Halliday, Jon, *Mao: The Unknown Story*, London, Jonathan Cape, 2004.

Chase, Alston, *Playing God in Yellowstone: The Destruction of America's First National Park*, New York, Harcourt Brace, 1986.

Chasemere v. Richards, [1859] 7 H.L. Cas. 349.

Christie, Ian, Warburton, Diane, and Real World Coalition, *From Here to Sustainability*, London, Earthscan, 2001.

Clark, Stephen, 'Gaia and the Forms of Life', in *Environmental Philosophy: A Collection of Readings*, eds. R. Elliot and A. Gare,

New York, University of Queensland Press, 1983.

Clausewitz, Carl von, *On War*, New York, Everyman's Library, 1993.

Clement, Matthew, 'Rice Imperialism: The Agribusiness Threat to Third World Rice Production', www.bulatlat.com, 8–14 February 2004.

Coase, Ronald, 'The Problem of Social Cost', *Journal of Law and Economics*, 3, October 1960.

Cobbett, William, *Rural Rides*, New York, Cosimo Classics, 2005.

Cohn, Norman, *The Pursuit of the Millennium*, London, Pimlico, 1993.

Cole, H. S. D., Freeman, C., Jahoda, M., and Pavitt, K. L. R., *Thinking About the Future: A Critique of the Limits to Growth*, London, Sussex University Press, 1973. Issued in US as *Models of Doom: A Critique of the Limits to Growth*, New York, Universe Books, 1975.

Colligan, Douglas, 'Brace Yourself for Another Ice Age', *Science Digest*, February 1973.

Common Tragedies website: commontragedies.wordpress.com.

Competitive Enterprise Institute website: cei.org.

Congdon, Tim, *The City of London under Threat*, London, Bruges Group, 2009.

Corell, R. W., Hassol, S. J., and Melillo, J., 'Emerging Challenges – Methane from the Arctic: Global Warming Wildcard', *UNEP Year Book 2008: An Overview of Our Changing Environment*, United Nations Environment Programme, Stevenage, 2008.

Costanza, Robert, and Perrings, Charles, 'A Flexible Assurance Bonding System for Improved Environmental Management', *Ecological Economics*, 2.1, April 1990, pp. 57–75.

Curtis, Glenn E., ed., *Poland: A Country Study*, Washington DC, GPO for the Library of Congress, Federal Research Division of the Library of Congress, 1992.

Curzon Price, Tony, 'Can Beauty be Preserved?', in Barnett and Scruton.

Dalrymple, Theodor, 'The Architect as Totalitarian', *City Journal*, 19.4, Autumn 2009.

Daly, Herman E., *Steady-State Economics: The Economics of Biophysical Equilibrium and Moral Growth*, San Francisco, W. H. Freeman, 1977.

Daly, Herman E., *Beyond Growth: The Economics of Sustainable Development*, Boston, Beacon Press, 2000.

Darwall, Stephen, *The Second-Person Standpoint: Morality, Respect, and Accountability*, Cambridge, MA, Harvard University Press, 1996.

Darwin, C., ed. Gillian Beer, *On the Origin of Species*, New York, Oxford University Press, 2008.

Darwin, C., ed. Michael T. Ghiselin, *The Descent of Man*, Mineola, NY, Dover, 2009.

Dasgupta, P., and Heal, G., *Economic Theory and Exhaustible Resources*, Cambridge University Press, 1995.

Dasgupta, Partha, and Heal, Geoffrey, 'The Optimal Depletion of Exhaustible Resources', *Review of Economic Studies*, Symposium on the Economics of Exhaustible Resources: 41, 1974, pp. 3–28.

David, Paul A., 'The Historical Origins of "Open Science": An Essay on Patronage, Reputation and Common Agency Contracting in the Scientific Revolution', *Capitalism and Society*, 3.2 Article 5, 2008, www.bepress.com/cas/vol3/iss2/art5.

Davies, Antony, and Yakolev, Pavel, 'Myths and Realities Surrounding the Estate Tax', American Family Business Foundation, www.nodeathtax.org, 2009.

Dawidoff, Nicholas, 'The Civil Heretic,' *New York Times Magazine*, 25 March 2009.

Dawkins, Richard, *The Selfish Gene*, 2nd ed., Oxford University Press, 2009.

DeMuth, Christopher C., and Ginsburg, Douglas H., 'Rationalism in Regulation', *Michigan Law Review*, 108.6, April 2010, pp. 877–912.

Diamond, Jared, *Collapse: How Societies Choose or Fail to Survive*, London, Allen Lane, 2005.

Dobson, Andrew, ed., *Fairness and Futurity: Essays on Environmental Sustainability*, Oxford University Press, 1999.

Douglas, Mary, and Wildavsky, Aaron, *Risk and Culture: An Essay on the Selection of Technological and Environmental Dangers*, Berkeley, University of California Press, 1983.

Drucker, Peter, *Post-Capitalist Society*, New York, Harper Business, 1993.

Durkheim, Émile, tr. Joseph W. Swain, *The Elementary Forms of the Religious Life*, Mineola, NY, Dover, 2008.

Durodié, Bill, 'Plastic Panics: European Risk Regulation in the Aftermath of BSE', in Morris.

Dworkin, Ronald, *Taking Rights Seriously*, London, Duckworth, 1977.

Ebbesmeyer, Curtis, and Scigliano, Eric, *Flotsametrics and the Floating World*, Washington DC, Smithsonian, 2009.

Ehrlich, Paul, *The Population Bomb*, Cutchogue, NY, Buccaneer Books, 1968.

Etherington, John, *The Wind Farm Scam*, London, Stacey International, 2009.

Evelyn, John, ed. Hunter, Alexander, *Silva; or, A Discourse of Forest-Trees*, York, T. Wilson & R. Spence, 1801.

Fairlie, Simon, *Low Impact Development: Planning and People in a Sustainable Countryside*, Charlbury, Jon Carpenter, 1996.

Fattal, Antoine, *Le statut légal des non-musulmans en pays d'Islam*, Beirut, Imprimerie Catholique, 1958.

Feisbach, Murray, *Ecocide in the USSR*, New York, Basic Books, 1992.

Fergusson, Adam, *The Sack of Bath*, Salisbury, Compton Russell, 1973.

Fleming, James Rodger, *Historical Perspectives on Climate Change*, New York, Oxford University Press, 1998.

Foreman, David, and Haywood, Bill, *Ecodefense: A Field Guide to Monkeywrenching*, 3rd ed., Chico, CA, Abbzug Press, 2002.

Fox, Warwick, *Toward a Transpersonal Ecology: Developing*

New Foundations for Environmentalism, Boston, Shambhala, 1990.

Frakes, L. A., *Climates Throughout Geologic Time*, Amsterdam, Elsevier Press, 1979.

Friedman, Milton, and Friedman, Rose, *Free to Choose: A Personal Statement*, New York, Harcourt Brace Jovanovich, 1980.

Friedman, Thomas, *Lexus and the Olive Tree*, rev. ed., London and New York, HarperCollins, 1999.

Furet, François, *Penser la révolution française*, Paris, Gallimard, 1978.

Garnaut, Ross, Howes, Stephen, Jotzo, Frank, and Sheehan, Peter, 'The Implications of Rapid Development for Emissions and Climate-change Mitigation', in Helm and Hepburn.

Garreau, Joel, *Edge City: Life on the New Frontier*, New York, Doubleday, 1991.

Geertz, Clifford, *The Interpretation of Cultures*, 1973, New York, Basic Books, reissued 2009.

Giddens, Anthony, *The Politics of Climate Change*, Cambridge, Polity, 2009.

Girard, René, *La Violence et le sacré*, Paris, Hachette, 1972.

Girard, René, *Des choses cachées depuis la fondation du monde*, Paris, Hachette, 1978.

Goldsmith, Zac, *The Constant Economy: How to Create a Stable Society*, London, Atlantic Books, 2009.

Goodman, Ellen, 'No Change in Political Climate', *Boston Globe*, 9 February 2007.

Goodstein, Eban S., *Economics and the Environment*, 5th ed., Hoboken, John Wiley & Sons, 2008.

Gosselin, Peter, *High Wire: The Precarious Financial Lives of American Families*, New York, Basic Books, 2008.

Graham, John D., and Wiener, Jonathan Baert, eds., *Risk vs. Risk: Tradeoffs in Protecting Health and the Environment*, Cambridge, MA, Harvard University Press, 1995.

Gray, John, *Beyond the New Right*, London and New York, Routledge, 1993.

Green, Kenneth P., *Plain English Guide to the Science of Climate Change*, Washington DC, Reason Public Policy Institute, 1997.

Green, Kenneth P., and Mathur, Aparna, 'A Green Future for Just Pennies a Day?', *The American*, 19 February 2010, www.american. com/archive/2010/february/a-green-future-for-just-pennies-a-day.

Gregg, Samuel, and Stoner, James, eds., *Profit, Prudence and Virtue: Essays in Ethics, Business and Management*, Exeter, Imprint Academic, 2009.

Gregg, Samuel, and Stoner Jr, James R., eds., *Rethinking Business Management: Examining the Foundations of Business Education*, Princeton, Witherspoon Institute, 2008.

Grünberg, Slawomir, dir., *Chelyabinsk : The Most Contaminated Spot on the Planet*, Log In Productions, 1995.

Hahn, Robert W., 'The Politics and Religion of Clean Air', *Cato Review of Business and Government*, 1990, www.cato.org/pubs/regulation/regv13n1/v13n1-3.pdf.

Hahn, Robert W., ed., *Risks, Costs, and Lives Saved: Getting Better Results from Regulation*, Oxford University Press, 1996.

Haidt, Jonathan, *The Happiness Hypothesis: Finding Modern Truth in Ancient Wisdom*, New York, Basic Books, 2005.

Haidt, Jonathan, and Graham, Jesse, 'Planet of the Durkheimians: Where Community, Authority and Sacredness are Foundations of Morality', in *Social and Psychological Bases of Ideology and System Justification*, eds. J. T. Jost, A. C. Kay and H. Thorisdottir, New York, Oxford University Press, 2009.

Hansen, James, *Storms of My Grandchildren: The Truth About the Coming Climate Catastrophe*, New York, Bloomsbury, 2009.

Hardin, Garret, 'The Tragedy of the Commons', *Science*, 162, 13 December 1968, pp. 1243–8.

Harvey, Graham, *The Killing of the Countryside*, London, Jonathan Cape, 1997.

Hayek, Friedrich A., *Individualism and Economic Order*, University of Chicago Press, 1948.

Hayward, Stephen, and Green, Kenneth P., 'Waxman-Markey: An Exercise in Unreality', *AEI Energy and Environment Outlook*, 3, July 2009, www.aei.org/outlook/100057.

Heckman, James J., Nelson, Robert L., and Cabatingan, Lee, *Global Perspectives on the Rule of Law*, London, Routledge, 2010.

Hegel, G. W. F., tr. Stephen Houlgate, *Outlines of the Philosophy of Right*, Oxford University Press, 2008.

Heidegger, Martin, *Poetry, Language, Thought*, New York, Harper & Row, 1971.

Heidegger, Martin, *The Question Concerning Technology and Other Essays*, New York, Harper & Row, 1977.

Heidegger, Martin, *Hölderlin's Hymn 'The Ister'*, trs. William McNeill and Julia Davis, Bloomington, Indiana University Press, 1996.

Heidegger, Martin, *Being and Time*, Harper Perennial Modern Thought ed., New York, Harper, 2008.

Held, David, McGrew, Anthony, Goldblatt, David, and Perraton, Jonathan, *Global Transformations: Politics, Economics, and Culture*, Cambridge, Polity, 1999.

Helm, Dieter, 'Climate-change Policy: Why Has So Little Been Achieved?', in Helm and Hepburn.

Helm, Dieter, and Hepburn, Cameron, eds., *The Economics and Politics of Climate Change*, Oxford University Press, 2009.

Hirsch, Fred, *Social Limits to Growth*, Cambridge, MA, Harvard University Press, 1976.

Hirst, Paul, 'Can Rutland learn from Jutland?', in Barnett and Scruton.

Hobbes, Thomas, ed. Aloysius Martinich, *Leviathan*, rev. ed., Peterborough, Ont., Broadview, 2010.

Hoff Sommers, Christina, *The War against Boys*, New York, Touchstone, 2001.

Hoffer, Eric, *The True Believer: Thoughts on the Nature of Mass Movements*, New York, Harper & Row, 1951.

Hollander, Jack M., *The Real Environmental Crisis: Why Poverty, not Affluence, is the Environment's Number One Enemy*, Berkeley, University of California Press, 2003.

Holling, C. S., 'Resilience and Stability of Ecological Systems', *Annual Review of Ecology and Systematics*, 4, November 1973, pp. 1–23.

Hoskins, W. G., *The Making of the English Landscape*, London, Hodder & Stoughton, 1955.

Houghton, Sir John, *Global Warming*, 4th ed., Cambridge University Press, 2010.

Hulme, Mick, *Why We Disagree About Climate Change*, Cambridge and New York, Cambridge University Press, 2010.

Husserl, Edmund, *Die Krisis der europäischen Wissenschaften und die transzendentale Phänomenologie: eine Einleitung in die phänomenologische Philosophie*, 1954, The Hague, Martinus Nijhoff, reissued 1962.

IPCC Report (2007): published by Cambridge University Press, available at www.ipcc.ch/pdf/assessment-report/ar$/wgl/ar4-wgl-spm.pdf.

Jacobs, Jane, *The Death and Life of Great American Cities*, 1961, New York, Random House, reissued 2002.

Jacoby, Henry D., Babiker, Mustafa H., Paltsev, Sergey, and Reilly, John M., 'Sharing the Burden of GHG Reductions', MIT Joint Program on the Science and Policy of Global Change, report no. 167, 2008.

Jamieson, Dale, 'The Ethics of Geo-Engineering', *People and Place*, 1.2, 13 May 2009, www.peopleandplace.net/perspectives/2009/5/13/the_ethics_of_geoengineering/print.

Jefferies, Richard, *The Amateur Poacher*, Cambridge University Press, 2001.

Jefferies, Richard, *The Story of My Heart: My Autobiography*, London, Macmillan, 1968.

Jenkins, Jennifer, *Remaking the Landscape: The Changing Face of Britain*, London, Profile Books, 2002.

Joisten, Karen, *Philosophie der Heimat: Heimat der Philosophie*, Berlin, Akademie Verlag, 2003.

Jonas, Hans, *The Imperative of Responsibility*, English translation, University of Chicago Press, 1984.

Jones, Laura, and Walker, Michael, eds., *The Case for Individual Transferable Quotas in the Salmon Fishery of British Columbia*, Vancouver, Fraser Institute, 1997.

Kant, Immanuel, tr. Nicholas Walker, *Critique of Judgment*, Oxford University Press, 2008.

Kauffman, Robert K., Kauppi, Heikki, Mann, Michael L. and Stock, James H., 'Reconciling Anthropogenic Climate Change with Observed Temperature 1998–2008', *Proceedings of The National Academy of Sciences*, July 19, 2011, vol. 108, no. 29.

Keeley, J. E., Carrington, M., and Trnka, S., 'Overview of Management Issues Raised by the 1993 Wildfires in Southern California', *Brushfires in California Wildlands: Ecology and Resource Management*, International Association of Wildland Fire, Fairfield, WA, 1995.

Keller, David R., ed., *Environmental Ethics*, Chichester, Wiley-Blackwell, 2010.

Kingsnorth, Paul, 'Cancun: Why You Should Care', *Ecologist*, 33.5, June 2003.

Kingsnorth, Paul, *Real England: The Battle Against the Bland*, London, Portobello Books, 2008.

Kirby, Alex, 'Brent Spar's Long Saga,' BBC News, http://news.bbc.co.uk/2/hi/science/nature/218527.stm, 25 November 1998.

Kirsch-Stracke, Roswitha, and Wiche, Julia, *Der Heimatbegriff in der nachhaltigen Entwicklung: Inhalte, Chancen und Risiken*,

Weikersheim, Margraf, 2005.

Kleckner, Dean, 'Species Law Was Its Own Worst Enemy', *Chicago Tribune*, 11 December 1993.

Klein, Naomi, *No Logo*, New York, Picador, 2000.

Knight, Richard Payne, *An Analytical Inquiry into the Principles of Taste*, London, 1805.

Korsgaard, Christine, *Creating the Kingdom of Ends*, Cambridge University Press, 1996.

Kotkin, Joel, *The Next Hundred Million: America in 2050*, New York, Penguin Books, 2010.

Kowalsky, Nathan, ed., *Hunting – Philosophy for Everyone: In Search of the Wild Life*, Oxford, Wiley-Blackwell, 2010.

Krebs, Angelika, *Ethics of Nature: A Map*, Berlin, Gruyter, 1999.

Krebs, Angelika, ed., *Naturethik: Grundtexte der gegenwärtigen tier- und ökoethischen Diskussion*, Frankfurt, Suhrkamp, 1977.

Krier, Leon, *Architecture: Choice or Fate*, London, Andreas Papadakis Publishers, 1998.

Krier, Leon, Thadani, Dhiru A., *et al.*, *The Architecture of Community*, Washington DC, Island Press, 2009.

Krugman, Paul, *The Self-Organizing Economy*, Cambridge, MA, Blackwell, 1996.

Krutilla, John V., 'Conservation Reconsidered', *American Economics Review*, 57, September 1967, pp. 787–96.

Kundera, Milan, *The Unbearable Lightness of Being*, New York, Harper & Row, 1984.

Kunstler, James Howard, *The Geography of Nowhere: The Rise and Decline of America's Man-Made Landscape*, New York, Simon & Schuster, 1993.

Kunstler, James Howard, 'Sprawl', *Salmagundi*, 152, Fall 2006.

Kunstler, James Howard, *The Long Emergency: Surviving the Converging Catastrophes of the Twenty-First Century*, New York, Grove Press, 2005.

Kurlansky, Mark, *Cod: A Biography of a Fish that Changed the World*, London, Vintage, 1999.

Lamb, Sir Hubert, *Climate: Past, Present and Future*, 2 vols., London, Methuen, 1972, 1977.

Lane, Lee, *Strategic Options for Bush Administration Climate Policy*, Washington DC, AEI Press, 2006.

Lane, Lee, Montgomery, David W., and Smith, Anne E., 'Institutions for Developing New Climate Solutions', Proceedings of the International Seminars on Planetary Emergencies, 42nd Session, 19 August 2009, www.aei.org/article/101809.

Latham, John, 'Amelioration of global warming by controlled enhancement of the albedo and longevity of low-level maritime clouds', *Atmospheric Science Letters*, 3.2–4, 2002, pp. 52–8.

Lea, Ruth, 'The Common Fisheries Policy and the Wreckage of an Industry', London, *Institute of Directors Policy Study*, December 2002.

Lenin, Vladimir I., 'What is to be done?', *Iskra*, 4, May 1901.

Leopold, Aldo, 'The Ecological Conscience', *Journal of Soil and Water Conservation*, 3, July 1948, pp. 109–12.

Leopold, Aldo, *A Sand County Almanac and Sketches Here and There*, 1949, New York, Oxford University Press, reissued 1993.

Lewis, Meriwether, and Clark, William, *The Journals of Lewis and Clark*, 1804–6, online at Project Gutenberg website: www.gutenberg.org/etext/8419.

Lieberman, Ben, 'The European Experience with Cap and Trade', Testimony before the Committee on Foreign Relations, United States Senate, 10 July 2009: www.heritage.org/Research/Testimony/The-European-Experience-with-Cap-and-Trade.

Lindzen, Richard S., 'Global Warming: The Origin and Nature of the Alleged Scientific Consensus', Proceedings of the OPEC Seminar on the Environment, 1992, Cato Institute website: www.cato.org/pubs/regulation/regv15n2/reg15n2g.html.

Lindzen, Richard S., and Choi, Yong-Sang, 'On the Determination of

Climate Feedbacks from ERBE Data', *Geophysical Research Letters*, 36.16, August 2009.

Locke, John, *Of Civil Government; Second Treatise*, Chicago, H. Regnery, 1971.

Lomborg, Bjørn, *The Skeptical Environmentalist: Measuring the Real State of the World*, Cambridge University Press, 2001.

Lovelock, James, *Gaia: A New Look at Life on Earth*, Oxford University Press, 1979.

Lovelock, James, *The Revenge of Gaia*, New York, Basic Books, 2006.

Lucas, John, 'Assess the Cost of Error', *Risk of Freedom Briefing*, 5, October 2000.

Lynas, Mark, *Six Degrees: Our Future on a Hotter Planet*, Washington DC, National Geographic, 2007.

Mabey, Richard, *The Common Ground: The Place for Nature in Britain's Future*, London, Hutchinson in association with the Nature Conservancy Council, 1980.

MacFarlane, Alan, *The Origins of English Individualism: The Family, Property and Social Transition*, Oxford, Blackwell, 1978.

MacFarquhar, Roderick, and Schoenhals, Michael, *Mao's Last Revolution*, Cambridge, MA, Belknap Press of Harvard University Press, 2006.

MacKay, David J. C., *Sustainable Energy – Without the Hot Air*, Cambridge, UIT Cambridge Ltd., 2009.

Maddox, J., *The Doomsday Syndrome*, London, Macmillan, 1972.

Maistre, Joseph, Comte de, *Le Principe Générateur des Constitutions*, Lyons, J. P. Pelagaud, 1809.

Maitland, F. W., eds. A. H. Chaytor and W. J. Whittaker, *Equity*, Cambridge University Press, 1909.

Maitland, F. W., eds. David Runciman and Magnus Ryan, *State, Trust and Corporation*, Cambridge University Press, 2003.

Malloch, Ted, *Spiritual Enterprise: Doing Virtuous Business*, New York and London, Encounter Books, 2008.

Malthus, T. R., *Essay on the Principle of Population*, London, Electric Book Co., 2001.

Mannison, Don, et al., *Environmental Philosophy*, Canberra, Australian National University, 1980.

Marchant, Gary E., and Mossman, Kenneth L., *Arbitrary and Capricious: The Precautionary Principle in the European Union Courts*, Washington DC, AEI Press, 2004.

Marcuse, Herbert, *One-Dimensional Man*, London, Sphere Books, 1964.

Marriott, Oliver, *Property Boom*, 2nd ed., New York, Woodhead Publishing, 1989.

Marsh, George P., *Man and Nature*, Whitefish, MT, Kessinger, 2008.

Martin, Calvin, *Keepers of the Game: Indian–Animal Relationships and the Fur Trade*, Berkeley, University of California Press, 1978.

Massingham, H. J., *The Wisdom of the Fields*, London, Collins, 1945.

Massingham, H. J., *The Faith of a Fieldsman*, London, Museum Press, 1951.

McCormick, John, *Acid Earth*, London, Earthscan, 1989.

McLaughlin, Andrew, 'The Heart of Deep Ecology', in Keller.

Meadows, Donella H., Meadows, Dennis L., Randers, Jørgen, and Behrens III, W. W., *The Limits to Growth*, London, Pan Books, 1972.

Merton, Robert K., 'The Unanticipated Consequences of Purposive Social Action', *American Sociological Review*,1.6, December 1936, pp. 894–904.

Meyer, Lukas, 'Intergenerational Justice', in online *Stanford Enyclopedia of Philosophy*, plato.stanford.edu/entries/justice-intergenerational/, 2009.

Meyer-Abich, Klaus M., *Aufstand für die Natur*, Munich, C. Hanser, 1990.

Michaels, Patrick J., and Balling, Robert, *The Satanic Gases: Clearing the Air About Global Warming*, Washington DC, Cato Institute, 2000.

Mill, J. S., *Principles of Political Economy*, new ed., Oxford University Press, 2008.

Mises, Ludwig von, tr. J. Kahane, *Socialism: An Economic and Sociological Analysis*, new ed., London, Jonathan Cape, 1951.

Mishan, E. J., *The Economic Growth Debate: An Assessment*, London, Unwin Hyman, 1977.

Mitchison, Denis, 'The Regulation of Clinical Trials', OpenDemocracy, 30 November 2009, www.opendemocracy.net/denis-mitchison/regulation-of-clinical-trials.

Mitscherlich, Alexander and Margarete, *Die Unfähigkeit ʒu trauern: Grundlagen kollektiven Verhaltens*, 1967, Munich, Piper, reissued 2007.

Monbiot, George, *The Age of Consent*, London, Harper Perennial, 2004.

Montford, Andrew, *The Hockey Stick Illusion*, London, Stacey International, 2010.

Morano, Marc, Climate Depot, http://climatedepot.com.

Morris, Julian, ed., *Rethinking Risk and the Precautionary Principle*, Oxford, Butterworth-Heinemann, 2000.

Morrow, David R., Kopp, Robert E., and Oppenheimer, Michael, 'Towards Ethical Norms and Institutions for Climate Engineering Research', *Environmental Research Letters*, 4, 2009, pp. 1–8.

Mulgan, Tim, *Future People: A Moderate Consequentialist Account of Our Obligations to Future Generations*, Oxford University Press, 2006.

Mumford, Lewis, *The City in History*, New York, Harcourt, Brace & World, 1937.

Murray, Charles, *Losing Ground: American Social Policy 1950–1980*, New York, Basic Books, 1984.

Naess, Arne, 'The Shallow and Deep, Long-Range Ecology Movements, a Summary,' *Inquiry*, 16, reprinted in Keller.

Nelson, Richard R., 'The Market Economy, and the Scientific Commons', working paper to the Laboratory of Economics and Management at Sant' Anna School of Advanced Studies, Pisa, November 2003, www.lem.sssup.it/WPLem/2003-24.html.

Nietzsche, Friedrich, *Beyond Good and Evil: Prelude to a Philosophy of the Future*, Arlington, VA, Richer Resources Publications, 2009.

Nordhaus, W. D., *Managing the Global Commons: The Economics of Climate Change*, Cambridge, MA, MIT Press, 1994.

Nordhaus, W. D, 'Global Warming Economics', *Science*, 294.5545, 9 November 2001, pp. 1283–4.

North, Douglass C., Wallis, John J., and Weingast, Barry R., *Violence and Social Orders*, Cambridge University Press, 2009.

North, Richard D., *Life on a Modern Planet: A Manifesto for Progress*, Manchester University Press, 1995.

Novalis, ed. Hans-Joachim Mähl, *Das allgemeine Brouillon: Materialien zur Enzyklopädistik 1798–1799*, Hamburg, F. Meiner, 1993.

Nye, Joseph S., and Donahue, John D., *Governance in a Globalizing World*, Washington DC, Brookings Institution Press, 2000.

O'Neill, John, 'The Varieties of Intrinsic Value', *The Monist*, reprinted 1992, Keller.

Oakeshott, Michael, *On Human Conduct*, Oxford, Clarendon Press, 1975.

Open Europe Blog Team, 'The Euro: Rewarding Bad Behaviour', openeuropeblog.blogspot.com/2009_12_01_archive.html.

Organization for Economic Co-operation and Development, *The Polluter Pays Principle: Definition, Analysis, Implementation*, Paris, OECD, 1975.

Oroussoff, Nicolai, 'Outgrowing Jane Jacobs and Her New York', *New York Times*, 30 April 2006.

Orr, David W., *Earth in Mind: On Education, Environment, and the Human Prospect*, Washington DC, Island Press, 1993.

Orr, David W., 'Four Challenges of Sustainability', *Conservation Biology*, 16. 6, 2002, pp. 1457–60.

Orwell, George, *My Country Right or Left 1940–1943: Collected Essays, Journalism and Letters of George Orwell*, vol. 2, New York, Harcourt, Brace, Jovanovich, 1968.

Ostrom, Elinor, *Governing the Commons: The Evolution of Institutions for Collective Action*, Cambridge University Press, 1990.

Packard, Vance, *The Hidden Persuaders*, 1953, Brooklyn, Ig Publishing, reissued 2007.

Parfit, Derek, *Reasons and Persons*, Oxford, Clarendon Press, 2007.

Parfit, Derek, 'Overpopulation and the Meaning of Life', in Singer, Peter.

Passmore, John, *Man's Responsibility for Nature: Ecological Problems and Western Traditions*, 2nd ed., London, Duckworth, 1974.

Pausanias, *Description of Greece*, vols. 1–5, New York, Gardners Books, 2007.

Pearce, David W., Markandya, Anil, and Barbier, Edward, *Blueprint for a Green Economy*, London, Earthscan, 1989.

Pearce, David W., and Turner, R. K., *Economics of Natural Resources and the Environment*, Hemel Hempstead, Harvester Wheatsheaf, 1990.

Pearce, David W., 'Book Review: Mark Sagoff, 2004, *Price, Principle and the Environment*', *Environmental & Resource Economics*, 31.3, 2005, pp. 385–8.

Pearce, Fred, *With Speed and Violence: Why Scientists Fear Tipping Points in Climate Change*, Boston and Uckfield, Beacon Press, 2007.

Pei, Minxin, *China's Trapped Transition*, Cambridge, MA, Harvard University Press, 2006.

Pei, Minxin, 'Will the Chinese Communist Party Survive the Crisis?', *Foreign Affairs*, 12 March 2009.

Peltzman, Sam, 'An Evaluation of Consumer Protection Legislation: The 1962 Drug Amendments', *Journal of Political Economy*, 81.5, September–October 1973, pp. 1049–91.

Peltzman, Sam, 'Toward a More General Theory of Regulation', *Journal of Law and Economics*, 19.2, August 1976, pp. 211–40.

Perrow, Charles, *The Next Catastrophe*, Princeton University Press, 2007.

Piechocki, Reinhard, *Landschaft-Heimat-Wildnis: Schutz der Natur – aber welcher und warum?* Munich, C. H. Beck, 2010

Pigou, Arthur C., *The Economics of Welfare*, London, Macmillan, 1920.

Pollitt, Hector, and Thoung, Chris, 'Modelling a UK 80% Greenhouse Gas Emissions Reduction by 2050', *New Scientist*, 3 December 2009.

Ponte, Lowell, *The Cooling*, Englewood Cliffs, NJ, Prentice-Hall, 1976.

Pretty, Jules, Ball, A. S., Lang, T., and Morison, J. I. L., 'Farm Costs and Food Miles: An Assessment of the Full Cost of the UK Weekly Food Basket', *Food Policy*, 30.1, February 2005, pp. 1–19.

Pride of Derby and Derbyshire Angling Association and Earl of Harrington v. British Celanese Ltd., the Derby Corporation and the British Electricity Authority, [1952] 1 All ER 179.

Priest, George L., 'The Invention of Enterprise Liability: A Critical History of the Intellectual Foundations of Modern Tort Law', *Journal of Legal Studies*, 14.3, December 1985, pp. 461–528.

Putnam, Robert, *Bowling Alone: The Collapse and Revival of American Community*, New York, Simon & Schuster, 2000.

Rackham, Oliver, *The History of the Countryside: The Full Fascinating Story of Britain's Landscape*, London, J. M. Dent, 1986.

Rahner, Karl, tr. W. T. O'Hare, *Hominization: The Evolutionary Origin of Man as a Theological Problem*, New York, Herder &Herder, 1965.

Rand, Ayn, *Atlas Shrugged*, New York, Random House, 2005.

Rasch, Philip J., *et al.*, 'An Overview of Geoengineering of Climate Using Stratospheric Sulphate Aerosols', *Philosophical Transactions of the Royal Society*, 366.1882, 13 November 2008, pp. 4007–37.

Rawls, John, *A Theory of Justice*, Cambridge, MA, Belknap Press of Harvard University Press, 2005.

Rayner, Steve, and Malone, Elizabeth, eds., *Human Choice and Climate Change, vol.1: The Societal Framework*, Columbus, OH, Batelle Press, 1998.

Raz, Joseph, *The Authority of Law*, 2nd ed., Oxford, Clarendon Press, 2009.

Reilly, Robert, *The Closing of the Muslim Mind*, Wilmington, DE, ISI Books, 2010.

Reitz, Edgar, dir., *Heimat*, 3 vols., Edgar Reitz Filmproduktion, 1984, 1992, 2004.

Revesz, Richard L., and Livermore, Michael A., *Retaking Rationality: How Cost-Benefit Analysis Can Better Protect the Environment and our Health*, Oxford University Press, 2008.

Ridley, Matt, *The Rational Optimist: How Prosperity Evolves*, London, Fourth Estate, 2010.

Ritson, Joseph, *Robin Hood: A collection of all the ancient poems, songs, and ballads*, Wakefield, E P Publishing, 1972.

Roberts, Donald, and Tren, Richard, with Bate, Roger, and Zambone, Jennifer, *The Excellent Powder: DDT's Political and Scientific History*, Indianapolis, Dog Ear Publishing, 2010.

Robock, Alan, 'Alan Robock's testimony on Geoengineering, 5 Nov. 2009', House Committee on Science and Technology Hearing, www.csp.rutgers.edu/csp-posts/archives/77.

Rolston III, Holmes, *Philosophy Gone Wild*, Buffalo, NY, Prometheus Books, 1989.

Rolston III, Holmes, 'Rights and Responsibilities on the Home Planet', *Yale Journal of International Law*, 18.1, 1993, pp. 251–79.

Ruskin, John, eds. E. T. Cook and Alexander Wedderburn, *The Works of John Ruskin*, 39 vols., London, George Allen, 1903–12.

Sagoff, Mark, *Price, Principle, and the Environment*, Cambridge University Press, 2004.

Salingaros, Nikos, *A Theory of Architecture*, Solingen, Umbau-Verlag, 2006.

Scanlon, Thomas, *What We Owe to Each Other*, Cambridge, MA, Belknap Press of Harvard University Press, 1998.

Schaar, John H., 'The Case for Patriotism', *New American Review*,17, May 1973, pp. 59–100.

Schama, Simon, *Landscape and Memory*, New York, Alfred Knopf, 1994.

Scheler, Max, tr. William W. Holdheim, *Ressentiment*, New York, Free Press of Glencoe, 1961.

Scheler, Max, tr. Peter Heath, *The Nature of Sympathy*, London, Routledge & Kegan Paul, 1979.

Schelling, Thomas, 'What Makes Greenhouse Sense?', *Foreign Affairs*, 81.3, May/June 2002, pp. 2–9.

Schlink, Bernhard, *Heimat als Utopie*, Frankfurt am Main, Suhrkamp, 2000.

Schulz, Max, 'Emptying Reservoirs in the Middle of a Drought', *American Spectator*, September 2009.

Schwartz, Joel M., and Hayward, Stephen F., *Air Quality in America*, Washington DC, AEI Press, 2007.

Schwarz, Michiel, and Thompson, Michael, *Divided We Stand: Redefining Politics, Technology and Social Choice*, University Park, Penn State University Press, 1990.

Scotese, Christopher R., 'The Paleomap Project', www.scotese.com/climate.htm.

Scruton, Roger, *The Aesthetics of Architecture*, Princeton University Press, 1979.

Scruton, Roger, *Animal Rights and Wrongs*, new ed., London, Continuum, 2003.

Scruton, Roger, *Art and Imagination: A Study in the Philosophy of Mind*, 1974, South Bend, IN, St Augustine's Press, reissued 1998.

Scruton, Roger, *Beauty*, Oxford University Press, 2009.

Scruton, Roger, *The Classical Vernacular: Architectural Principles in an Age of Nihilism*, Manchester, Carcanet, 1992.

Scruton, Roger, *The Meaning of Conservatism*, Harmondsworth, Penguin Books, 1980.

Scruton, Roger, *Modern Culture*, London, Continuum, 2004.

Scruton, Roger, *The Need for Nations*, London, Civitas, 2006.

Scruton, Roger, *The Palgrave Macmillan Dictionary of Political Thought*, London, Palgrave Macmillan, 2007.

Scruton, Roger, *The Philosopher on Dover Beach*, South Bend, IN, St Augustine's Press, 1999.

Scruton, Roger, *The West and the Rest: Globalization and the Terrorist Threat*, Wilmington, DE, ISI Books, 2002.

Scruton, Roger, 'Hayek and Conservatism', in *The Cambridge Companion to Hayek*, ed. Edward Feser, Cambridge University Press, 2007.

Scruton, Roger, 'The Sacred Pursuit', in Kowalsky.

Scruton, Roger, 'Virtue and Profit', in Gregg and Stoner, *Profit and Prudence*.

Seel, Martin, *Eine Ästhetik der Natur*, Frankfurt am Main, Suhrkamp, 1991.

Self, Will, *The Book of Dave*, London, Viking, 2006.

Selye, Hans, *The Physiology and Pathology of Exposure to Stress: A Treatise Based on the Concepts of the General-Adaptation-Syndrome, and the Diseases of Adaptation*, Montreal, Acta, 1950.

Sen, Amartya, *The Idea of Justice*, London, Allen Lane, 2009.

Sessions, George, *Deep Ecology for the Twenty-First Century*, Boston, Shambhala, 1995.

Shutkin, William A., *The Land that Could Be: Environmentalism and Democracy in the Twenty-First Century*, Cambridge, MA, MIT Press, 2001.

Sikora, R. I., and Barry, Brian, eds., *Obligations to Future Generations*, Philadelphia, University of Pennsylvania Press, 1978.

Silber, John, *Architecture of the Absurd*, New York, Quantuck Lane Press, 2007.

Singer, Fred S. and Avery, Dennis, *Unstoppable Global Warming: Every 1,500 Years*, New York, Rowman and Littlefield, 2007

Singer, Fred S., Starr, Chauncey, and Revelle, Roger, 'What to Do about Greenhouse Warming: Look Before You Leap', *Cosmos: A Journal of Emerging Issues*, 1, April 1991, pp. 28–33.

Singer, Peter, ed., *Applied Ethics*, Oxford University Press, 1987.

Sloterdijk, Peter, *Du mußt dein Leben ändern*, Frankfurt am Main, Suhrkamp, 2009.

Smith, John Maynard, *Evolution and the Theory of Games*, Cambridge University Press, 1982.

Sokal, Alan D., and Bricmont, Jean, *Fashionable Nonsense: Postmodern Intellectuals' Abuse of Science*, new ed., London, Profile, 2003.

Solomon, Lawrence, 'Avertible Catastrophe', *National Post*, 25 June 2010.

Solomon, Lawrence, *The Deniers: The World-Renowned Scientists Who Stood Up Against Global Warming Hysteria, Political Persecution, and Fraud – and Those Who are Too Fearful to Do So*, Minneapolis, Richard Vigilante, 2008.

Solomon, S., Qin, D., Manning, M., Chen, Z., Marquis, M., Averyt, K. B., Tignor, M., and Miller, H. L., eds., *Contribution of Working Group I to the Fourth Assessment Report of the Intergovernmental Panel on Climate Change*, Cambridge University Press, 2007.

Spaemann, Robert, 'Technische Eingriffe in die Natur als Problem der politischen Ethik', in Birnbacher, ed.

Spaemann, Robert, tr. Oliver O'Donovan, *Persons: The Difference between Someone and Something*, Oxford University Press, 2006.

Spencer, Roy W., *Climate Confusion: How Global Warming Hysteria Leads to Bad Science, Pandering Politicians and Misguided Policies that Hurt the Poor*, New York, Encounter, 2008.

Spencer, Roy W., and Braswell, William D., 'Potential Biases in Feedback Diagnosis from Observations Data: A Simple Model Demonstration', *Journal of Climate*, 21, November 2008, pp. 5624–8.

Spengler, John D., et al., *Summary of the Symposium on Health Aspects of Exposure to Asbestos in Buildings*, Cambridge, MA, Harvard University Energy and Environmental Policy Center, 1989.

Sperber, Dan, *Explaining Culture: A Naturalistic Approach*, Oxford, Blackwell, 1995.

Stein, Edith, *On the Problem of Empathy*, 2nd ed. in English, The Hague, Martinus Nijhoff, 1970.

Stern, David I., 'The Environmental Kuznets Curve', 2006, www.ecoeco.org/pdf/stern.pdf.

Stern, Nicholas, *The Economics of Climate Change*, Cambridge University Press, 2007.

Stiglitz, Joseph, *Globalization and Its Discontents*, London, Penguin, 2002.

Stiglitz, Joseph, *Making Globalization Work*, New York and London, W. W. Norton, 2006.

Stone, Christopher D., 'Should Trees Have Standing? Toward Legal Rights for Natural Objects', *Southern California Law Review*, 45, 1972, pp. 450–501.

Strawson, P. F., 'Freedom and Resentment', in *Freedom and Resentment and Other Essays*, London, Methuen, 1974.

Sturt, George, *Change in the Village*, Dover, NH, Caliban Books, 1984.

Sullivan, Walter, 'Scientists Ask Why World Climate Is Changing; Major Cooling May Be Ahead', *New York Times*, 21 May 1975.

Sunstein, Cass, ed., *Behavioural Law and Economics*, Cambridge, Cambridge University Press, 2000

Sunstein, Cass, et al., *Punitive Damages: How Juries Decide*, University of Chicago Press, 2002.

Svensmark, Henrik, and Calder, Nigel, *The Chilling Stars: A New Theory of Climate Change*, Thriplow, Icon Books, 2007.

Sylvan, Richard, and Bennett, David, *The Greening of Ethics*, Cambridge, White Horse Press, 1994.

Taylor, Bron, *Dark Green Religion: Nature Spirituality and the Planetary Future*, Berkeley, University of California Press, 2009.

Tengs, Tammy, 'Optimizing Societal Investments in the Prevention of Premature Death', A Thesis Submitted to the Faculty of the Harvard School of Public Health in Partial Fulfillment of the Requirements for the Degree of Doctor of Science in the Field of Health Policy and Management, 1994.

Thomas, David, 'Anti-Christ of the Green Religion', *Daily Telegraph*, 20 January 2002.

Thomas, Sir Keith, *Man and the Natural World: Changing Attitudes in England 1500–1800*, Harmondsworth, Allen Lane, 1983.

Thompson, M. G., and Rayner, S., 'Cultural Discourses', in Rayner and Malone.

Tocqueville, Alexis, Comte de, tr. Elizabeth Rawlings, abridged with an introduction by Michael Kammen, *Democracy in America*, Boston, Bedford/St Martin's, 2009.

Tooby, John, and Cosmides, Leda, Introduction to Berkow *et al.*

Transco plc v. Stockport Metropolitan Borough Council, [2003] UKHL 61.

Tullock, Gordon, 'The Welfare Costs of Tariffs, Monopolies, and Theft', *Western Economic Journal*, 5.3, June 1967, pp. 224–32.

Turner, Michael, *Enclosures in Britain*, London, Macmillan, 1984.

United Nations Conference on Environment and Development, *Rio Declaration on Environment and Development*, New York, United Nations Publications, 1992.

United Nations Development Programme Regional Bureau for Arab States, *Arab Human Development Report 2009: Challenges to Human Security in the Arab Countries*, New York, United Nations Publications, 2009, arab-hdr.org/publications/other/ahdr/ahdr2009e.pdf.

Vitousek, P. M., Ehrlich, P. R., Ehrlich, A. H., and Mason, P., 'Human Appropriation of the Products of Photosynthesis', *BioScience*, 36.6, June 1986, pp. 368–73.

Walters, Simon, 'George Osborne Unveils £500m Bonfire of the Quangos', *Daily Mail*, 23 May 2010.

Ward, Colin, *Arcadia for All: The Legacy of a Makeshift Landscape*, new ed., Nottingham, Five Leaves Publications, 2004.

Ward, Colin, and Crouch, David, *The Allotment: Its Landscape and Culture*, 3rd ed., Nottingham, Five Leaves Publications, 1997.

Weston, Jessie L., *From Ritual to Romance*, Cambridge University Press, 1920.

Wiggins, David, *Needs, Values, Truth: Essays in the Philosophy of Value*, Oxford University Press, 1987.

Wiggins, David, 'An Idea We Cannot Do Without', in *The Philosophy of Need*, ed. Soran Reader, Cambridge University Press, 2004.

Wiggins, David, 'Solidarity and the Root of the Ethical', *Tijdschrift voor filosofie*, 71, 2009, pp. 239–69.

Wildavsky, Aaron, *Searching for Safety*, New Brunswick, Transaction Books, 1988.

Wildavsky, Aaron, and Wildavsky, Adam, 'Riskless Society', in *The Concise Encyclopedia of Economics*, ed. David R. Henderson, Indianapolis, Liberty Fund, 1998.

Wilde, Gerald J. S., *Target Risk: Dealing with the Danger of Death, Disease and Damage in Everyday Decisions*, Toronto, PDE Publications, 1994.

Williams, Bernard, *Making Sense of Humanity, and Other Philosophical Papers*, Cambridge University Press, 1995.

Williams-Ellis, C., *Britain and the Beast*, London, J. M. Dent, 1937.

Wilson, James Q., *The Moral Sense*, New York, Simon &Schuster, 1993.

Wolf, Martin, *Fixing Global Finance*, expanded and updated ed., Baltimore, Johns Hopkins University Press, 2010.

World Commission on Environment and Development, *Our Common Future*, 1987, found at UN Documents: Gathering a Body of Global Agreements, www.un-documents.net/wced-ocf.htm.

World Resources Institute, *World Resources 1992–93: Guide to Global Environment*, New York, Oxford University Press, 1992.

Worley, William S., *J. C. Nichols and the Shaping of Kansas City*, Columbia, MO, University of Missouri Press, 1990.

Worpole, Ken, *Richer Futures: Fashioning a New Politics*, 2nd ed., London, Earthscan, 1999.

Worpole, Ken, *Last Landscapes*, London, Reaktion Books, 2003.

Wright, Patrick, 'An Encroachment too Far', in Barnett and Scruton.

Zamoyski, Adam, *Holy Madness: Romantics, Patriots, and Revolutionaries, 1776–1871*, New York, Penguin Books, 2001.

Zeng, N., Ding, Y., Pan, J., Wang, H., and Gregg, J., 'Climate Change – the Chinese Challenge', *Science*, 319.5864, February 2008, pp. 730–31.

Index

Abbey, Edward, 360
accountability, 89, 95–7, 183,
    204–5, 208, 212, 218, 405
acidification, 53
acquis communautaire, 313–4
Adams, Ansel, 285, 359
Adams, John, (Geographer) 73, 134
Adams, John, (Composer) 285
adaptation, 55–6, 64–7, 78, 83, 88,
    134, 194, 210f, 213, 219, 281, 283
Addison, Joseph, 328
Adorno, Theodor W., 244
advertising, 259–260
aesthetic judgment, 260, 274–9,
    384–5
Africa, 16, 149, 256, 303, 403,
    406–7
ageing, 393–4
agricultural subsidies, 165, 350,
    351–2, 355
agriculture, 164–5, 232–3, 250,
    332–3, 350, 351–5, 395–8
alarms, 39–40, 81–4
Albrecht, Glenn, 210n
Alexander, Christopher, 271
Amazon, (rainforest) 32, 368

America (USA), 22–3, 24, 57–8,
    79, 85, 98f, 119–20, 146, 158, 169,
    170, 175–6, 219, 238, 241, 256,
    257, 259, 261, 267–70, 274, 282,
    284f, 293, 303, 318, 320, 356–375,
    394, 397, 398, 403
American Climate and Energy
    Security Act, 57–8
anarchism, 101–2
Anderson, Terry, 94n, 141n, 162
Anglers Conservation Association,
    161, 164, 338
angling, 161–3
animal rights, 113–4, 162–3, 199
Apel, Karl-Otto, 203n
Aquinas, St Thomas, 187
Arabia, 16, 257, 368
architecture, 274–84, 287, 338,
    343–4, 364
Aristotle, 13n, 121–2, 139, 186,
    409f, 412
Arnold, Matthew, 339
Aron, Leon, 93
Arrow, Kenneth J., 171n, 179, 184n,
    390n
asbestos, 119–20

Attlee, Clement R., Earl, 293
Augustine, St, 238
Austen, Jane, 221, 330
Australia, 219, 256
Austrian economics, 219–20
Avery, Alex, 397n
Axelrod, Robert, 143

Baird Callicott, J., 196
Balfour, Lady Eve, 5, 353
Balling, Robert C., 45
bankruptcy, 181
Barber, Samuel, 228
Barker, Paul, 270–271
Barrell, John, 331n
Barry, Brian, 187n
Bate, Roger, 159n
Bath Preservation Society, 285–6
Baudelaire, Charles, 261
Bauhaus, 277–8, 279, 351
Baum-Snow, Nathaniel, 268n
beauty, 5, 214, 253–291, 330f, 356
Beck, Ulrich, 128–9
Beckel, J. Eric, 63n
Beckerman, W., 14n
Beeching, Richard, Lord, 348
Belgium, 312, 345
Belien, Paul, 312n
Benedict, Ruth, 209
Benjamin, Asher, 276
Bennett, David, 85n
Bentham, Jeremy, 333, 371–2
Bergman, Ingmar, 228
Bergson, Henri, 233
Bergsten, Fred C., 93n
Berry, Wendell, 6, 164, 165n, 285, 355, 363
Bewick, Thomas, 328
big business, 178–182, 250–51, 322, 348
big trade unions, 348
biodiversity, 1, 59, 69–70, 165, 198, 351, 355

Birnbacher, Dieter, 190n, 192, 236n
Blackburn, Colin, Lord (Mr Justice Blackburn), 152–3
Blair, Tony, (Prime Minister) 104
Body, Sir Richard, 350
Bonevac, Daniel, 382n
Booker, Christopher, 40, 51n, 84n, 86n, 101, 383n
Borromini, Francesco, 275
Bové, José, 258
Bowlby, John, 222, 226–7
Boy Scouts, 365
Bramwell, Anna, 25n
Braswell, William D., 51n
Brecht, Bertolt, 393
Brent Spar oil platform, 30f
Bricmont, Jean, 248n
Britain (UK), 24, 32, 64–7, 79, 80, 146, 159f, 165, 176, 256, 257, 279, 285, 293, 314, 316, 318, 323, 364, 385–6, 394, 400, 406–7
British Field Sports Society, 163
British Medical Association, 65–6
Brody, Hugh, 147, 286
Brooks, Arthur, 176n, 379n
Broome, John, 212n
Brower, David, 359n
Brower, Michael, 378n
Bruegman, Robert, 270–271
Bruntland, Gro Harlem, 381, 382
Buber, Martin, 230
Buchanan, J. M., 90
Bunting, Basil, 332
Bureau of Land Management and Forest Service (US), 146
bureaucracy, 90–120
Burke, Edmund, 13n, 19, 26, 27, 28, 102, 174–5, 215–7, 220, 237, 253, 330, 343, 349, 365

Calder, Nigel, 52n
Campaign for the Protection of
Rural England, 250, 344
Campbell, Thomas, 332
Canada, 29, 33, 394
Canon Law, 310
cap and trade, 303, 314, 388
capitalism, 75, 244f
Carbon Sequestration Leadership
Forum, 323
carbon tax, 387–391, 395
care, 232–4
Carlson, Allen, 363
Carlyle, Thomas, 339
Carson, Rachel, 164, 352, 411
Ceaușescu, Nicolae, 366
Cézanne, Paul, 228
Chakraborty, R. N., 147n
Chang, Jung, 296n
Charitable Uses Act (England), 33
charity, 33
Chasemere v. Richards, 160
Chernobyl, 93
Chernyshevsky, Nikolay
Gavrilovitch, 83
China, 6f, 58, 61–2, 91, 92n, 295–7,
300–303, 368, 391
Choi, Yong-Sang, 51n
Chomsky, Noam, 248, 249n
Christie, Ian, 4, 80
cities, 265–274, 363–9
civil association, 11, 27–8, 32–3, 67,
89, 97, 170, 218, 335, 348–9, 353,
365–6
Cixous, Hélène, 248
Clare, John, 332
Clark, Stephen, 411n
Clark, William, 148, 357
Clausewitz, Carl von, 116
clean energy, 383–7
Clement, Matthew, 395n
climate change, 1, 38–71, 87–8, 136,

295–7, 300–306, 323, 374–5, 383,
401–2
Club of Rome, 377–8
Coase, Ronald Harry, 155–6, 157n,
388
Cobbett, William, 65, 243, 333
Coke of Holkham, Thomas, Earl of
Leicester, 333
Cole, H. S. D., 15n, 378n
Coleridge, Samuel Taylor, 338
collectivism, 25
Colligan, Douglas, 40n
Common Agricultural Policy
(EU), 353–4
Common Fisheries Policy, 140, 141,
147
common law, 141, 152–162, 221,
297, 319, 334, 336
commons, 141–8
Commons, Open Spaces and
Footpaths Preservation Society,
336
communism, 92–3, 243, 277, 293,
294–7, 366–7
competition and cooperation, 144ff
Condorcet, Nicolas, Marquis de,
184n
Confucianism, 296–7, 302
Confucius, 187
conservatism, 2–4, 7–14, 18, 22, 32,
67–8, 76, 89–90, 221, 246, 251,
376–401
American vs European, 12–13
Conservative Party (UK), 348
Constable, John, 227, 329, 331
consumerism, 27, 81, 244–5, 260
Convention on Biodiversity, 69–70
Cooper, James Fenimore, 243, 358
Copenhagen Climate Change
Conference (2009), 70, 302
Corell, R.W., 54n
Corot, Jean-Baptiste, 228

Corporate Social Responsibility, 178
Cosmides, Leda, 210
cosmopolitanism, 321–2, 395
cost–benefit analysis, 112f, 188, 191, 200, 212
Costanza, Robert, 123
Cotman, John Sell, 329
Countryman, The, 294
Countryside Alliance, 337n
Countryside Restoration Trust (UK), 250, 346, 397
Cowper, William, 332
Crabbe, Rev. George, 221
Crome, John, 227, 329, 331
Crouch, David, 80n
cultural theory, 72–7, 209f
culture, 209–11
Curzon Price, Tony, 4, 355–6

Daly, Herman, 380–381
Darwall, Stephen, 203–4, 205, 208, 230n
Darwin, Charles, 211
Dasgupta, P., 149n
David, Paul A., 390
Davies, Brian, 28–9
Dawidoff, Nicholas, 45n
Dawkins, Richard, 40–41
death taxes, 341–2
deep ecology, 85–6, 195–6, 288–9
Deleuze, Gilles, 248
democracy, 14–17, 25, 30, 93–4, 239–40, 304
DeMuth, Christopher C., 4, 110n, 113n, 154n
Denmark, 318, 356, 383, 387
Diamond, Jared, 56, 148
Dickens, Charles, 66, 227
discount rates, 189–90
Dobson, Andrew, 207n
doomsday literature, 41–2, 84, 86

Douglas-Home, Jessica, 367
Douglas, Mary, 72–3
Drucker, Peter, 150n
Durkheim, Émile, 86, 209
Durodié, Bill, 108n
Dutilleux, Henri, 285
Dworkin, Ronald, 372
Dyson, Freeman, 45n

Earth First!, 30, 36, 360–61
Easter Island, 56, 150
Eastwood, John, 160–161
Ebbesmeyer, Curtis, 69n
ecofascism, 196
economic growth, see growth
economics and the environment, 26, 58–60, 184–6, 214, 254n
economics of climate change, 48, 58–9
egalitarianism, 73–9, 81, 97, 172–3
Ehrlich, Anne, 379
Ehrlich, Paul, 39, 359, 379
Eliot, T. S., 234–5
Emerson, Ralph Waldo, 243, 285, 358
Empson, Sir William, 380
endangered species legislation, 98–101
endowment effect, 157n
England, 22–3, 33, 141, 161–3, 170, 249–50, 294, 326–355, 398
English Law, 33, 310, 316
Enlightenment, 36–7, 253, 406
enterprise liability, 154
entropy, 9–11, 23–4
Environmental Protection Agency (US), 112, 131, 158–9, 168, 169, 360, 388
Epictetus, 186
equity, 160, 162, 172, 217–8, 221, 333f
Esterson, Aaron, 249n

Etherington, John, 384
ethics, 62–3, 185–208, 213, 409–413
European Court of Human Rights, 317, 370–71
European Court of Justice, 106–7, 316
European Union, 22, 91, 98, 107–9, 117, 131, 140, 166, 249, 304, 307, 312–7, 322, 353–4, 367, 371, 388, 397
Evelyn, John, 328, 331, 332, 344
evolutionary psychology, 210–213, 225–6
externalising costs, 17f, 95, 122–3, 151–9, 164–6, 167f, 181–2
externalities, 17, 151–9, 173, 388
Exxon-Valdez case, 154, 157

Factory Acts (UK), 66
factory labour, 66
Fairlie, Simon, 80, 102n, 400
Family Farmers Association (UK), 397
Fannie Mae and Freddie Mac, 175–6
fatalism, 73–5
Fattal, Antoine, 311n
Federal Emergency Management Agency, 176
Feisbach, Murray, 6n
Fergusson, Adam, 286n
fisheries, 140–147, 313
Fleming, James Rodger, 41n
Food and Drug Administration (US), 131
Food Family Farming Foundation (US), 363
foot and mouth disease, 111
Foreman, David, 360
Forestry Commission (UK), 94–5
forests, 94–5, 327–8, 335–6, 359–60
Forster, E. M., 345

Foucault, Michel, 248, 249n
Fox, Warwick, 195
Frakes, L. A., 52n
France, 316, 326, 356, 364, 389
Frankfurt School, 244
free enterprise, 7, 9, 31–2, 78, 273
free rider problem, 18, 102, 139
French Revolution, 74, 82, 102, 174, 215
Freud, Sigmund, 231
Friedman, Milton, 13n
Friedman, Rose, 13n
Friedman, Thomas, 308n
Friendly Societies (England), 65
Friends of the Earth, 30, 31, 384
friendship, 253–5
Fukushima Daiichi, 118
functionalism in architecture, 266–8
Furet, François, 82n

Gaia hypothesis, 85, 255, 288–9
Game Conservancy Association (UK), 163, 337–8
game theory, 142–3, 185
Garden City Association, 344
Gardiner, Rolf, 5
Garnaut, Ross, 403n
Garreau, Joel, 271
Gaskell, Elizabeth Cleghorn (Mrs Gaskell), 66
Geertz, Clifford, 209
Geo-engineering, 53, 54, 61–2, 63, 68, 323, 402
George III, King, 333
Germany, 6, 25, 26, 118–9, 235–6, 364
Gęscińska, Alicja, 4
Giddens, Tony, Lord, 47, 48
Gierke, Otto Friedrich von, 13n
Ginsburg, Douglas H., 113n, 154n
Giono, Jean, 6, 228

Girard, René, 213n
Girondins, 82
globalization, 21–24, 307–323
GM crops, 106, 123–4, 178
goals vs. side-constraints, 273–4,
    281–2, 347
Goldblatt, David, 308n
Goldsmith, Zac, 140n, 377, 379n
Goodman, Ellen, 47n
Goodstein, Eban S., 59n, 184n
Gore, Al, 42, 47, 49, 56
Gosselin, Peter, 177n
Graham, Jesse, 77n, 226n
Graham, John D., 131n
Gray, John, 6n, 10n, 34, 178
Greece, 318, 389
green belts, 345
Green Party, UK, 7
Green, Kenneth P., 4, 47, 57n, 59n
Greenpeace, 30–31, 33, 36, 62n,
    308, 384
Greenwood myth, The, 327–8
growth, 14–17, 377–82
Grünberg, Slawomir, 93
Guild of St George, 339

Hahn, Robert W., 168n
Haidt, Jonathan, 77n, 226n
Halliday, Jon, 296n
Hansen, James, 44–5, 47, 55
Hardin, Garrett, 18n, 139, 155n
Harvey, Graham, 165n, 350, 355
Hayek, Friedrich A., 181n, 219
Hayward, Stephen, 4, 57n, 131n,
    169n
Heal, G., 149n
health and safety, 98, 119–121, 131,
    166–7, 169, 315, 398, 399
Heaney, Seamus, 285
Hegel, Gottfried Wilhelm
    Friedrich, 19, 27, 28n, 208n, 222,
    224–5, 227, 237

Heidegger, Martin, 6, 229, 232–3,
    243, 245, 259
Heimat, 26–7, 209–252, 228, 233,
    235–6
Heimatgefühl, 26, 27, 236–9, 341,
    375
Held, David, 308n
Helm, Dieter, 49n, 55n, 58n, 59n,
    404n
Hepburn, Cameron, 49n, 55n, 404n
heresy, 86–7
Hesiod, 228
hierarchy, 73–5, 97
High Wycombe Society, 346
Hill, Octavia, 341
Hinduism, 195, 238
Hirsch, Fred, 378–9
Hirst, Paul, 356
Hitler, Adolf, 83, 191
Hobbes, Thomas, 18n, 222, 223
'hockey-stick' graph, 46n
Hoffer, Eric, 86n
Hoffmann, Leonard, Lord, 154n
Hogarth, William, 330
Hölderlin, Johann Christian
    Friedrich, 232n, 233
Holland, 326, 345
Hollander, Jack M., 14n, 39n, 142n
Holling, C. S., 64n, 55n, 73, 130
home, 25–6, 171, 210, 225–7, 232–3,
    236–9, 246, 262–7, 290, 412–3
homeostasis, 11, 30, 35–6, 96–7,
    129–30, 132, 135, 138–182, 290,
    325, 349, 355
Homer, 227, 238
hominization, 213
homo economicus, 11, 184, 213, 231
Hopkins, Gerard Manley, 332
Hopkins, Keriann, 4
Horkheimer, Max, 244
Hoskins, W. G., 350
Houghton, Sir John, 48

Howard, Sir Ebenezer, 270, 344
Hudson River painters, 285, 358, 359
Hudson, Kimberly, 4
Hulme, Mick, 42n, 72n
Hume, David, 27
Hungary, 354
Hunter-gatherers, 147, 286–7, 357
Hunter, Alexander, 328
Hunter, Sir Robert, 341
hunting, 29, 115, 148, 163–4, 332, 336f
Hussein, Saddam, 304
Husserl, Edmund, 228–9, 232
Huxley, Aldous, 190

Iceland, 145, 323
immigration, 391–4
incentives, 55, 90–91, 97, 98–9, 133, 149, 305, 386
India, 300, 302–3
Individual Transferable Quotas (ITQ), 145f
individualism, 73–9, 81, 84, 97
Industrial Revolution, 64–7, 332, 333–4
inheritance, 216–7, 234–5
Inshaw, David, 285
instrumental values, 197–8, 201, 231, 254
instrumentalization, 245, 259
inter-generational justice, 207–8
Intergovernmental Panel on Climate Change (IPCC), 44f, 48–51, 404
International Fund for Animal Welfare, 28–30, 33, 308
international law, 311–12
internationalism, 78, 235, 295, 308–323, 369–70
intrinsic values, 197–8, 201, 206, 231, 237, 254

Inuit (people), 29, 33, 147–8, 286
Iragaray, Luce, 248
Ishido, Allen, 99
Islamic society, 16, 240, 310–11
Italy, 314, 318

Jacobins, 82
Jacobs, Jane, 265, 266, 268, 269, 273
Jacoby, Henry D., 404n
Jamieson, Dale, 62n
Japan, 118
Jean Paul (Johann Paul Friedrich Richter), 243
Jefferies, Richard, 79, 293, 294, 340
Jefferson, Thomas, 41, 357, 358
Jenkins, Dame Jennifer, 51n
Jenkins, Sir Simon, 351n
Joisten, Karen, 233, 236
Jonas, Hans, 6, 126, 133, 136, 205–6, 208, 231, 234, 235, 284
Jones, Laura, 145n
Joyce, James, 227
justice, 206–7, 224, 403–8

Kahneman, Daniel, 157n
Kant, Immanuel, 97n, 201–3, 205, 253, 254n, 309, 409f
Kaufmann, Robert K., 62n
Keeley, J. E., 100n
Keller, David R., 186n
Keohane, Robert O., 308n
Keynes, John Maynard, Lord, 10
Kingsnorth, Paul, 21n, 293, 319n
Kirsch-Stracke, Roswitha, 236n
Kleckner, Dean, 100n
Klein, Naomi, 259
Knight, Richard Payne, 328, 329n
Korda, Alexander, 329
Korsgaard, Christine, 202n, 205
Kotkin, Joel, 269–70, 274
Krebs, Angelika, 4, 186n, 196n,

203, 236, 254n
Krier, Leon, 271, 272, 273
Kristeva, Julia, 248
Kropotkin, Prince Peter, 79
Krugman, Paul, 271
Krutilla, John V., 150
Kundera, Milan, 257
Kunstler, James Howard, 268–9, 271n, 272, 273, 294
Kurlansky, Mark, 140n
Kurzweil, Raymond, 190
Kuznets curve, 14
Kuznets, Simon, 14
Kyoto Protocol, 15, 55, 61, 70, 302–3, 307, 314, 388, 404

Labour Party (UK), 29, 80, 294, 348, 369
Laing, R. D., 249n
Lamb, Sir Hubert, 41n
landscape painting, 329–30
Lane, Lee, 4, 391n
Latham, John, 62n
Lawrence, D. H., 227
Le Corbusier (Charles-Édouard Jeanneret), 276, 278–9
Lea, Ruth, 313n
League of Women Voters (US), 365
Leal, Donald, 94n, 141n, 162
left versus right, 5–8, 35–7, 42, 74–8, 97, 113, 172–3, 184, 238, 246, 292
legislation, 370–373
Lenin, Vladimir Ilyich, 83, 84, 191, 277, 385
Leopold, Aldo, 6n, 79, 195, 196, 199–200, 255, 361, 363
Lewis, Meriwether, 148, 357
liberalism, 10–11
Lieberman, Ben, 314n
Limbaugh, Rush, 42

limited liability, 178–9
'limits to growth' debate, 15, 377–382
Lindzen, Richard, 45, 47, 51n
litigation, 119–20, 263–4
Livermore, Michael A., 113n
Lloyd-George, David, Earl, 341–2
Lloyd-Wright, Frank, 276
locality, 20–27, 36, 143–5, 290–91, 293, 309–310, 318–9, 392–3, 396–9
localization, 395–400
Lofoten fishery, 142, 145
Lomborg, Bjørn, 46–7
Lovelock, James, 85n, 195, 255
low-impact development, 400
Lucas, John, 116n
Lynas, Mark, 43–4, 47, 53, 67

Maastricht Treaty, 320
Mabey, Richard, 350, 355
MacFarlane, Alan, 141n, 334n
MacFarquhar, Roderick, 296n
MacKay, David J. C., 52n, 55n, 61n, 118n, 383n, 385–6
MacKaye, Benton, 361
Maistre, Joseph, Comte de, 19, 27
Maitland, F. W., 218, 335n
Malloch, Ted, 91n
Malory, Sir Thomas, 327
Malthus, Rev. Thomas, 333, 377, 378n, 380
Mansart, Jules Hardouin, 275
Mao Zedong, 83, 296, 297
Marchant, Gary E., 107n
Marcuse, Herbert, 244
market failure, 138, 141, 173
markets, 7–8, 11, 13, 26, 34, 64, 76, 91, 96, 132, 138–82, 183, 219–20
Marriott, Oliver, 351n
Marsh, George Perkins, 359–60
Martin, Calvin, 147n

Marx, Karl, 244
Massingham, H. J., 5, 95n, 294,
   340, 345
Masters of Foxhounds Association,
   163
Mathur, Aparna, 59n
Matson, Pamela, 379
Matthews, David, 285
McGrew, Anthony, 308n
McLaughlin, Andrew, 196n
Meadows, D. H., 15n, 378n
Medecins sans Frontières, 318
Merkel, Angela, 118
Merton, Robert K., 132n
Messiaen, Olivier, 285
Meyer-Abich, Klaus Michael, 85,
   195, 411n
Meyer, Hannes, 277
Meyer, Lukas, 207n
Michaels, Patrick J., 45
Mickiewicz, Adam, 284
Mihai Eminscu Trust (Romania),
   367
Mill, John Stuart, 380
Milton, John, 328
Mises, Ludwig von, 181n, 219
Mishan, E. J., 15n
Mitchison, Denis, 131n
modernism in architecture, 276f,
   346–7
Monbiot, George, 21, 36–7, 79n,
   308n
Monet, Claude, 228
Montford, Andrew, 46
Montgomery, David, 301n
Montreal Protocol on Ozone
   Substances That Deplete the
   Ozone Layer, 305
moral hazard, 175–7, 179
Morano, Marc, 49
Morris, William, 340, 343
Morrow, David R., 62n

Möser, Justus, 13n
Mossman, Kenneth L., 107n
motor industry, 179–80
Mugabe, Robert, 299
Muir, John, 243, 285, 357, 358
Mulgan, Tim, 187n
multiculturalism, 369, 393
multinationals, 31f, 36, 258, 307–8,
   322, 366–7
Mumford, Lewis, 269
Murray, Charles, 177n, 226n
mutual aid, 79–80, 293

Naess, Arne, 86, 195
Namibia, 33
NASA, 44, 46
nation state, 22, 31–2, 68–7,
   308–323, 401, 404
National Association of Realtors
   (US), 364
National Council of Ramblers'
   Federations (UK), 343
National Family Farm Coalition
   (US), 363
National Geographic Society (US),
   363
National Park Service (US), 357,
   362
National Trails system (US), 357
National Trust (UK), 250, 341–2,
   358, 385
nationalism, 20–21
nations, 19–27, 70f, 173, 240–242,
   375, 401
Naturalists Trusts (UK), 340
need, 125–67, 200–202
negative feedback, 12, 96–7, 135,
   136, 157, 162, 165, 182, 388, 392
Nelson, Richard R., 390
Němcová, Božena, 227
Neo-liberalism, 34, 178
New Republic, 292

New Urbanism, 271–2, 364
New Zealand, 145
NGOs, 26, 28–37, 54–5, 57, 89, 115,
    117, 250, 251, 302, 341
Nichols J. C., 264
Nietzsche, Friedrich Wilhelm,
    77–8, 84, 410
Nordhaus, W. D., 15n, 59
North, Douglass C., 298
North, Richard D., 40, 51n, 69n,
    84n, 86n, 101, 359n, 362n, 383n
Norway, 24, 118, 142, 318
nostalgia, 234, 237, 247, 349
Novalis (G. P. F. Freiherr von
    Hardenburg), 237
nuclear power, 118–9, 383
Nye, Joseph S., 308n

O'Neill, John, 254n
Oakeshott, Michael, 11n, 13n, 251
Office of Information and
    Regulatory Affairs (US), 112
oikophilia, 3, 25–7, 163, 214–9, 227,
    231, 233–5, 242, 246, 253–91, 296,
    302, 326–75, 339–40, 349, 358,
    363, 366, 368, 369, 393, 402, 413
oikophobia, 27, 247–51, 296, 351,
    369, 377
oil spills, 1, 32, 124–5, 131–2, 136,
    154–5, 379
Olmsted, Frederick Law, 270
Olympic Movement, 317–8
open access orders, 298f
open science regime, 390–91
Organization for Economic
    Cooperation and Development,
    382
original sin, 87
Orousoff, Nicolai, 265n
Orr, David, 79n, 381–2
Orwell, George (Eric Blair), 247,
    293

'Ossian' (James MacPherson), 330
Ostrom, Elinor, 24n, 143–4, 147,
    156, 170, 171, 356
Owen, Robert, 338

Pachauri, Rajendra, 49
Packard Foundation, 367
Packard, Vance, 259
Page, Robin, 346
Pareto, Vilfredo, Marchese, 381n
Parfit, Derek, 190–191
Parr, Doug, 62n
Passmore, John, 197
patents, 389–91
patriotism, 171, 236, 242, 249–50,
    292–3
pattern books, 276
Pausanias, 284, 286
Pearce, David W., 58n, 60n, 388
Pearce, Fred, 54n
Pearl Harbor (attacks on), 117
Pei, Minxin, 297n, 300n
Peltzman, Sam, 131n, 133, 134n, 386
permaculture, 398
perpetuity, 299–300, 301
Perraton, Jonathan, 308n
Perrow, Charles, 176n
person and personality, 229–32,
    238, 256
phenomenology, 228–9, 232f,
    237–8
philosophy, 3
phthalates, 108–9
picturesque, 329
Piechocki, Reinhard, 236n
piety, 19, 224–5, 263, 283–91
Pigou, Arthur Cecil, 155, 388, 391
Pilger, John Richard, 249n
Pius XI, Pope, 320
planning, 265–74, 277–8, 280, 285,
    344, 346–7, 351, 364, 368–9, 371,
    399

plastic pollution, 1, 69, 165–6, 306–7, 315–6
Pol Pot, 83
Poland, 92, 354
political correctness, 248
politics, 34f
Pollitt, Hector, 59n
'polluter pays' principle, 382
Ponte, Lowell, 40
population growth, 16, 39, 333, 359, 377–9, 392–4
Portugal, 318
practical reason, 2, 3, 18–19, 73–9, 104–136, 184–6, 188–94, 201–3, 325
Pre-Raphaelite Brotherhood, 340
Precautionary Principle, 70n, 104–28
preference orderings, 184, 185, 201, 212, 214
Pretty, Jules, 355n, 397
Pride of Derby case, 161
Priest, George L., 154n
Prisoner's Dilemma, The, 18, 139, 142–3
property rights, 9, 140–150, 333f
Proust, Marcel, 227, 284
psychology, 3
public goods, 138–9
public spirit, 171, 317–9
Pugin, Augustus, 338, 343
Pushkin, Alexander Sergeyevich, 125
Putnam, Robert, 170n, 365–6, 368, 399

Quangos, 173n
Quincy Library Group, 356

Rackham, Oliver, 95n, 340, 341n, 350
Rahner, Karl, 213n

railways, 65, 287, 338–40, 348
Rand, Ayn, 13n, 84
Rasch, Philip J., 54n
rational self-interest, 18, 19
Ravenna Park Seattle, 94
Rawls, John, 18n, 206–7, 222, 223, 405
Rawnsley, Canon Hardwicke, 341
Rayner, S., 74n
Raz, Joseph, 373
Rechtsgefühl, 309
Red Cross, 33, 317, 365
regulation, 1, 101, 105–130, 156f, 183
Reilly, Robert, 311n
Reitz, Edgard, 27, 228
religion, 64, 85–7, 88, 224, 240, 263, 288–9
rent seeking, 17, 90–91, 102, 297, 299
research, 389–91
resilience versus interception, 130f, 135, 392
resilience, 64, 127, 176–7, 325
resource depletion, 149–51
responsibility, 138, 183, 203, 204, 205–7, 208, 212, 214, 224, 230ff, 242, 392
ressentiment, 77–8, 89
Revelle, R., 62
Revesz, Richard L., 113n
revolutionary politics, 82–4, 102, 217, 296
ribbon development, 345
Ricq, Charles, 355
Ridley, Matt, 66n, 378n, 381n, 384
right versus left, see left versus right
rights of way, 336
rights, 188, 192, 194, 198–201, 204, 212, 222, 310–374
Rilke, Rainer Maria, 88, 289–90

Rio Declaration 1992, 70, 117
risk, 73–4, 84–5, 104–136
risk, disaggregation of, 109–112,
    392
Ritson, Joseph, 328
Roberts, Donald, 411n
Robespierre, Maximilien de, 82
Robin Hood myth, 328
Robock, Alan, 62
Rolston III, Holmes, 186n, 195,
    199n
Roman Empire, 127, 310
Roman law, 310, 317
Romania, 354, 366–8
Roosevelt, Franklin D., 110n, 117
Rousseau, Jean-Jacques, 174, 243,
    253
Routley, Richard, see Sylvan
Routley, Val, 85n
Royal Society for the Protection of
    Birds, 337
rule of law, 8, 64, 76–7, 93, 139,
    240, 273, 298, 308–9, 407
Ruskin, John, 243, 287–8, 338, 339,
    343, 358
Russia, 149, 364, 368
Russian Constructivists, 279
Rylands v. Fletcher, 152–4

sacredness, 284–7
sacrifice, 127, 201, 209, 210, 213,
    214, 246
Sagoff, Mark, 4, 60n, 115n, 185n,
    254n, 283, 356–7
Salingaros, Nikos, 271
Salisbury, Robert, 3rd Marquess of,
    10
Salt, Titus, 338
salvationism, 81–5, 86, 288
San Joaquin Valley, California, 99
sanctions, 304
Sartre, Jean Paul, 83, 248

Scanlon, Tim, 200
Schaar, John, 292–3
Schama, Simon, 284, 327n
Scheler, Max, 77, 203n, 205n,
    229–30, 235
Schelling, Thomas, 110n, 304
Schiller, Johann Christoph
    Friedrich von, 253
Schlegel, August Wilhelm, 243
Schlegel, Karl Wilhelm Friedrich,
    243
Schlink, Bernard, 26, 236–7
Schmitt, Carl, 83
Schoenhals, Michael, 296n
Schulz, Max, 99
Schwartz, Joel M., 131n, 169n
Schwarz, Michiel, 9n, 72
science, 64, 72, 229, 230, 390–91
Scigliano, Eric, 69n
Scotese, Christopher R., 52n
Scott, Sir Walter, 328, 330
Scruton, Jack, 294–5
Seel, Martin, 255n
Selborne Society, 32, 337
Self, Will, 67
Selye, Hans, 96n
Sen, Amartya, 171n, 405–6
Sessions, George, 86n
settlement, 232–4, 242, 246,
    265–70, 272–3, 274, 281
Seurat, Georges, 228
Shaftesbury, 3rd Earl of, 328
Shakespeare, William, 327
Shariah law, 310–311
Shaw-Lefevre, George, 336
Shell Oil, 30f
Shoard, Marion, 164, 165n, 350, 355
Shutkin, William A., 24n, 364
Sibelius, Jean, 228
Sicily, 318
Sierra Club, 115, 358–9
Sikora, R. I., 187n

Silber, John, 276n
Singer, Fred S., 46, 62n
Singer, Peter, 186n, 193
sinks and residues, 122–4, 151, 164, 166
Sloterdijk, Peter, 88n, 410n
Slow, Robert 381n
Smith, Adam, 27, 405
Smith, John Maynard, 143
smog, 135–6, 168, 301
social capital, 23, 217, 342
social choice theory, 60, 171n, 184n, 185
social contract, 18, 174, 222–4
social justice, 21, 75–9, 80, 385
social rationality, 73
socialism, 6–7, 11–12, 17, 21f, 77f, 80–81, 91f, 102, 277, 279–80, 431
Society for the Preservation of the Commons of London, 336
Society for the Protection of Ancient Buildings, 343
Soil Association, 353
Sokal, Alan, 248n
solastalgia, 210n
Solomon, Lawrence, 125n
Solomon, Robert, 46, 50
Somerville, William, 332
Sommers, Christina Hoff, 121n
Southern Agrarians, 6
sovereignty, 319–321
Soviet Union, 6f, 39, 91, 93, 154–5, 181n, 218, 257
Spaemann, Robert, 190n, 230n
Spain, 143, 314, 318
Spencer, Roy, 46, 51n
Spengler, John D., 120n
Sperber, Dan, 40–41
St Just, Louis Antoine de, 82
Stalin, Joseph, 83, 191, 199
Starr, C., 62n
steady state economy, 380

Stein, Edith (St Teresa Benedict), 229
Steiner, Rudolf, 5, 351, 397
Stendhal (Henri Bayle), 326
Stern, David I., 14
Stern, Nicholas, Lord, 48, 55n, 59, 189, 404n
stewardship, 12, 71, 138–182, 197, 235, 376f, 413
Stiglitz, Joseph, 23n
Stockholm Conference 1982, 105
Stone, Christopher D., 199n
Strawson, Sir Peter, 205n
Street, A. G., 345
Stubbs, George, 330
Sturt, George (George Bourne), 293
sublime, the, 330–331
subsidiarity, 320
subsidies, 164–9, 396–7
suburbanization, 268–72, 274
Sullivan, Walter, 40n
Sunstein, Cass, 158n
supermarkets, 167, 168, 178, 250, 322, 394, 395, 412
sustainability, 21f, 381–2
Sweden, 24, 118, 318
Switzerland, 143–4, 219, 318, 356, 394, 399
Sylvan, Richard, 85n, 196
Syria, 299

Tate, Allen, 6
Taylor, Bron, 85n
technology, 232–3, 243–7
technophilia, 27, 232f, 245
Tengs, Tammy, 158n
Tennyson, Alfred, Lord, 332
Terence (Plubius Terentius Afer), 91
territory, 19f, 22, 171, 239–42, 284–6, 308f, 311–2

Theocritus, 228
thermodynamics, 10, 26
Thibon, Gustave, 6
Thomas, David, 47n
Thomas, Edward, 340
Thomas, Sir Keith, 148, 327n, 328,
    331n, 340n
Thomas, Rev R. S., 332
Thompson, Michael, 9n, 73, 74n
Thomson, James, 332
Thoreau, Henry David, 6, 243,
    284, 357, 358, 363
Thoung, Chris, 59n
Tickell, Sir Crispin, 51n
time preference, 189
time, 233–5
'tipping points', 53–4, 63, 74
Tocqueville, Alexis, Comte de, 27,
    170n, 365
Tooby, John, 210
tort law, 152–162, 172, 221, 392
Town and Country Planning
    Association, 344
Trade-Related Intellectual
    Property Rights, 395
tradition, 219–21
tragedy of the commons, 18,
    139–146, 356
transition towns, 400
transnational government, 307–8,
    311–316
treaties, 15f, 61, 67–8, 295–324, 401
Treaty of Rome, 317
Trevelyan, G. M., 344, 345
tribal society, 240, 286–7
Trotsky, Leon (Lev Davidovich
    Bronshtein), 83
trust law (see also equity), 334–5
trusteeship, 25–6, 174–5, 217–8
Tullock, Gordon, 90
Turkish law, 311
Turner, R. K., 58n

uglification, 257
United Nations, 22, 44, 249, 307,
    318
Utilitarianism, 187–198

Vaughan Williams, Ralph, 228
Vitousek, Peter, 379
volunteers, 170–171, 173–4, 218–9,
    361, 365–6

Wagner, Richard, 227
Wales, Charles, Prince of, 271, 346
Wallace, Alfred Russel, 211
Wallis, John Joseph, 298
Walters, Simon, 174n
Walton, Izaak, 162, 163, 331
Wandervogel movement, 6
Ward, Colin, 79–80
Webb, Philip, 343
Webber, Melvin M., 347
Weber, Max, 298n
Weingast, Barry R., 298
Welty, Eudora, 285
Wensleydale, James Parke, Lord,
    160
Weston, Jessie L., 327
White, Rev. Gilbert, 332
Wicke, Julia, 236n
Wiener, Jonathan Baert, 131n
Wiggins, David, 4, 125–6, 133, 136
Wildavsky, Aaron, 9n, 64n, 72–3,
    112, 115, 116n, 130f, 135
Wildavsky, Adam, 9n
Wilde, Gerald, 134
Wilderness Society (US) 357, 361
wilderness, 197–8, 330f, 357–9,
    359–63
Williams-Ellis, Sir Clough, 344–5
Williams, Sir Bernard, 196n, 361
Wilson, E. O., 195
Wilson, James Q., 226n
Wilson, Richard, 330

Winchilsea, Anne Finch, Countess of, 332
wind power, 301, 383–5
windows, 281–2
witch hunts, 86–7
Wojtyła, Karol (Pope John Paul II), 205n
Wolf, Martin, 179n
Women's Institute, 32–3, 35, 250, 342–3
Wordsworth, William, 162–3, 227, 243, 253, 338, 339
World Bank, 14n, 23, 308
World Commission on Environment and Development, 381
World Meteorological Organization, 44
World Resources Institute, 6n
World Trade Organization, 22, 23, 305, 319, 395
World Wildlife Fund, 384
Worley, William S., 364
Worpole, Ken, 80, 293
Wright, Patrick, 5, 25
Wyler, Steve, 400

Yellowstone National Park, 357, 362–3
Yellowstone Park Foundation, 363
Young, Arthur, 333
Youth Hostel Association, 343

Zamoyski, Count Adam, 20n
Zeng, Ning, 302n
Zero-sum thinking, 114f, 373
Zimbabwe, 299
Zinn, Howard, 83, 248, 249n
zoning, 267–70, 281, 363, 394